Handbook
of Christian
Apologetics

HUNDREDS OF ANSWERS
TO CRUCIAL QUESTIONS

Peter Kreeft & Ronald K. Tacelli

IVP Academic
An imprint of InterVarsity Press
Downers Grove, Illinois

InterVarsity Press
P.O. Box 1400, Downers Grove, IL 60515-1426
World Wide Web: www.ivpress.com
E-mail: email@ivpress.com

InterVarsity Press® *is the book-publishing division of InterVarsity Christian Fellowship/USA*®, *a movement of students and faculty active on campus at hundreds of universities, colleges and schools of nursing in the United States of America, and a member movement of the International Fellowship of Evangelical Students. For information about local and regional activities, write Public Relations Dept., InterVarsity Christian Fellowship/USA, 6400 Schroeder Rd., P.O. Box 7895, Madison, WI 53707-7895, or visit the IVCF website at <www.intervarsity.org>.*

Cover design: Cindy Kiple
Cover images: cross: Photodisc Collection/Getty Images
         three crosses, two Jesuses, one baby Christ: istockphoto.com
         Jesus mosaic: Photodisc

ISBN 978-0-8308-1774-0

Printed in the United States of America ∞

Library of Congress Cataloging-in-Publication Data

Kreeft, Peter.
    Handbook of Christian apologetics/Peter Kreeft and Ronald K.
Tacelli.
      p. cm.
    Includes bibliographical references.
    ISBN 0-8308-1774-3
    1. Apologetics—20th century.   I. Tacelli, Ronald K. (Ronald
Keith), 1947-   II. Title.
    BT1102.K724   1994
    239—dc20
                                      94-415
                                        CIP

P   41   40   39   38   37   36   35   34   33

Y   25   24   23   22   21   20   19   18

To Salvatore M. Bellino
"Uncle Sully" who was always there

To John Kreeft
who had a large role in shaping this book
and a larger role in shaping
one of its authors

A Personal Preface

Our compelling reasons for writing this book are three:

1. We are certain that the Christian faith is true.

2. We are only a little less certain that the very best thing we can possibly do for others is to persuade them of this truth, in which there is joy and peace and love incomparable in this world, and infinite and incomprehensible in the next.

3. We are a little less certain, but still confident, that honest reasoning can lead any open-minded person to this very same conclusion.

Part 1
INTRODUCTION

Outline of Chapter 1
The Nature, Power & Limitations of Apologetics

1. About this book

2. About reason

☐ We need to restore the older notion of reason as

    more than subjective

    more than calculative

☐ We therefore use an Aristotelian logic of terms and essences

☐ We believe faith and reason are allies

☐ We must distinguish objective reason from subjective reason, which is clouded by passion, prejudice, ignorance and ideology

☐ *Non*rational factors in arguments (e.g., beauty) are not *ir*rational

☐ Reason is the friend, not the enemy, of

    authority

    faith

    hope

    love

    symbolism

☐ A minilesson in logic:

    terms must be clear

    premises must be true

    arguments must be logically valid

☐ We have included many merely probable arguments as converging clues

☐ We should distinguish the questions of

    truth

    knowledge

    certainty

    proof

    method

☐ A *summa*-style format for a complete argument is outlined

3. About apologetics

☐ Answers to objections to doing apologetics

    Life and love are more important than rational argument

    People don't decide what to believe by logical reasoning
☐ Reasons for apologetics
    To unbelievers: to lead up to faith
    To believers: to build up faith and aid love
    To engage in spiritual warfare
☐ Concerning methodology
    We do not assume any school of methodology

    The arguments in this book should be used with sensitivity to personal
    and social contexts
☐ Apologetics is especially needed today, when our civilization is in
    social crisis
    intellectual crisis
    spiritual crisis
☐ We confine ourselves to arguing for "mere Christianity"

CHAPTER 1
The Nature, Power
& Limitations of
Apologetics

W E ARE WRITING THIS BOOK BECAUSE WE HAVE BEEN BESIEGED WITH RE
quests for it.

We both teach philosophy of religion at Boston College, and students often ask us where they can find a book that lists, outlines or summarizes all the major arguments for all the major Christian teachings that are challenged by unbelievers today—such as the existence of God, the immortality of the soul, the trustworthiness of Scripture, and the divinity and resurrection of Christ—and answers the strongest and commonest objections against these doctrines. We were amazed to find that no such book exists! There are thousands of books on apologetics, and some very good ones, but not one of them summarizes apologetic arguments as Aquinas summarized theological arguments in his *Summa Theologiae* and *Summa Contra Gentiles*. This book is written to begin to fill that vacuum.

We even thought of titling it *Summa Apologetica,* but our publisher wisely rejected that title as unmarketable. Comparison with Aquinas's *Summas* may seem arrogant, even ludicrous; but we mean it to refer to the genus, not the genius, of Aquinas's works.

There were many *summas,* or summaries, in the Middle Ages, which condensed many arguments into a small space, carefully organizing and succinctly explaining them. A *summa* is meant to function as a digest or mini-encyclopedia. It need not be read in order from beginning to end. It can be used as a reference book or handbook. That genus is at least as useful today as it was in the Middle Ages, for two reasons. For one thing, we moderns, like the medievals, respect scientific order, clarity, rationality and structure. (It is a popular but wholly indefensible myth that the medieval mind was unscientific, irrational, unquestioning, vague or crude. If anything, it was rational to a fault. It was the mind of a librarian, positively reveling in order.)

The second reason is that we moderns are all terribly busy (though our technology should give us great leisure!) and we want time-saving devices, digests and "bottom-line" summaries. Yet that desire is not fulfilled in modern apologetics. The contents of that noble art are usually diffused, not collected. Most apologetics books make ten points in fifty pages. This book aims to make fifty points in ten pages.

One point of comparison with a medieval *summa*, then, is the genus: summary. A second is that, like a *summa*, it is written "for beginners" (as Aquinas said in the preface to his *Summa Theologiae*); that is, for a general audience rather than for a scholarly and specialized one. It means to bridge the gap between the scholarly and the popular which so sadly divides and weakens modern theology and philosophy. A third point of comparison with a medieval *summa* is the division into small, bite-sized chunks. This follows from the previous point: since we are beginners, we need (but seldom get) the aid of clear outlining, numbering and divisions. Descartes was right in this, at least. The second step of his famous "Method" notes that a difficult problem is made much easier by analyzing it into smaller pieces and steps, and taking each one by one.

The fact that this book is so carefully outlined, however, will count *against* it in some people's minds. There will be some readers and reviewers who will accuse us of "black and white thinking" simply because we argue logically about religion. They will trot out epithets like "narrow," "simplistic," "cut and dried" and "rationalistic," because they mistakenly assume (1) that religion must be irrational and (2) that to write clearly is to ignore mystery.

About Reason

They probably pick up this latter assumption from reading twentieth-century philosophy. Philosophy in our century is seldom both clear and profound, both respectful of reason and respectful of mystery at the same time, as medieval philosophy was. Throughout this century the English Channel has divided two philosophical styles more deeply than did the Iron Curtain. We find clarity at the expense of profundity in most of the English analytical tradition, and profundity without clarity in most of the continental existential and phenomenological tradition. Our intent here is to bridge the channel by bridging the ages; to return to the medieval enterprise of arguing rationally about the great mysteries; to turn back a clock that is keeping bad time.

Restoring the Older Notion of Reason

To make this restoration possible, another restoration is necessary: a restoration of the older, larger notion of reason itself. This means essentially two things:

1. seeing our subjective, psychological, human processes of reasoning as participations in and reflections of an objective rational order, a *logos*, a "Reason" with a capital *R;* and

2. seeing reason not as confined to reasoning, calculating—what scholastic logic calls "the third act of the mind"—but as including "the first act of the mind": apprehension, intellectual intuition, understanding, "seeing," insight, contemplation.

Using Aristotelian Logic

These two positions we take concerning the nature of reason lie behind our use of Aristotelian logic. This is a logic of (linguistic) terms, which express (mental) concepts, which represent (real) essences, or the natures of things. (The Greek word *logos* has all three of these meanings.) Many modern philosophers are suspicious and skeptical of the venerable and commonsense notion of things having real essences or natures and of our ability to know them. Aristotelian logic assumes the existence of essences and our ability to know them, for its basic units are terms, which express concepts, which express essences. But modern symbolic logic does not assume what philosophers call metaphysical realism (that essences are real), but implicitly assumes instead metaphysical nominalism (that essences are only *nomina*, names, human labels), since its basic units are not terms but propositions. Then it relates these propositions in argumentative structures just as a computer can do: if *p*, then *q; p;* therefore *q*.

The human mind is indeed a computer—we do compute, after all—but it is much more than that. We can also "see," or understand. Behind our use of Aristotelian logic is our hope that all our arguing will begin and end with seeing, with insight. Thus, we usually begin by defining terms and end by trying to bring the reader to the point of seeing objective reality as it is.

Faith and Reason Are Allies

We do not believe reason should usurp the primacy of faith, hope and love. We agree with classical Christian orthodoxy as expressed in medieval formulas like *fides quaerens intellectum* ("faith seeking understanding") and *credo ut intelligam* ("I believe in order that I may understand"). That is to say that when faith comes first, understanding follows, and is vastly aided by faith's tutelage. But we also agree with the classical position's contention that many of the things God has revealed to us to be believed, such as his own existence and some of his attributes, can also be proved by human reason, properly used. We could not have written this book if we did not believe that. After we believe, we can and should "be ready to make [a] defense" for our faith (1 Pet 3:15).

Objective vs. Subjective Reason

However, we must not naively identify objective rationality with subjective rationality. (See chap. 16 on objective truth.) Truth is objective, but people usually aren't! We are obviously living in a fallen world, not a perfect world, one where people's exercise of reason is expressed in various forms of irrationality. An argument that is in itself perfectly rational and valid will often fall on ears deafened by prejudice, passion, ignorance, misunderstanding, incomprehension or ideology.

The last of these seems especially dangerous today. Usually, people seem to choose what to believe not by looking at the evidence but by looking at ideological labels, especially "liberal" or "conservative," or by asking which group of people they want to be associated with, or by vague feelings and associations evoked by an idea within their consciousness, rather than by looking at the idea itself and at the reality it points to outside their consciousness.

We need not and should not employ any of these substitutes for reason in order to "make contact with" or "be relevant to" those who are doing so. We make contact and relevance not by changing rationality into irrationality but by changing irrationality into rationality. That is what education is. That is the goal of this book.

Nonrational Arguments Are Not Irrational

However, the *non*rational is broader than the *ir*rational, and often extremely important, even in arguments. For instance, arguments have an aesthetic dimension too, and the beauty of an argument can move us more powerfully than we realize.

A good argument is effective partly because it is like a diamond. Like a diamond, its light is beautiful and reflects the light of day, of objective reality. Like a diamond, it cannot originate light, only reflect it from its source in reality. Like a diamond, it is precious. Like a diamond, it is hard, not easily cut, not easily refuted; it cuts through other, softer materials, refuting and conquering error.

Reason as Friend

Reason is the friend of all other ways of knowing which are not irrational but nonrational. These nonrational ways of knowing must be distinguished from their irrational counterfeits:

1. Reason is the friend of divine authority, which can neither deceive nor be deceived, but not necessarily of human authority, fads and fashions.

2. Reason is the friend of faith in this divine authority, but not of naiveté. Thus reason leads to the faith and away from the cults.

3. Reason is the friend of hope, but not of human wishful thinking.

4. Reason is the friend of *agapē* (love) but not of *eros* (selfish passion).

5. Reason is the friend and complement to imagery, symbol and myth, which also reveal truth, but not to impossible imaginings, esoteric fantasies or misty pseudomysticisms.

A Minilesson in Logic

The inherent structure of human reason manifests itself in three acts of the mind: (1) understanding, (2) judging and (3) reasoning. These three acts of the mind are expressed in (1) terms, (2) propositions and (3) arguments. Terms are either clear or unclear. Propositions are either true or untrue. Arguments are either logically valid or invalid.

A term is clear if it is intelligible and unambiguous. A proposition is true if it corresponds to reality, if it says what is. An argument is valid if the conclusion follows necessarily from the premises. If all the terms in an argument are clear, and if all the premises are true, and if the argument is free from logical fallacy, then the conclusion must be true.

These are the essential rules of reason, in apologetics and in any other field of argument. They are not rules of a game that we invented and can change. They are rules of reality.

Not only reason but even language is more than a "game" (Wittgenstein's influential but misleading term); it has an inherent structure, for it is an expression of reason, which has an inherent structure. (In Greek, the same word, *logos*, means "objective intelligible structure," "reason as revealing that structure" and "word or speech as expressing reason.")

We write in terms, propositions and arguments because we think in concepts, judgments and reasoning; and we do this because the reality we think about includes essences, facts and causes. Terms express concepts which express essences. Propositions express judgments which express facts. And arguments express reasoning which expresses causes, real "becauses" and "whys."

Arguments are like eyes: they see reality. The arguments in this book demonstrate that the essential Christian doctrines are true, unless they are bad arguments; that is, ambiguous, false or fallacious. To disagree with the conclusion of any argument, it must be shown that either an ambiguous term or false premise or a logical fallacy exists in that argument. Otherwise, to say "I still disagree" is to say "You have proved your conclusion true, but I am so stubborn and foolish that I will not accept this truth. I insist on living in a false world, not the true one."

Probable Arguments and Converging Clues

In this book we have set ourselves the double task of (1) negative refutation by exposing at least one of these three possible mistakes in each of the most important objections we are aware of to the fundamental doctrines of Christianity, and (2) providing positive arguments for these doctrines, either probable or demonstrative, that are free from these three mistakes.

We have included some arguments which we regard as probable but not certain, for these also count, as significant *clues*, especially when considered cumulatively. Ten converging clues are almost as convincing as one demonstrative argument in most areas of life (e.g., in court, at war or in love). Even where we believe there are some demonstrative arguments available, we have added many such "clue" arguments, especially for the two key issues of the existence of God and life after death, in order to present a more complete case, to "cover the waterfront."

Questions About Arguments

We need to distinguish three related questions about arguments, since understanding what these questions involve will help you to understand our procedure in this book.

1. Is this argument probable *or* demonstratively certain?

Sometimes we can draw a conclusion not from premises known with certainty to an equally certain conclusion, but from various convergent clues to a *reasonable* (or *probable*) conclusion. Juries do this all the time. They decide that someone is guilty beyond a reasonable doubt; they weigh the evidence with scrupulous care; but still a wrong verdict is *conceivable*. Drawing a probable or reasonable conclusion is not like doing logic or mathematics. Plato said long ago that most of our knowledge is "right opinion." And in this life it couldn't really be otherwise.

2. *Is the certainty of a demonstrative argument merely* psychological? *Or is another kind of certainty meant?*

Psychological certainty is what we call *certitude:* a *feeling* of certainty. And this is not what we mean by the certainty that belongs to a solid demonstrative argument. Instead, we mean that the premises are *known* to be true, that the conclusion really does follow from these premises, and that the conclusion is therefore true and equally *known* to be true. Obviously, not all arguments that produce a feeling of certitude are demonstratively certain. Nor do all demonstratively certain arguments *in fact* produce a feeling of certitude. Most of us have had the experience of approaching an argument with great feelings of skepticism, and only later, after much painful thought, coming to see that its premises are certainly true and its conclusion certainly follows from them. Our feelings of certitude can shift in a way that real certainties cannot.

3. *Is* empirical *demonstration the only kind possible? Or is there another kind?*

There must be another kind; for there can't be an empirical demonstration that the only kind of demonstration is empirical. Philosophy claims to have proofs—proofs giving us certain knowledge—that are not empirical or experimental. In fact, what counts today as the scientific method doesn't even claim to deliver what we mean by certain knowledge.

What about the arguments in this book? There are many *probable* arguments, arguments from converging clues. We can only hope our readers will find them as reasonable and persuasive as we do. There are other arguments whose conclusions, we claim, are known with *certainty*. This certainty may not produce in you immediate feelings of *certitude*. But this by itself says more about you than about these arguments; it does not show that they fail to demonstrate their conclusions (though it might spur you on to demonstate that failure!). At the very least, you need to ponder these arguments, and your reaction to them, with great care. Finally, it goes without saying that our demonstrative proofs are not *empirical* or *experimental;* they proceed by methods proper to philosophy. To those who prefer the methods of natural science we say: Then be scientific! *Read* the proofs! *Look* at them carefully! *See* whether they work!

A Summa-Style Format

We make no apology for the "rationalistic" format. In fact, we apologize for not adhering to it more strenuously. We believe that the wise old saying "If a thing is worth doing, it's worth doing well" is true of reasoning too.

Ideally, the complete format for a good argument includes the following parts, and we have attempted to follow this format as much as possible.

A. The whole science or study (apologetics) is divided into important issues, one for each chapter. (These correspond to the "questions" in the *Summa.*)

B. Each chapter is divided into a number of distinct, specific controversial questions which have two possible answers, or sides. (These questions correspond to the "articles" in the *Summa.*) Sometimes a chapter will have only one such question, such as: Does God exist?

C. Each question can be further divided into seven parts. These seven things must be done in order to settle an argument completely.

1. Definition of terms and the meaning of the question

2. The importance of the question, the difference it makes

3. Objections to the Christian answer to the question

4. Answers to each of these objections

5. Arguments for the Christian answer from premises accepted by the unbeliever as well as by the believer

6. Objections to *these* arguments

7. Answers to each of these objections

We must answer both our opponents' own arguments in step (4) and their objections to our arguments in step (7). Their arguments against Christianity come in step (3) and we must show each of these to contain ambiguities, falsehoods or fallacies. Their criticisms of our arguments in step (6) take the form of their claiming to find ambiguities, falsehoods or fallacies in *our* arguments.

A very demanding reader will fault us for not insisting on all parts of this format for each question. Most readers will be a bit put out that we come so close to it—much more so than any other nontechnical book in the field today. We attempt to bridge the gap between the popular and the technical, the amateur and the professional, so we compromise a bit of the ideal format for easier readability.

About Apologetics
Answers to Objections to Doing Apologetics
Most people scorn or ignore apologetics because it seems very intellectual, abstract and rational. They contend that life and love and morality and sanctity are much more important than reason.

Those who reason this way are right; they just don't notice that they are *reasoning*. We can't avoid doing it, we can only avoid doing it well. Further, reason is a friend, not an enemy, to faith (see chap. 2) and to sanctity, for it is a road to truth, and sanctity means loving God, who is Truth.

Not only does apologetic reasoning lead to faith and sanctity, but faith and sanctity also lead to apologetic reasoning. For sanctity means loving God, and loving God means obeying God's will, and God's will is for us to *know* him and to be "ready to give a reason for the hope that is in you" (1 Pet 3:15).

Finally, the fact that apologetics is not nearly as important as love does not mean it is not very, very important. The fact that health is not as important as wisdom does not mean health is not very important—much more important than money, for instance.

All the arguments in this book, and in all the books on apologetics ever written, are worth less in the eyes of God than a single act of love to him or to your neighbor. But if even one of these arguments is a good one, it alone is worth more than the price in dollars that you paid for this whole book.

Another, deeper reason why some people scorn apologetic reasoning is that they decide whether to believe or not with their hearts much more than with their heads. Even the most perfect argument does not move people as much as emotion, desire and concrete experience. Most of us know that our heart is our center, not our head. But apologetics gets at the heart *through* the head. The head is important precisely because it is a gate to the heart. We can love only what we know.

Further, reason at least has veto power. We can't believe what we know to be untrue, and we can't love what we believe to be unreal. Arguments may not bring you to faith, but they can certainly keep you away from faith. Therefore we must join the battle of arguments.

Arguments can bring you to faith in the same sense as a car can bring you to the sea. The car can't swim; you have to jump in to do that. But you can't jump in from a hundred miles inland. You need a car first to bring you to the point where you *can* make a leap of faith into the sea. Faith *is* a leap, but a leap in the light, not in the dark.

The head is like the navigator. The heart is like the captain. (What Scripture means by "heart" is closer to "will" than "feelings.") Both are indispensable. Each obeys the other in a different way.

Reasons for Doing Apologetics

The first reason, for the Christian, is out of obedience to God's will, announced in his Word. Refusal to give a reason for faith is disobedience to God. There are also at least two practical reasons for doing apologetics: to convince unbelievers and to instruct and build up believers.

Even if there were no unbelievers to persuade, we should still give reasons for faith, for faith does not remain alone but produces reasons just as it produces good works. Faith educates reason and reason explores the treasure of the "faith that was once for all entrusted to the saints" (Jude 3).

Furthermore, faith for a Christian is faith in a God who is himself love, our lover and our beloved; and the more our hearts love someone, the more our minds want to know about our beloved. Faith naturally leads to reason through the agency of love. So faith leads to reason, and reason leads to faith—that is what this book tries to show. Thus reason and faith are friends, companions, wedded partners, allies.

Apologetics is also like war, for the two friends, faith and reason, have common enemies. Apologetic arguments are like military hardware. Note how Paul describes the spiritual warfare of which apologetics is a part:

> Indeed, we live as human beings, but we do not wage war according to human standards; for the weapons of our warfare are not merely human, but they have divine power to destroy strongholds. We destroy arguments and every proud obstacle raised up against the knowledge of God, and we take every thought captive to obey Christ. (2 Cor 10:3-5)

In this warfare we defend reason as well as faith, for reason is the friend of truth, and un*faith* is un*true*. In defending the faith we take back territory of the mind that is rightfully ours, or rather God's. All territory is God's. As Arthur Holmes said, "All truth is God's truth."

But the warfare is against unbelief, not unbelievers, just as insulin is against diabetes, not diabetics. The goal of apologetics is not victory but truth. Both sides win. Abraham Lincoln's saying also applies to apologetic arguments: "The best way to conquer your enemy is to make him your friend."

We invite critics, skeptics, unbelievers and believers in other religions to dialogue with us and write to us—for the sake of our mutual pursuit of truth, and for the (much less important) sake of improving future editions of this book. One of the few things in life that cannot possibly do harm, in the end, is the honest pursuit of the truth.

Concerning Methodology

An introduction to apologetics usually deals with methodology. We do not. We believe that nowadays second-order questions of method often distract attention from first-order questions of truth. Our intent is to get "back to basics." We have no particular methodological axe to grind. We try to use commonsense standards of rationality and universally agreed principles of logic in all our arguing. We collect and sharpen arguments like gem collectors collecting and polishing gems; readers can set them into various settings of their own.

But we must say one thing about method: how *not* to use this book.

We have said that apologetic arguments are like military hardware. That is a dangerous metaphor, for they are never to be used to hit people over the head. Argumentation is a human enterprise that is embedded in a larger social and psychological context. This context includes (1) the total psyches of the two persons engaged in dialogue, (2) the relationship between the two persons, (3) the immediate situation in which they find themselves, and (4) the larger social, cultural and historical situation surrounding them. Even national, political, racial and sexual factors influence the apologetic situation. One should not use the same arguments in discussion with a Muslim woman from Tehran that one would use with an African-American teenager from Los Angeles.

In other words, though arguments are weapons, they are more like swords than bombs. Bombs are rather indiscriminate in their targets. It also matters little who drops a bomb. But it matters enormously who wields a sword, for a sword is an extension of the swordsman. Thus, an argument in apologetics, when actually used in dialogue, is an extension of the arguer. The arguer's tone, sincerity, care, concern, listening and respect matter as much as his or her logic—probably more. The world was won for Christ not by arguments but by sanctity: "What you are speaks so loud, I can hardly hear what you say."

The Need for Apologetics Today

Apologetics is especially needed today, when the world stands at a triple crossroads and crisis.

1. Western civilization is for the first time in its history in danger of dying. The reason is spiritual. It is losing its life, its soul; that soul was the Christian faith. The infection killing it is not multiculturalism—other faiths—but the monoculturalism of secularism—no faith, no soul. Our century has been marked by genocide, sexual chaos and money-worship. Unless all the prophets are liars, we are doomed unless we repent and "turn back the clock" (not technologically but spiritually). The church of Christ will never die, but our civilization will. If the gates of hell will not prevail against the church, this world certainly won't. We do apologetics not to save the church but to save the world.

2. We are not only in a civil, cultural crisis, but also a philosophical, intellectual one. Our crisis is "a crisis of truth" (to use Ralph Martin's title). Increasingly, the very idea of objective truth is being ignored, abandoned or attacked—not only in practice but even in theory, directly and explicitly, especially by the educational and media establishments, who mold our minds. (See chap. 16 for a defense of this foundational idea of objective truth.)

3. Finally, the deepest level of our crisis is not cultural or intellectual but spiritual. At stake are the eternal souls of men and women for whom Christ died. Some think the end is near. We are skeptical of such predictions, but we know one thing with certainty: each individual is nearing the end, death and eternal judgment, every day. Our civilization may last for another century, but you will not. You will soon stand naked in the light of God. You had better learn to love and seek that light while there is still time, so that it will be your joy and not your fear forever. It is unfashionable today to put such things in print—a fact that says volumes about the spiritual sanity of our ostrichlike age.

This book tries to be a road map in the search for truth about God. Road maps are useful at any time, but especially in this time when the landscape seems to have changed so radically that many wander around lost, and when the old maps have been scorned, mutilated or discarded.

Mere, or Orthodox, Christianity

We confine ourselves in this book to the core beliefs common to all orthodox Christians—what C. S. Lewis called "mere Christianity." By *mere* we do not mean some abstract "lowest common denominator," but the heart or essence of the faith, as summarized in the Apostles' Creed. This ancient and unchanging core unites diverse believers with each other and against unbelievers within many churches and denominations as well as without. Liberal (or modernist or demythologist or revisionist) theologians will not like this book, especially its arguments for miracles, the reliability of Scripture, the reality of the resurrection, the divinity of Christ and the reality of heaven and hell. We invite them to join the self-confessed unbelievers in trying to refute these arguments. We also invite them to begin practicing more accurate "truth in labeling" in describing their own position.

Liberal readers may stigmatize this book as "conservative" or "right-wing." Neither term is accurate or appropriate.

"Conservative," as opposed to "progressive," refers to something in time and history; not eternal truths, but opinions or ways of the past as against the future. What is "progressive" at one time becomes "conservative" at another. Whether God, heaven or miracles exist is a question not about timebound opinions, but about unchanging realities.

"Right-wing" refers to a post-French-Revolution political orientation, as opposed to "left-wing" (more or less socialistic), which has nothing to do with Christian apologetics. The truth or falsity of socialism in politics does not follow from the existence or nonexistence of God.

The correct theological term for many who label themselves "liberal" or "left-wing" or "progressive" theologians is "heretics." By definition, a heretic is one who dissents from an essential doctrine (from the Greek *haireomai*, "to pick out for oneself"). Since most heretics today no longer believe in the very idea of essential doctrines, they do not accept the label.

They also have a strong case in the press because the church still smells from the smoke of the Inquisition, when it made the very same mistake contemporary liberals make: confusing heresies with heretics. The Spanish Inquisition wrongly destroyed heretics in order rightly to destroy heresies; modern "liberals" wrongly love heresies in order rightly to love heretics.

Apologetics defends orthodox Christianity. Dissenters don't believe in apologetics for orthodox Christianity because they do not believe in orthodox Christianity. They believe in apologizing for it, not apologetics for it.

Some of the conclusions we argue for are proper to Christianity alone (e.g., the divinity of Christ). Some are also taught by other theistic religions, especially Judaism and Islam (e.g., a Creator-God). Some are taught by all or nearly all the world's religions (e.g., life after death). One of them is even shared by theists and clear-minded, honest atheists, but widely denied today: the existence of objective truth. Logically, this should be our first topic. But since it is the most abstract of all our topics, we have placed it in the last chapter so that readers would not be daunted.

Questions for Discussion

1. What is apologetics? What is religion? What is their relation?

2. Is there anything distinctively Christian about apologetics? Why or why not? Do all religions include apologetics? Why or why not?

3. How much do you think natural human reason can accomplish in religion? In general?

4. What good does it do to argue for your faith? What harm can it do?

5. What is the point of, or the reason for, the difference between the premodern notion of "reason" and the modern notion? What are the pluses and minuses of each?

6. How do you think reason is related to (a) authority, (b) love, (c) intuition, (d) mysticism, (e) symbolism, (f) hope?

7. How useful are merely probable arguments?

8. Can there be truth without knowledge? Knowledge without certainty? Certainty without proof? Proof without the scientific method? Why or why not?

9. Should methodology be a first and important question? Why or why not?

10. Is apologetics more or less appropriate today than in the Middle Ages?

11. Is Christian apologetics naturally and properly "conservative" or "liberal"? Why? Define these terms theologically.

12. Why do you think Luther called reason "the Devil's whore"? Isn't reason fallen along with the rest of human nature? If so, how can we trust it?

13. If we need God to validate reason and reason to validate God, how do we escape circular reasoning? Since any proof of God is by definition rational, if God does not validate reason, what else can? Reason itself? Something subrational? Our brain-computers were programmed either by God (a good spirit), the Devil (an evil spirit) or blind chance (no spirit, no mind); only in the first case are they trustworthy. Doesn't this lead us straight into circular reasoning?

14. Why do you suppose Aquinas said that "to impugn human reason is to impugn God"? What are some consequences that follow if that is believed?

Outline of Chapter 2
Faith & Reason

1. The importance of the question

2. Definitions

☐ Faith

The *object* of faith is all the things revealed by God

The *act* of faith includes

emotional trust

intellectual belief

volitional love and obedience

the heart's fundamental acceptance

☐ Reason

The *object* of reason is all truths that can be

understood by reason alone

discovered by reason alone

proved by reason alone

The *act* of reason is all the acts of

understanding truths

discovering truths

proving truths

3. The relation between the objects of faith and reason

Five possible answers

☐ Rationalism

☐ Fideism

☐ Identity of faith and reason

☐ Dualism

☐ Partially overlapping: there are three classes of truths

Known by faith and not by reason

Known by both faith and reason

Known by reason and not by faith

4. Why faith and reason can never contradict each other

☐ Only falsehood can contradict truth

☐ God is the single teacher in both faith and reason

5. Objections

☐ How can we understand God's infinitely superior mind by our reason?

☐ Isn't it humble to demean reason's powers?

☐ Isn't it proud to claim reason can know much about God?

☐ Why are there rationally brilliant unbelievers?

☐ Aren't Christians' reasons really rationalizations?

☐ Doesn't reason take away the merit of faith?

Postscript

CHAPTER 2
Faith
& Reason

I N A SENSE THE MARRIAGE OF FAITH AND REASON IS THE MOST IMPORTANT
question in apologetics because it is the overall question. If faith and
reason are not wedded partners, if faith and reason are divorced or
incompatible, like cats and birds, then apologetics is impossible. For apologetics is the attempt to ally reason to faith, to defend faith with reason's
weapons.

Definitions
It is especially crucial to clarify our definitions of *faith* and *reason,* because
these terms are often used either vaguely or equivocally. Defining removes
vagueness. Distinguishing two possible meanings and confining ourselves
to one at a time removes equivocation.

Faith
We must distinguish the *act* of faith from the *object* of faith, believing from
what is believed.

1. The object of faith means all the things believed. For the Christian,
this means everything God has revealed in the Bible; Catholics include all
the creeds and universal binding teachings of the church as well. This faith
(the object, not the act) is expressed in propositions. Propositions are not
expressions of the act of believing but expressions of the content believed.
Liturgical and moral acts express the act of believing. However, the propositions are not the ultimate objects of faith, but only the proximate objects

of faith. They are manifold, but the ultimate object of faith is one. The ultimate object of faith is not words but God's Word (singular)—indeed, God himself. The propositions are the map or structure of faith; God is the real existing object of faith. (God is also the author of faith—both the revealer of the objective doctrines believed and the one who inspires the heart to make the free choice to believe them.)

It is equally wrong to stop at propositions and not have your faith reach out to the living God, or to denigrate propositions as dispensable or even harmful to living faith. Without a live relationship to the living God, propositions are pointless, for their point is to point beyond themselves to God. ("A finger is good for pointing to the moon, but woe to him who mistakes the finger for the moon," according to a wise Zen saying.) But without propositions, we cannot know or tell others what God we believe in and what we believe about God.

2. The act of faith is more than merely an act of belief. We believe many things—for example, that the Bulls will beat the Celtics, that the President is not a crook, that Norway is beautiful—but we are not willing to die for these beliefs, nor can we live them every moment. But religious faith is something to die for and something to live every moment. It is much more than belief, and much stronger, though belief is one of its parts or aspects.

We can distinguish at least four aspects or dimensions of religious faith. Ranked on a hierarchy from less to more important and essential, and less to more interior—that is, as coming from ever more central aspects of the human self—they are (a) emotional faith, (b) intellectual faith, (c) volitional faith and (d) heart faith.

a. Emotional faith is feeling assurance or trust or confidence in a person. This includes hope (which is much stronger than just a wish) and peace (which is much stronger than mere calm).

b. Intellectual faith is belief. This is stronger than emotional faith in that it is more stable and unchanging, like an anchor. My mind can believe while my feelings are shaken. This belief, however, is held tight, unlike a mere opinion. The old definition of intellectual faith was "the act of the intellect, prompted by the will, by which we believe everything God has revealed on the grounds of the authority of the One who revealed it." It is this aspect of faith that is formulated in propositions and summarized in creeds.

c. Volitional faith is an act of the will, a commitment to obey God's will. This faith is faithfulness, or fidelity. It manifests itself in behavior, that is, in good works. Just as a hope deeper than a wish is central to emotional faith, and a belief deeper than an opinion is central to intellectual faith, so a love deeper than a feeling is central to volitional faith. For the root of volitional faith—the will—is the faculty or power of the soul that is closest to the prefunctional root and center called the "heart" (d).

The intellect is the soul's navigator, but the will is its captain. The intellect is its Mr. Spock, the will is its Captain Kirk, and the feelings are its Dr. McCoy. The soul is an "Enterprise," a real starship. The will can command the intellect to think, but the intellect cannot command the will to will, only inform it, as a navigator informs the captain. Yet the will cannot simply make you believe. It can't force the intellect to believe what appears to it to be false, or to disbelieve what seems to it to be true. Belief is what happens when you decide to be honest and put your mind in the service of truth. (See Aquinas, *Summa Theologiae*, I, 82, 3-4 on the relationship between intellect and will.)

d. Faith begins in that obscure mysterious center of our being that Scripture calls the "heart." *Heart* in Scripture (and in the church fathers, especially Augustine) does not mean feeling or sentiment or emotion, but the absolute center of the soul, as the physical heart is at the center of the body. The heart is where God the Holy Spirit works in us. This is not specifiable as a kind of interior *object*, as emotions, intellect and will are, because it is the very self, the I, the subject, the one whose emotions and mind and will they are.

"Keep your heart with all vigilance," advised Solomon, "for from it flow the springs of life" (Prov 4:23). With the heart we choose our "fundamental option" of yes or no to God, and thereby determine our eternal identity and destiny.

The faith-works controversy that sparked the Protestant Reformation was due largely to an equivocation on the word *faith*. If we use "faith" as Catholic theology does—see the old Baltimore Catechism definition of faith in section (b) above—and as Paul did in 1 Corinthians 13—that is, if we mean intellectual faith—then faith alone is not sufficient for salvation, for "Even the demons believe—and shudder" (Jas 2:19). Hope, and above all love, need to be added to faith (1 Cor 13:13). But if we use "faith" as Luther did, and as Paul did in Romans and Galatians, that is, as heart-faith, then this is saving faith. It is sufficient for salvation, for it necessarily produces the good works of love just as a good tree necessarily produces good fruit. Protestants and Catholics agree on this. The Pope even told the German Lutheran bishops so over a decade ago, and they were startled and delighted. The two churches issued a public Joint Statement on Justification, a statement of agreement. Protestants and Catholics do not have essentially different religions, different ways of salvation. There are real and important differences, but this most central issue is not one of them.

Reason

Here again we must distinguish the subjective, personal *act* of reason from the *object* of reason.

1. The object of reason means all that reason can know. This includes three kinds of things, corresponding to the "three acts of the mind" in classical Aristotelian logic. It means all the truths that can be (a) *understood* by reason (that is, by human reason alone without faith in divine revelation), (b) *discovered* by human reason to be true and (c) *proved* logically, without any premises assumed by faith in divine revelation. (See figure 1 on page 33.)

a. For instance, we can understand what a star is made of by human reason alone, and this is not part of divine revelation. We can also understand why the universe is so well ordered: human reason tells us that there must be a superhuman intelligence behind its design. This second example is also part of divine revelation, while the first is not. A third case: we cannot understand what God's plan to save humanity is by human reason alone, only by divine revelation.

b. As to the second "act of the mind"—we can discover that the planet Pluto exists by human reason alone, and this is not part of divine revelation. We can also discover the historical existence of Jesus by human reason alone, by historical research. But this truth is also part of divine revelation, while the first is not. But we cannot discover by reason alone that God loves us so much that he died for us. We can know this only by faith in divine revelation.

c. Finally, we can prove the Pythagorean theorem in geometry by human reason alone, and this is not part of revelation. We can also prove by reason alone that the soul does not die as the body dies, by good philosophical arguments (see chap. 10). This is also part of revelation. But we cannot prove that God is a Trinity; we can only believe it because God revealed it.

2. The act of reason, as distinct from the object of reason, means all the subjective, personal acts of the mind by which we (a) understand, (b) discover or (c) prove any truth. The ancient meaning of *reason* included all three of these "acts of the mind," classically called (a) "simple apprehension," (b) judgment and (c) reasoning. But the meaning of reason narrowed in modern times, beginning with Ockham's nominalism in the fourteenth century and Descartes's rationalism in the seventeenth, to mean only the

Figure 1

	Understanding	Discovering	Proving
By reason alone and not part of revelation	What a star is made of	That Pluto exists	The Pythagorean theorem
By reason and by faith in divine revelation	Why the universe is so well ordered	The historical existence of Jesus	That the soul does not die
Not by reason, only by faith in divine revelation	God's plan to save us	How much God loves us	God is a Trinity

"third act of the mind," reasoning, calculating, proving. We use the older, broader meaning of reason here.

Reason is relative to truth; it is a way of knowing truth: understanding it, discovering it or proving it. Faith is also relative to truth; it is a way of discovering truth. No human being ever existed without some faith. We all know most of what we know by faith; that is, by belief in what others—parents, teachers, friends, writers, society—tell us. Outside religion as well as inside it, faith *and* reason are roads to truth.

The Relation Between the Objects of Faith and Reason

Having defined our two terms, we are ready to ask the question about the relation between them. When we ask this question, we do not mean "What is the *psychological* relation between the *act* of faith and the *act* of reason?" but "What is the *logical* relation between the *object* of faith and the *object* of reason?" How are these two sets of truths—those knowable by unaided human reason and those knowable by faith in divine revelation—related?

There are always five possible answers to the question of the relation between any two classes or sets of things:

1. All *A*'s are *B*'s but not all *B*'s are *A*'s.

2. All *B*'s are *A*'s but not all *A*'s are *B*'s.

3. All *A*'s are *B*'s and all *B*'s are *A*'s.

4. No *A*'s are *B*'s and no *B*'s are *A*'s.

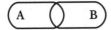

5. Some but not all *A*'s are *B*'s
and some but not all *B*'s are *A*'s.

Applied to the faith-reason question, the five possibilities come out as follows:
1. All that is known by faith is also known by reason, but not all that is known by reason is known by faith. Faith is a subclass of reason.

2. All that is known by reason is also known by faith, but not all that is known by faith is known by reason. Reason is a subclass of faith.

3. All that is known by faith is known by reason too, and all that is known by reason is known by faith. Faith and reason are interchangeable.

4. Nothing that is known by faith is known by reason, and nothing that is known by reason is known by faith. Faith and reason are mutually exclusive.

5. Some but not all that is known by faith is also known by reason, and some but not all that is known by reason is also known by faith. Faith and reason partly overlap.

Keep in mind here that *reason* can mean one, two or all three of the objects of the three "acts of the mind": what can be understood, discovered or proved by reason.

Let us now consider each of these five possible answers.

1. Rationalism

Rationalism holds that everything we know by faith can also be understood, or discovered, or proved by reason, but not vice versa. Faith is a subclass or subdepartment of reason.

Very few Christian thinkers have claimed this. Anselm seems to have been one, for he tried to prove even the doctrines of the Trinity and the Incarnation by strict rational philosophical arguments, what he called "necessary reasons."

Hegel was a very different kind of rationalist. He radically reinterpreted the content of revelation to fit his philosophy (e.g., he denied creation out of nothing and Christ's unique divinity). This is Christian rationalism only if we stretch the term *Christian* beyond any useful historical definition. Hegel believed that the historic Christian faith, traditionally interpreted, was a primitive, only symbolically or mythically true precursor of his philosophy. Today Hegel's kind of rationalism is quite popular, but Anselm's is (as far as we know) totally extinct.

2. Fideism

Fideism contends that the only knowledge, or at least the only certain knowledge, we can have is by faith. While rationalism denies the existence of any truths of faith unprovable by reason, fideism denies the existence of any certain truths attainable by reason without faith.

Now there is no explicitly *religious* faith involved in knowing things like the existence of Pluto or the Pythagorean theorem. Therefore fideism must mean either that all such truths, outside religion, are uncertain, or that if they are certain they come under some kind of nonreligious faith.

The first choice seems simply ridiculous. We may not be certain that the sun will rise tomorrow, but we are certain that $2 + 2 = 4$. We do have some certainties. Therefore it must mean that all certainties come from some nonreligious faith. The main candidate for this "nonreligious faith" is faith in reason itself.

Pascal, for instance, argued that to trust reason in the first place must itself be an act of faith, and not rationally provable. For if trust in reason were proved by reason, we would be committing the logical fallacy of "begging the question," assuming what we are supposed to prove. Pascal further argued that if the source of our reason is not an intelligent and trustworthy God, but blind chance or some untrustworthy evil spirit, then our reason is not trustworthy at all. Who would trust a computer programmed by chance or a deceiver? But how do we know there is a good and trustworthy God who created and designed human reason? If we try to prove such a God by our reason, we again beg the question and argue in a circle. We try to validate God by reason and reason by God. The only way out, argued Pascal, is a nonrational leap of faith in the beginning.

We think this argument is a strong one, but it does not necessarily lead to practical fideism: the refusal to try to prove any of the doctrines of faith. It only contends that the ultimate *theoretical* justification for reason cannot be reason itself. Pascal himself offered many rational arguments for his faith in the *Pensées*.

3. Identity of Faith and Reason
Position 3, that of an identity between what is knowable by faith and what is knowable by reason, is a logical possibility, but no one we know of has ever held it.

4. Dualism
Dualism is a popular position today because it reflects the "separation of church and state," religion and philosophy, sacred and secular, that characterizes the modern era. Dualism simply divorces faith and reason, placing them into two different compartments. It usually does this by (a) reducing reason to scientific, mathematical and empirical reasoning, and (b) reducing faith to a personal, subjective attitude. Thus reason and faith correspond to the public and private sectors.

It seems reasonable to hold such dualism if you believe some esoteric Eastern religion based on private mystical experience; but unreasonable if you are a Christian, a Jew or a Muslim (all of whom have been called "the

People of the Book"), someone who believes in a religion of public, propositional revelation.

It also seems cowardly not to meet the unbeliever's challenge to fight on a common field (reason) but instead to withdraw to a private one (faith as conceived here in a merely subjective way—a fundamental misunderstanding of "faith," judged by historic Christian standards).

5. Partial Overlapping

Most people would agree with us that the fifth position is the most reasonable and correct one. It distinguishes three different kinds of truths:

a. truths of faith and not of reason,
b. truths of both faith and reason, and
c. truths of reason and not of faith.

Truths of faith alone are things revealed by God but not understandable, discoverable or provable by reason (e.g., the Trinity or the fact that Christ's death atoned for our sins). Truths of both faith and reason are things revealed by God but also understandable, discoverable or provable by reason (e.g., the existence of one God, or an objective moral law, or life after death). Truths of reason and not of faith are things not revealed by God but known by human reason (e.g., the natural sciences). If this is the correct position, it follows that the Christian apologist has two tasks: to prove all the propositions in class *b* and to answer all objections to the propositions in class *a*.

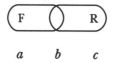

a   b   c

We cannot prove the propositions in class *a* (e.g., the Trinity), but we can answer all objections to them. For example, suppose a Unitarian objects to the Trinity because "it splits God into triplets." We can show that this is a misunderstanding; it does not mean three Gods, but one God in three Persons. Or suppose a logician says it is a contradiction to call anything both one and three. We can reply that God is one nature, not three, and three persons, not one. This is not a contradiction, any more than we are: we are two natures (spirit and animal, mind and matter, soul and body) but one person.

Christian thinkers do not all agree about how many of the propositions of faith can be proved by reason, but most have held that some could (thus apologetics is possible) but not all (thus apologetics is limited).

The doctrine of the Fall teaches that human nature, and thus human reason, is corrupted, but still valid and usable—like a crippled body. It can walk, unlike rocks, but not well. We must distinguish reason *de facto* ("in reality," or "in fact") and reason *de jure* ("by law," or "by right"), or reason in its everyday use and reason in itself, or reason improperly used and reason properly used. Used properly, it is powerful but not all-powerful. Reason can persuade you to walk to the beach, but you must make the leap of faith into the sea of the living God. Fideism says it can't even bring you to the beach; rationalism says it can put you into the sea.

Why Faith and Reason Can Never Contradict Each Other

There are two basic questions about the relation between faith and reason:

1. How much of the faith can reason prove?
2. Can faith and reason ever contradict each other?

We've already seen that there are different answers to question 1—all, some, none—and that the best answer seems to be *some*. Now what of the other question?

Only Falsehood Can Contradict Truth

Aquinas's answer to this question in *Summa Contra Gentiles* I, 7 seems to us irrefutably true:

> The truth that the human reason is naturally endowed to know cannot be opposed to the truth of the Christian faith. For that with which the human reason is naturally endowed is clearly most true; so much so, that it is impossible for us to think of such truths as false. [If we only understand the meaning of the terms in such self-evident propositions as "The whole is greater than the part" or "What has color must have size," we cannot think them false.] Nor is it permissible to believe as false that which we hold by faith, since this is confirmed in a way that is so clearly divine. [It is not our faith but its object, God, that justifies our certainty.] Since, therefore, only the false is opposed to the true, as is clearly evident from an examination of their definitions, it is impossible that truth of faith should be opposed to those principles that the human reason knows naturally.

Thus, either Christianity is false, or reason is false, or—if both are true—

there can never be any real contradiction at all between them, since truth cannot contradict truth.

Aquinas is speaking of faith and reason objectively, not subjectively. The objective stock of propositions revealed by God for us to believe, and the objective stock of propositions provable by our reason properly used, do not contain any contradictions. But subjectively, we fallen humans can easily err. We can misunderstand the faith, and we can misuse our reason. *Opinions* can certainly contradict faith, but reason itself cannot.

God Is the Teacher in Both

Aquinas gives a second, equally compelling reason for the same conclusion:

> Furthermore, that which is introduced into the soul of the student by the teacher is contained in the knowledge of the teacher—unless his teaching is fictitious, which it is improper to say of God. Now the knowledge of the principles that are known to us naturally [rationally self-evident propositions] has been implanted in us by God; for God is the Author of our nature. These principles, therefore, are also contained by the divine Wisdom. Hence, whatever is opposed to them is opposed to the divine Wisdom and therefore cannot come from God. That which we hold by faith as divinely revealed, therefore, cannot be contrary to our natural knowledge.

Many will follow Aquinas so far, but balk at his next point. Yet this next point follows necessarily from the previous one:

> From this we evidently gather the following conclusion: whatever arguments are brought forward against the doctrines of faith are conclusions incorrectly derived from the first and self-evident principles embedded in [rational human] nature. Such conclusions do not have the force of demonstration; they are arguments that are either probable or sophistical [fallacious]. And so there exists the possibility to answer them.

In other words, every possible argument against every Christian doctrine has a rational mistake in it somewhere, and therefore can be answered by reason alone.

If this were not so, if Aquinas is wrong here, then one of those arguments from unbelievers against one of the doctrines of Christianity, at least, would really and truly prove the doctrine to be false, that is, prove Christianity untrue. Aquinas's optimistic view of the marriage between faith and reason necessarily follows from the simple premise that Christianity is true. Thus "Christian irrationalism" is self-contradictory.

Remember, however, that we (and Aquinas) are not claiming that all

Christian doctrines can be proved by reason, only that every argument against them can be disproved. Nor are we claiming that any given person can disprove them. Reason is flawless, de jure, but reasoners are not, de facto.

Aquinas's confidence is also confirmed by experience and history. For nearly two millennia, orthodox Christians have found it true. Today thousands of thoughtful converts repeat the same threefold process of discovery that Justin Martyr wrote of in the second century in his autobiographical *First Apology:*

1. A man seeks the truth by the unaided effort of reason, and is disappointed.

2. It is offered him by faith, and he accepts.

3. And, having accepted, he finds that it satisfies his reason. (See E. Gilson, *The Spirit of Medieval Philosophy,* chap. 2)

There is an even earlier testimony to this pattern. The first Christian apologist, Paul, expresses it in 1 Corinthians 1:20-25:

Where is the one who is wise? Where is the scribe? Where is the debater of this age? Has not God made foolish the wisdom of the world? For since, in the wisdom of God, the world did not know God through wisdom, God decided, through the foolishness of our proclamation, to save those who believe. For Jews demand signs and Greeks desire wisdom, but we proclaim Christ crucified, a stumbling block to Jews and foolishness to Gentiles, but to those who are the called, both Jews and Greeks, Christ the power of God and the wisdom of God. For God's foolishness is wiser than human wisdom, and God's weakness is stronger than human strength.

If the divinely revealed gospel, "God's foolishness," is wiser than the best human philosophical wisdom, then human wisdom must be more foolish than the gospel. There are three ways to be foolish: (a) to misapprehend or misunderstand or fail to grasp; (b) to be ignorant, to fail to know or discover, and (c) to be illogical and fail to prove, to commit a fallacy. At least one of these follies, or mistakes, corresponding to the three "acts of the mind," must be present in every argument against the truth, and therefore also against the truth of the Christian faith. And since these three follies are follies of reason, right reason can refute them.

The sword of reason is in itself undefeatable and can cut through all the objections to the faith. But any given human reasoner, like any given swordsman, can use it badly, that is, irrationally. The Fall weakened our arms that wield the sword, but the sword itself remains sharp.

Objections

Objection 1: *But God's ways and mind and nature are infinitely far above ours; how can we expect to understand them?*

Reply: But we *can* understand what he has revealed to us. Otherwise he is a poor teacher. A good teacher communicates effectively, translating the advanced truths he knows into the proper level of understanding for his students. We cannot completely understand divine truth, of course. We *know* God by revelation, but we do not *comprehend* him. We touch him but we do not surround him or define him with our reason.

Objection 2: *Isn't it humble to demean the powers of human reason?*

Reply: Reason is created and designed by God. It is part of God's image in us. It is God's opus, not ours. (Did we invent the human soul?) We do not praise an artist by demeaning his work.

We must distinguish reason de jure from reason de facto and be aware of the great limits of the latter. The proper place for humility is regarding our use of God's gifts (including reason), not regarding those gifts themselves. If your mother knitted you a beautiful sweater and someone saw you wearing it and said "That sweater is beautiful!" it would not be humility to reply, "No, it's not really very beautiful at all."

Objection 3: *But you are claiming a lot for human reason even de facto, as used in practice. Isn't it proud to think human reason can know a lot about God?*

Reply: It is more arrogant to say that we know so much about the limits of reason that we can lay down limits in advance for reason. If we know so little, how do we know how little we can know? It is more proud to use reason to limit reason than just to use reason. It is also self-contradictory, for "to draw a limit to thought you must think both sides of that limit" (Wittgenstein).

Objection 4: *What about all those intellectually brilliant unbelievers, the counterexamples to Justin Martyr? If Christianity is so reasonable, why did Celsus, Plotinus, Hobbes, Machiavelli, Voltaire, Rousseau, Goethe, Melville, Jefferson, Shaw, Russell, Franklin, Sartre, Camus, Nietzsche, Marx, Freud and Skinner all reject it?*

Reply A: Christianity is reasonable but it is not obvious. It is more like $E = MC^2$ than like $2 + 2 = 4$.

Reply B: If Christianity is so irrational, why have so many brilliant minds accepted it? The assortment of unbelievers mentioned above is easily overcome by Paul, John, Augustine, Aquinas, Anselm, Bonaventura, Scotus, Luther, Calvin, Descartes, Pascal, Leibniz, Berkeley, Galileo, Copernicus,

Kepler, Newton, Newman, Lincoln, Pasteur, Kierkegaard, Shakespeare, Dante, Chesterton, Lewis, Solzhenitsyn, Tolstoy, Dostoyevsky, Tolkien, da Vinci, Michelangelo, T. S. Eliot, Dickens, Milton, Spenser and Bach, not to mention a certain Jesus of Nazareth.

Reply C: Brilliant minds often reject Christianity because they don't *want* it to be true, because it is no longer fashionable or because it commands obedience, repentance and humility.

Objection 5: *But aren't Christians' reasons really rationalizations? Aquinas didn't really arrive at the existence of God by means of the reasoning in his five proofs; he learned it from his mother. Then, as an adult, he looked for some reasons to confirm the faith he had already adopted for nonlogical reasons. That's not reasoning but rationalizing.*

Reply A: Even if that were all Aquinas did, it would not invalidate his proofs. An irrational subjective motive does not necessarily mean an irrational objective argument. Suppose Einstein had discovered that $E = MC^2$ because he was a Nazi who wanted to invent the atom bomb to conquer the Allies and win the world for Hitler. That bad motive would not mean that E does *not* equal MC^2. The objection commits "the genetic fallacy": confusing the psychological origin of an idea with its logical validity.

Reply B: Looking for good reasons for your faith can be perfectly honest if you are also open to reasons against it, as Aquinas certainly was. The objections against the many doctrines he defends in the *Summa* are manifold, fairly stated and objectively answered.

Reply C: Although Aquinas first learned about God by faith, Aristotle didn't. He knew nothing of the Scriptures, but much about God. History proves that human reason unaided by faith in divine revelation can come to know the existence and some of the attributes of God—for example, that he is one, eternal, perfect, intelligent and the uncaused cause. Aristotle did just that. His reasoning was not rationalizing, for he had no faith to rationalize (except faith in reason itself).

Revelation takes us for an easy ride up the mountain of truth in a divinely provided helicopter. Reason struggles and scrambles up the hard, slow footpath, and doesn't get nearly as far up. Neither way invalidates the other. But millions can get to the top in the helicopter, while only a few Aristotles can get more than a few feet up the path by walking.

Objection 6: *Doesn't reason take away the merit of faith? There is nothing praiseworthy in believing something because you see it, whether with your eyes or with your* *mind; but it is praiseworthy to trust a friend. To prove what you believe removes your merit, or praiseworthiness, in believing it; so it is not advantageous.*

Reply A: Since we are supposed to grow up and figure things out for ourselves, understanding and proving our faith *is* praiseworthy. Our parents don't want us to remain children who don't understand them but can only trust them. (Nor do they want us to stop trusting them.) What is praiseworthy is obeying God's will in all things, including his will for us to grow up.

Reply B: Reason is not more perfect virtue than faith, but it is more perfect knowledge. Faith is secondhand knowledge, through authority. In heaven there will be no need for faith. We will see and understand for ourselves. Insofar as we can do this on earth, this is progress, for heaven is the standard of real progress.

To add reason to faith is progress, but to demand reason before faith is not. If I demand proof before trusting you, that means I trust you less. But to desire to rationally understand the one I trust is not a weakening of the trust.

Reply C: Finally, we still need faith even after we know a truth by reason, to stave off irrational doubts. Reason and faith are not rivals but allies against irrational doubts, passion, prejudice, propaganda, fear, folly, fantasy and fallacy.

Postscript

There is a far harder task than the one this chapter has dealt with. This chapter showed that there can never be any real contradiction between faith and reason, between Christian revelation and true philosophy or true science. It was about the task of being both a full Christian and a full philosopher or scientist. That task is easy. What is harder, and more precious, is to be a Christian philosopher or a Christian scientist.

The greatness of giants like Augustine and Aquinas was not merely that they solved problems and resolved apparent contradictions between faith and reason, Christianity and philosophy; but that they married them, united them, permeated their philosophy with the light of faith. They were not, like Descartes, just philosophers who happened to be Christians or Christians who happened to be philosophers, but Christian philosophers.

How do you do that? It takes more than a chapter in a book to say. Read them and see. You learn more about what a good marriage is by living in one than by reading all the books in the world about it. The same is true of the marriage between faith and reason. Through the magic of books, the masters still converse with us. We are invited to "come and see." The best way to become a good student, and then a good teacher, of Christian apologetics is to go to the masters to be taught, to sit at their feet. Even dwarves like us, if we have the good sense to do that, can become farsighted like eagles.

Questions for Discussion

1. Is the question of the relation between faith and reason more important for the Middle Ages or for the present? Why?

2. What exactly is "faith"? Does the answer to this question depend on which religion you believe? On whether or not you believe in any religion? Is faith the common factor in all religions?

3. How much of faith can reason prove? Why do you think that? How many objections against faith can reason disprove? Why do you think that?

4. What are the reasons for believing each of the five answers to the question of the relation between faith and reason (pp. 34-35)? How would you answer these reasons, or arguments, for the four answers or positions with which you disagree?

5. Evaluate Aquinas's three arguments (pp. 38-39).

6. Evaluate the answers to each of the six objections (pp. 41-43).

7. How could we recast the question of the relation between faith and reason if we meant by these two terms the subjective psychological acts rather than the objective content?

Part 2
GOD

Outline of Chapter 3
Twenty Arguments for the Existence of God

1. The argument from change
2. The argument from efficient causality
3. The argument from time and contingency
4. The argument from degrees of perfection
5. The design argument
6. The kalām argument
7. The argument from contingency
8. The argument from the world as an interacting whole
9. The argument from miracles
10. The argument from consciousness
11. The argument from truth
12. The argument from the origin of the idea of God
13. The ontological argument

    Anselm's version

    Modal version

    Possible worlds version

14. The moral argument
15. The argument from conscience

    Addendum on religion and morality

16. The argument from desire
17. The argument from aesthetic experience
18. The argument from religious experience
19. The common consent argument
20. Pascal's Wager

CHAPTER 3
Twenty Arguments
for the Existence
of God

I N THIS SECTION YOU WILL FIND ARGUMENTS OF MANY DIFFERENT KINDS for the existence of God. And we make to you, the reader, an initial appeal. We realize that many people, both believers and nonbelievers, doubt that God's existence can be demonstrated or even argued about. You may be one of them. You may in fact have a fairly settled view that it can*not* be argued about. But no one can reasonably doubt that attention to these arguments has its place in any book on apologetics. For very many have believed that such arguments are possible, and that some of them actually work.

They have also believed that an effective rational argument for God's existence is an important first step in opening the mind to the possibility of faith—in clearing some of the roadblocks and rubble that prevent people from taking the idea of divine revelation seriously. And in this they have a real point. Suppose our best and most honest reflection on the nature of things led us to see the material universe as self-sufficient and uncaused; to see its form as the result of random motions, devoid of any plan or purpose. Would you then be impressed by reading in an ancient book that there exists a God of love, or that the heavens proclaim his glory? Would you be disposed to take that message seriously? More likely you would excuse yourself from taking seriously anything claimed as a communication from the Creator. As one person put it: I cannot believe that we are adopted children of God, because I cannot believe there is anyone to do the adopting.

It is this sort of cramped and constricted horizon that the proofs presented in this chapter are trying to expand. They are attempts to confront us with the radical insufficiency of what is finite and limited, and to open our minds to a level of being beyond it. If they succeed in this—and we can say from experience that some of the proofs do succeed with many people—they can be of very great value indeed.

You may not feel that they are particularly valuable to you. You may be blessed with a vivid sense of God's presence; and that is something for which to be profoundly grateful. But that does not mean you have no obligation to ponder these arguments. For many have not been blessed in that way. And the proofs are designed for them—or some of them at least—to give a kind of help they really need. You may even be asked to provide that help.

Besides, are any of us really in so little need of such help as we may claim? Surely in most of us there is something of the skeptic. There is a part of us tempted to believe that nothing is ultimately real beyond what we can see and touch; a part looking for some reason, beyond the assurances of Scripture, to believe that there is more. We have no desire to make exaggerated claims for these demonstrations, or to confuse "good reason" with "scientific proof." But we believe that there are many who want and need the kind of help these proofs offer more than they might at first be willing to admit.

A word about the organization of the arguments. We have organized them into two basic groups: those which take their data from without—cosmological arguments—and those that take it from within—psychological arguments. The group of cosmological arguments begins with our versions of Aquinas's famous "five ways." These are not the simplest of the arguments, and therefore are not the most convincing to many people. Our order is not from the most to the least effective. The first argument, in particular, is quite abstract and difficult.

Not all the arguments are equally demonstrative. One (Pascal's Wager) is not an argument for God at all, but an argument for faith in God as a "wager." Another (the ontological argument) we regard as fundamentally flawed; yet we include it because it is very famous and influential, and may yet be saved by new formulations of it. Others (the argument from miracles, the argument from religious experience and the common consent argument) claim only strong probability, not demonstrative certainty. We have included them because they form a strong part of a cumulative case. We believe that only some of these arguments, taken individually and separately, demonstrate the existence of a being that has some of the properties only God can have (no argument proves all the divine attributes); but all twenty taken together, like twined rope, make a very strong case.

1. The Argument from Change

The material world we know is a world of change. This young woman came to be 5'2", but she was not always that height. The great oak tree before us grew from the tiniest acorn. Now when something comes to be in a certain state, such as mature size, that state cannot bring itself into being. For until it comes to be, it does not exist, and if it does not yet exist, it cannot cause anything.

As for the thing that changes, although it *can be* what it will become, it *is not yet* what it will become. It actually exists right now in this state (an acorn); it will actually exist in that state (large oak tree). But it is not actually in that state now. It only has the potentiality for that state.

Now a question: To explain the change, can we consider the changing thing alone, or must other things also be involved? Obviously, other things must be involved. Nothing can give itself what it does not have, and the changing thing cannot have now, already, what it will come to have then. The *result* of change cannot actually exist *before* the change. The changing thing begins with only the potential to change, but it needs to be acted on by other things outside if that potential is to be made actual. Otherwise it cannot change.

Nothing changes itself. Apparently self-moving things, like animal bodies, are moved by desire or will—something other than mere molecules. And when the animal or human dies, the molecules remain, but the body no longer moves because the desire or will is no longer present to move it.

Now a further question: Are the other things outside the changing thing also changing? Are its movers also moving? If so, all of them stand in need right now of being acted on by other things, or else they cannot change No matter how many things there are in the series, each one needs something outside itself to actualize its potentiality for change.

The universe is the sum total of all these moving things, however many there are. The whole universe *is* in the process of change. But we have already seen that change in any being requires an outside force to actualize it. Therefore, there is some force outside (in addition to) the universe, some real being transcendent to the universe. This is one of the things meant by "God."

Briefly, if there is nothing outside the material universe, then there is nothing that can cause the universe to change. But it does change. Therefore there must be something in addition to the material universe. But the universe is the sum total of all matter, space and time. These three things depend on each other. Therefore this being outside the universe is outside matter, space and time. It is not a changing thing; it is the unchanging Source of change.

2. The Argument from Efficient Causality

We notice that some things cause other things to be (to begin to be, to continue to be, or both). For example, a man playing the piano is causing the music that we hear. If he stops, so does the music.

Now ask yourself: Are all things caused to exist by other things right now? Suppose they are. That is, suppose there is no Uncaused Being, no God. Then nothing could exist right now. For remember, on the no-God hypothesis, all things need a present cause outside of themselves in order to exist. So right now, all things, including all those things which are causing other things to be, need a cause. They can give being only so long as they are given being. Everything that exists, therefore, on this hypothesis, stands in need of being caused to exist.

But caused by what? Beyond everything that is, there can only be nothing. But that is absurd: all of reality dependent—but dependent on nothing! The hypothesis that all being is caused, that there is no Uncaused Being, is absurd. So there must be something uncaused, something on which all things that need an efficient cause of being are dependent.

Existence is like a gift given from cause to effect. If there is no one who has the gift, the gift cannot be passed down the chain of receivers, however long or short the chain may be. If everyone has to borrow a certain book, but no one actually *has* it, then no one will ever *get* it. If there is no God who has existence by his own eternal nature, then the gift of existence cannot be passed down the chain of creatures and we can never get it. But we do get it; we exist. Therefore there must exist a God: an Uncaused Being who does not have to receive existence like us—and like every other link in the chain of receivers.

Question 1:

Why do we need an uncaused cause? Why could there not simply be an endless series of things mutually keeping each other in being?

Reply: This is an attractive hypothesis. Think of a single drunk. He could probably not stand up alone. But a group of drunks, all of them mutually supporting each other, might stand. They might even make their way along the street. But notice: Given so many drunks, and given the steady ground beneath them, we can understand how their stumblings might cancel each other out, and how the group of them could remain (relatively) upright. We could not understand their remaining upright if the ground did not support them—if, for example, they were all suspended several feet above it. And of course, if there were no actual drunks, there would *be* nothing to understand.

This brings us to our argument. Things have got to exist in order to be mutually dependent; they cannot depend upon each other for their entire being, for then they would have to be, simultaneously, cause and effect of each other. *A* causes *B, B* causes *C,* and *C* causes *A.* That is absurd. The argument is trying to show why a world of caused causes can be *given*— or can *be there*—at all. And it simply points out: If *this* thing can exist only because something else is *giving* it existence, then there must exist something whose being is not a gift. Otherwise *everything* would need at the same time to be given being, but nothing (in addition to "everything") could exist to give it. And that means nothing would actually *be.*

Question 2:
Why not have an endless series of caused causes stretching backward into the past? Then everything would be made actual and would actually be—even though their causes might no longer exist.
Reply: First, if the kalām argument (argument 6) is right, there could not exist an endless series of causes stretching backward into the past. But suppose that such a series could exist. The argument is not concerned about the past, and would work whether the past is finite or infinite. It is concerned with what exists *right now.*

Even as you read this, you are dependent on other things; you could not, right now, exist without them. Suppose there are seven such things. If these seven things did not exist, neither would you. Now suppose that all seven of them depend for their existence *right now* on still other things. Without these, the seven you now depend on would not exist—and neither would you. Imagine that the entire universe consists of you and the seven things sustaining you. If there is nothing besides that universe of changing, dependent things, then the universe—and you as part of it—could not be. For everything that is would *right now* need to be given being; but there would be nothing capable of giving it. And yet you *are* and it *is.* So there must in that case exist something besides the universe of dependent things—something not dependent as they are.

And if it must exist in that case, it must exist in this one. In our world there are surely more than seven things that need, *right now*, to be given being. But that need is not diminished by there being more than seven. As we imagine more and more of them—even an infinite number, if that were possible—we are simply expanding the set of beings that stand in need. And this need—for being, for existence—cannot be met from within the imagined set. But obviously it *has* been met, since contingent beings exist. Therefore there is a source of being on which our material universe right now depends.

3. The Argument from Time and Contingency

1. We notice around us things that come into being and go out of being. A tree, for example, grows from a tiny shoot, flowers brilliantly, then withers and dies.

2. Whatever comes into being or goes out of being does not have to be; its nonbeing is a real possibility.

3. Suppose that nothing has to be; that is, that nonbeing is a real possibility for everything.

4. Then right now nothing would exist. For

5. If the universe *began* to exist, then all being must trace its origin to some past moment before which there existed—literally—nothing at all. But

6. From nothing nothing comes. So

7. The universe could not have begun.

8. But suppose the universe *never* began. Then, for the infinitely long duration of cosmic history, all being had the built-in possibility not to be. But

9. If in an infinite time that possibility was never realized, then it could not have been a real possibility at all. So

10. There must exist something which *has* to exist, which *cannot not exist.* This sort of being is called *necessary.*

11. Either this necessity belongs to the thing in itself or it is derived from another. If derived from another there must ultimately exist a being whose necessity is not derived, that is, an absolutely necessary being.

12. This absolutely necessary being is God.

Question 1:

Even though you may never in fact step outside your house all day, it was possible *for you to do so. Why is it impossible that the universe still* happens *to exist, even though it was* possible *for it to go out of existence?*

Reply: The two cases are not really parallel. To step outside your house on a given day is something that you may or may not choose to do. But if nonbeing is a real possibility for you, then you are the kind of being that *cannot* last forever. In other words, the possibility of nonbeing must be built-in, "programmed," part of your very constitution, a necessary property. And if all being is like that, then how could anything still exist after the passage of an infinite time? For an infinite time is every bit as long as forever. So being must have what it takes to last forever, that is, to stay in existence for an infinite time. Therefore there must exist within the realm of being something that does not tend to go out of existence. And this sort of being, as Aquinas says, is called "necessary."

4. The Argument from Degrees of Perfection

We notice around us things that vary in certain ways. A shade of color, for example, can be lighter or darker than another; a freshly baked apple pie is hotter than one taken out of the oven hours before; the life of a person who gives and receives love is better than the life of one who does not.

So we arrange some things in terms of more and less. And when we do, we naturally think of them on a scale approaching most and least. For example, we think of the lighter as approaching the brightness of pure white, and the darker as approaching the opacity of pitch black. This means that we think of them at various "distances" from the extremes, and as possessing, in degrees of "more" or "less," what the extremes possess in full measure.

Sometimes it is the literal distance from an extreme that makes all the difference between "more" and "less." For example, things are more or less hot when they are more or less distant from a source of heat. The source communicates to those things the quality of heat they possess in greater or lesser measure. This means that the degree of heat they possess is caused by a source outside of them.

Now when we think of the goodness of things, part of what we mean relates to what they are simply as beings. We believe, for example, that a relatively stable and permanent way of being is better than one that is fleeting and precarious. Why? Because we apprehend at a deep (but not always conscious) level that being is the source and condition of all value; finally and ultimately, being is *better* than nonbeing. And so we recognize the inherent superiority of all those ways of being that expand possibilities, free us from the constricting confines of matter, and allow us to share in, enrich and be enriched by, the being of other things. In other words, we all recognize that intelligent being is better than unintelligent being; that a being able to give and receive love is better than one that cannot; that our way of being is better, richer and fuller than that of a stone, a flower, an earthworm, an ant, or even a baby seal.

But if these degrees of perfection pertain to being and being is *caused* in finite creatures, then there must exist a "best," a source and real standard of all the perfections that we recognize belong to us *as beings*.

This absolutely perfect being—the "Being of all beings," "the Perfection of all perfections"—is God.

Question 1:
The argument assumes a real *"better." But aren't all our judgments of comparative value merely subjective?*

Reply: The very asking of this question answers it. For the questioner would not have asked it unless he or she thought it really better to do so than not, and really better to find the true answer than not. You can speak subjectivism but you cannot live it.

5. The Design Argument
This sort of argument is of wide and perennial appeal. Almost everyone admits that reflection on the order and beauty of nature touches something very deep within us. But are the order and beauty of the product of intelligent design and conscious purpose? For theists the answer is yes. Arguments for design are attempts to vindicate this answer; to show why it is the most reasonable one to give. They have been formulated in ways as richly varied as the experience in which they are rooted. The following displays the core or central insight.

1. The universe displays a staggering amount of intelligibility, both within the things we observe and in the way these things relate to others outside themselves. That is to say: the way they *exist* and *coexist* display an intricately beautiful order and regularity that can fill even the most casual observer with wonder. It is the norm in nature for many *different* beings to work together to produce the same valuable end—for example, the organs in the body work for our life and health. (See also argument 8.)

2. Either this intelligible order is the product of chance or of intelligent design.

3. Not chance.

4. Therefore the universe is the product of intelligent design.

5. Design comes only from a mind, a designer.

6. Therefore the universe is the product of an intelligent Designer.

The first premise is certainly true—even those resistant to the argument admit it. The person who did not would have to be almost pathetically obtuse. A single protein molecule is a thing of immensely impressive order; much more so a single cell; and incredibly much more so an organ like the eye, where ordered parts of enormous and delicate complexity work together with countless others to achieve a single certain end. Even chemical elements are ordered to combine with other elements in certain ways and under certain conditions. Apparent disorder is a problem precisely because of the overwhelming pervasiveness of order and regularity. So the first premise stands.

If all this order is not in some way the product of intelligent design—then what? Obviously, it "just happened." Things just fell out that way "by chance." Alternatively, if all this order is not the product of blind, purposeless forces, then it has resulted from some kind of purpose. That purpose can only be intelligent design. So the second premise stands.

It is of course the third premise that is crucial. Ultimately, nonbelievers tell us, it is indeed by chance and not by any design that the universe of our experience exists the way it does. It just happens to have this order, and the burden of proof is on believers to demonstrate why this could not be so by chance alone.

But this seems a bit backward. It is surely up to nonbelievers to produce a credible alternative to design. And "chance" is simply not credible. For we can understand chance only against a background of order. To say that something happened "by chance" is to say that it did not turn out as we would have expected, or that it did turn out in a way we would not have expected. But expectation is impossible without order. If you take away order and speak of chance alone as a kind of ultimate source, you have taken away the only background that allows us to speak meaningfully of chance at all. Instead of thinking of chance against a background of order, we are invited to think of order—overwhelmingly intricate and ubiquitous order—against a random and purposeless background of chance. Frankly, that is incredible. Therefore it is eminently reasonable to affirm the third premise, not chance, and therefore to affirm the conclusion, that this universe is the product of intelligent design.

Question 1:
Hasn't the Darwinian theory of evolution shown us how it is possible for all the order in the universe to have arisen by chance?

Reply: Not at all. If the Darwinian theory has shown anything, it has shown, in a general way, how species may have descended from others through random mutation; and how survival of these species can be accounted for by natural selection—by the fitness of some species to survive in their environment. In no way does it—can it—account for the ubiquitous order and intelligibility of nature. Rather, it presupposes order. To quote a famous phrase: "The survival of the fittest presupposes the arrival of the fit." If Darwinians wish to extrapolate from their purely biological theory and maintain that all the vast order around us is the result of random changes, then they are saying something which no empirical evidence could ever confirm; which no empirical science could ever demonstrate; and which, on the face of it, is simply beyond belief.

Question 2:

Maybe it is only in this region of the universe that order is to be found. Maybe there are other parts unknown to us that are completely chaotic—or maybe the universe will one day in the future become chaotic. What becomes of the argument then?

Reply: Believers and nonbelievers both experience the same universe. It is this which is either designed or not. And this world of our common experience is a world of pervasive order and intelligibility. That fact must be faced. Before we speculate about what will be in the future or what may be elsewhere in the present, we need to deal honestly with what is. We need to recognize in an unflinching way the extent—the overwhelming extent— of order and intelligibility. Then we can ask ourselves: Is it credible to suppose that we inhabit a small island of order surrounded by a vast sea of chaos—a sea which threatens one day to engulf us?

Just consider how in the last decades we have strained fantastically at the limits of our knowledge; we have cast our vision far beyond this planet and far within the elements that make it up. And what has this expansion of our horizons revealed? Always the same thing: *more*—and not *less*—intelligibility; *more*—and not *less*—complex and intricate order. Not only is there no reason to believe in a surrounding chaos, there is every reason not to. It flies in the face of the experience that all of us—believers and nonbelievers—share in common.

Something similar can be said about the future. We know the way things in the universe have behaved and are behaving. And so, until we have some reason to think otherwise, there is every reason to believe it will continue on its orderly path of running down. No speculation can nullify what we know.

And, anyway, exactly what sort of chaos is this question asking us to imagine? That effect precedes cause? That the law of contradiction does not hold? That there need not be what it takes for some existing thing to exist? These suggestions are completely unintelligible; if we think about them at all, it is only to reject them as impossible. Can we imagine less order? Yes. Some rearrangement of the order we experience? Yes. But total disorder and chaos? That can never be considered as a real possibility. To speculate about it as if it were is really a waste of time.

Question 3:
But what if the order we experience is merely a product of our minds? Even though we cannot think utter chaos and disorder, maybe that is how reality really is.
Reply: Our minds are the only means by which we can know reality. We have no other access. If we agree that something cannot exist in thought, we cannot go ahead and say that it might nevertheless exist in reality. Because then we would be thinking what we claim cannot be thought.

Suppose you claim that order is just a product of our minds. This puts you in a very awkward position. You are saying that we must think about reality in terms of order and intelligibility, but things may not exist that way in fact. Now to propose something for consideration is to think about it. And so you are saying: (a) we must think about reality in a certain way, but (b) since we think that things may not in fact exist that way, then (c) we need not think about reality the way we must think about it! Are we willing to pay that high a price to deny that the being of the universe displays intelligent design? It does not, on the face of it, seem cost-effective.

6. The Kalām Argument
The Arabic word *kalām* literally means "speech," but came to denote a certain type of philosophical theology—a type containing demonstrations that the world could not be infinitely old and must therefore have been created by God. This sort of demonstration has had a long and wide appeal among both Christians and Muslims. Its form is simple and straightforward.

1. Whatever begins to exist has a cause for its coming into being.

2. The universe began to exist.

3. Therefore, the universe has a cause for its coming into being.

Grant the first premise. (Most people—outside of asylums and graduate schools—would consider it not only true, but certainly and obviously true.)

Is the second premise true? Did the universe—the collection of all things bounded by space and time—begin to exist? This premise has recently received powerful support from natural science—from so-called Big Bang Cosmology. But there are philosophical arguments in its favor as well. Can an infinite task ever be done or completed? If, in order to reach a certain end, infinitely many steps had to precede it, could the end ever be reached? Of course not—not even in an infinite time. For an infinite time would be unending, just as the steps would be. In other words, no end would ever be reached. The task would—could—never be completed.

But what about the step just before the end? Could *that* point ever be reached? Well, if the task is really infinite, then an infinity of steps must also have preceded *it*. And therefore the step just before the end could also never be reached. But then neither could the step just before *that* one. In fact, no step in the sequence could be reached, because an infinity of steps must always have preceded any step; must always have been gone through one by one before it. The problem comes from supposing that an infinite sequence could ever reach, by temporal succession, any point at all.

Now if the universe never began, then it always was. If it always was, then it is infinitely old. If it is infinitely old, then an infinite amount of time would have to have elapsed before (say) today. And so an infinite number of days must have been completed—one day succeeding another, one bit of time being added to what went before—in order for the present day to arrive. But this exactly parallels the problem of an infinite task. If the present day has been reached, then the actually infinite sequence of history has reached this present point: in fact, has been completed up to this point—for at any present point the whole past must already have happened. But an infinite sequence of steps could never have reached this present point—or any point before it.

So, either the present day has not been reached, or the process of reaching it was not infinite. But obviously the present day *has* been reached. So the process of reaching it was not infinite. In other words, the universe began to exist. Therefore, the universe has a cause for its coming into being, a Creator.

Question 1:

Christians believe they are going to live forever with God. So they believe the future will be endless. How come the past cannot also be endless?

Reply: The question really answers itself. Christians believe that their life with God will never end. That means it will never form an actually completed infinite series. In more technical language: an endless future is potentially—but never actually—infinite. This means that although the future will never cease to expand and increase, still its actual extent will always be finite. But that can only be true if all of created reality had a beginning.

Question 2:

How do we know that the cause of the universe still exists? Maybe it started the universe going and then ceased to be.

Reply: Remember that we were seeking for a cause of spatio-temporal being. This cause created the entire universe of space and time. And space and time themselves must be part of that creation. So the cause cannot be another spatio-temporal being. (If it were, all the problems about infinite duration would arise once again.) It must somehow stand outside the limitations and constraints of space and time.

It is hard to understand how such a being could "cease" to be. We know how a being within the universe ceases to be: it comes in time to be fatally affected by some agency external to it. But this picture is proper to us, and to all beings limited in some way by space and time. A being not limited in these ways cannot "come" to be or "cease" to be. If it exists at all, it must exist eternally.

Question 3:

But is this cause God—a he and not a mere it?

Reply: Suppose the cause of the universe has existed eternally. Suppose further that this cause is not personal: that it has given rise to the universe, not through any choice, but simply through its being. In that case it is hard to see how the universe could be anything but infinitely old, since all the conditions needed for the being of the universe would exist from all eternity. But the kalām argument has shown that the universe cannot be infinitely old. So the hypothesis of an eternal impersonal cause seems to lead to an inconsistency.

Is there a way out? Yes, if the universe is the result of a free personal choice. Then at least we have some way of seeing how an eternal cause could give rise to a temporally limited effect. Of course, the kalām argument does not prove everything Christians believe about God, but what proof does? Less than everything, however, is far from nothing. And the kalām argument proves something central to the Christian belief in God: that the universe is not eternal and without beginning; that there is a Maker of heaven and earth. And in doing so, it disproves the picture of the universe most atheists wish to maintain: self-sustaining matter, endlessly changing in endless time.

7. The Argument from Contingency

The basic form of this argument is simple.

1. If something exists, there must exist what it takes for that thing to exist.

2. The universe—the collection of beings in space and time—exists.

3. Therefore, there must exist what it takes for the universe to exist.

4. What it takes for the universe to exist cannot exist within the universe or be bounded by space and time.

5. Therefore, what it takes for the universe to exist must transcend both space and time.

Suppose you deny the first premise. Then if X exists, there need not exist what it takes for X to exist. But "what it takes for X to exist" means the immediate condition(s) for X's existence. You mean that X exists *only if* Y. Without Y, there can be no X. So the denial of premise 1 amounts to this: X exists; X can only exist if Y exists; and Y does not exist. This is absurd. So there must exist what it takes for the universe to exist. But what does it take?

We spoke of the universe as "the collection of beings in space and time." Consider one such being: yourself. You exist, and you are, in part at least, material. This means that you are a finite, limited and changing being, for matter is a principle of limitation and change. Because you are limited and changing, you know that right now, as you read this book, you are dependent for your existence on beings outside you. Not your parents or grandparents. They may no longer be alive, but you exist *now.* And right now you depend on many things in order to exist—for example, on the air you breathe. To be dependent in this way is to be contingent. You exist if something else right now exists.

But not everything can be like this. For then everything would need to be given being, but there would be nothing capable of giving it. There would not exist what it takes for anything to exist. So there must be something that does not exist conditionally; something which does not exist only if something else exists; something which exists in itself. What it takes for this thing to exist could only be this thing itself. Unlike changing material reality, there would be no distance, so to speak, between *what* this thing is and *that* it is. Obviously the collection of beings changing in space and time cannot be such a thing. Therefore, what it takes for the universe to exist cannot be identical with the universe itself or with a part of the universe.

Question 1:

But why should we call this cause "God"? Maybe there is something unknown that grounds the universe of change we live in.

Reply: True. And this "unknown" is God. What we humans know directly is this sensible changing world. We also know that there must exist whatever it takes for something to exist. Therefore, we know that neither this changing universe as a whole nor any part of it can be itself what it takes for the universe to exist. But we have no such direct knowledge of the cause of changing things. We know that there must exist a cause; we know that this cause cannot be finite or material—that it must transcend such limitations. But what this ultimate cause is in itself remains, so far, a mystery.

There is more to be said by reason; and there is very much more God has made known about himself through revelation. But the proofs have given us some real knowledge as well: knowledge that the universe is created; knowledge that right now it is kept in being by a cause unbounded by any material limit, that transcends the kind of being we humans directly know. And that is surely knowledge worth having. We might figure out that someone's death was murder and no accident, without figuring out exactly who did it and why, and this might leave us frustrated and unsatisfied. But at least we would know what path of questioning to pursue; at least we would know that *someone* did it.

So it is with the proofs. They let us know that at every moment the being of the universe is the creative act of a Giver—a Giver transcending all material and spiritual limitations. Beyond that, they do not tell us much about *what* or *who* this Giver is—but they point in a very definite direction. We know that this Ultimate Reality—the Giver of being—cannot be material. And we know the gift which is given includes personal being: intelligence, will and spirit. The infinite transcendent cause of these things cannot be less than they are, but must be infinitely more. How and in what way we do not know. To some extent this Giver must always remain unknown to human reason. We should never expect otherwise. But reason can at least let us know that "someone did it." And that is of great value.

8. The Argument from the World as an Interacting Whole

Norris Clarke, who taught metaphysics and philosophy of religion for many years at Fordham, has circulated privately an intriguing version of the design argument. We present it here, slightly abridged and revised, for your reflection.

Starting Point. This world is given to us as a dynamic, ordered system of many active component elements. Their natures (natural properties) are ordered to interact with each other in stable, reciprocal relationships which we call physical laws. For example, every hydrogen atom in our universe is ordered to combine with every oxygen atom in the proportion of 2:1 (which implies that every oxygen atom is reciprocally ordered to combine with every hydrogen atom in the proportion of 1:2). So it is with the chemical valences of all the basic elements. So too all particles with mass are ordered to move toward every other according to the fixed proportions of the law of gravity.

In such an interconnected, interlocking, dynamic system, the active nature of each component is defined by its relation with others, and so presupposes the others for its own intelligibility and ability to act. Contemporary science reveals to us that our world-system is not merely an aggregate of many separate, unrelated laws, but rather a tightly interlocking whole, where relationship to the whole structures and determines the parts. The parts can no longer be understood apart from the whole; its influence permeates them all.

Argument. In any such system as the above (like our world) no component part or active element can be self-sufficient or self-explanatory. For any part presupposes all the other parts—the whole system already in place—to match its own relational properties. It can't act unless the others are there to interact reciprocally with it. Any one part could be self-sufficient only if it were the cause of the whole rest of the system—which is impossible, since no part can act except in collaboration with the others.

Nor can the system as a whole explain its own existence, since it is made up of the component parts and is not a separate being, on its own, independent of them. So neither the parts nor the whole are self-sufficient; neither can explain the actual existence of this dynamically interactive system.

Three Conclusions

1. Since the parts make sense only within the whole, and neither the whole nor the parts can explain their own existence, then such a system as our world requires a *unifying efficient cause* to posit it in existence as a unified whole.

2. Any such cause must be an *intelligent cause*, one that brings the system into being according to a unifying idea. For the unity of the whole—and of each one of the overarching, cosmic-wide, physical laws uniting elements under themselves—is what determines and correlates the parts. Hence it must be somehow actually present as an effective organizing factor. But the unity, the wholeness, of the whole transcends any one part, and therefore cannot be contained in any one part. To be actually present all at once as a whole this unity can only be the unity of an organizing unifying idea. For only an idea can hold together many different elements at once without destroying or fusing their distinctness. That is almost the definition of an idea. Since the actual parts are spread out over space and time, the only way they can be together at once as an intelligible unity is within an idea. Hence the system of the world as a whole must live first within the unity of an idea.

Now a real idea cannot actually exist and be effectively operative save in a real mind, which has the creative power to bring such a system into real existence. Hence the sufficient reason for our ordered world-system must ultimately be a creative ordering Mind. A cosmic-wide order requires a cosmic-wide Orderer, which can only be a Mind.

3. Such an ordering Mind must be independent of the system itself, that is, *transcendent;* not dependent on the system for its own existence and operation. For if it were dependent on—or part of—the system, it would have to presuppose the latter as already existing in order to operate, and would thus have to both precede and follow itself. But this is absurd. Hence it must exist and be able to operate prior to and independent of the system.

Thus our material universe necessarily requires, as the sufficient reason for its actual existence as an operating whole, a Transcendent Creative Mind.

9. The Argument from Miracles

1. A miracle is an event whose only adequate explanation is the extraordinary and direct intervention of God.

2. There are numerous well-attested miracles.

3. Therefore, there are numerous events whose only adequate explanation is the extraordinary and direct intervention of God.

4. Therefore God exists.

Obviously if you believe that some extraordinary event is a miracle, then you believe in divine agency, and you believe that such agency was at work in this event. But the question is: Was this event a miracle? If miracles exist, then God must exist. But do miracles exist?

Which events do we choose? In the first place, the event must be extraordinary. But there are many extraordinary happenings (e.g., numerous stones dropping from the sky in Texas) that do not qualify as miracles. Why not? First, because they could be caused by something in nature, and second, because the context in which they occur is not religious. They qualify as mere oddities, as "strange happenings"; the sort of thing you might expect to read in *Believe It or Not,* but never hear about from the pulpit. Therefore the meaning of the event must also be religious to qualify as a miracle.

Suppose that a holy man had stood in the center of Houston and said: "My dear brothers and sisters! You are leading sinful lives! Look at yourselves—drunken! dissolute! God wants you to repent! And as a sign of his displeasure he's going to shower stones upon you!" Then, moments later—thunk! thunk! thunk!—the stones began to fall. The word "miracle" might very well spring to mind.

Not that we would *have* to believe in God after witnessing this event. But still, if that man in Texas seemed utterly genuine, and if his accusations hit home, made us think "He's right," then it would be very hard to consider what happened a deception or even an extraordinary coincidence.

This means that the setting of a supposed miracle is crucially important. Not just the physical setting, and not just the timing, but the personal setting is vital as well—the character and the message of the person to whom this event is specially tied. Take, for example, four or five miracles from the New Testament. Remove them completely from their context, from the teaching and character of Christ. Would it be wrong to see their religious significance as thereby greatly diminished? After all, to call some happening a miracle is to interpret it religiously. But to interpret it that way demands a context or setting which invites such interpretation. And part of this setting usually, though not always, involves a person whose moral authority is first recognized, and whose religious authority, which the miracle seems to confirm, is then acknowledged.

Abstract discussions of probability usually miss this factor. But setting does play a decisive role. Many years ago, at an otherwise dull convention, a distinguished philosopher explained why he had become a Christian. He said: "I picked up the New Testament with a view to judging it, to weighing its pros and cons. But as I began to read, I realized that *I* was the one being judged." Certainly he came to believe in the miracle-stories. But it was the character and teaching of Christ that led him to accept the things recounted there as genuine acts of God.

So there is not really a proof *from* miracles. If you see some event as a miracle, then the activity of God is seen *in* this event. There is a movement of the mind from this event *to* its proper interpretation as miraculous. And what gives impetus to that movement is not just the event by itself, but the many factors surrounding it which invite—or seem to demand—such interpretation.

But miraculous events exist. Indeed, there is massive, reliable testimony to them across many times, places and cultures.

Therefore their cause exists.

And their only adequate cause is God.

Therefore God exists.

The argument is not a proof, but a very powerful clue or sign. (For further discussion, see chap. 5 on miracles.)

10. The Argument from Consciousness

When we experience the tremendous order and intelligibility in the universe, we are experiencing something intelligence can grasp. Intelligence is part of what we find in the world. But this universe is not itself intellectually aware. As great as the forces of nature are, they do not know themselves. Yet we know them *and* ourselves. These remarkable facts—the presence of intelligence amidst unconscious material processes, and the conformity of those processes to the structure of conscious intelligence—have given rise to a variation on the first argument for design.

1. We experience the universe as intelligible. This intelligibility means that the universe is graspable by intelligence.

2. Either this intelligible universe and the finite minds so well suited to grasp it are the products of intelligence, or both intelligibility and intelligence are the products of blind chance.

3. Not blind chance.

4. Therefore this intelligible universe and the finite minds so well suited to grasp it are the products of intelligence.

There are obvious similarities here to the design argument, and many of the things we said to defend that argument could be used to defend this one too. For now we want to focus our attention on step 3.

Readers familiar with C. S. Lewis's *Miracles* will remember the powerful argument he made in chapter three against what he called "naturalism": the view that everything—including our thinking and judging—belongs to one vast interlocking system of physical causes and effects. If naturalism is true, Lewis argued, then it seems to leave us with no reason for *believing* it to be true; for all judgments would equally and ultimately be the result of nonrational forces.

Now this line of reflection has an obvious bearing on step 3. What we mean by "blind chance" is the way physical nature must ultimately operate if "naturalism" is true—void of any rational plan or guiding purpose. So if Lewis's argument is a good one, then step 3 stands: blind chance cannot be the source of our intelligence.

We were tempted, when preparing this section, to quote the entire third chapter of *Miracles*. This sort of argument is not original to Lewis, but we have never read a better statement of it than his, and we urge you to consult it. But we have found a compelling, and admirably succinct version (written almost twenty years before *Miracles)* in H. W. B. Joseph's *Some Problems in Ethics* (Oxford University Press, 1931). Joseph was an Oxford don, senior to Lewis, with whose writings Lewis was certainly familiar. And undoubtedly this statement of the argument influenced Lewis's later, more elaborate version.

> If thought *is* laryngeal motion, how should any one think more truly than the wind blows? All movements of bodies are equally necessary, but they cannot be discriminated as true and false. It seems as nonsensical to call a movement true as a flavour purple or a sound avaricious. But what is obvious when thought is said to *be* a certain bodily movement seems equally to follow from its being the effect of one. Thought called knowledge and thought called error are both necessary results of states of brain. These states are necessary results of other bodily states. All the bodily states are equally real, and so are the different thoughts; but by what right can I hold that my thought is knowledge of what is real in bodies? For to hold so is but another thought, an effect of real bodily movements like the rest. . . . These arguments, however, of mine, if the principles of scientific [naturalism] . . . are to stand unchallenged, are themselves no more than happenings in a mind, results of bodily movements; that you or I think them sound, or think them unsound, is but another such happening; that we think them no more than another such happening is itself but yet another such. And it may be said of any ground on which we may attempt to stand as true, *Labitur et labetur in omne volubilis aevum* ["It flows and will flow swirling on forever" (Horace, *Epistles,* I, 2, 43)]. (*Some Problems in Ethics,* pp. 14-15)

11. The Argument from Truth

This argument is closely related to the argument from consciousness. It comes mainly from Augustine.

1. Our limited minds can discover eternal truths about being.

2. Truth properly resides in a mind.

3. But the human mind is not eternal.

4. Therefore there must exist an eternal mind in which these truths reside.

This proof might appeal to someone who shares a Platonic view of knowledge—who, for example, believes that there are Eternal Intelligible Forms which are present to the mind in every act of knowledge. Given that view, it is a very short step to see these Eternal Forms as properly existing within an Eternal Mind. And there is a good deal to be said for this. But that is just the problem. There is too much about the theory of knowledge that needs to be said before this could work as a persuasive demonstration.

12. The Argument from the Origin of the Idea of God

This argument, made famous by René Descartes, has a kinship to the ontological argument (13). It starts from the idea of God. But it does not claim that real being is part of the content of that idea, as the ontological argument does. Rather it seeks to show that only God himself could have caused this idea to arise in our minds.

It would be impossible for us to reproduce the whole context Descartes gives for this proof (see his third Meditation), and fruitless to follow his scholastic vocabulary. We give below the briefest summary and discussion.

1. We have ideas of many things.

2. These ideas must arise either from ourselves or from things outside us.

3. One of the ideas we have is the idea of God—an infinite, all-perfect being.

4. This idea could not have been caused by ourselves, because we know ourselves to be limited and imperfect, and no effect can be greater than its cause.

5. Therefore, the idea must have been caused by something outside us which has nothing less than the qualities contained in the idea of God.

6. But only God himself has those qualities.

7. Therefore God himself must be the cause of the idea we have of him

8. Therefore God exists.

Consider the following common objection. The idea of God can easily arise like this: we notice degrees of perfection among finite beings—some are more perfect (or less imperfect) than others. And to reach the idea of God, we just project the scale upward and outward to infinity. Thus there seems to be no need for an actually existing God to account for the existence of the idea. All we need is the experience of things varying in degrees of perfection, and a mind capable of thinking away perceived limitations.

But is that really enough? How can we think away limitation or imperfection unless we first recognize it as such? And how can we recognize it as such unless we already have some notion of infinite perfection? To recognize things as imperfect or finite involves the possession of a standard in thought that makes the recognition possible.

Does that seem farfetched? It does not mean that toddlers spend their time thinking about God. But it does mean that, however late in life you use the standard, however long before it comes explicitly into consciousness, still, the standard must be there in order for you to use it. But where did it come from? Not from your experience of yourself or of the world that exists outside you. For the idea of infinite perfection is already presupposed in our thinking about all these things and judging them imperfect. Therefore none of them can be the origin of the idea of God; only God himself can be that.

13. The Ontological Argument

The ontological argument was devised by Anselm of Canterbury (1033-1109), who wanted to produce a single, simple demonstration which would show *that* God is and *what* God is. Single it may be, but far from simple. It is, perhaps, the most controversial proof for the existence of God. Most people who first hear it are tempted to dismiss it immediately as an interesting riddle, but distinguished thinkers of every age, including our own, have risen to defend it. For this very reason it is the most intensely philosophical proof for God's existence; its place of honor is not within popular piety, but rather textbooks and professional journals. We include it, with a minimum of discussion, not because we think it conclusive or irrefutable, but for the sake of completeness.

Anselm's Version

1. It is greater for a thing to exist in the mind *and* in reality than in the mind alone.

2. "God" means "that than which a greater cannot be thought."

3. Suppose that God exists in the mind but not in reality.

4. Then a greater than God *could* be thought (namely, a being that has all the qualities our thought of God has *plus* real existence).

5. But this is impossible, for God is "that than which a greater cannot be thought."

6. Therefore God exists in the mind and in reality.

Question 1:

Suppose I deny that God exists in the mind?

Reply: In that case the argument could not conclude that God exists in the mind and in reality. But note: the denial commits you to the view that there is no concept of God. And very few would wish to go that far.

Question 2:

Is it really greater for something to exist in the mind and in reality than in the mind alone?

Reply: The first premise of this argument is often misunderstood. People sometimes say: "Isn't an imaginary disease better, and in that sense greater, than a real one?" Well it certainly is better—and so a greater thing—for *you* that the disease is not real. But that strengthens Anselm's side of the argument. Real bacteria *are* greater than imaginary ones, just because they have something that imaginary ones lack: real being. They have an independence, and therefore an ability to harm, that nothing can have whose existence is wholly dependent on your thought. It is this greater level of independence that makes them greater *as beings.* And that line of thinking does not seem elusive or farfetched.

Question 3:

But is real being just another "thought" or "concept"? Is "real being" just one more concept or characteristic (like "omniscience" or "omnipotence") that could make a difference to the kind of being God is?

Reply: Real being does make a real difference. The question is: Does it make a *conceptual* difference? Critics of the argument say that it does not. They say that just because real being makes all the difference it cannot be one more quality among others. Rather it is the condition of there being something there to have any qualities at all. When the proof says that God is the greatest being that can be "thought," it means that there are various *perfections* or *qualities* that God has to a degree no creature possibly could, qualities that are supremely admirable. But to say that such a being *exists* is to say that there really *is* something which is supremely admirable. And that is not one more admirable *quality* among others.

Is it greater to exist in reality as well as in the mind? Of course, incomparably greater. But the difference is not a conceptual one. And yet the argument seems to treat it as if it were—as if the believer and the nonbeliever could not share the same *concept* of God. Clearly they do. They disagree not about the content of this concept, but about whether the kind of being it describes really exists. And that seems beyond the power of merely conceptual analysis, as used in this argument, to answer. So question 3, we think, really does invalidate this form of the ontological argument.

Modal Version
Charles Hartshorne and Norman Malcolm developed this version of the ontological argument. Both find it implicitly contained in the third chapter of Anselm's *Proslogion.*

1. The expression "that being than which a greater cannot be thought" (GCB, for short) expresses a consistent concept.

2. GCB cannot be thought of as:

   a. necessarily nonexistent; or as

   b. contingently existing; but only as

   c. necessarily existing.

3. So GCB can only be thought of as the kind of being that cannot not exist, that must exist.

4. But what must be so is so.

5. Therefore, GCB (i.e., God) exists.

Question:
Just because GCB must be thought of as existing, does that mean that GCB really exists?

Reply: If you must think of something as existing, you cannot think of it as not existing. But then you cannot deny that GCB exists; for then you are thinking what you say cannot be thought—namely, that GCB does not exist.

Possible Worlds Version
This variation on the modal version has been worked out in great detail by Alvin Plantinga. We have done our best to simplify it.

Definitions:
Maximal excellence: To have omnipotence, omniscience and moral perfection in some world

Maximal greatness: To have maximal excellence in every possible world.

1. There is a possible world (W) in which there is a being (X) with maximal greatness.

2. But X is maximally great only if X has maximal excellence in every possible world.

3. Therefore X is maximally great only if X has omnipotence, omniscience and moral perfection in every possible world.

4. In W, the proposition "There is no omnipotent, omniscient, morally perfect being" would be impossible—that is, necessarily false.

5. But what is impossible does not vary from world to world.

6. Therefore, the proposition, "There is no omnipotent, omniscient, morally perfect being" is necessarily false in this actual world, too.

7. Therefore, there actually exists in this world, and must exist in every possible world, an omnipotent, omniscient, morally perfect being.

14. The Moral Argument

1. Real moral obligation is a fact. We are really, truly, objectively obligated to do good and avoid evil.

2. Either the atheistic view of reality is correct or the "religious" one.

3. But the atheistic one is incompatible with there being moral obligation.

4. Therefore the "religious" view of reality is correct.

We need to be clear about what the first premise is claiming. It does not mean merely that we can find people around who claim to have certain duties. Nor does it mean that there have been many people who thought they were obliged to do certain things (like clothing the naked) and to avoid doing others (like committing adultery). The first premise is claiming something more: namely, that we human beings really are obligated; that our duties arise from the way things really are, and not simply from our desires or subjective dispositions. It is claiming, in other words, that moral values or obligations themselves—and not merely the belief in moral values—are objective facts.

Now given the fact of moral obligation, a question naturally arises. Does the picture of the world presented by atheism accord with this fact? The answer is no. Atheists never tire of telling us that we are the chance products of the motion of matter: a motion which is purposeless and blind to every human striving. We should take them at their word and ask: Given this picture, in what exactly is the moral good rooted? Moral obligation can hardly be rooted in a material motion blind to purpose.

Suppose we say it is rooted in nothing deeper than human willing and desire. In that case, we have no moral standard against which human desires can be judged. For every desire will spring from the same ultimate source—purposeless, pitiless matter. And what becomes of obligation? According to this view, if I say there is an obligation to feed the hungry, I would be stating a fact about my wants and desires and nothing else. I would be saying that I want the hungry to be fed, and that I choose to act on that desire. But this amounts to an admission that neither I nor anyone else is really obliged to feed the hungry—that, in fact, no one has any real obligations at all. Therefore the atheistic view of reality is not compatible with there being genuine moral obligation.

What view is compatible? One that sees real moral obligation as grounded in its Creator, that sees moral obligation as rooted in the fact that we have been created with a purpose and for an end. We may call this view, with deliberate generality, "the religious view." But however general the view, reflection on the fact of moral obligation does seem to confirm it.

Question 1:

The argument has not shown that ethical subjectivism is false. What if there are no objective values?

Reply: True enough. The argument assumes that there are objective values; it aims to show that believing in them is incompatible with one picture of the world, and quite compatible with another. Those two pictures are the atheistic-materialistic one, and the (broadly speaking) religious one. Granted, if ethical subjectivism is true, then the argument does not work. However, almost no one is a consistent subjectivist. (Many *think* they are, and *say* they are—until they suffer violence or injustice. In that case they invariably stand with the rest of us in recognizing that certain things ought never to be done.) And for the many who are not—and never will be—subjectivists, the argument can be most helpful. It can show them that to believe as they do in objective values is inconsistent with what they may also believe about the origin and destiny of the universe. If they move to correct the inconsistency, it will be a move toward the religious view and away from the atheistic one.

Question 2:

This proof does not conclude to God, but to some vague "religious" view. Isn't this "religious" view compatible with very much more than traditional theism?

Reply: Yes indeed. It is compatible, for example, with Platonic idealism, and many other beliefs that orthodox Christians find terribly deficient. But this general religious view is incompatible with materialism, and with any view that banishes value from the ultimate objective nature of things. That is the important point. It seems most reasonable that moral conscience is the voice of God within the soul, because moral value exists only on the level of persons, minds and wills. And it is hard, if not impossible, to conceive of objective moral principles somehow floating around on their own, apart from any persons.

But we grant that there are many steps to travel from objective moral values to the Creator of the universe or the triune God of love. There is a vast intellectual distance between them. But these things are compatible in a way that materialism and belief in objective values are not. To reach a personal Creator you need other arguments (cf. arguments 1-6), and to reach the God of love you need revelation. By itself, the argument leaves many options open, and eliminates only some. But we are surely well rid of those it does eliminate.

15. The Argument from Conscience

Since moral subjectivism is very popular today, the following version of, or twist to, the moral argument should be effective, since it does not presuppose moral objectivism. Modern people often say they believe that there are no universally binding moral obligations, that we must all follow our own private conscience. But that very admission is enough of a premise to prove the existence of God.

Isn't it remarkable that no one, even the most consistent subjectivist, believes that it is ever good for anyone to deliberately and knowingly disobey his or her own conscience? Even if different people's consciences tell them to do or avoid totally different things, there remains one moral absolute for everyone: never disobey your own conscience.

Now where did conscience get such an absolute authority—an authority admitted even by the moral subjectivist and relativist? There are only four possibilities.

1. From something less than me (nature)

2. From me (individual)

3. From others equal to me (society)

4. From something above me (God)

Let's consider each of these possibilities in order.

1. How can I be absolutely obligated by something less than me—for example, by animal instinct or practical need for material survival?

2. How can I obligate myself absolutely? Am I absolute? Do I have the right to demand absolute obedience from anyone, even myself? And if I am the one who locked myself in this prison of obligation, I can also let myself out, thus destroying the absoluteness of the obligation which we admitted as our premise.

3. How can society obligate me? What right do my equals have to impose their values on me? Does quantity make quality? Do a million human beings make a relative into an absolute? Is "society" God?

4. The only source of absolute moral obligation left is something superior to me. This binds my will, morally, with rightful demands for complete obedience.

Thus God, or something like God, is the only adequate source and ground for the absolute moral obligation we all feel to obey our conscience. Conscience is thus explainable only as the voice of God in the soul. The Ten Commandments are ten divine footprints in our psychic sand.

Addendum on Religion and Morality

In drawing this connection between morality and religion, we do not want to create any confusion or misunderstanding. We have not said that people can never *discover* human moral goods unless they acknowledge that God exists. Obviously they can. Believers and nonbelievers can know that knowledge and friendship, for example, are things that we really ought to strive for, and that cruelty and deceit are objectively wrong. Our question has been: which account of the way things really are best makes sense of the moral rules we all acknowledge—that of the believer or that of the nonbeliever?

If we are the products of a good and loving Creator, this explains why we have a nature that discovers a value that is really there. But how can atheists explain this? For if atheists are right, then no objective moral values can exist. Dostoyevsky said, "If God does not exist, everything is permissible." Atheists may know that some things are not permissible, but they do not know why.

Consider the following analogy. Many scientists examine secondary causes all their lives without acknowledging the First Cause, God. But, as we have seen, those secondary causes could not *be* without the First Cause, even though they can be *known* without knowing the First Cause. The same is true of objective moral goods. Thus the moral argument and the various metaphysical arguments share a certain similarity in structure.

Most of us, whatever our religious faith, or lack of it, can recognize that in the life of someone like Francis of Assisi human nature is operating the right way, the way it ought to operate. You need not be a theist to see *that* St. Francis's life was admirable, but you do need to be a theist to see *why*. Theism explains that our response to this believer's life is, ultimately, our response to the call of our Creator to live the kind of life he made us to live.

There are four possible relations between religion and morality, God and goodness.

1. Religion and morality may be thought to be independent. Kierkegaard's sharp contrast between "the ethical" and "the religious," especially in *Fear and Trembling*, may lead to such a supposition. But (a) an amoral God, indifferent to morality, would not be a wholly good God, for one of the primary meanings of "good" involves the "moral"—just, loving, wise, righteous, holy, kind. And (b) such a morality, not having any connection with God, the Absolute Being, would not have absolute reality behind it.

2. God may be thought of as the inventor of morality, as he is the inventor of birds. The moral law is often thought of as simply a product of God's choice. This is the Divine Command Theory: a thing is good only because God commands it and evil because he forbids it.

If that is all, however, we have a serious problem: God and his morality are arbitrary and based on mere power. If God commanded us to kill innocent people, that would become good, since *good* here means "whatever God commands." The Divine Command Theory reduces morality to power.

Socrates refuted the Divine Command Theory pretty conclusively in Plato's *Euthyphro*. He asked Euthyphro, "Is a thing pious because the gods will it, or do the gods will it because it is pious?" He refuted the first alternative, and thought he was left with the second as the only alternative.

3. But the idea that God commands a thing *because* it is good is also unacceptable, because it makes God conform to a law higher than himself, a law that overarches God and humanity alike. The God of the Bible is no more separated from moral goodness by being under it than he is by being over it. He no more obeys a higher law that binds him, than he creates the law as an artifact that could change and could well have been different, like a planet.

4. The only rationally acceptable answer to the question of the relation between God and morality is the biblical one: morality is based on God's eternal nature. That is why morality is essentially unchangeable. "I am the Lord your God; sanctify yourselves therefore, and be holy, for I am holy" (Lev 11:44). Our obligation to be just, kind, honest, loving and righteous "goes all the way up" to ultimate reality, to the eternal nature of God, to what God is. That is why morality has absolute and unchangeable binding force on our conscience.

The only other possible sources of moral obligation are:

a. My ideals, purposes, aspirations, and desires, something created by my mind or will, like the rules of baseball. This utterly fails to account for why it is always wrong to disobey or change the rules.

b. My moral will itself. Some read Kant this way: I impose morality on myself. But how can the one bound and the one who binds be the same? If the locksmith locks himself in a room, he is not really locked in, for he can also unlock himself.

c. Another human being may be thought to be the one who imposes morality on me—my parents, for example. But this fails to account for its binding character. If your father commands you to deal drugs, your moral obligation is to disobey him. No human being can have absolute authority over another.

d. "Society" is a popular answer to the question of the origin of morality; "this or that specific person" is a very unpopular answer. Yet the two are the same. "Society" only means more individuals. What right do they have to legislate morality to me? Quantity cannot yield quality; adding numbers cannot change the rules of a relative game to the rightful absolute demands of conscience.

e. The universe, evolution, natural selection and survival all fare even worse as explanations for morality. You cannot get more out of less. The principle of causality is violated here. How could the primordial slime pools gurgle up the Sermon on the Mount?

Atheists often claim that Christians make a category mistake in using God to explain nature; they say it is like the Greeks using Zeus to explain lightning. In fact, lightning should be explained on its own level, as a material, natural, scientific phenomenon. The same with morality. Why bring in God?

Because morality is more like Zeus than like lightning. Morality exists only on the level of persons, spirits, souls, minds, wills—not mere molecules. You can make correlations between moral obligations and persons (e.g., persons should love other persons), but you cannot make any correlations between morality and molecules. No one has even tried to explain the difference between good and evil in terms, for example, of the difference between heavy and light atoms.

So it is really the atheist who makes the same category mistake as the ancient pagan who explained lightning by the will of Zeus. The atheist uses a merely material thing to explain a spiritual thing. That is a far sillier version of the category mistake than the one the ancients made; for it is possible that the greater (Zeus, spirit) caused the lesser (lightning) and explains it; but it is not possible that the lesser (molecules) adequately caused and explains the greater (morality). A good will might create molecules, but how could molecules create a good will? How can electricity obligate me? Only a good will can demand a good will; only Love can demand love.

16. The Argument from Desire

1. Every natural, innate desire in us corresponds to some real object that can satisfy that desire.

2. But there exists in us a desire which nothing in time, nothing on earth, no creature can satisfy.

3. Therefore there must exist something more than time, earth and creatures, which can satisfy this desire.

4. This something is what people call "God" and "life with God forever."

The first premise implies a distinction of desires into two kinds: innate and externally conditioned, or natural and artificial. We naturally desire things like food, drink, sex, sleep, knowledge, friendship and beauty; and we naturally shun things like starvation, loneliness, ignorance and ugliness. We also desire (but not innately or naturally) things like sports cars, political office, flying through the air like Superman, the land of Oz and a Red Sox world championship.

Now there are differences between these two kinds of desires. We do not, for example, for the most part, recognize corresponding states of deprivation for the second, the artificial, desires, as we do for the first. There is no word like "Ozlessness" parallel to "sleeplessness." But more importantly, the natural desires come from within, from our nature, while the artificial ones come from without, from society, advertising or fiction. This second difference is the reason for a third difference: the natural desires are found in all of us, but the artificial ones vary from person to person.

The existence of the artificial desires does not necessarily mean that the desired objects exist. Some do; some don't. Sports cars do; Oz does not. But the existence of natural desires does, in every discoverable case, mean that the objects desired exist. No one has ever found one case of an innate desire for a nonexistent object.

The second premise requires only honest introspection. If someone denies it and says, "I am perfectly happy playing with mud pies, or sports cars, or money, or sex, or power," we can only ask, "Are you, *really?*" But we can only appeal, we cannot compel. And we can refer such a person to the nearly universal testimony of human history in all its great literature. Even the atheist Jean-Paul Sartre admitted that "there comes a time when one asks, even of Shakespeare, even of Beethoven, 'Is that all there is?' "

The conclusion of the argument is not that everything the Bible tells us about God and life with God is really so. What it proves is an unknown X, but an unknown whose *direction*, so to speak, is known. This X is *more:* more beauty, more desirability, more awesomeness, more joy. This X is to great beauty as, for example, great beauty is to small beauty or to a mixture of beauty and ugliness. And the same is true of other perfections.

But the "more" is infinitely more, for we are not satisfied with the finite and partial. Thus the analogy (X is to great beauty as great beauty is to small beauty) is not proportionate. Twenty is to ten as ten is to five, but infinity is not to twenty as twenty is to ten. The argument points down an infinite corridor in a definite direction. Its conclusion is not "God" as already conceived or defined, but a moving and mysterious X which pulls us to itself and pulls all our images and concepts out of themselves.

In other words, the only concept of God in this argument is the concept of that which transcends concepts, something "no eye has seen, nor ear heard, nor the human heart conceived" (1 Cor 2:9). In other words, this is the real God.

C. S. Lewis, who uses this argument in a number of places, summarizes it succinctly:

> Creatures are not born with desires unless satisfaction for these desires exists. A baby feels hunger; well, there is such a thing as food. A duckling wants to swim; well, there is such a thing as water. Men feel sexual desire; well, there is such a thing as sex. If I find in myself a desire which no experience in this world can satisfy, the most probable explanation is that I was made for another world. (*Mere Christianity*, Bk. III, chap. 10, "Hope")

Question 1:

How can you know the major premise—that every *natural desire has a real object—is universally true, without* first *knowing that this natural desire also has a real object? But that is the conclusion. Thus you beg the question. You must know the conclusion to be true before you can know the major premise.*

Reply: This is really not an objection to the argument from desire only, but to *every* deductive argument whatsoever, *every* syllogism. It is the old saw of John Stuart Mill and the nominalists against the syllogism. It presupposes empiricism—that is, that the *only* way we can ever know anything is by sensing individual things and then generalizing, by induction. It excludes deduction because it excludes the knowledge of any universal truths (like our major premise). For nominalists do not believe in the existence of any universals—except one (that all universals are only names).

This is very easy to refute. We can and do come to a knowledge of universal truths, like "all humans are mortal," not by sense experience alone (for we can never sense *all* humans) but through abstracting the common universal essence or nature of humanity from the few specimens we do experience by our senses. We know that all humans are mortal because humanity, as such, involves mortality, it is the *nature* of a human being to be mortal; mortality follows necessarily from its having an animal body. We can understand that. We have the power of understanding, or intellectual intuition, or insight, in addition to the mental powers of sensation and calculation, which are the only two the nominalist and empiricist give us. (We share sensation with animals and calculation with computers; where is the distinctively human way of knowing for the empiricist and nominalist?)

When there is no real connection between the nature of a proposition's subject and the nature of the predicate, the only way we can know the truth of that proposition is by sense experience and induction. For instance, we can know that all the books on this shelf are red only by looking at each one and counting them. But when there is a real connection between the nature of the subject and the nature of the predicate, we can know the truth of that proposition by understanding and insight—for instance, "Whatever has color must have size," or, "A Perfect Being would not be ignorant."

Question 2:
Suppose I simply deny the minor premise and say that I just don't observe any hidden desire for God, or infinite joy, or some mysterious X that is more than earth can offer?

Reply: This denial may take two forms. First, one may say, "Although I am not perfectly happy now, I believe I would be if only I had ten million dollars, a Lear jet, and a new mistress every day." The reply to this is, of course, "Try it. You won't like it." It's been tried and has never satisfied. In fact, billions of people have performed and are even now performing trillions of such experiments, desperately seeking the ever-elusive satisfaction they crave. For even if they won the whole world, it would not be enough to fill one human heart.

Yet they keep trying, believing that "If only . . . Next time . . ." This is the stupidest gamble in the world, for it is the only one that consistently has *never* paid off. It is like the game of predicting the end of the world: every batter who has ever approached that plate has struck out. There is hardly reason to hope the present ones will fare any better. After trillions of failures and a one hundred percent failure rate, this is one experiment no one should keep trying.

A second form of denial of our premise is: "I am perfectly happy now." This, we suggest, verges on idiocy or, worse, dishonesty. It requires something more like exorcism than refutation. This is Merseult in Camus's *The Stranger.* This is subhuman, vegetation, pop psychology. Even the hedonist utilitarian John Stuart Mill, one of the shallowest (though cleverest) minds in the history of philosophy, said that "it is better to be Socrates dissatisfied than a pig satisfied."

Question 3:

This argument is just another version of Anselm's ontological argument (13), which is invalid. You argue to an objective God from a mere subjective idea or desire in you.

Reply: No, we do not argue from the idea alone, as Anselm does. Rather, our argument first derives a major premise from the real world of nature: that nature makes no desire in vain. Then it discovers something real in human nature—namely, human desire for something more than nature— which nature cannot explain, because nature cannot satisfy it. Thus, the argument is based on observed facts in nature, both outer and inner. It has data.

17. The Argument from Aesthetic Experience

There is the music of Johann Sebastian Bach.
Therefore there must be a God.
You either see this one or you don't.

18. The Argument from Religious Experience

Some sort of experience lies at the very core of most people's religious faith. Most of our readers have very likely had such an experience. If so, you realize, in a way no one else can, its central importance in your life. That realization is not itself an *argument* for God's existence; in fact, in the light of it you would probably say that there is no need for arguments. But there is in fact an argument for God's existence constructed from the data of such experiences. It is not an argument which moves from your own personal experience to your own affirmation that God exists. As we said, you most probably have no need for such an argument. Instead, this argument moves in another direction: from the widespread *fact* of religious experience to the affirmation that only a divine reality can adequately explain it.

It is difficult to state this argument deductively. But it might fairly be put as follows.

1. Many people of different eras and of widely different cultures claim to have had an experience of the "divine."

2. It is inconceivable that so many people could have been so utterly wrong about the nature and content of their own experience.

3. Therefore, there exists a "divine" reality which many people of different eras and of widely different cultures have experienced.

Does such experience prove that an intelligent Creator-God exists? On the face of it this seems unlikely. For such a God does not seem to be the object of all experiences called "religious." But still, he is the object of many. That is, many people understand their experience that way; they are "united with" or "taken up into" a boundless and overwhelming Knowledge and Love, a Love that fills them with itself but infinitely exceeds their capacity to receive. Or so they claim. The question is: Are we to believe them?

There is an enormous number of such claims. Either they are true or not. In evaluating them, we should take into account:

1. the *consistency* of these claims (are they self-consistent as well as consistent with what we know otherwise to be true?);

2. the *character* of those who make these claims (do these persons seem honest, decent, trustworthy?); and

3. the *effects* these experiences have had in their own lives and the lives of others (have these persons become more loving as a result of what they experienced? More genuinely edifying? Or, alternatively, have they become vain and self-absorbed?).

Suppose someone says to you: "All these experiences are either the result of lesions in the temporal lobe or of neurotic repression. In no way do they verify the truth of some divine reality." What might your reaction be? You might think back over that enormous documentation of accounts and ask yourself if that can be right. And you might conclude: "No. Given this vast number of claims, and the quality of life of those who made them, it seems incredible that those who made the claims could have been so wrong about them, or that insanity or brain disease could cause such profound goodness and beauty."

It is impossible to lay down ahead of time how investigation into this record of claims and characters will affect all individuals. You cannot say ahead of time how it will affect you. But it *is* evidence; it has persuaded many; and it cannot be ignored. Sometimes—in fact, we believe, very often—that record is not so much faced as dismissed with vivid trendy labels.

19. The Common Consent Argument

This proof is in some ways like the argument from religious experience (18) and in other ways like the argument from desire (16). It argues that:

1. Belief in God—that Being to whom reverence and worship are properly due—is common to almost all people of every era.

2. Either the vast majority of people have been wrong about this most profound element of their lives or they have not.

3. It is most plausible to believe that they have not.

4. Therefore it is most plausible to believe that God exists.

Everyone admits that religious belief is widespread throughout human history. But the question arises: Does this undisputed fact amount to evidence in favor of the *truth* of religious claims? Even a skeptic will admit that the testimony we have is deeply impressive: the vast majority of humans have believed in an ultimate Being to whom the proper response could only be reverence and worship. No one disputes the reality of our feelings of reverence, attitudes of worship, acts of adoration. But if God does not exist, then these things have never once—*never once*—had a real object. Is it really plausible to believe that?

The capacity for reverence and worship certainly seems to belong to us by nature. And it is hard to believe that this natural capacity can never, in the nature of things, be fulfilled, especially when so many testify that it has been. True enough, it is *conceivable* that this side of our nature is doomed to frustration; it is *thinkable* that those millions upon millions who claim to have found the Holy One who is worthy of reverence and worship were deluded. But is it *likely?*

It seems far more likely that those who *refuse* to believe are the ones suffering from deprivation and delusion—like the tone-deaf person who denies the existence of music, or the frightened tenant who tells herself she doesn't hear cries of terror and distress coming from the street below and, when her children awaken to the sounds and ask her, "Why is that lady screaming, Mommy?" tells them, "Nobody's screaming; it's just the wind, that's all. Go back to sleep."

Question 1:

But the majority is not infallible. Most people were wrong about the movements of the sun and earth. So why not about the existence of God?

Reply: If people were wrong about the theory of heliocentrism, they still experienced the sun and earth and motion. They were simply mistaken in thinking that the motion they perceived was the sun's. But if God does not exist, what is it that believers have been experiencing? The level of illusion goes far beyond any other example of collective error. It really amounts to collective psychosis.

For believing in God is like having a relationship with a person. If God never existed, neither did this relationship. You were responding with reverence and love to no one; and no one was there to receive and answer your response. It's as if you believe yourself happily married when in fact you live alone in a dingy apartment.

Now we grant that such mass delusion is conceivable, but what is the *likely* story? If there were no other bits of experience which, taken together with our perceptions of the sun and earth, make it most likely that the earth goes round the sun, it would be foolish to interpret our experience that way. How much more so here, where what we experience is a relationship involving reverence and worship and, sometimes, love. It is most reasonable to believe that God really is there, given such widespread belief in him—unless atheists can come up with a very persuasive explanation for religious belief, *one that takes full account of the experience of believers* and shows that their experience is best explained as delusion and not insight. But atheists have never done so.

Question 2:

But isn't there a very plausible psychological account of religious belief? Many nonbelievers hold that belief in God is the result of childhood fears; that God is in fact a projection of our human fathers: someone "up there" who can protect us from natural forces we consider hostile.

Reply A: This is not really a naturalistic *explanation* of religious belief. It is no more than a statement, dressed in psychological jargon, that religious belief is false. You begin from the assumption that God does not exist. Then you figure that since the closest earthly symbol for the Creator is a father, God *must* be a cosmic projection of our human fathers. But apart from the assumption of atheism, there is no compelling evidence at all that God is a mere projection.

In fact, the argument begs the question. We seek psychological explanation only for ideas we already know (or presume) to be false, not those we think to be true. We ask, "Why do you think black dogs are out to kill you?

Were you frightened by one when you were small?" But we never ask, "Why do you think black dogs *aren't* out to kill you? Did you have a nice black puppy once?"

Reply B: Though there must be something of God that is reflected in human fathers (otherwise our symbolism for him would be inexplicable), Christians realize that the symbolism is ultimately inadequate. And if the Ultimate Being is mysterious in a way that transcends all symbolism, how can he be a mere projection of what the symbol represents? The truth seems to be—and if God exists, the truth is—the other way around: our earthly fathers are pale projections of the Heavenly Father. It should be noted that several writers (e.g., Paul Vitz) have analyzed atheism as itself a psychic pathology: an alienation from the human father that results in rejection of God.

20. Pascal's Wager

Suppose you, the reader, still feel that all of these arguments are inconclusive. There is another, different kind of argument left. It has come to be known as Pascal's Wager. We mention it here and adapt it for our purposes, not because it is a proof for the existence of God, but because it can help us in our search for God in the absence of such proof.

As originally proposed by Pascal, the Wager assumes that logical reasoning by itself cannot decide for or against the existence of God; there seem to be good reasons on both sides. Now since reason cannot decide for sure, and since the question is of such importance that we must decide somehow, then we must "wager" if we cannot prove. And so we are asked: Where are you going to place your bet?

If you place it with God, you lose nothing, even if it turns out that God does not exist. But if you place it against God, and you are wrong and God does exist, you lose everything: God, eternity, heaven, infinite gain. "Let us assess the two cases: if you win, you win everything, if you lose, you lose nothing."

Consider the following diagram.

The vertical lines represent correct beliefs, the diagonals represent incorrect beliefs. Let us compare the diagonals. Suppose God does not exist and I believe in him. In that case, what awaits me after death is not eternal life but, most likely, eternal nonexistence. But now take the other diagonal: God, my Creator and the source of all good, does exist; but I do not believe in him. He offers me his love and his life, and I reject it. There are answers to my greatest questions, there is fulfillment of my deepest desires; but I decide to spurn it all. In that case, I lose (or at least seriously risk losing) everything.

The Wager can seem offensively venal and purely selfish. But it can be reformulated to appeal to a higher moral motive: If there is a God of infinite goodness, and he justly deserves my allegiance and faith, I risk doing the greatest injustice by not acknowledging him.

The Wager cannot—or should not—coerce belief. But it can be an incentive for us to search for God, to study and restudy the arguments that seek to show that there is Something—or Someone—who is the ultimate explanation of the universe and of my life. It could at lease motivate "The Prayer of the Skeptic": "God, I don't know whether you exist or not, but if you do, please show me who you are."

Pascal says that there are three kinds of people: those who have sought God and found him, those who are seeking and have not yet found, and those who neither seek nor find. The first are reasonable and happy, the second are reasonable and unhappy, the third are both unreasonable and unhappy. If the Wager stimulates us at least to seek, then it will at least stimulate us to be reasonable. And if the promise Jesus makes is true, all who seek will find (Mt 7:7-8), and thus will be happy.

Questions for Discussion

1. Why might someone think that the whole question of this chapter, whether God's existence can be proved, is trivial, unimportant, distracting or wrongheaded? How might such a person's argument(s) be answered?

2. Could there be an argument for God's existence that does not fit into either of the two categories here, cosmological (external) or psychological (internal)?

3. How psychologically forceful and how psychologically impotent is a valid argument for God's existence to an atheist? What does the answer to that question depend on? (There are many answers to this question; mention as many as you can. Which do you think is the most important one?)

4. How can anything be "outside" the universe if "the universe" = "everything in space and time and matter"? What is meant by "outside" here? Can you give any

analogy or parallel situation where a term is used like this?

5. Why are there more than twenty arguments for and only one against God (the problem of evil)? (See chap. 6.)

6. What commonsense meaning of *cause* do these cosmological arguments use (especially 2)? What alternative meanings of *cause* have some philosophers preferred? How do they change or invalidate the cosmological argument(s)? How could these alternatives be refuted? (Hume's is the most famous.)

7. Does the answer to question 2 after argument 2 prove that God is creating the world right now?

8. Would alternative theories of time change or invalidate any of the cosmological arguments?

9. Does the simple answer to question 1 after argument 4 refute subjectivism? If not, where is the error in it? If so, why are there so many subjectivists?

10. Why is the design argument the most popular?

11. What is the relation between *intelligibility* and *intelligence*? Are *intelligibility*, *design* and *order* interchangeable concepts?

12. Isn't there a *tiny* chance that the universe just happened by chance? A quintillion monkeys typing for a quintillion years will eventually produce *Hamlet* by chance. Couldn't this book have been caused by an explosion in a print factory?

13. Regarding argument 10, how do we know the universe is not conscious or aware?

14. Does the answer to question 3 of argument 6 prove God is a person?

15. Sartre wrote: "There can be no eternal truth because there is no eternal Consciousness to think it." What is the implied premise of his argument and of proof 11?

16. Does argument 12 presuppose "innate ideas"? If not, how and when did the idea of God get into our minds?

17. Why is it that you can tell a lot about a philosopher's metaphysics by knowing whether or not he or she accepts the ontological argument? What do Anselm, Descartes, Spinoza, Leibniz and Hegel have in common? What doctrine of Thomistic metaphysics enables Thomas to criticize Anselm's argument?

18. Can you refute the modal and possible worlds versions of the ontological argument?

19. Can an atheist believe in real moral obligation (argument 14)? If so, how? Do most atheists believe in real moral obligation?

20. Is the argument from conscience any stronger if you admit objective moral laws?

21. How would *you* formulate the relationship between religion and morality? Between God and morality?

22. Does everyone have the desire mentioned in premise 2 of argument 16? If so, must atheists suppress and ignore it?

23. Would nominalists be able to escape argument 16? (Cf. question 1.)

24. Can you formulate argument 17 logically?

25. Why is religious experience any more of an argument for the real existence of God than any common delusion, illusion, fantasy or dream for its object? Are we arguing here from idea to reality, as in the ontological argument?

26. Why is the common consent argument hardly ever used today, whereas it was very popular in the past?

27. Is Pascal's "Wager" dishonest? Why or why not? Read Pascal's version of it in the *Pensées*; what do you find there that is significant that is not included here?

28. Do you know of, or can you imagine, any other argument for God's existence?

29. Which of these twenty arguments do you find the most powerful?

30. How would an atheist answer each one of these twenty arguments? (Remember, there are only three ways of answering any argument.)

Outline of Chapter 4
The Nature of God

1. The mystery of God
2. Language about God
3. The attributes of God
   - ☐ God exists absolutely
   - ☐ God is infinite
   - ☐ God is one
   - ☐ God is spiritual
   - ☐ God is eternal
   - ☐ God is transcendent and immanent
      Note on panentheism
   - ☐ God is intelligent
   - ☐ God is omniscient and omnipotent
   - ☐ God is good
4. Mystery and revelation
5. Is God a "he"?

CHAPTER 4
The Nature
of God

Y OU MAY HAVE NOTICED THAT MOST OF THE PROOFS PRESENTED IN CHAP-
ter three begin with things familiar to us—our experience of change,
for example, or of living a moral life. They call to our attention certain
features of these familiar things that are puzzling; certain features about
which we can—and should—ask questions. Now if the questions raised in
the proofs are real ones—questions like: How come the material universe
exists?—if they are of a sort that admit some kind of answer, then we can
see, if we reflect, that the answer is not to be found within the world of finite
and familiar things. In other words, anything that answers the question is
going to be of a kind altogether *unfamiliar* to us. This is as it should be.
For it is the most familiar and natural features of the things in our world
that pressed these questions on us in the first place. If the answer were of
the familiar kind, then it would not really be an answer at all; another
question could be raised about *it*. So the answer to our question, which we
call "God," is an answer we can never fully understand. We know that our
questions are valid, and that there is some answer to them. We give to it
the name "God," knowing that whatever answers our question is and must
always remain beyond our comprehension. That is what we mean by calling
God a "mystery."

Language About God
If this is the case, then how can we speak of God? If God is so mysterious,
how can language, which fundamentally refers to the world of our familiar
experience, ever properly be used of him? This a fair question, but not a

hopelessly unanswerable one, as some have thought. For it is the legitimacy of certain questions about the experienced world that allows us to think in a systematic way about God. God is the answer to these questions. He is the cause of these phenomena. And by meditating on his effects we can know *something* of their cause, shed *some* light on God himself—even though it be only a pinpoint of light.

Something similar happens in science. For example, physicists notice certain regularly occurring effects and give a name to what produces them. They have no direct observation of the causes they name, and in fact they know that some of them cannot ever be observed. But they have no trouble in calling by name what produces these effects—and even in ascribing unusual properties to such theoretical entities on the basis of their observation.

But here the similarity ends. After all, gluons and muons are part of the physical world and share its fundamental properties; God, on the other hand, is the Creator of the world. He cannot exist in the same way that the physical world exists. For as we have stressed repeatedly, it is just those properties essential to the physical world that raise the question whose answer is God. Some writers on the divine nature give the impression that God himself has sat for their portrait. We hope to create no such impression. We simply want to start from the discussion of God's existence, reflect on the demonstrations found there, and ask what they imply about the One whose existence they demonstrate.

The Attributes of God
God Exists Absolutely

By this we do not mean merely that God is always there or that he does not tend to go out of existence. These things are true, in a sense. But we mean something more.

God is the source of being, or existence, for all things. Looking at the universe we see that in every creature there is a distinction between its *essence* and its *existence*; that there is a difference between *what* things are and the fact *that* they are. That is why, as we saw, limited things are by nature existential zeros, why they have a need for being that they cannot themselves supply.

If God is the answer to this question about finite being, then he cannot suffer from this same need. In other words, in God there can be no such distance between *what* he is and *that* he is. That he exists is not a happy accident, not due to some other being as his cause. Being must be inseparable from what he is; it must belong to him by nature. More radically put. God must be identical with the fullness of being. That is what we mean by saying that God exists absolutely.

God Is Infinite

We saw that it is finite or limited being that poses a question for us, that seems to require a condition or cause for its existence. So God cannot be limited or finite. In other words, God must be infinite, utterly limitless.

People often think that by the infinity of God is meant immense size or endless duration—as if God were older than anyone could count or bigger than anyone could measure. But by saying God is infinite we mean that we must deny of God the kinds of limitation (like age or size) that raised a question about finite being. Think of it this way. If something is limited, it is limited in terms of something else—it *is not* what or where the other *is*. So limitation involves *non*being. But God, if he exists, is the very fullness of being. So there can be no limitation in God. He must be without limit; that is, God must be infinite.

God Is One

If God is infinite, can there be many Gods? Obviously not. We have already seen that God must exist without limit. But if he is without limit, there cannot be more than one God. For if there were, there would have to be some difference between them, and this would involve nonbeing; the one could *not* be what or where the other was. But if that were so, then neither one could be the limitless fullness of being. And this would mean that what we call "God" is not the ultimate answer to our question about finite being after all. But if "God" is the answer to that question, then he must be the limitless fullness of being and cannot be limited by another God outside himself. So God must be one.

God Is Spiritual

By saying God is spiritual, we mean that God is not a material being. To be a material being is to be a body of some kind. But a body is always limited and subject to change. To be subject to change in this way is *not to be* what one *will become*. And therefore to be subject to change involves *nonbeing*. And since to be a body is to be subject to change, therefore to be a body involves nonbeing. Now God is the limitless fullness of being, so God cannot be a body. In fact, God cannot be material at all—at least not as matter is normally understood. God must be immaterial, that is, spiritual.

God Is Eternal

Since God is not material, he is not spatially limited. That must be true, for God is the Creator of space and all the constantly changing material things which occupy it. Now the measure of that change is what we call "time." Is God in time? Can he be temporally limited?

We experience ourselves as temporally limited. But most of us believe that human beings are more than just material things, and that something more is what we call "spirit." But our spirits or souls are finite in nature and tied to our body's matter. And therefore time is an intimate part of the way we experience our being—even our spiritual being. It takes time to think, as well as (for us) to be. That is why we can often feel separated from ourselves by vast physical, intellectual and moral distances in time ("How small—naive—carefree I was back then!").

God cannot be subject to time. For God is the Creator of everything that changes: everything that raises a question about its own being. All beings subject to time raise that question. God cannot be like that.

This unboundedness by time is called "eternity." Boethius's famous definition of eternity goes like this: Life without limits, possessed perfectly and as a simultaneous whole. His words are very suggestive. But they clearly convey one essential thing: God is not bound by the kind of changing being which time measures. That is what we mean in the first place when we say that God is *e-ternal* (nontemporal).

The Incarnation does not contradict this; rather, it presupposes it. The Incarnation means that God took upon himself, in Christ, a human nature, which included time, space and matter. This presupposes that the divine nature is different from human nature. Part of that difference has traditionally been seen as God's not being limited by time, space and matter. Only if a bird *doesn't* swim in the ocean but flies in the air can it *enter* the ocean from above; only because God is *not* temporal, can he *become* temporal.

God Is Transcendent and Immanent

God cannot be a *part* of the universe. If he were, he would be limited by other parts of it. But God is the *Creator* of all things, giving them their total being. He cannot be one of them, or the totality of them—for each one of them, and so the totality of them, must be given being, must receive being from God. So God must be *other* than his creation. This is what we mean by the *transcendence* of God.

At the same time God must exist *in* all things. They cannot be set over against him, for then he would be limited by them. Shakespeare was limited by his contemporaries but not by his creations; by Marlowe but not by Hamlet. God is the Creator, the giver of the total being to all things. As such he must be active in giving them what they need to be and to act. If God were not actively communicating being to all things, they would cease to be. So God must be present to all things at their deepest core, existence itself "In him we live and move and have our being." In other words, God is immanent.

Note how this affirmation of God's transcendence and immanence avoids the one-sided pitfalls of pantheism (which identifies God with material nature) and deism (which makes God remote from creation, as if he could wind it up and let it run on its own).

Note on Panentheism

In recent years, the doctrine of God's eternity has lost favor with some Christian philosophers and theologians. A number of them maintain that God exists everlastingly in time. Others argue that, since the creation of the world, God exists in time only. Still others have embraced panentheism, the doctrine that all things exist in God—a kind of compromise between theism and pantheism. It does not identify God with the material universe (as pantheism does), but neither does it hold that there actually exists an eternal God, transcendent to creation (as theism does).

Panentheists believe that the material universe constitutes God, but that God is more than the material universe. There is an eternal, necessary and unchanging (i.e., "abstract") aspect to God's being, but there is also the way God concretely and actually exists—namely, as the vital force, the "soul"—of this dynamically changing world. And thus the world is necessarily involved in what God actually is. He cannot concretely exist except as vitalizing the world; nor can the world exist except as vitalized by God. Each needs the other. And just as the real world changes from one state to another, so the actual being of God must change as well. Thus panentheism is one way of making God temporal.

Any orthodox Christian who maintains that God is somehow in time must also have ready some analysis of time that does not involve any lack or incompletion of being—the kind of imperfection that, when noticed in material being, indicates the need for a Creator. In that case they mean by time something different from what we (and others) mean by it when we say that God is eternal. And so the differences between us might be merely verbal. We might be quibbling over a technical point and not a central Christian doctrine.

Panentheism, on the other hand, is clearly heretical. For it asserts as part of its doctrine that the material universe does not demand a Creator, merely a vivifier, a kind of "world-soul." This is not only unorthodox, it seems positively irrational. For if our analysis of finite being is right (cf. arguments 1-8 in chap. 3 for the existence of God), then the world does raise a much deeper and more radical question about itself, namely: Why does it exist at all, rather than not? And if that is a real question, and if God is its answer, then the world and God cannot be codependent. For God is the Creator; the world depends on him for its *total* being.

God Is Intelligent

God is the creator and sustainer of all things. He is, for example, the creator and sustainer of all physical and chemical elements and all living organisms. Now every one of these things has an intelligible structure, and fits within a system of intelligible structure—a system in which things act and react with each other in certain specific ways determined by the system. This intelligible correlation of part with part (of which our intelligence grasps the tiniest measure) is something established by God. An intelligible correlation of part with part is the kind of thing we normally refer to as a "plan," as an "act of intelligence." So it is reasonable to affirm that all the vast intelligibility, which the world is given by its Creator, is the work of intelligence, and therefore, that the Creator is intelligent.

There is a second argument for God's being intelligent. Something which distinguishes persons from nonpersons is self-possession. Personal intelligence can unify a diversity and hold it together, as in a work of art or a scientific theory. And that single center which holds many things together with itself allows us to escape the sheer externality of matter, and to use, work, and control those things which have no intelligence. But then God, who is utterly immaterial, and who controls and unifies the whole of creation can surely not be unintelligent. His intelligence cannot be like ours, because ours is tied in a way to matter. It must be infinitely greater. But still it is reasonable to hold that the answer to our question, the mystery we call "God," is intelligent.

Finally, we human beings respond to certain goods, to real values. These are not things we have created, but things we discover, like the value of life or love or honesty. If God creates both the human nature which responds to those goods, and also these goods themselves, it is reasonable to think of God as intelligently *designing* this congruence between what we are and the goods we need for fulfillment.

God Is Omniscient and Omnipotent

To say that God is omniscient and omnipotent means that there can be no real barriers to God's knowing or acting. Apart from himself, God has created everything there is to be known and sustains it in being. So is it conceivable that there is something he could not know or not have power over? It is impossible to think of something as thwarting God's will, unless God himself allows the thwarting—as in the human free choice to sin. But that is a circumstance that *requires* omnipotence, and therefore is not an argument against it.

God Is Good

God, as we have just seen, is the source of all that we recognize as good. Now let us go a step further. God is the source of all being. Therefore God cannot be evil in any way, for whether an evil is moral or physical, it is properly understood in terms of what should be there but is not. A thing is good *of its kind* (and that qualification is important) if it succeeds in being that kind of thing to the fullest. It is bad if it fails. Now there can be no question of failure on the part of the Creator; God *is* to the fullest. And insofar as goodness is one with perfect being, God is the perfect good.

Mystery and Revelation

You may be dissatisfied with some of what you find in this section on the nature of God. Some may think too much is claimed. But if you look back over what we have said, you will find that the results are mainly negative. We have taken pains to say what the Creator is *not* and cannot be. It is because God is the Creator that we must deny certain things about him. For example, we argued that God is not material, he is spiritual. We use the word *spiritual* to denote his complete immateriality because we use it to denote that part of us which is furthest removed from what we take to be material being.

But *how* God lives his life we do not, and cannot, as mere philosophers, pretend to know. All we know is that God is not bound by matter, and that if what we call "spirit" is that which escapes the constraints of material limitation, then God is spirit—though infinitely more free from that limitation than we are, with an intensity incalculably richer than our own. Therefore, "spirit" is not used *univocally* (i.e., with the same meaning) of God and us; nor is it used *equivocally* (i.e., with two completely different meanings). Rather, it is used *analogically* (i.e., in a way partly the same and partly different).

Note the movement of thought from affirmation to negation and back again. Note also that what controls this movement at every stage is our realization that God is the creative cause of all things.

1. God is the fullness of being. (affirmation)
2. God is immaterial. (negation)
3. God is spiritual. (affirmation)
4. God is not spiritual as we are. (negation)
5. God's spiritual being is infinitely greater and richer than our own. (reaffirmation)

We can reasonably assert *that* these things are true; but we do not, and cannot, know how. The life of God remains a mystery.

But some may think that we have claimed too little. They see a great distance here between the loving Father revealed in Scripture and the infinitely mysterious Creator revealed in philosophical speculation. And we admit this: the kind of love revealed in Jesus is far greater than what we could hope to know from philosophy. That is precisely why Jesus revealed the Father to us. If we could learn all we need to know about God from philosophy, we would have no need of divine revelation. Having said this, what philosophy has given us is not without worth. It shows that, at every moment of our existence, we depend on our Creator for everything: our existence, our intelligence, the intelligibilities our intelligence grasps, the goods we strive for—even the free choices by which we strive for them. Philosophy shows that this Creator infinitely exceeds whatever level of spiritual unity we might possess, and that it is reasonable to view God's action as intelligent, good and providential. True, it does not show the level of love that was revealed in Christ. But it leaves the way open for that possibility. It also discourages idolatry: our cutting God down to our own size, reducing to a measurable distance, so to speak, the height from which he sees us. God cannot be greater than us by any finite measure. He is not in competition with any created thing.

Whatever we have is a gift. Nothing is our own. Philosophy can help us to see all that, and so to be grateful for something we too often take for granted: our very being.

Is God a "He"?

The hottest controversy today about God concerns the traditional exclusive use of the pronoun *he*. Nearly all Christians admit that (1) God is not literally male, since he has no biological body, and (2) women are not essentially inferior to men. Those are red herrings.

There are, however, two reasons for defending the exclusive use of masculine pronouns and imagery for God. One issue is whether we have the authority to change the names of God used by Christ, the Bible and the church. The traditional defense of masculine imagery for God rests on the premise that the Bible is divine revelation, not culturally relative, negotiable and changeable. As C. S. Lewis put it, "Christians believe God himself has told us how to speak of him."

The other reason for calling God "he" is historical. Except for Judaism, all other known ancient religions had goddesses as well as gods. The Jewish revelation was distinctive in its exclusively masculine pronoun because it was distinctive in its theology of the divine transcendence. That seems to be the main point of the masculine imagery. As a man comes into a woman from without to make her pregnant, so God creates the universe from without rather than birthing it from within and impregnates our souls with grace or supernatural life from without. As a woman cannot impregnate herself, so the universe cannot create itself, nor can the soul redeem itself.

Surely there is an inherent connection between these two radically distinctive features of the three biblical or Abramic religions (Judaism, Christianity and Islam): their unique view of a transcendent God creating nature out of nothing and their refusal to call God "she" despite the fact that Scripture ascribes to him feminine *attributes* like compassionate nursing (Is 49:15), motherly comfort (Is 66:13) and carrying an infant (Is 46:3). The masculine pronoun safeguards (1) the transcendence of God against the illusion that nature is born from God as a mother rather than created and (2) the grace of God against the illusion that we can somehow save ourselves—two illusions ubiquitous and inevitable in the history of religion.

Questions for Discussion

1. How is God a *mystery?* Are there any other "mysteries" in this sense besides God? What other meanings does the term often have?

2. How can we formulate just where, between total unintelligibility and total intelligibility, the concept of God lies? How does Aquinas's theory of analogy address this question? (Compare the section on mystery and revelation.)

3. Can we imagine "absolute existence"? Can we imagine "existence" at all? How can we conceive what we cannot imagine? What do we conceive about "absolute existence"?

4. Does God's infinity mean he is *everything?* If so, how is theism different from pantheism? If not, why do so many people think this?

5. Does God's oneness mean *uniqueness* or *indivisibility* (or both)? Explain what these mean.

6. What does *spirit* mean? Why do materialists not believe it exists? Why do many materialists believe the term is unintelligible and meaningless?

7. What is eternity? Is it more than "having no beginning and no end"? Can there be anything *between* time and eternity? Can you imagine eternity? What is analogous to it?

8. How can an eternal being become temporal in the Incarnation? How can the same person have two contrary natures, eternal and temporal? What other cases or analogies are like this?

9. Is anything besides God both transcendent and immanent?

10. "God can be totally immanent only because he is totally transcendent. The very same fact about him enables him to be both." Explain.

11. What is the relation between panentheism and "process theology"?

12. How must divine intelligence be different from human intelligence in more than just degree or quantity?

13. If *omnipotent* means "able to do anything," can God make a rock bigger than he can lift?

14. What practical, existential consequences follow from the three attributes of omniscience, omnipotence and goodness taken together?

15. What must *good* mean when predicated of God? Compare a good God, a good man, a good doggie, a good gun and a good belch.

16. Why is there a need for revelation?

17. How can our very being be a gift? To whom, if the recipient has no being yet?

18. How do those feminists who want to revise biblical language about God answer the two arguments presented (the question of authority and the historical precedent)?

Part 3
GOD & NATURE

Outline of Chapter 5
Four Problems of Cosmology

Introduction

1. Creation and Evolution

☐ Is creation possible?

☐ What difference does the doctrine of creation make?

☐ Is evolution possible?

☐ What difference does the theory of evolution make?

☐ Does evolution contradict creation?

2. Providence and freedom

3. Miracles

☐ Two questions about miracles

☐ Have miracles actually occurred in history?

☐ Arguments for the possibility of miracles

☐ Objections against miracles

Miracles violate the principle of the uniformity of nature.

It is more probable that the "miracle" did not occur than that a law of nature was really violated.

To accept miracles is to abandon the scientific method.

Miracles are an affront to the glory of God, the designer of nature.

How can we know that it is God, and not another spiritual being, who has intervened in the natural order?

4. Angels

☐ What are angels?

☐ Do angels exist?

☐ Why is it important to believe in angels?

CHAPTER 5
Four Problems
of Cosmology

A LL FOUR OF THE PROBLEMS OF COSMOLOGY—CREATION AND EVOLUTION, providence and freedom, miracles and angels—concern God's relationship with the cosmos or nature or the universe. All of them can be addressed either at great length or in brief. We choose the latter way because we feel that all four issues have been made unnecessarily complex. On the other hand, the problem of evil, the subject of chapter six, is the perennial Problem Number One facing the theist, and merits its own entire, rather long and complex, chapter. (But since it concerns what seems to be the badness of creation and the goodness of the Creator, we realize that the problem of evil, like the four problems treated in this chapter, is also a problem of cosmology: a problem about the relation between God and nature.)

Creation and Evolution
There is much to be said about the issue of creation and evolution. However, here we only summarize the answers to five essential questions: (1) Is creation possible? (2) What difference does creation make? (3) Is evolution possible? (4) What difference does evolution make? (5) Does evolution contradict creation?

Is Creation Possible?
When Jewish and Christian theologians first talked to Greek philosophers, the Greeks thought the biblical notion that God created the world *ex nihilo*

("out of nothing") was absurd and irrational, because it violated a law of nature that *ex nihilo nihil fit* ("out of nothing nothing comes"). The reply was (and is) that:

1. It is indeed a law of nature, but the laws of nature cannot be expected to bind the transcendent Creator of nature.

2. The reason for this is that all of nature and all powers in nature are finite, but God is infinite; no finite power can produce the infinite change from nonbeing to being, but infinite power can.

3. The idea of God creating out of nothing is not irrational because it does not claim that anything ever popped into existence without an adequate cause. God did not pop into existence, and nature did have an adequate cause: God.

(The question "If God made everything, who made God?" is like asking "Who made circles square?" It assumes a self-contradiction: that the uncreated Creator is a created creature. It extends the law about changing things—that every change needs a cause—beyond its limits, to the unchanging Source of change. God does not need a cause, or a maker, because he is not made or changed. He changes other things, but is not himself changed by anything. There is nothing that comes to be in him, nothing that needs a cause for its coming-into-being.)

What Difference Does the Doctrine of Creation Make?

It makes a difference to our concept of God. If God is the Creator, he must be: (1) infinitely powerful; (2) immeasurably wise (to create this whole universe and all its parts, including its design, laws and structures); (3) a great artist ("Poems are made by fools like me, but only God can make a tree"); and (4) totally generous, since the all-sufficient, perfect Being couldn't have created out of need (e.g., boredom or loneliness).

It also makes a difference to our concept of nature. If nature is created by God, it is (1) intelligible (it is no accident that science arose in the theistic West, not the pantheistic East); (2) good (thus Christianity has always condemned all forms of Manichaeism and gnosticism as heresy); and (3) real (the East often sees nature as an unreal illusion projected by unenlightened consciousness).

Finally, the doctrine of creation affects our concept of ourselves. If we owe our very existence to God, then (1) we have no rights over against God. This startling conclusion necessarily follows from the doctrine of Creation. Shakespeare has rights over against Marlowe, and Hamlet has rights over against Laertes, but how could Hamlet have rights over against Shakespeare? (2) Our existence is meaningful if we are in a play, a divine design, deliberately created rather than blindly evolved. (3) And if we owe God our very existence, we owe him everything. Nothing is our own—no part of our time, or our money, or even our thoughts.

No idea in the history of human thought has ever made more difference than the idea of Creation.

Is Evolution Possible?

If it were impossible, that impossibility would have to come either from the creature or from the Creator.

Scientists and philosophers do not all agree about whether evolution is possible, whether the nature of species makes evolution impossible or not. The jury is still out, though many people on both sides feel absolutely and totally convinced.

There is no impossibility on the side of the Creator. If God wanted to arrange for species to evolve from each other by natural means, he certainly could have created such a world.

So as far as either scientists or theologians know, evolution is *possible*. Whether it is *actual*, whether it actually happened, is undecided. The theory is indeed in scientific trouble. Perhaps it can be salvaged. That is for science to decide.

What Difference Does Evolution Make?

What makes a great difference is not evolution as such but two other ideas that are often identified with it: natural selection and materialism.

Natural selection basically means "the survival of the fittest." According to Darwin, it is the mechanism by which species evolved. Now this could be one of two things. It could be the means God used, the force he implanted in nature from the beginning—in which case natural selection is a part of divine design. Or it could mean a way of *eliminating* divine design. For Darwin and most of his followers right down to the present, it has usually meant the second.

The elimination of divine design does indeed make a difference. If it is true that we evolved simply by blind chance, not divine design, then our lives have no overarching meaning, no preset divine plan, no script. The only meaning, purpose or values that exist are the ones we invent for ourselves. These can never be right or wrong, justified or not justified by a higher standard than our own desires, which created them. Thus there is no real reason to prefer Christian ethics to Stalinist ethics, for instance, except one's own desires themselves. Desire becomes its own reason, its own justification.

Does evolution involve materialism? Not necessarily. The evolution of the body seems to make no difference if the soul is distinguished from the body. But if there is no soul, or if the soul is something that naturally emerged from the body and naturally evolves, then there is no essential difference between humans and apes. Our bodies are essentially the same kind of thing as ape bodies. If we have no souls or if our souls are also essentially the same as ape souls, then there is no reason to expect anyone to act essentially different from apes. (This may explain much current social history!) What makes a difference is not where the body came from, but whether there is a soul, and where *it* came from.

Does Evolution Contradict Creation?

What we have said above, and elsewhere in this book, seems to show clearly that the answer is no. God created the universe at the beginning of time; the *universe* could not possibly have evolved, because there was nothing for it to have evolved from, and not even any time for it to have evolved in. But what about *life* evolving? God may have created organic life directly or he may have evolved it from inorganic life by natural processes; nothing we know for sure in either theology or science, God or nature, makes us absolutely certain of either answer.

Now the human body is one form of organic life. If organic life-forms evolved by natural selection, the human body may have done so too. Or God may have created it directly. Certainly, a God who creates a whole universe from nothing can perform miracles within that universe, including creating that comparatively little thing called a human body, if that is what he wished to do. Nothing we know about either nature or God seems to make it impossible for our bodies either to have evolved, or to have been created directly.

The soul, however, cannot evolve. Spirit cannot evolve from matter; it would be easier to get blood from a stone. No matter how many atoms you line up, or how complicated their lineup, you cannot get a wholly different thing—thought, consciousness, reason, self-awareness—from mere bits of matter. *Awareness of the material universe is not one more part of that universe.* The knowledge of a thing is not one of the thing's parts, it is transcendent to the thing, an addition from without. Science can say absolutely nothing about where souls come from, for souls simply are not the sort of thing you can see or measure. (For more on creation and evolution, see pp. 218-20.)

Providence and Freedom

God knows all things and his knowledge is eternal. Therefore he must know what we are going to choose before we ever choose it. But then how can we choose anything freely? Being free seems to involve an alternative; I may choose the path of vice or virtue. But if it has been determined from eternity that I will choose one path rather than another, there is really nothing for me to genuinely choose. God, in creating me, seems also to have created all my choices. So my choices turn out not to be mine at all but really God's. Two terrifying conclusions seem to follow: (1) if God exists, human freedom is impossible; and (2) God is the author of sin. Such is the problem of providence and freedom.

Our reply will be brief. First, when we say that God's knowledge is eternal or that he knows from all eternity the choices you are going to make, we do not mean that he knows at a time in the distant past that you will do something in the future and that this knowledge *determines* you to do it. We mean instead that the *kind* of knowledge God has (like the kind of being he has) is not limited in any way by temporal constraints as our knowledge is. Time is the measure of moving, changing beings; in other words, time is a creature every bit as much as these things are. God, the Creator, is beyond such measure. His being transcends time and all such temporal categories.

We naturally think of God's eternity as if it were a temporal extension stretching infinitely back into the past and forward into the future. That is because our language reflects the kind of being we have: finite, changing, timebound. We know that God's being cannot really be like that, and therefore that his knowledge cannot really look forward or back. He sees in a single and eternal act of vision all our free choices *as they really exist*, embedded in their times and places and circumstances. And he can have this eternal vision because every creature is "embedded" in him, the Creator, the Source of all being.

Second, if God created us to be free, our freedom is a created gift. That is to say, God's creating and conserving power must be present in all our free acts. There can be no human freedom which is absolute in the sense that it eliminates the need for God. If God is really the Creator, the source of the being of all things, he must also give being to our freedom. His power cannot be an impediment to our free acts, as it would be if he were just another, but supremely powerful, creature—like a Cosmic Hypnotist, making us do his bidding, when we think we are acting on our own. Creatures can act on their own only with respect to other creatures; but never with respect to the Creator. Without God there would be no freedom for us to have. And there would be no "us" to have it.

A great deal of technical theology has been written about the problems of providence and freedom. We decline to enter those dark and still turbulent waters. But as Christians we offer this thought: If God really is intimately involved in giving being to our free choices, to all our actions, think what a terrible thing sin must be. God has committed himself to create and sustain those of us who use the gift of freedom to hurt others and to hate God himself. The power of those who drove the nails into his beloved Son's hands and feet came ultimately from him. If freedom has a terrible price, surely God pays more than his share.

Miracles

We begin with a preliminary definition. A miracle is: *a striking and religiously significant intervention of God in the system of natural causes.*

Note two things here: (1) the concept of miracles presupposes, rather than sets aside, the idea that nature is a self-contained system of natural causes. Unless there are regularities, there can be no exceptions to them. (2) A miracle is not a contradiction. A man walking through a wall is a miracle. A man both walking and not walking through a wall at the same time and in the same respect is a contradiction. God can perform miracles but not contradictions—not because his power is limited, but because contradictions are meaningless.

Two Questions About Miracles

We must distinguish the philosophical question—Are miracles possible?—from the historical question—Are miracles actual? Has there ever really been such an intervention? The answer to the second question requires a knowledge of events in history. It also requires not philosophical, but historical investigation. What the philosopher and apologist can do is argue for the *possibility* of miracles. For nearly all those people who deny that miracles have actually happened have done so because of some philosophical argument which is supposed to prove that miracles *cannot* happen.

Obviously, you cannot believe miracles have happened without believing that a miracle-worker exists. Thus all who believe in miracles believe in some kind of God. But not everyone who believes in God believes in miracles. If there is a God, miracles are *possible*. But perhaps God did not choose to actualize this possibility.

Have Miracles Actually Occurred in History?

There are some who believe that God exists but has never worked a miracle in the entire course of human history. Others disbelieve in God *and* miracles, sometimes arguing that the absence of miracles is a reason for not believing in God (as the absence of footprints on a beach is a reason for not believing that people have just been walking there).

You may well ask: How could anyone justify so strong a claim as that whether or not there is a God, no miracles have *ever* happened in the entire course of human history? Did they examine *every* alleged miracle story, sift through *all* the evidence on a case-by-case basis? Of course not; that kind of investigation would take lifetimes. How then could such a claim ever be justified? Only if there exist arguments showing that miracles are impossible or vastly improbable. That would obviously free us from the need to take any evidence for miracles seriously, because we would already know that it is not really worth considering at all.

Thus we must consider the question of the philosophical *possibility* of miracles before investigating the historical question of their *actuality*. Logically, there are four possibilities:

1. If miracles are not possible, then they cannot be actual. That we know.

2. And if they are actual, then they are possible. That we know.

3. But if they are possible, we do not yet know whether they are actual.

4. And if they are not actual, we still do not yet know whether they are possible.

Arguments for the Possibility of Miracles

This section addresses only the *possibility* of miracles, to open the way to the historical investigation of their actuality. There are two arguments for the possibility of miracles: one from the side of God, the miracle-worker, or the cause, and the other from the side of the world, or the effect. We must show that both are open, not closed, to miracles.

First, there is no defense against miracles in God's nature, no assurance that God would *not* work a miracle. For if there is a God, he is omnipotent (cf. chap. 4), and thus able to work miracles. Whether he would freely choose to do so or not is not a matter we can know a priori, for it would depend on his free choice. An omnipotent God could not be compelled to work or not work a miracle. So there is no obstacle to miracles in God. If there is a God, miracles are possible.

Second, there is no obstacle to or defense against miracles on the part of the world of nature. If God created it in the first place, that is, if nature is open to the possibilities of existing or not existing, then it is open to the possibilities of containing miracles or not containing them. In other words, if God can bang out the Big Bang of creation, he can certainly add some smaller bangs of miracles. If the author can create the play, he can change it too. And if the play is dependent on God, its author, for its very existence, then it is also dependent on him for whatever else he may want to do in it.

Objections Against Miracles

The main task of the apologist, with regard to miracles, is to answer all the objections that seek to prove that miracles are impossible. Remember, the objector here is not a historian who has investigated every event in all of human history and concluded that not one of them is miraculous. We do not have to meet the objection on the historical level by showing that some particular events have been miraculous. Rather, the objections operate on the philosophical level, the level of possibility. Each objection tries to prove that miracles are impossible (or overwhelmingly improbable). If miracles are impossible, then they are not actual, and if no miracles ever actually happened, then Christianity is false. For the fundamental claims and doctrines of Christianity are all miracles: Incarnation, resurrection, salvation, inspiration. If any one of these objections is valid, the whole of Christianity is refuted.

Objection 1:

Miracles violate the principle of the uniformity of nature.

Reply: What is meant by the "uniformity of nature"? If it means that we can explain whatever happens wholly in terms of the system of natural causes, then the objection begs the question. It amounts to saying "miracles violate the principle that miracles never happen."

Objection 2:

A miracle, by definition, must violate some law of nature, and therefore must be a maximally improbable event. But then it is always more likely that the event never really occurred as described (or remembered), or that it did not really violate the laws of nature.

Reply A: A miracle does not "violate" the laws of nature—any more than a school principal violates the schedule of classes by cancelling gym for a special assembly. *Violations* take place whenever someone who has to follow or uphold an established order fails or refuses to do so—for example, when the gym teacher cancels classes on his own to lead his students in an hour of spontaneous prayer. But the principal has done nothing like that if he modifies the schedule *within the limits of his authority.*

Now the Creator of the universe has authority over all creation. It is truly odd to call his suspending this or that regularly observed sequence a "violation," as if it were something he should feel guilty or embarrassed about. A miracle violates nothing. When one happens, God has (mercifully) modified the schedule of the day.

Reply B: Why are miracles called "maximally improbable"? They are certainly unusual, but how do we know whether they are *likely* to happen or not? Only if we have already decided whether or not it is likely that God exists—or that he would ever work a miracle. In that case calling miracles "maximally improbable" is not a neutral description: it stacks the deck *against* them. For it places every report of miracles in a setting where it is most likely that God does not exist or does not intervene in the system of natural causes, and therefore that the event reported is not a miracle at all. Hence the conclusion that reports of miracles should be disbelieved is really assumed in, and assured by, the words used in the premises to describe them.

Reply C: We are creatures of habit. Life is one darn thing after another— often the same sort of darn thing. We expect that today is going to be pretty much like yesterday, and we know that people, including ourselves, are given to exaggeration and deceit. So we naturally approach stories of "signs and wonders" with deep suspicion. Our experience of humanity teaches us to have our guard up much of the time. And when we hear of "miracles" from people of questionable or unstable character, we dismiss them as mere oddities, frauds or delusions. But when an event seems for its setting so right, and the person to whom it is imputed so noble, then it seems to demand a more serious response. The place of *fittingness* has not often enough been acknowledged in discussions of miracles. But surely it is a key factor in the way we concretely assess events we hear about—or even witness. (For more on this, cf. the argument from miracles in chap. 3.)

Objection 3:
To accept miracles would be to abandon the method by which science operates.

Reply: Nonsense. All the natural sciences operate by assuming certain things as given: the world of matter, natural causes operating within that world, and an order or regularity that makes empirical investigation possible. That is why questions like: "How come the world of matter exists at all—rather than nothing?" or "What caused the Big Bang—the absolute beginning of all material being?" are not, strictly speaking, questions within physical science. This does not mean that such questions are unreal, only that science as such cannot answer them. A scientist who believes that God caused the universe to exist has not abandoned scientific method, but merely acknowledged its limits.

Consider the following example. A doctor witnesses a most unusual event: a patient of his with terminal AIDS is suddenly cured after bathing in the waters of Lourdes. He thinks: "Some cause has reversed the progress of this disease—but what exactly was it?" So he sets out in search of this unknown cause. He checks on all the drugs the patient had taken before, during and after the pilgrimage. He investigates the water of the shrine to see whether some as-yet-unknown element in it is able to destroy the AIDS virus. After weeks of fruitless labor, he begins to wonder whether even this terrible disease could be psychosomatically reversed. Finally, he throws up his hands and admits that *as a scientist* he can find no plausible *empirical* explanation. This is a possible scenario. But there is another.

Suppose that while visiting Lourdes to gather water for testing, the doctor finds himself deeply moved, even shaken, by the faith of the pilgrims he sees there. He has already been impressed by the faith-filled charity which radiates from his newly-cured patient who was once so bitter and self-absorbed. He feels the same thing here at the shrine, only in almost overwhelming intensity. So he inquires about the message of Lourdes, then about Christianity. Finding no plausible empirical explanation, he comes to believe, *as a person who is also a scientist*, that God did specially intervene in curing his patient of AIDS, and that no description of the event which left God out would be adequate. But notice: he did not come to disbelieve in empirical explanation. He did not cease to be a scientist. He simply acknowledged that empirical explanation has its limitations, and believed that, in this case, the true explanation transcended them.

Objection 4:
Miracles are an affront to the glory of God. If he designed the system of nature, and then has to intervene in its regular workings he must be an incompetent architect.
Reply: This argument would only be true if God designed a system in which he *should* never intervene—in which he should never answer prayers or reveal himself in special and spectacular ways. If you acquired a newly-built house and found it had no bathrooms, that would indeed reflect badly on the architect. For the concrete design of the house would lack what it

unquestionably ought to have. But if miracles happen, then God did not design a system in which he should never intervene. The intervention is part of the plan; he designed it that way.

Is anyone in a position to say God ought *not* to have designed the system this way? We do not, and cannot, know the extent of God's creation. There may be worlds in which there are no specially answered prayers, no interventions in the system of natural causes. How can we really know that it was wrong for him to have created a world in which he does intervene?

Objection 5:
How can we ever know that it is God and not a mere god (or even demon) who is responsible for this or that striking intervention in the natural order of things?
Reply: Here again context is crucially important. When we consider, for example, the extraordinary deeds attributed to Jesus, and the special relationship he claimed to have with "the Father" (i.e., God), it is difficult to avoid one of three conclusions. Either Jesus was a sincere lunatic, or a demonic fraud, or he really was the Son of God—and his extraordinary deeds were in the fullest sense miracles. This triple possibility arises not merely from the deeds considered by themselves; it arises primarily from the life, character and message of the one who performed them.

And so, in the following chapters we will ask you to consider carefully and honestly the character of Christ, as well as the character of the testimony left behind about him. We will try, on the basis of the evidence, to make a case for the miracle of the Incarnation (that, in Jesus, the divine Word became flesh; cf. chap. 7), and the resurrection (that three days after his crucifixion Jesus really did rise from the dead; cf. chap. 8).

Angels
Popular books on angels are now suddenly very fashionable (though serious religious and theological books are not). This is clearly because "nature abhors a vacuum" spiritually as well as physically. Pop spirituality rushes in to fill a religious need. And in the devotional lives of many ordinary Christians there can be no doubt that belief in angels has grown cold. Why is that? There seem to be several reasons. To many, such belief seems a distraction from the central fact of revelation—the victory of Christ over sin and death. And not a few associate devotion to angels with superstition, fanaticism and that standard example of vain theological dispute: How many angels can dance on the head of a pin? (Or is it: How many pins can stick in the head of an angel?)

We do not intend to argue directly against this trend. We wish merely to note it—and to note that Jesus and his disciples shared a different view. So in this section we state, briefly and simply, the traditional Christian teaching on angels, and suggest why a strong belief in them can help both our devotion to Christ and our understanding of the world he redeemed.

What Are Angels?

Angels are finite spirits (Col 1:16; Heb 1:14). Their very name (Greek: *angelos*) denotes the function Scripture most often describes them as serving—heavenly messengers. They far exceed humans in power and intelligence (1 Pet 1:12; 2 Pet 2:11), and have a will capable of disobedience (Jude 6). It follows that angels are *personal* beings; Scripture even tells us the names of some—for example, Gabriel (Dan 8:16) and Michael (Dan 10:13, 21). Since angels are spirits, they have no flesh or bones (Lk 24:39) and are naturally invisible (Num 22:31). They do not marry and reproduce (Mt 22:30; Mk 12:25), nor do they die (Lk 20:36). They seem to be organized in a hierarchy that includes archangels (Jude 9), principalities and powers (Eph 3:10). There are also cherubim and seraphim (Gen 3:22-24; Is 6:1-3; cf. Rev 4 and 5), whose function it is to praise and worship God and to guard his holiness. Some angels are described as having power over the forces of nature, a power exercised in order to chastise God's enemies or guard his elect (cf. Gen 19:1-13; 2 Sam 24:15-16; 2 Kings 19:35). Among guardian angels there are those who watch over individuals (Mt 18:10; Heb 1:14) and those assigned to watch over whole nations (Dan 10—12).

Not all angels are good. Some have turned their wills against God, and therefore against his truth and goodness. These evil spirits are called *demons*. Like good angels, demons seem to be organized in ranks (Eph 6:11-12). They do the bidding of Satan, the prince of demons and the prince of this world (Mt 12:22-24; Jn 12:31). These ranks of demons war against the will of God (Rev 16:12-16). They use their great intelligence to deceive and discourage individuals (2 Cor 4:4; 1 Thess 2:18; Eph 6:11-12; 1 Tim 4:1); they use their influence over the nations to lead them disastrously astray (Rev 20:3); and they use their power over the forces of nature to inflict pestilence and disease (see Mt 9:32-33).

But Satan and his legions can succeed only in minor skirmishes; the war has already been won. Through Christ's death and resurrection the world of Satan's dominion has been overcome (1 Jn 5:4-5) and its bitter fruit of sin and death definitively vanquished (1 Cor 15:50-57). God even uses demonic assaults to accomplish his purposes (1 Sam 16:14-23). And on the last day, Satan and the other evil spirits will be cast into everlasting fire (Mt 25:31-46).

Do Angels Exist?

1. A look at any Bible concordance reveals how intimately belief in angels is woven into the fabric of Scripture. It is clearly and constantly taught throughout Scripture that God works through these spiritual intermediaries. Expunge them as inessential and you seem to be left with a document in tatters.

2. Belief in angels was not universal in Jesus' day. The Sadducees, for example, disbelieved in angels as well as the resurrection. While siding against the Sadducees on the resurrection, Jesus went out of his way to side against them on the reality of angels as well (see Mk 12:25). His teaching about angels was unprecedented in the ancient world; he said "these little ones"—that is, children, and perhaps the uneducated—have angels who "continually see the face of my Father in heaven" (Mt 18:10). No Jew had ever taught that angels behold the face of God—even the seraphim must shield their eyes from his glory (Is 6:2). If angels do not exist, then Jesus was *wrong* when he taught these things. And if he was wrong, then he was not a fully trustworthy teacher. Is any Christian ready to believe that?

3. It is not only Christians, Jews and Muslims who believe in angels. Pagans have believed in them as well. Aristotle, for example, argued that there are immaterial beings responsible for the motion of the heavens (see *Metaphysics* 12:8), and Plotinus said that there are "guardian spirits" (see *Enneads* 3:4). Why has it seemed to so many, whatever their religious convictions (or lack of them), that the class of intelligent beings is not exhausted by us humans: that there *ought to exist* intelligences "other" and "higher" than our own? Benedict Ashley has provided an impressive answer:

> [It is] uncomfortable to the modern mind . . . to suppose that we human beings are the only intelligences in the universe. To understand this discomfort, which has resulted in the proliferation of science fiction fantasies about life in other worlds and in perfectly serious efforts of scientists to communicate with other humanoids, we should note that one of the modes of creative thinking that has paid off richly in science, although of course it always requires testing against the evidence, is *extrapolation* or pattern thinking. For example, Mendelejeff's periodic table was based on symmetrical arrangement of known elements according to their properties, but it contained blanks. Eventually it was possible to fill in these blanks by the discovery of new elements. Again, the table

of possible kinds of crystalline structures was first worked out mathe-matically from known types and the blanks were eventually all filled in by new discoveries. Our evolutionary view of the world presents us with a great variety of kinds of primary units from atoms to the most complex of living forms. We are always looking for "missing links" to complete this pattern. Whenever we find a new type of living thing we immediately suspect that we will soon discover that it has "radiated" in a number of genera and species adapted to the various possible environmental niches.

Therefore, when we discover that in our visible universe there is a type of organism, the human species, which introduces a wholly new prin-ciple of behavior, namely abstract, symbolically expressed, creative thought, we naturally conjecture that the very limited exemplification of this type of life found only in the single human species cannot be the only one. If we also accept that the world has been created by a God who is an infinite intelligence, we are even more struck by the immense gap that lies between these two extremes of mental power, the human and the divine. Undoubtedly this gap must still puzzle us today, just as it puzzled ancient people the world over, and even more so because we have greater awareness both of the wonderful scale of natural forms and of the vast differences between the human beings who have attained to scientific understanding and technological control of the world and the other animals. (*Theologies of the Body*, chap. 13)

Why Is It Important to Believe in Angels?

Those engaged in war need to know who their enemy is. It is folly to move forward into battle ignorant of what you will face there, oblivious to the strength of the troops arrayed against you, without a true assessment of the forces you have with you to meet the advancing threat. That seems obvious; simple common sense. But remember that right now—even as you read— all of us on earth are in the midst of a spiritual war. Christians know that victory is theirs in Christ, but they must still engage the enemy in combat. What enemy? Scripture is bracingly clear:

Put on the whole armor of God, so that you may be able to stand against the wiles of the devil. For our struggle is not against enemies of blood and flesh, but against the rulers, against the authorities, against the cosmic powers of this present darkness, against the spiritual forces of evil in the heavenly places. Therefore take up the whole armor of God, so that you may be able to withstand on that evil day, and having done everything, to stand firm. Stand therefore, and fasten the belt of truth around your waist, and put on the breastplate of righteousness. As shoes for your feet put on whatever will make you ready to proclaim the gospel of peace. With all of these, take the shield of faith, with which you will be able to quench all the flaming arrows of the evil one. (Eph 6:11-16)

Part of the armor God gives us is the knowledge that we struggle against a more-than-human enemy, and are helped by more-than-human allies. The demons and the angels are here surrounding us, moving swiftly on the field of battle. There is no possible advantage in pretending otherwise.

Questions for Discussion

1. If the laws of nature (e.g., *ex nihilo nihil fit*) cannot be expected to bind the Creator of nature (p. 105), why can we use the category of *causality* to relate God and creatures in the cosmological arguments (chap. 3)? How is causality different from *ex nihilo nihil fit*? Don't we illegitimately extend both when referring them to God?

2. Why is the change from nonbeing to being (i.e., the act of creation) infinite?

3. If the question "Who made God?" is self-contradictory (p. 105), why does it seem so natural and proper that many people ask it?

4. Evaluate the idea that "we have no rights over against God" (p. 105). Give *reasons*.

5. Why are many Christians unwilling to believe that God could have used evolution by natural selection, if this is possible?

6. If creation and evolution are as easily reconciled as this chapter says, why do so many on both sides think otherwise? And why has Darwinism led so many people away from religious faith? What is its existential bite?

7. Evaluate the argument against the evolution of the soul (p. 107).

8. Distinguish *providence* from *predestination*.

9. What is the evidence for the reality of free will?

10. What other meanings of *freedom* are there besides free will?

11. How does God's transcendence reconcile freedom and providence? That is, if God were part of nature, the following ideas would be mutually contradictory: (1) God is the First Cause of everything in nature, and (2) human choices are free. Why does transcendence make the difference? Does the analogy of an author and his characters help?

12. Using the analogy from question 11, would a miracle be like an author changing his text? Would the Incarnation be like the author including himself as one of his characters? Is there any reason this would not be possible?

13. Do any disbelievers in miracles think they are *possible*? If not, does this mean that disbelief in miracles is never a result of scientific, empirical investigation of the data, but only of philosophical prejudice or presupposition?

14. How could a disbeliever in miracles justify his universal negative? Why is a universal negative the hardest kind of proposition to prove? When can it be proved? How could an atheist justify his universal negative? Imagine a dot in a circle. You are the dot. Inside the circle are all your knowledge and experience. Outside the circle is everything else. Surely, there is much more outside than inside. So how could you *know* there are no miracles, or no God? If you have never been to Iceland, how do you know miracles don't happen in Iceland?

15. What is the most popular psychological motive, as distinct from logical argument, for disbelieving in miracles?

16. Are there any other arguments you can think of for or against miracles?

17. Why do so many who believe in God disbelieve in angels? Why do many believe in angels but not demons?

18. Why do some people believe humans become angels after death? Is this possible? Why or why not?

19. Is there any proof of the existence of angels? Is there a good probable argument for them other than the arguments used in this chapter?

20. Are there any other existential consequences, individual or societal, of believing or disbelieving in angels? Suppose you really believed you and your life were surrounded by real, present and powerful spirits who knew you and either helped or harmed you. How would your everyday consciousness be changed? How much of modernity can be explained by this change in reverse?

Outline of Chapter 6
The Problem of Evil

1. The importance of the problem of evil
   - ☐ It is the only apparent proof of atheism
   - ☐ It is universal
   - ☐ It is a practical problem
2. The forms of the problem of evil
   - ☐ That *any* evil disproves an all-good God
   - ☐ That an unnecessary *amount* of evil disproves God
   - ☐ That the *unjust distribution* of evil disproves God

   Answers: original sin and vicarious atonement
3. The levels of the problem of evil
   - ☐ Emotional
   - ☐ Intellectual

     Intuitive

     Argumentative
   - ☐ Dramatic
4. The dilemma of evil
   - ☐ Saying yes (condoning) or no (condemning)

   Answers: forgiveness and separating sins from sinners
5. Four logical formulations of the problem of evil
   - ☐ Aquinas
   - ☐ Augustine
   - ☐ C. S. Lewis
   - ☐ The problem clarified
6. Five possible solutions to the problem of evil
   - ☐ Atheism
   - ☐ Pantheism
   - ☐ Naturalism
   - ☐ Idealism
   - ☐ Theism
7. Six methodological principles for approaching the problem of evil
   - ☐ Begin with data, not theory

☐ Do not compromise the data

☐ Think clearly, concretely and simply

☐ Think logically

☐ Do not try to be original

☐ Begin with real definitions

8. Definitions of key terms

☐ Evil

Evil is not a being

Evil is twofold: moral and physical

The Fall connects sin and suffering

☐ Free will (vs. determinism)

☐ Omnipotence (not extending to contradictions)

☐ Goodness (vs. kindness)

☐ Happiness (vs. contentment)

9. Solutions to the problem of evil

10. A problem remaining

11. Practical application

CHAPTER 6
The Problem
of Evil

T HE PROBLEM OF EVIL IS UNIQUELY IMPORTANT FOR THREE VERY SERIOUS reasons.

First, it is the apparent proof of atheism. There are many proofs or apparent proofs of theism (chap. 3 reviewed twenty of them), but there is only one argument that even claims to prove there is no God. There are many other arguments against theism, but none of them amounts to a proof or demonstration. For instance, there are objections to all the arguments *for* theism, but even if they are successful, these objections only refute the arguments as invalid and inconclusive. They do not thereby *dis*prove God's existence. There are also alternative explanations for religious belief and experience, such as Freud's, but even if these were successful and irrefutable, they would only provide an alternative hypothesis; they would not *dis*prove the theistic hypothesis. There are also serious practical and personal objections against faith, such as observed wickedness and hypocrisy among believers, and the inconvenience and shock to one's ego of having to repent of cherished sins. But these do not prove that God does not exist.

A second reason why the problem of evil is uniquely important is because it is universal. Everyone wonders why bad things happen to good people; some wonder why bad things happen at all.

Incidentally, this very wonder hints at a solution to the problem of evil. The fact that we do not naturally accept this world full of injustice, suffering, sin, disease and death—that we spontaneously cheer the poet (Dylan Thomas) when he says, so irrationally yet nobly: "Do not go gentle into that good night / Rage, rage against the dying of the light"—the very fact of our outrage at evil is a clue that we are in touch with a standard of goodness by which we judge this world as defective, as falling drastically short of the mark. The fact that we judge something evil might even be developed into an argument for the existence of the standard of Perfect Goodness implied in our judgment, and thus for the existence of the God of perfect goodness whom evil's existence seems to disprove.

Thirdly, and most importantly, the problem of evil is not merely a theoretical problem but an intensely practical one. It is not merely the alienation between two concepts, God and evil, but the alienation between a little child and her father when she looks up through tears and asks him, "Why did you let me hurt so bad?" The heart of the problem is not found in words like ours, in a book, but in the words from the cross: "My God, my God, why have you forsaken me?" It is a problem not on paper but on wood.

The Forms of the Problem of Evil

Three forms of the problem of evil must be distinguished:

1. It may be claimed that *any* evil disproves an all-good God.

2. Or it may be claimed that the *amount* of evil, the superfluity and needlessness and pointlessness of much evil, disproves God.

3. Or it may be claimed that the *unjust distribution* of evil disproves God—not that bad things happen, or even that so many bad things happen, but that they happen to good people just as much as to bad people.

Since the first claim is the simplest and clearest (and in that sense the strongest), we will concentrate on it. But we also here briefly indicate the lines of a solution to the second and third claims.

As to the second claim, that there is too much evil for a world controlled by a good God, a fair question is: How much evil would be too much? Would a Holocaust of six million disprove God but not a Holocaust of six thousand?

Theologians in Boston are developing a new argument for atheism: the argument from the seventy-five-year-long failure of the Red Sox to win a world championship—a failure marked by the weirdest, almost supernatural "bad luck" in baseball history. One wonders, however, whether a world with just one Red Sox championship in seventy-five years would be compatible with a good God? Would it require two? Three?

A second and more serious reply to the argument that there is too much evil in our world for there to be a God is: How do we know how much evil is too much? These objectors seem to assume implicitly that since they cannot understand why so much evil is permitted, it could not possibly be permitted by God; that is, they assume that only the evil which they can understand as necessary or justified is compatible with God. But if only such evil did exist, it would be strong evidence against God. For if there is a God, his wisdom must be infinitely superior to ours, and we will not understand all his ways.

This is the only answer Job got, and Job was satisfied, for he was a good philosopher. This posture is not blind fideism but eminent reasonableness. Who are we, the players on the stage, to tell off the author of the play? How pitiful the sight of the pot trying to lecture the potter. We cannot explain the particular evils we see, but we *can* explain why we cannot explain them.

The third form of the problem is the unjust distribution of evil. The sunlight and the plague fall on the just and the unjust alike. To this most mysterious aspect of evil we reply with two of the most mysterious doctrines in Christianity: original sin and vicarious atonement.

Both doctrines are mysteries of solidarity, stemming from a time before modern individualism. Behind these two ideas is a vision of the human race as a single organism or body, with each of us an organ or cell; a tree with each of us a leaf. Recapturing this ancient vision is our main doorway to understanding these two ideas and how they explain the problem of evil.

We still preserve a little of this old vision, unconsciously. Suppose you suddenly found out that Adolf Hitler was your grandfather. Wouldn't you feel ashamed? But you did not collaborate in his atrocities. Yet you feel a family solidarity in sin. Or in virtue; if a family member becomes a hero, you feel proud, even though you are not a hero.

But Hitler *is* your relative, only a little less close than your grandfather. So is Mother Teresa. Everyone on earth is literally related to everyone else. Original sin is not a doctrine as foreign to our real lives as we initially may think. When a pregnant mother takes drugs, her baby is born an addict. That is original sin: spiritual and moral heredity.

To think of heredity as exclusively material and biological is to assume an unreal dualism, as if we were soul-ghosts in body-machines. This same dualism leads us to interpret the biblical principle that the sins of the fathers are visited on the children to the third and fourth generations (Ex 20:5; 34:6-7; Num 14:18; Deut 5:9) as a purely spiritual principle. But it means something more simple and obvious: that when three or four generations live together, the great-grandfather's sins will affect his great-grandchildren. Even with nuclear families, if your father was abused as a child, it will be harder for him not to abuse you, and harder for you not to abuse your children. There is nothing ethereal about original sin.

The only two ways God could have avoided having the human race fall into this sin, which becomes hereditary and innate, would be (1) not to give us free will in the first place, that is, to create animals, not humans; or (2) to create us like angels: radically individual, not in a family, not in a hereditary oneness. The very best things in life come to us through our families, but so do the very worst.

The other Christian doctrine that addresses the problem of the unjust distribution of evil is the doctrine of vicarious atonement. Just as there is a solidarity in sin throughout the human race, there is also a solidarity in redemption. Just as the sins of the guilty can harm the innocent, so the sufferings and virtue of the innocent can help redeem the guilty.

It is these two central mysteries of solidarity that Ivan Karamazov rebels against in Dostoyevsky's great novel *The Brothers Karamazov*. Ivan's atheism is the deepest kind. He does not reject God as such, but he rejects God's world. It is a world run by a divine justice that is too mysterious for his rationalistic mind; a world in which bad things happen to good people and good things happen to bad people. Ivan's brother is found guilty of a murder he did not commit but accepts his suffering anyway, while Ivan is not punished for a murder he *was* responsible for, and he cannot accept this.

Vicarious atonement means that even the sufferings that do not seem to do anyone any good, may do someone some good, may help atone for sin in some invisible way, through human solidarity. For the Redeemer was literally our brother, and his suffering saved his whole family. We can now share in Christ's work and suffer for each other. Calvary was not a freak, an exception; it was the hub of the wheel, the center of the system, the trunk of the tree. (See Col 1:24.)

But the two mysteries of original sin and vicarious atonement cannot be explored or explained adequately here. We have only indicated or hinted at a solution through them. We see them more deeply and truly in concrete stories than in abstract concepts; in novels more than philosophy. We suggest Dostoyevsky's *The Brothers Karamazov*, Charles Williams's *Descent into Hell*, C. S. Lewis's *Till We Have Faces*, J. R. R. Tolkien's *The Lord of the Rings* and George Bernanos's *Diary of a Country Priest*.

The Levels of the Problem of Evil

The problem of evil may arise on three levels of consciousness.

First, there is the immediate, emotional, "gut" level. When the doctor tells you that your child is dying, you learn by experience where the problem of evil is; then evil is not a concept, like a cloud in your head, but an immediate reality, like an iron ball in your gut.

Then there is the intellectual level. This is first intuitive before it is calculative or argumentative. You seem to see, intuitively, a glaring incompatibility between evil and an all-good God. You see it, and then you work it out in an argument. This is the level on which philosophers and theologians especially work: argument. Though this is not the deepest level, it is crucial because it seems that evil disproves God; and if God is disproved, then he is unreal; and if God is gone, everything is gone.

The deepest level, however, is the level that appears in Scripture and in life: the level of actual events, of story, of drama. Evil does not just "exist," it *happens*. Its solution, then, must also *happen* in the same world in which evil happens. It is not enough that it be true in a timeless sense; it also must be true in a timely sense.

The Dilemma of Evil

The primary place where evil exists, then, is within the drama of human history. But that is precisely where the problem seems the most insolvable, even if a clever philosopher "solves" it intellectually. It seems inevitable that evil will succeed in destroying good. Good seems like delicate china: precious but fragile. Evil seems like a bull in a china shop: strong and triumphantly destructive. To use another metaphor, it takes a lifetime of careful balancing to keep the ball of goodness in the air, and only one moment of relaxed vigilance to drop it. One cruel word can ruin a friendship, one affair can ruin a marriage, and one psychotic's finger on a nuclear button can ruin a world. As Ecclesiastes puts it, one fly spoils a whole barrel of ointment (10:1).

The greatest good of all is love, and nothing seems more weak and vulnerable than love, nothing more easily betrayed than trust, nothing more easily disappointed than hope.

The problem is solved by concretizing it, by looking at how Christ solved it. Let us move not from general problem to general answer but from general problem to specific problem to specific answer to general answer. How did Christ solve the dilemma of evil?

A dilemma was posed to Christ: What do you say, should the adulteress be stoned or not? If Christ said to stone her, he was cruel; if he said not to stone her, he was indulgent. If he said to stone her, he betrayed his own teaching of forgiveness; if he said not to stone her, he betrayed Moses' (and God's) law. If he said to stone her, the Roman state had grounds against him, for they denied the right of capital punishment to the Jews. If he said not to stone her, the Jewish authorities had grounds against him, for Moses ordered stoning for adultery.

Or similarly, should taxes be paid to Caesar or not? If Christ said yes, he was treasonously supporting the Jews' enslaver. If he said no, he was treasonously disobeying Roman law. For Jesus' stunning answers, see John 8:1-11 and Matthew 22:15-22, 46.

These and many similar examples allow us to generalize Christ's answer to the dilemma of evil. The dilemma is: Yes or no? Yes to evil condones it; no condemns it. The Sadducees, the liberals of their day, condoned some evils (like divorce and disbelief in the supernatural), while the Pharisees, the conservatives of their day, condemned all evils. How did Jesus distinguish himself from both with the same stroke?

To love evil is to become evil, to succumb to it. But to hate evil is also to succumb to it. For it is practically impossible (1) to avoid Pharisaic self-righteousness and (2) to hate sins without hating sinners. Finally, (3) to hate at all is to become hard and dark and negative; even hating evil hardens us into haters.

Jesus' simple answer was, in one word, *forgiveness*. Forgiveness neither condemns nor condones. It admits that evil is evil; it doesn't say, with the bland indifference of pop psychology, "there's nothing to forgive." It dissolves the glue between the sinner and the sin and sets the sinner free. Repentance does the same thing from the side of the sinner. Repentance and forgiveness work together like a reverse epoxy.

It seems impossible for God to solve the dilemma of justice versus mercy, but we know from the Gospel account how he does it. The problem is that he cannot, it seems, do both; he must either exact the just penalty for sin—death—or not. Mercy seems a relaxation of justice, and justice a refusal of mercy. Either you punish or you don't. The laws of logic seem to prevent God from being both just and merciful at the same time, just as the laws of physics prevent a body from being two different places at the same time.

God solves this dilemma on Calvary. Full justice is done: sin is punished with the very punishment of hell itself—being forsaken of God (Mt 27:46). But mercy and forgiveness are also enacted. The trick is to give *us* the mercy and *him* the justice.

One way of explaining how it "works" that may be helpful is the following. One body cannot be in two places at once, but two different bodies can. The sinner with his sin cannot receive simultaneously just punishment and merciful forgiveness; but Christ's vicarious atonement separates the sin

from the sinner. We can only mentally distinguish the sin from the sinner;
Christ really separates them. The sin receives its just punishment in his own
divine person on the Cross, and we sinners receive mercy and forgiveness
in our own persons.

That is why the biblical formula for what we must do to be saved from
sin is "repent and believe." Objectively salvation was accomplished by
Christ on the cross, but subjectively we must accept him and his separation
of sin from sinner. Our repentance and faith is our yes to this; our impenitence and unbelief is our no.

Four Logical Formulations of the Problem of Evil

Let us now back up and begin again with our problem on a logical level.
How shall we most powerfully formulate the problem of evil as an argument
against the existence of God?

1. Aquinas, in the *Summa,* comes the closest to capturing the intuitive,
preargumentative point of the problem of evil in a logical formulation:

> If one of two contraries is infinite, the other is completely destroyed.

> But "God" means infinite goodness.

> If, therefore, God existed, there would be no evil discoverable in the
> world.

> But there is evil.

> Therefore God does not exist. *(Summa Theologiae* I, 2, 3, obj. I)

2. A slightly more "unpacked" version is the following dilemma, first
formulated, we believe, by Augustine:

> If God is all-good, he would will all good and no evil.

> And if God were all-powerful, he would accomplish everything he
> wills.

> But evil exists as well as good.

> Therefore either God is not all-powerful, or not all-good, or both.

3. C. S. Lewis uses a more anthropomorphic, psychological version of
this dilemma in formulating *The Problem of Pain:*

> If God is all-good, he wants his creatures to be happy.

> And if he is all-powerful, he can do whatever he wants.

> But the creatures are not happy.

> Therefore God lacks either goodness or power or both.

4. Finally, we may set up the problem in such a way as to clarify and
classify the different possible solutions, in this way:

> There seems to be a logical contradiction built in to affirming all four
> of the following propositions:

(1) God exists.
(2) God is all-good.
(3) God is all-powerful.
(4) Evil exists.

Affirm any three and you must deny the fourth, it seems.

If God exists, wills all-good, and is powerful enough to get everything he wills, then there would be no evil.

If God exists and wills only good, but evil exists, then God does not get what he wills. Thus he is not all-powerful.

If God exists and is all-powerful and evil exists too, then God wills evil to exist. Thus he is not all-good.

Finally, if "God" means "a being who is both all-good and all-powerful," and nevertheless evil exists, then such a God does not exist.

Five Possible Solutions

In light of this last formulation of the problem, there are five possible solutions: atheism, pantheism, naturalism, idealism and biblical theism.

1. Atheism is the denial of proposition 1, that God exists.

2. Pantheism is the denial of proposition 2, that God is good and not evil.

3. Modern naturalism and ancient polytheism both deny proposition 3, that God is all-powerful. Ancient polytheism limited God's power by splitting God up into many little gods, some good, some evil. (A very simple and obvious solution to the problem of evil; why doesn't it occur to people today, we wonder?) Modern naturalism, such as "process theology," does the same thing by reducing God to a being of time and growth and imperfection and weakness.

4. Idealism here means the denial of real evil. It comes in various forms, such as Advaita Hinduism, Christian Science and much New Age thinking, all of which say evil is an illusion of unenlightened human consciousness.

5. Finally, biblical theism (orthodox Christianity, Judaism and Islam) affirms all four propositions and denies they are logically contradictory. This can be done if and only if there are some ambiguous terms. We shall try to show in the next few pages that the terms *good, evil, all-powerful* and *happy* are used ambiguously.

Six Methodological Principles

Before we attempt to solve this notorious problem, we should pause to remember a few indispensable rules of method. We need not have a full-blown methodology in place beforehand. In fact, we are suspicious of those who do, for method is meant to serve and be subordinate to subject matter, and to emerge out of it. But there are certain basic methodological principles that we ignore at our own peril. Here are six of them.

1. We must begin with data, not with theories. Theology, like every science, has *data*, basic *givens.* In addition to experience, both religious and nonreligious, theology has the data of faith, that is, the data received by faith, as the data of astronomy are received by telescopes. These data are the contents of divine revelation, for example, of the Scriptures. For Catholics they include the church's authoritative interpretations of Scripture.

The problem of evil arises from the data, from the apparent contradiction between two sets of data, namely the experience of real evil and the revelation of an all-good, all-loving, all-just God who created and omnipotently controls the universe. If either set of data could be denied, the problem would be solved. Atheism denies the datum of revelation that there is a real God. Idealism denies the data of experience that there is real evil. These are cheap, simple solutions, we think. We are in the market for a better and more costly one. We shall have to spend more time and thought to find it.

2. We should not minimize, compromise or water down the data. Pantheism and naturalism do just that. They reduce the all-good and all-powerful God which our data deliver to either a pantheistic pudding equally inclusive of good and evil like lumps in the tapioca, or to a "Force" in nature, or the cosmos, which is unable to create the cosmos out of nothing and unable miraculously and supernaturally to turn the forces of evil in the cosmos to good.

When Augustine faced the apparent contradiction between divine grace and human free will *(On Grace and Free Will),* his most important move was his first, his methodology. He did not minimize either half of his apparently contradictory data. Instead, he reflected deeply on, and explored both halves of, his data, so that after this double journey he could emerge from these two deep caves, these two great mysteries, into the light of day with the insight that grace and free will are really two sides of the same coin. This insight was not available on shallower levels of looking at the data. His solution came from looking into his data more deeply.

Specifically, it worked like this. On the shallow level, it looks like a question of whether God pulls my strings or I pull my own strings. But by going more deeply into the double data, Augustine came to realize two things, one about grace and the other about free will. First, grace is an "interior master" rather than an exterior one; grace deals with nature according to its nature, "grace perfects nature." And "nature" for humans means human nature, which includes free will as part of its essence. Second, true freedom is not just indetermination, freedom *from* all influence, but self-determination, self-realization, self-perfection; freedom *for* the realization of our end and destiny. And this comes only from God, our Author and Designer, our Savior from the sin that blocks this self-realization. Thus, the two parts of the problem become the two parts of the solution.

But this coming-together could not have happened if Augustine had been impatient with paradox and minimized or compromised his paradoxical data. Augustine's method seems to us paradigmatic and archetypical for the Christian theologian. In fact, all great Christian thinkers have used it—in modern times, especially Pascal, Kierkegaard, Dostoyevsky, Chesterton and C. S. Lewis.

3. We must not use the typical style found in scholarly dissertations and articles. Rather, we should strive to think and write clearly, simply, directly, concretely and specifically, and to translate abstract, technical terminology into ordinary language. Polysyllabic jargon is like long freight trains: they put the mind to sleep as you wait for them to cross the road. They are like magical incantations that go on by themselves and have a life of their own. But one-syllable words force the gray matter to make connections. If you can't translate it into words a fisherman would understand, you don't understand it yourself. We propose the radical exercise of translating Christian apologetics into language the apostles (some of whom were fishermen, remember) would understand.

4. We should think logically; that is to say, the threefold logical structure of thought itself should always be in the background. We should habitually check the clarity of our terms, the truth of our premises and the validity of our arguments, and remember that there are three and only three ways to answer any argument: find an ambiguous term, a false premise or a logical fallacy. Argumentation is really much simpler, not more complex, than most people think.

5. We should not try to be original, or avant-garde, or "politically correct," or peer-popular, or anything except *true.* C. S. Lewis said no one who tried to be original ever succeeded. Only when you seek the truth, not caring who saw or said it before you, will you be original.

6. We should begin with definitions—that is, *real* definitions, not just nominal ones: definitions of real things, not just fussing over words and usage. In modern logic, modern philosophy and modern life, the most neglected mental act is the one needed for real definitions, "the first act of the mind," "simple apprehension" or understanding of an essence, a nature, a *what*, a unit of meaning which can be defined.

All judging and reasoning begins with understanding its terms. Augustine resolved the problem of grace and free will not by reasoning but by understanding. We will try to resolve the problem of evil in the same way.

We begin by defining the terms used in this debate.

Definitions

This section will take up most of our time and space because this is where the problem begins, and therefore this is where it must end. We need to understand at least five key terms: *evil, omnipotence, good, happiness* and *free will*. The most important one for the problem of evil, of course, is *evil*.

Evil

The two most common misunderstandings about evil that make the problem more difficult than it needs to be are (1) the tendency to see evil as a being and (2) the confusion between two very different kinds of evil, physical evil and moral evil.

1. Evil is not a being, thing, substance or entity. This was Augustine's great breakthrough *(Confessions)* that liberated him from Manichaean dualism (the belief in two ultimate beings, one good, one evil). He realized that all being is good metaphysically, or ontologically, or in its being. For all being is either the Creator or his creature. He himself is good, and he declared everything he created good (Genesis 1). And that is all the being there is.

If evil were a being, the problem of evil would be insolvable, for then either God made it—and thus he is not all-good—or else God did not make it—and thus he is not the all-powerful creator of all things. But evil is not a thing. Things are not evil in themselves. For instance, a sword is not evil. Even the stroke of the sword that chops off your head is not evil in its being—in fact, unless it is a "good" stroke, it will not chop your head off. Where is the evil? It is in the will, the choice, the intent, the movement of the soul, which puts a wrong order into the physical world of things and acts: the order between the sword and an innocent's neck rather than a murderer's neck or an innocent's bonds.

Even the devil is good in his being. He is a good thing gone bad—in fact, a very good thing gone very bad. If he had not had the greatest ontological goodness (goodness in his being) of a powerful mind and will, he could never have become as morally corrupt as he is. "Lilies that fester smell far worse than weeds." *Corruptio optimi pessima*, "the corruption of the best things are the worst things." To be morally bad, you must first be ontologically good.

Even physical evil is not a thing. The lack of power in a paralyzed limb is physical evil, but it is not a thing, like another limb. Blindness is a physical evil, but it is not a thing, like an eye. The cataract that causes the evil is not itself the evil.

Is evil then merely subjective? A fantasy, an illusion? No, for if it were a mere subjective illusion, then the fact that we fear this mere illusion would be really evil. As Augustine says, "thus either the evil that we fear is real, or the fact that we fear it is evil."

Evil is real, but it is not a real *thing*. It is not subjective, but it is not a substance. Augustine defines evil as disordered love, disordered will. It is a wrong relationship, a nonconformity between our will and God's will. God did not make it; we did. That is the obvious point of Genesis 1 and 3, the stories of God's good creation and humanity's evil fall.

The point, once seen, is so simple and obvious that we take it for granted. But without it, we would very likely embrace one of two popular heresies: either (1) the idea that we, not God, are the creators of good, the denial of Genesis 1, or (2) the idea that God, not we, is the creator of evil, the denial of Genesis 3. (New Age pantheistic idealism combines both of these heresies.)

2. The second major confusion about evil is to fail to distinguish between moral evil and physical evil, sin and suffering, the evil we actively do and the evil we passively suffer, the evil we freely will and the evil that is against our will, the evil we *are* directly responsible for and the evil we are not.

We need two different explanations for these two different kinds of evil, to explain both their causes and their cures. The origin of sin is human free will. The immediate origin of suffering is nature, or rather the relationship between ourselves and nature. We stub our toe, or get pneumonia, or drown.

Thus God is off the hook for sin, but not for suffering, it seems—unless the origin of suffering can also be traced to sin. This is what the story in Genesis 3 does. Without explaining how, it tells us that the thorns and thistles and the sweat of the brow and the pain of childbirth all are the result of our sin.

Connecting Suffering with Sin: The Fall

This is not as fanciful as most people think, if we remember the principle of psychosomatic unity. This principle, affirmed by just about every one of the hundreds of schools of psychology, affirms that we are not ghosts in machines, souls imprisoned in bodies, or angels in disguise, but soul-body ("psycho-somatic") unities. Our souls or psyches or personalities are our form and our bodies are our matter, much as in a poem the meaning is the form and the sounds or syllables are the matter.

Once we grant this principle, it makes sense that if the soul becomes alienated from God by sin, the body will become alienated, too, and experience pain and death as sin's inevitable consequences. These are not external, arbitrary punishments added on. Spiritual death (sin) and physical death go together because our spirits (souls, consciousness) and bodies go together. This is not original. We learned it from Genesis 3.

But it makes a difference how we interpret this story. There are three ways, and our solution is available only within two of the three ways. First, there is what we may call the fundamentalist interpretation: historical and literal. Second, there is the traditional interpretation: historical but symbolic rather than literal. Third, there is the modernist or liberal interpretation: nonhistorical and nonliteral.

According to the traditional interpretation, which we espouse here, the crucial question is whether the Fall actually happened in human history, not how literally you interpret the garden, the snake, the trees or the fruit. For if the modernist is right and Genesis 3 is only a fable that teaches that each of us sins, and that Adam and Eve are only symbols for Joe and Mary, then we have two terrible consequences.

First, if there never was a real time of innocence, then God did not make us good, as Genesis 1 says he did. If from the beginning we were sinners, then we can trace sin back to our beginning; and "in the beginning, God." Thus God is to blame for creating sinners.

Second, if the Fall is only what each one of us does, why have none of us ever resisted the forbidden fruit? If out of ten billion people, ten billion choose A and no one chooses B, we can hardly believe we have unfettered freedom to choose between A and B. If the drama in Eden is only the drama of today in symbol, why isn't it dramatic today, why isn't it "iffy," why doesn't anyone ever choose innocence?

There are two powerful arguments for the historical truth of Genesis 3. First, nearly every tribe, nation and religion throughout history have a similar story. One of the most widespread "myths" (sacred stories) in the world is the myth of a past paradise lost, a time without evil, suffering or death. The mere fact that everyone innately believes the same thing does not prove that it is true, of course; but it is at least significant evidence. And if we assume what Chesterton calls "the democracy of the dead" and extend the vote to everyone, not just to "the small and arrogant oligarchy of the living," the few lucky ones who happen to be walking about in the strangest, most secularized society in history, it puts the onus of proof on the small modern minority who scorn the universal myth.

A second piece of experiential evidence for a historical time of innocence and a historical Fall are the four most salient facts about the human condition:

1. All desire perfect happiness.
2. No one is perfectly happy.
3. All desire complete certainty and perfect wisdom.
4. No one is completely certain or perfectly wise.

The two things we all want are the two things no one has. We behave as if we remember Eden and can't recapture it, like kings and queens dressed in rags who are wandering the world in search of their thrones. If we had never reigned, why would we seek a throne? If we had always been beggars, why would we be discontent? People born beggars in a society of beggars accept themselves as they are. The fact that we gloriously and irrationally disobey the first and greatest commandment of our modern prophets (the pop psychologists)—that we do *not* accept ourselves as we are—strongly points to the conclusion that we must at least unconsciously desire, and thus somehow remember, a better state.

To help understand Creation and the Fall, the image of three iron rings suspended from a magnet is helpful. The magnet symbolizes God; the first ring, the soul; the middle ring, the body; and the bottom ring, nature. As long as the soul stays in touch with God, the magnetic life keeps flowing through the whole chain, from divine life to soul life, body life and nature life. The three rings stay harmonized, united, magnetized. But when the soul freely declares its independence from God, when the first iron ring separates from the magnet, the inevitable consequence is that the whole chain of rings is demagnetized and falls apart. When the soul is separated from God, the body is separated from the soul—that is, it dies—and also from nature—that is, it suffers. For the soul's authority over the body is a delegated authority, as is humanity's authority over nature. When God the delegator is rejected, so is the authority he delegated. If you rebel against the king, his ministers will no longer serve you. Thus both suffering and sin are traced to man, not God.

There are three ways of explaining how this may have happened. The first and simplest is that the "thorns and thistles" were there before the Fall but they only hurt afterward. The second is that fallen angels had already corrupted the earth, but God protected Adam and Eve in a special garden; they abandoned this protection when they abandoned God the protector. (This theory was held by some of the church fathers; we wonder whether there is any good theological or scientific disproof of it, or if it is just unfashionable to take seriously the work of demons.) The third is that Adam was the priest of the world, and the Fall was like saying a Black Mass, perverting everything. The bottom line is, of course, that we do not know and can only speculate about how it happened.

What is not at all speculative is that Christianity takes evil more seriously than most other religions. Even physical evil. Christianity takes the whole physical world more seriously than do the typically Oriental, Platonic or New Age philosophies. It regards as radically inadequate that high-minded, idealistic solution to the problem of evil that Socrates made famous: the identification of the self merely with the soul, not the body. From that idealism there logically follows the principle that "no evil can possibly happen to a good man" (i.e., a good soul). For the evil that happens to us passively is only physical evil, or suffering.

Christianity, on the other hand, believes in God's creation of matter and even incarnation in a human body. Bodies are not illusions, not evil, not trivial, not secular, and not outside our essence, our identity. The evil we do is not just spiritual but physical, bodily evil, for our bodies are parts of us. So the evils we do—sins—are also evils others suffer. Each evil is like a stone thrown into a pond, sending consequences rippling outward to the farthest limits of physical interconnectedness.

To the question of why bad things happen to good people Socrates replies that they never do! Christianity disagrees. Its answer is that there are among us no "good people," that is, innocent people. We are involved in a physical world with our evil, which is like that stone tossed into the pond. The two great mysteries of solidarity, original sin (solidarity in sin) and vicarious atonement (solidarity in salvation) mean that even the "innocents" among us, our small children, are involved in this double drama.

Free Will

Perhaps the clearest way to define our second crucial term, *free will*, is to contrast it with the philosophy that denies it. That is determinism.

According to determinism, everything we do can be totally accounted for by two causes: heredity plus environment. Free will adds a third cause to our actions: our wills, which in turn are not entirely the result of heredity plus environment. Thus the formula for determinism is:

$$H + E = A$$

That is, heredity plus environment equals the human act. The formula for the alternative philosophy of free will is:

$$H + E < A$$

That is, heredity plus environment together are less than the human act. Instead,

$$H + E + FW = A$$

Heredity plus environment plus free will equals the human act. Heredity and environment *condition* our acts, but they do not *determine* them, as the paints and the frame condition a painting but do not determine it. They are *necessary* causes but not *sufficient* causes of freely chosen acts.

The simplest argument for the existence of free will is observation of how we use words. We praise, blame, command, counsel, exhort and moralize to each other. Doing these things to robots is absurd. We do not hold machines morally responsible for what they do, no matter how complicated the machines are. If there is no free will, all moral meaning disappears from language—and from life.

There is another form of determinism that denies free will. This is divine determinism, as seen in some (but not all) forms of Calvinism. According to this Calvinism we are pots and God is the potter; we are only instrumental causes, like the mud in the potter's hands, totally determined by the First Cause. Other Christians have taken the more pervasive scriptural image of the parent-child relationship as closer to the truth—we are not God's artifacts but his children—and ascribed free choice to the human will. In other words, God's created causal chains include one link—the human will—which is more than just one more link in a one-directional vertical chain. It hops "sideways," so to speak, and creates its own new chains of effects.

C. S. Lewis had one of the simplest and clearest ways of expressing the doctrine of human free will and moral responsibility that is implied in the Genesis 3 account of our "free fall." He said, "If there are other intelligent beings on other planets, it is not necessary to suppose that they have fallen like us."

The next question is: Why did God give us free will and allow us to misuse it? The question is misleading. One gives a polish to a table, or a pony to a schoolboy, but one does not give three sides to a triangle or free will to a human being. Free will is part of our essence. There can be no human being without it. The alternative to free will is not being a human but an animal or a machine.

Omnipotence

A third term in need of definition is the term *omnipotent,* for the problem of evil is the apparent incompatibility of evil with a God who is all-powerful as well as all-good. If "all things are possible with God," why didn't God create a world without sin?

The answer is that he *did,* according to Genesis 1 and 2. Evil's source is not God's power but man's freedom. Then why didn't God create a world without human freedom? Because that would have been a world without humans, a world without hate but also without love. Love too proceeds only from free will. Animals cannot love, they can only like, or be affectionate. But isn't a world with free human beings but no sin possible? It is indeed. And God created just such a world. But such a world—a world in which no-sin is freely possible, is necessarily a world in which sin is also freely possible. And if there are human beings at all, that is, creatures with free will, then it is up to their free choice whether that possibility of sin is freely actualized or not.

To put it another way, even omnipotence could not have created a world in which there was genuine human freedom and yet no possibility of sin, for our freedom includes the possibility of sin within its own meaning. "All things are possible with God" indeed; but a meaningless self-contradiction is not any thing at all. One such meaningless self-contradiction is a world in which there is real free choice—that is, the possibility of freely choosing good or evil—and at the same time no possibility of choosing evil. To ask why God didn't create such a world is like asking why God didn't create colorless color or round squares.

Not all Christian thinkers agree with this concept of omnipotence. Some argue that God's power is limited by nothing, not even the laws of our logic. This view seems motivated by piety and the desire to credit God with every possible perfection. But a pious motive does not excuse a mental confusion. We believe this is a misunderstanding both of God and logic.

It is a misunderstanding of God in that it is not a divine perfection to create or perform a meaningless self-contradiction. It is rather God's consistency—his never contradicting himself—that is a perfection. There is also a misunderstanding here of what logic means. The law of noncontradiction is not "our" logic. It is not an artificial rule, like playing nine and not ten innings in baseball. It is an objective truth about everything. We discover it; we do not invent it. Nor is it a mere tautology, a verbal repetition like X = X. It is a universal, eternal, objective truth about all reality. It is based on the nature of God as one and identical and consistent with himself. To relativize or subjectivize or humanize the law of noncontradiction is to demean a divine attribute. *That* is impious.

Thus, even an omnipotent God cannot forcibly prevent sin without removing our freedom. This "cannot" does not mean that his power meets some obstacle outside himself, but rather (as Lewis said) that "nonsense does not cease to be nonsense when we add the words 'God can' before it."

This notion of God's omnipotence as not extending to self-contradictions explains necessary physical evil as well as moral evil. Even omnipotence cannot avoid all physical evil if it creates a finite world that is not infinitely perfect.

More specifically, let us distinguish two kinds of physical evil: (1) the imperfections, weaknesses, diseases and deaths of nonhuman things, and (2) the suffering of human beings. The first is inherent in any finite, created world. The second is a necessary consequence of sin, as we saw with our image of the magnet and three iron rings (p. 135). Because of the body-soul unity, soul-evil necessarily has body-consequences.

At first, God's omnipotence seems to contribute to the making of the problem of evil, for there seems to be a contradiction between evil and an omnipotent God. But in reality, omnipotence contributes to the *solution* to the problem of evil, by enabling God to providentially bring good even out of evil, to make all things work together for a good end for all who love him, who freely choose to enter his plan (Rom 8:28). For them, it is true, as Boethius says, that "all fortune is good fortune." God's solution to evil is like a fairy tale; he "writes straight with crooked lines." In his painting, each dark shadow contributes to the overall light; in his plot, every terrible event aids the wonderfulness of the End. We are not yet at the End, so this cannot yet be seen or proved. But it can be believed and lived, as the "theological virtue" of hope.

Goodness

First, we must be clear that *goodness* means more than "kindness." Kindness is the will to free the loved one from pain. Sometimes, to be good is *not* to be kind. Dentists, surgeons, athletic trainers, teachers and parents all know that. If goodness meant only kindness, a God who tolerated pain in his creatures when he could abolish it would not be an all-good God. A Christ who healed only a few thousand people in a world where millions were hurt would not be all-good either.

But the more deeply we love, the more we go beyond mere kindness. We are merely kind to a stranger's children, but are more demanding to our own. We are merely kind to animals; we kill them to prevent pain. (Hence most advocates of euthanasia believe humans to be merely clever, evolved animals.) But we have higher hopes for humans: we hope not just for freedom from pain but also freedom from vice and ignorance and sin.

God allows suffering and deprives us of the lesser good of pleasure in order to help us toward the greater good of moral and spiritual education. Even the pagans knew that: the gods teach wisdom through suffering. Aeschylus wrote:

Day by day, hour by hour,
Pain drips upon the heart
As, against our will, and even in our own despite
Comes Wisdom from the awful grace of God.

God let Job suffer not because he lacked love but precisely out of his love, to bring Job to the point of the Beatific Vision of God face to face (Job 42:5), which is humanity's supreme happiness. Job's suffering hollowed out a big space in him so that a big piece of God and joy could fill it. Job's experience is paradigmatic for all saintly suffering.

A further question is whether any suffering would have been necessary for us if we had not fallen. Would we still have to have suffered to be trained in wisdom? Is the explanation of suffering as "soul-making" limited to a fallen world, where sinners have to learn "the hard way"? If Adam had not fallen, would it still have been painful for him to sacrifice his will to God's will? We do not claim to know the answer (though we suspect it is no). In either case God is "off the hook." He allows only the evil that can work for a greater good for us. Not all that we do is good, but all that God does is good, including *not* miraculously interfering to deliver us from all evil. That would be like parents doing all their children's homework problems for them.

Happiness

We now come to our fifth ambiguous term, *happiness*. As with omnipotence and goodness, the ambiguity is between the shallow, popular meaning and the deeper, more philosophical meaning. The shallow meaning creates the problem of evil; the deeper meaning solves it.

The shallow meaning of happiness (which is our modern meaning) is first of all subjective. Happiness in this sense is a feeling. If you feel happy, you are happy. Second, this happiness is only a present, temporary phenomenon. Feelings come and go, and so does the feeling of happiness. Third, this happiness is largely a matter of "hap," that is, chance or fortune. It is "good luck." It is not under our control. Finally, its source is external. It consists in things like winning the lottery, or the Super Bowl, or bodily pleasures, or prestige, or health. It is money, sex and power, never poverty, chastity and obedience.

The older, deeper meaning of happiness is evident in the Greek word *eudaimonia*. This is, first of all, an objective state, not just a subjective feeling. It's not true that if only you feel happy, you are happy. A grown man sitting in the bathtub all day playing with his rubber ducky may be content, but he is not happy. A Nero gloating over the Christians he killed may be pleased, but he is not happy. Happiness is to the soul what health is to the body. You can feel healthy without being healthy, and you can feel happy without truly being happy. You can also be happy without feeling happy, as Job was, learning wisdom through suffering. Jesus' saying "Blessed [objectively happy] are those who mourn [feel subjectively unhappy]" (Mt 5:4) assumes such a distinction.

In the second place, true happiness is a permanent state, a matter of a lifetime, not a fleeting moment. It is also under our control, our choice. Its main sources are wisdom and virtue, both of which are good habits we create in ourselves by practice, not gifts of fortune passively received. Finally, happiness' source is internal, not external. It is a good soul, not a good bank account, that makes you happy.

Divine providence arranges our lives in light of true happiness as our end, because God is good and loving. This does not necessarily include happiness in the shallow sense. In fact, to be truly happy, we need to be deprived of much happiness in the shallow sense. For true happiness requires wisdom, and wisdom requires suffering. As Rabbi Abraham Heschel says so simply, "The man who has not suffered, what can he possibly know, anyway?"

Deep happiness is in the spirit, not the body or even the feelings. It is like an anchor that holds fast and calm on the bottom even while storms rage on the surface. God allows physical and emotional storms to strengthen the anchor; fires to test and harden our mettle. Our souls must become bright, hard, sharp swords. That is our destiny and his design. We are not toys; we are swords. And that requires tempering in the fire. The sword of the self is to sing in the sun eternally, like the seraphim. If we could catch even a glimpse of this heavenly destiny, if we understood why we are destined to judge angels (1 Cor 6:3), we would not see a problem in the sufferings of Job. Teresa of Ávila said that the most miserable earthly life, seen from the perspective of heaven, looks like one night in an inconvenient hotel.

Solutions to the Problem of Evil

Where are we now? Have these five definitions enabled us to construct a solution to the problem of evil?

Better than that. The definitions, which we thought would be preliminary tools for constructing a solution, turn out to contain the solution. The problem is now not so much solved as dissolved, like a fog. Once we see clearly, we need not construct clever, elaborate arguments any more.

There are six problems: the nature, origin and end of spiritual evil and of physical evil.

1. The nature of spiritual evil is sin, separating ourselves from God.

2. The origin of spiritual evil is human free will.

3. The end for which God allows spiritual evil is to preserve human free will, that is, human nature.

4. The nature of our physical evil is suffering.

5. The origin of physical evil is spiritual evil. We suffer because we sin.

6. The end or use of physical evil is spiritual discipline and training for our own ultimate perfection and eternal joy. (It also is just punishment for sin and a deterrence from sin.)

A Problem Remaining

A problem remains. It is an in-house problem, so to speak. It is a tension, a contrast in emphasis, between two elements within our many-faceted solution. This remaining problem is brought about by an embarrassment of riches, so to speak. But if this section confuses you, please forget it.

The tension is between appealing to free choice and appealing to divine providence and grace to solve the problem of evil. Let's first look at this tension regarding sin, and then suffering.

Sin is explained, on the one hand, by our free will. On the other hand, God's providential plan foresaw and used even sin. God brings good out of evil, and makes all things work together for good for those who love him.

Even sin, through the golden door of repentance, becomes "behovable," as Julian of Norwich said, that is, good for something. But only by the power of God.

The argument between those who emphasize free will and those who emphasize providence is largely one of emphasis, for both are parts of our scriptural data. The difference in emphasis is between those who see human history as a novel, written by God, and those who see it as a play, enacted by man. The two images are not exclusive. The novel, though completely the author's creation, is about free people, not trees or robots; and though the play has a script, the actors are free to obey the script or not. If the emphasis is on God's predestination, our attitude to life will emphasize trust and faith and acceptance and hope; while if the emphasis is on human free will, our attitude to life will emphasize morality and spiritual warfare and the will to make the right choices. The first emphasizes wisdom, the second morality; the first contemplation, the second action; the first seeing, the second doing; the first faith, the second works. They are two sides of the same Christian coin.

We find the same tension between the emphasis on free will and the vision of a necessary divine plan when we look at physical evil. The free-will origin of physical evil, or suffering, is our sin. But there is also another origin of suffering: it is built (by God) into a finite universe. If there are going to be animals with pain nerves, there is going to be pain. The tension here can come to the point with a question like this one: If Adam had stubbed his toe on a rock before he ate the forbidden fruit, would it have hurt? We think the answer is probably: Physically, yes; mentally, no. Pain is ninety percent mental, some claim; and to a pure soul, physical pain registers very differently than to a soul fallen into fear, lust, greed and egotism. But this is speculation, not certainty.

Practical Application

More important than evil as an argument against the existence of God is evil as a broken relationship with God, a spiritual divorce. Therefore, more important than a logical answer to the problem of evil theoretically is a personal answer to the problem of evil practically. More important than an apologist is a Savior.

The theoretical problem produces in us ignorance and questioning. The practical problem produces in us sin and guilt. Christ came to solve the second problem, not the first. Christ was not a philosopher.

Guilt can be removed only by God, because guilt is the index of a broken covenant with God. Shame is only the index of a horizontal, human fear or fracture, but guilt is vertical, supernatural. A good psychologist can set you free from shame but not from guilt. He can even set you free from guilt feelings, but not from real guilt. He can give you anesthetics but cannot cure your disease. Psychology can make you feel good, but only religion—relationship with God—can make you be good.

That's why God sent his Son; no one but Jesus Christ could take away our sin and guilt. Faith in his atoning sacrifice is the only answer to the real problem of evil. Our only hope is not a good answer but "good news," the gospel. The great theologian Karl Barth was asked in his old age what was the most profound idea he had ever had, in his many years of theologizing. He instantly replied, "Jesus loves me."

Questions for Discussion

1. Can you think of any other argument for atheism besides the problem of evil?

2. Do you think the problem of evil is the main reason people lose their faith or never begin to believe? What might be a more widespread reason for both?

3. Do you think the second form of the problem (the *amount* of evil) can be justified by specifying a "proper" amount of evil which would be compatible with a good God? Doesn't it seem that we come to some point at which we naturally say "too much"? (For example, there certainly seems to be a significant difference between a head cold and a Holocaust, with regard to disproving God.)

4. Can you think of any other answer to the problem of the seemingly unjust distribution of evil besides original sin and vicarious atonement?

5. Why is the vision of solidarity which underlies these two doctrines less popular to modern consciousness than it was to ancient consciousness?

6. Evaluate the notion of spiritual heredity.

7. If you were God, how would you make a better world?

8. Did God create the best of all possible worlds? If not, how can he be maximally good if he deliberately preferred the worse to the better? If so, why can we imagine a possible world better than this one?

9. Why is goodness so fragile and vulnerable to evil?

10. What exactly is forgiveness?

11. Is it always right to love sinners and hate sins? If so, why is this simple distinction not universally admitted and used? How should we apply this distinction to controversial issues like abortion, war, divorce, sodomy, contraception, fornication?

12. Can you think of any other solution to the problem of evil besides the ones here?

13. Is it really possible to "begin with data, not theories"? Many philosophers (Kant, Dewey, Derrida) say no. Why? Must there be raw, uninterpreted data if we

are to answer the question yes?

14. Is there controversy about any of the other principles of method (p. 130)?

15. The classical Augustinian teaching is that evil is real but is not a being—if this is true, why do so many thinkers still not accept it and say that either (A) since evil is not a being, it is not real (New Age or Eastern monism) or (B) since it is real, it is a being (popular dualism)? What consequences do each of these three positions—classical Augustinian theism, monism and dualism—entail regarding Satan and evil spirits?

16. With regard to the distinction between physical evil and moral evil:

A. If this is true, why do many not accept it and say either

(1) that since we are morally evil, we are metaphysically evil, or (2) that since we are not metaphysically evil, we are not morally evil, or even (3) that we are not morally evil but we are metaphysically evil (Freud, Marx, Gould)?

B. What are the consequences of a worldview in which

(1) there is no evil, metaphysical or moral

(2) we are metaphysically evil

(3) we are not morally evil

(4) (2) and (3) together

17. What are the reasons most modern minds disbelieve the Genesis 3 account of the Fall? Evaluate these reasons. How would the disbeliever in the traditional interpretation of Genesis 3 answer the four arguments (p. 134), namely, "two terrible consequences" and "two powerful arguments" two paragraphs later? Which of the three explanations of how physical evil arose (p. 136) do you think is most likely? Why?

18. Summarize the arguments on each side of the free will versus determinism dispute.

19. What does *free will* mean? What does it not mean?—that is, what is the most common misunderstanding of this idea (for example, in Sartre)?

20. Define the two different Christian concepts of omnipotence. (Luther, Calvin and Descartes teach the one rejected here.) What reasons might one have for preferring this alternative (Luther-Calvin-Descartes)? Evaluate these reasons. How would this position explain evil without the classical doctrine of omnipotence as not extending to contradictories?

21. Why must goodness be more than kindness? Why do many people identify goodness with kindness?

22. If we hadn't fallen, do you think there would still be any suffering? Why or why not?

23. What are the controverted *presuppositions* behind the classical, as distinct from the modern, notion of happiness?

24. Would you prefer a world in which God allowed less suffering and more happiness in the modern sense? Why or why not?

25. After the solution summarized on page 142, do you see any other problems

remaining besides the one noted? What is your solution to the remaining problems?

26. Do you agree with the distinction between psychology and religion with regard to guilt? Why or why not?

27. Is Karl Barth's solution to the problem of evil (p. 144) simplistic or profound? Why? Distinguish "simplistic" from "simple."

Part 4
GOD & GRACE

Outline of Chapter 7
The Divinity of Christ

1. The issue: *What* is Christ?
2. The importance of the issue: The essence of orthodox Christianity
3. The difficulty with the doctrine: The shock and apparent contradiction
4. Some clues to the possibility of the doctrine in
   - ☐ Myth
   - ☐ Art
   - ☐ Logic
5. Arguments for Christ's divinity
   - ☐ Christ's trustworthiness
   - ☐ The impossibility of the alternative
6. The main argument
   - ☐ The dilemma: Lord or liar?
   - ☐ The trilemma: Lord, liar or lunatic?
   - ☐ The quadrilemma: Lord, liar, lunatic or myth?
   - ☐ The quintilemma: Lord, liar, lunatic, myth or guru?
   - Summary
7. Conclusions: Why many are not persuaded by these arguments
   - ☐ Not for rational reasons
   - ☐ Because of Christians, not Christianity
   - ☐ Fear of the church
   - ☐ Moral reluctance
   - ☐ Fear of the supernatural
   - ☐ Pride
   - ☐ Intellectually unfashionable
   - ☐ American notions of equality
8. Some scriptural data

CHAPTER 7
The Divinity
of Christ

USTON SMITH NOTES, IN *THE WORLD'S RELIGIONS*, THAT ONLY TWO PEOPLE ever astounded their contemporaries so much that the question they evoked was not *"Who* is he?" but *"What* is he?" They were Jesus and Buddha. The answers these two gave were exactly opposite. Buddha said unequivocally that he was a mere man, not a god—almost as if he foresaw later attempts to worship him. Jesus, on the other hand, claimed in many ways to be divine.

The problem of Jesus' identity emerges from the data. The data are the four Gospels, which inform us about the claims he made about himself and the claims others made about him. In all four Gospels the claim is shockingly strong. (See pp. 173-74.)

Jesus called himself the "Son of God"—that is, of the same nature as God. A son is of the same nature, the same species, the same essence, as his father. Jesus called God his Father: "I and the Father are one" (Jn 10:30) and "Whoever has seen me has seen the Father" (Jn 14:9).

He also claimed to be sinless: "Which of you can convict me of sin?" He claimed to forgive sins—all sins, against everyone. The Jews protested: "Who can forgive sins but God alone?" They were much more clear-thinking theologians than the modernists, who "nuance" this claim. The only one who has the right to forgive all sins is the only One who is offended in all sins, namely, God. I have a right to forgive you for your sins against me, but not for your sins against others.

Jesus claimed to save us from sin and death. He said, "I am the resurrection and the life. He who believes in me will never die." He said he had come from heaven, not just earth, and that he would return again from heaven at the end of the world to judge everyone. Meanwhile, he gave us his flesh to eat, and said that this would give us eternal life.

Jesus changed Simon's name to Peter. For a Jew, changing names was something only God could do, for your name was not just a human, arbitrary label, but your real identity, which was given to you by God alone. In the Old Testament, only God changed names, and destinies—Abram became Abraham, Sarai became Sarah, Jacob became Israel. An orthodox Jew who got his name legally changed was excommunicated.

Jesus kept pointing people to himself, saying "Come unto me." Buddha said, "Look not to me; look to my *dharma* (doctrine)." Buddha also said, "Be ye lamps unto yourselves." Jesus said, "I am the light of the world."

Buddha, Confucius, Muhammad and other religious founders performed no miracles and did not rise from the dead. Jesus offered his many miracles and his resurrection as evidence for his divinity.

Most clearly and shockingly of all, he invited crucifixion (or stoning) by saying: "Very truly, I tell you [i.e., I am not exaggerating or speaking symbolically here; take this in all its force], before Abraham was, *I am*" (Jn 8:58). He spoke and claimed the sacred name that God revealed to Moses, the name God used to name himself (Ex 3:14). If he was not God, no one in history ever said anything more blasphemous than this; by Jewish law, no one ever deserved to be crucified more than Jesus.

Who then was Jesus, really?

You cannot even ask the question without implicitly choosing among answers. The very wording of the question, in the past tense ("Who *was* Jesus?") or the present ("Who *is* Jesus?"), presupposes its own answer. For those who believe his claim do not say that he *was* divine, but *is* divine. Divinity does not change or die or disappear into the past. Furthermore, if he really rose from the dead, he still *is*, and is very much alive today.

The Importance of the Issue
The issue is crucially important for at least six reasons.

1. The divinity of Christ is the most distinctively Christian doctrine of all. A Christian is most essentially defined as one who believes this. And no other religion has a doctrine that is even similar. Buddhists do not believe that Buddha was God. Muslims do not believe that Muhammad was God: "There is no God but Allah, and Muhammad is his prophet."

2. The essential difference between orthodox, traditional, biblical, apos tolic, historic, creedal Christianity and revisionist, modernist, liberal Christianity is right here. The essential modernist revision is to see Christ simply as the ideal man, or "the man for others"; as a prophet, rabbi, philosopher, teacher, social worker, psychologist, psychiatrist, reformer, sage or magician—but not God in the flesh.

3. The doctrine works like a skeleton key, unlocking all the other doctrinal doors of Christianity. Christians believe each of their many doctrines not because they have reasoned their own way to them as conclusions from a theological inquiry or as results of some mystical experiences, but on the divine authority of the One who taught them, as recorded in the Bible and transmitted by the church.

If Christ was only human, he could have made mistakes. Thus, anyone who wants to dissent from any of Christ's unpopular teachings will want to deny his divinity. And there are bound to be things in his teachings that each of us finds offensive—if we look at the totality of those teachings rather than confining ourselves to comfortable and familiar ones.

4. If Christ is divine, then the incarnation, or "enfleshing" of God, is the most important event in history. It is the hinge of history. It changes everything. If Christ is God, then when he died on the cross, heaven's gate, closed by sin, opened up to us for the first time since Eden. No event in history could be more important to every person on earth than that.

5. There is an unparalleled present existential bite to the doctrine. For if Christ is God, then, since he is omnipotent and present right now, he can transform you and your life right now as nothing and no one else possibly can. He alone can fulfill the psalmist's desperate plea to "create in me a clean heart, O God" (Ps 51:10). Only God can create; there is even a special word in Hebrew for it *(bara')*.

6. And if Christ is divine, he has a right to our entire lives, including our inner life and our thoughts. If Christ is divine, our absolute obligation is to believe everything he says and obey everything he commands. If Christ is divine, the meaning of freedom becomes conformity to him.

The Difficulty of the Doctrine

Christians ought to realize how difficult, how scandalous, how objectionable, how apparently unbelievable and absurd this doctrine is bound to appear to others. They ought to realize this for two reasons: for apologetic purposes to understand the state of mind of prospective converts; and for purposes of appreciating their own belief in all its astounding character—something that dulls with familiarity.

The difficulty is a double one. First, there is the immediate, instinctive, intuitive shock. Everyone who met Jesus was shocked. No one understood him—his disciples, his enemies, Jews, Gentiles, Greeks, Romans, Sadducees, Pharisees, the pious, the impious, the learned, the unlearned, liberals, conservatives—no one. No one had ever met anyone like Jesus before. "Never has anyone spoken like this" (Jn 7:46).

Second, on the reflective, rational level his claim seems patently absurd. It is the claim of a man who came from a woman's womb, grew from a baby, got hungry and tired and angry, suffered and died—to be divine! It is not only intuitively shocking, it seems logically self-contradictory. Humans by essence are temporal, finite, fallible and mortal; God by essence is eternal, infinite, infallible and immortal. How can one person have two opposite essences simultaneously? It sounds like a round square.

The answer to this latter question required many centuries and many church councils, and can hardly be adequately explained here. But we note that it is not a simple self-contradiction to say that one person can have two natures, though it *is* a simple self-contradiction to say that that person is both one person and two persons, or one nature and two natures, at the same time. There is even something of an analogy in ourselves—we are both material and immaterial, spatial and nonspatial, visible and invisible—for we are both body and soul.

Our argument for the truth of this doctrine consists of two steps. The first step is preliminary and consists of six clues. These clues merely show the *possibility* of God becoming man. The second step attempts to demonstrate that this actually happened in Jesus. In other words, the second step will be so unfashionably ambitious as to attempt to demonstrate that Jesus is indeed God and do so by rational, logical, philosophical argument.

Some Clues to the Possibility of the Doctrine

1. C. S. Lewis calls the Incarnation "myth become fact." Scattered generously throughout the myths of the ancient world is the strange story of a god who came down from heaven. Some tell of a god who died and rose for the life of man (e.g., Odin, Osiris and Mesopotamian corn gods). Just as the Garden of Eden story and the Noah's flood story appear in many different cultures, something like the Jesus story does too.

For some strange reason, many people think that this fact—that there are many mythic parallels and foreshadowings of the Christian story—points to the *falsehood* of the Christian story. Actually, the more witnesses tell a similar story, the more likely it is to be *true*. The more foreshadowings we find for an event, the more likely it is that the event will happen.

2. There is an analogy in art to the possibility of the Incarnation; an answer to the objection that it is impossible and self-contradictory. Suppose an author inserted himself into his own novel or play or movie as one of his own characters. This character would have a double nature, and would have "come down from heaven," so to speak—the heaven of the author's mind—yet he would be a completely human character interacting with the other characters in the story. Alfred Hitchcock frequently did this, inserting himself into his own movies as a character for a fleeting moment. If he can do it, why can't God?

3. Which brings us to the very simple and logical argument: How do you, the critic who says the Incarnation is impossible, know so much that you can tell God what he can or cannot do? The skeptic should be more skeptical of himself and less skeptical of God. If the objection is that the doctrine of the Incarnation claims too much, claims to know too much, the response is that to deny it claims to know much more. (Logically, a universal negative proposition is the hardest kind to prove.)

4. The same point can be put more positively. If a being exists worthy of the name "God," that being must be omnipotent, that is, able to do anything that is intrinsically possible, anything that is meaningful, anything that does not involve a self-contradiction (like a rock that is not a rock, or a rock too heavy for infinite power to lift). But the Incarnation, however miraculous, is not a self-contradiction. Therefore the Incarnation is possible.

5. It is possible not only from the side of the Creator but also from the side of the creature. A human being can be transformed, taken up into God somewhat as subhuman food is transformed into the human body, physical sounds are transformed into spiritual music; form and color become art, natural affection becomes charity, or ego-consciousness becomes mystical experience. This principle of transformation runs throughout the world. Evolution, if it really happened, is an example of it. One might almost view Jesus as the next step in evolution. (The difference, of course, is that evolution—if it happens—happens by nature, while the Incarnation happened by supernatural grace. The point here is that both are *possible.*)

6. Finally, the fact that it is possible for one person to have two opposite natures can be seen (as we saw above) in the most familiar of all things: yourself. You are one person, yet you both are and are not spatially measurable. The gap between our physical and spiritual natures, between a few million electrons zapping across the synapses of Einstein's brain and his

discovery that $E = MC^2$, is hardly more startling than the gap between the two natures of Christ.

(Note: this is *not* meant to imply that Christ's divinity and humanity are to be identified with his soul and body, or that they are related in just the same way as our soul and our body.)

Arguments for Christ's Divinity

We now move to stronger arguments: arguments for the actuality, not just the possibility, of Christ's divinity.

Christ's Trustworthiness

Everyone who reads the Gospels agrees that Jesus was a good and wise man, a great and profound teacher. Most nonreligious people, and even many people of other religions, like Gandhi, see him as history's greatest moral teacher. He is, in short, eminently trustworthy.

But what a trustworthy teacher teaches can be trusted. If he is trustworthy, then we should trust him, especially about his own identity. If we do not trust him about that, then we cannot say he is trustworthy, that is, wise and good.

In fact, if we do not trust him even to know who he is, then he certainly is *not* trustworthy, wise and good. If there is any one thing that disqualifies a person from being trustworthy, it is not knowing himself. A man who thinks he is God when he is not God clearly does not know himself!

The size of the gap between what you are and what you think you are is a pretty good index of your insanity. If I believe I am the best writer in America, I am an egotistical fool, but I am not insane. If I believe I am Napoleon, I am probably near the edge. If I believe I am the archangel Gabriel, I am probably well over it. And if I believe I am God? . . . Would you send your children to Sunday school to be taught by a man who thought he was God?

Why then did anyone believe Jesus' claim to be God?

The psychological, personal, motivational reason—as distinct from the objective, logical, theological reason—is because he was so good and wise and trustworthy. This is the same reason so many believed Buddha's almost equally incredible claim: that we are all living in perpetual illusion; that all our thoughts are false; that you and I and space and time and past and future and matter and soul are all illusions; and that the only thing that is real is totally nameless and indescribable, except to say *sunyata* ("emptiness") and *neti, neti* ("not this, not that"). They believed this doctrine not because *it* seemed true but because *Buddha* seemed true. How could he deceive or be deceived? He was "holy to his fingertips." The same psychological principle explains how Christians, from twelve apostles 2000 years ago to a billion believers today, believe this even more astonishing claim: they believe *it* because they believe *him.* To deny it, you would have to deny him. And that is unthinkable.

There is an instructive parallel in Lewis's *The Lion, the Witch and the Wardrobe.* Lucy has entered another world, Narnia, through a wardrobe, and told her siblings about it. They disbelieve her, of course. A wise old professor adjudicates the argument by asking Peter, Lucy's older brother, whether Lucy is a liar. Peter is confident she is not; he knows her too well. Well, then, is she insane? It is obvious from her behavior that she is not. Then there is only one possibility left, concludes the professor: Lucy must be telling the truth.

If Peter knows Lucy better than he knows the universe, it is more reasonable for him to believe Lucy and change his beliefs about the universe than vice versa. If we know the humanity and trustworthiness of Jesus better than we know what is possible for God to do, it is reasonable for us to believe Jesus and change our theological expectations, rather than vice versa.

The Impossibility of the Alternative

What is the alternative to this conclusion that Jesus is God? What do unbelievers say to this argument? Jesus claimed to be God, and Jesus is believable, therefore Jesus is God. The conclusion follows from the premises. Which premise can be denied?

Concerning the first one—that Jesus claimed to be God—perhaps the New Testament texts lie. Perhaps traditional Christianity is a myth, a fairy tale, a fantasy. But this raises questions even more unanswerable than the question of how a man could be God. Here are seven such questions.

1. If the Gospels lie, who invented the lie and for what reason? Was it Jesus' apostles? What did they get out of the lie? Martyrdom—hardly an attractive temptation. A liar always has some selfish motive.

2. Why did thousands suffer torture and death for this lie if they knew it was a lie? As Pascal points out, the human heart is very fickle, especially the heart of a liar; all the enemies of Christianity needed to do to destroy this new religion from the beginning was to produce one confession from one of Jesus' disciples that it was all a lie, a hoax. They used many forms of torture and bribery. They never succeeded.

3. What force sent Christians to the lions' den with hymns on their lips? What lie ever transformed the world like that? What lie ever gave millions a moral fortitude and peace and joy like that? Christianity conquered the world mainly through the force of sanctity and love. Saints, not theologians, converted the world. You can fake theology, but you cannot fake sanctity. Saints are not liars and liars are not saints.

4. If it was not a deliberate lie but a hallucination or a myth sincerely mistaken for a literal truth, then who were the naive fools who first believed it? There isn't another idea a Jew would be less likely to believe. Imagine this: the transcendent God who for millennia had strictly forbidden his chosen people to confuse him with a creature as the pagans did—this Creator-God became a creature, a man—a crucified criminal. Hardly a myth that arises naturally in the Jewish mind!

5. And if it was not the Jews but the Gentiles who started the myth, where did the myth come from in the New Testament? Of the twenty-seven books of the New Testament, twenty-five were written by Jews.

6. Whether Jews or Gentiles started the myth, they could not have done so during the lifetime of those who knew the real Jesus, for it would have been publicly refuted by eyewitnesses who knew the facts. Other religious founders, like Buddha and Muhammad, were indeed "divinized" by later myths, but at least two or three generations (more usually two or three centuries) had to pass before such myths could be believed. But the "myth" of Jesus' divinity goes back to the very earliest times and documents.

7. Why has the "myth" continued to attract the brightest minds in history? If you pit Paul of Tarsus, John the Evangelist, Justin Martyr, Clement of Alexandria, John Damascene, Origen, Augustine, John Chrysostom, Boethius, Erigena, Anselm, Abelard, Aquinas, Bonaventura, Scotus, Ockham, Nicholas of Cusa, Cajetan, Luther, Calvin, Kepler, Ignatius Loyola, Dante, da Vinci, Michelangelo, Descartes, Pascal, Leibniz, Berkeley, Copernicus, Newton, Kierkegaard, Newman, Pasteur, Jaspers, Marcel, Galileo, Tolstoy, Chesterton, Dostoyevsky, T. S. Eliot and C. S. Lewis against Machiavelli, Hobbes, Renan, Freud, Darwin, Marx, La Mettrie, Skinner, Nietzsche, Sartre, Bertrand Russell, Ayer, Paine and the ACLU, it would hardly be a fair fight.

Aquinas argues that if the Incarnation did not really happen, then an even more unbelievable miracle happened: the conversion of the world by the biggest lie in history and the moral transformation of lives into unselfishness, detachment from worldly pleasures and radically new heights of holiness by a mere myth.

The fundamental difficulty unbelievers have is with the *data*. How can they explain the data of history: a good and wise man who claimed to be God? No one has ever satisfactorily answered the simple question: If Jesus is not God, as Christians say he is, then who is he? If any answer to that question had even a specious staying power, it would have served as a mainstay of all unbelievers' arguments for all time. But hypothesis after weak hypothesis is tried, and each fares about as well as fog on a sunny morning.

The Main Argument

There are only five possible answers to the question: If Jesus is not God, what is he? The bottom line on the argument for Christ's divinity is that:

1. Jesus was either Lord, liar, lunatic, guru or myth.

2. He could not possibly be a liar, lunatic, guru or myth.

3. Therefore "Jesus is Lord" (the earliest Christian creed).

This argument can best be understood if it is developed slowly, step by step, from its simplest to its most complex form.

The Dilemma: Lord or Liar?

The dilemma is as old as the earliest Christian apologists: *Aut deus aut homo malus,* "Either God or a bad man." That is the classic argument. Spelled out, it looks like this:

1. Jesus was either God (if he did not lie about who he was) or a bad man (if he did).

2. But Jesus was not a bad man.

3. Therefore Jesus was (is) God.

Few would challenge the second premise. But if the first premise is added, the conclusion necessarily follows. Therefore, non-Christians must challenge the first premise. What justifies this premise?

Common sense. Someone who claims to be God and is not, is not a good man but a bad man. Merely a "good man" is one thing Jesus could not possibly be. By claiming to be God he eliminated that possibility. For a liar is not a good man, and one who lies about his essential identity is a liar, and a mere man who claims to be God lies about his essential identity.

It is attractive and comfortable to say that Jesus was neither a bad man nor God, but a good man. To say he was a bad man offends Christians, and to say he was God offends non-Christians. To say neither offends no one. Therefore non-Christians want to say neither.

But that position offends logic.

The Trilemma: Lord, Liar or Lunatic?

Perhaps Jesus was neither God nor a liar. Perhaps he sincerely believed he was God.

But if Jesus wasn't really God, then he was still a bad man, even though sincere. He was not morally bad (he did not deliberately deceive people); he was mentally bad (he was deceived himself). A lunatic may not be wicked, but he is not much more trustworthy than a liar.

Either Jesus believed his own claim to be God or he did not. If he did, he was a lunatic. If he did not, he was a liar. Unless, of course, he was (is) God.

Why could he not be either a liar or a lunatic? Because of his character. There are two things everyone admits about Jesus' character: he was wise and he was good. A lunatic is the opposite of wise, and a liar is the opposite of good.

There are lunatics in asylums who sincerely believe they are God. The "divinity complex" is a recognized form of psychopathology. Its character traits are well known: egotism, narcissism, inflexibility, dullness, predictability, inability to understand and love others as they really are and creatively relate to others. In other words, this is the polar opposite of the personality of Jesus! More than any other man in history, Jesus had the three essential virtues every human being needs and wants: wisdom, love and creativity. He wisely and cannily saw into people's hearts, behind their words. He solved insolvable problems. He also gave totally to others, including his very life. Finally, he was the most creative, interesting, unpredictable man who ever lived. No one—believer, unbeliever or agnostic—was ever bored by him. The common verb predicated of those who met Jesus was *thaumazō*, "to wonder." Lunatics are not wonderful, but Jesus was the most wonderful person in history. If that were lunacy, lunacy would be more desirable than sanity.

If, on the other hand, Jesus was a liar, then he had to have been the most clever, cunning, Machiavellian, blasphemously wicked, satanic deceiver the world has ever known, successfully seducing billions into giving up their eternal souls into his hands. If orthodox Christianity is a lie, it is by far the biggest and baddest lie ever told, and Jesus is the biggest and baddest liar.

But in every way Jesus was morally impeccable. He had all the virtues, both soft and hard, tender and tough. Further, he died for his "lie." What would motivate a selfish, evil liar to do that? We have never known anyone who thought Jesus was a deliberate liar. That would be more bizarre than calling Mother Teresa a party animal.

But if Jesus must be either Lord, liar or lunatic, and he cannot be either liar or lunatic, then he must be Lord.

He claimed to be God. Either he was, or he wasn't. If he wasn't, he either knew that he wasn't or he didn't. These are the only possibilities. The first means he is Lord, the second means he is a liar, and the third means he is a lunatic.

Let us go slowly and carefully here, for this is the most important question in the world, and we do well to fear rushing and missing something much more than repeating something. Let us review the evidence so far.

Why couldn't Jesus be a liar?

1. Because he has the wrong psychological profile. He was unselfish, loving, caring, compassionate, and passionate about teaching truth and helping others to truth. Liars lie for selfish reasons, like money, fame, pleasure or power. Jesus gave up all worldly goods, and life itself.

2. Because there is no conceivable motive for his lie. It brought him hatred, rejection, misunderstanding, persecution, torture and death.

3. Because he could not have hoped that his "lie" would be successful, for the Jews were the least likely people in the world to have worshiped a man, and Jesus, as a Jew, would have known that. In fact, we see him at every step of his life's way fully knowing and predicting his own execution, and claiming that he came to earth precisely for that reason: to suffer and die. He perfectly lived out Mother Teresa's saying: God did not put me here to be successful, but to be faithful.

Suppose it was not Jesus himself but his disciples who invented the "lie"? The same arguments apply to the disciples, or to whoever first invented the "lie."

1. They do not manifest the psychological traits of liars.

2. There was no motive—they all got out of it the same thing Jesus did: suffering and death. They proved their sincerity by their martyrdom.

3. They could not have believed it would be successful because they would have known how every Jew would be shocked and horrified at this blasphemy.

Why couldn't Jesus be a lunatic?

1. Because the psychological profiles are opposite. The lunatic lacks the very qualities that shine in Jesus: practical wisdom, tough love, and unpredictable creativity.

2. When we meet a lunatic, we are uncomfortable because we feel superior to him; when his enemies met Jesus, they were uncomfortable for the opposite reason. A lunatic does not make you feel personally challenged, only embarrassed and, eventually, bored. But Jesus made everyone feel challenged and uncomfortable, never bored. A lunatic is like darkness, Jesus was like light. A lunatic is like a man asleep, Jesus was the most wide awake of all men.

3. No Jew could sincerely think he was God. No group in history was less likely to confuse the Creator with a creature than the Jews, the only people who had an absolute, and absolutely clear, distinction between the divine and the human.

What if it was his disciples who were the lunatics, or the sincerely deceived ones? Suppose his divinity was their own idea that they read back into him and wrote back into the texts of the Gospels? The same arguments apply to whoever "invented" Christianity, whether it was Jesus, his apostles, the early church, philosophers, popes or the Mafia.

1. The writers of the Gospels certainly were not lunatics. If they invented their Jesus, they invented the most compelling fictional character in history. No lunatic could have invented a single chapter of the Gospels, much less all of it.

2. Nor could lunacy have changed so many lives for the better for so many centuries. Consider the enormity of the lunacy of confusing a man with God, then consider the enormity of the change wrought in millions of lives by this "lunacy" (read, e.g., Augustine's *Confessions*), and you will see the size of the camel you have to swallow to avoid swallowing the gnat of faith.

3. Whoever was first "deceived," what accounts for the deception? It is as hard to account for the origin of the lunacy as to account for the origin and motivation of the "lie."

These, then, are the objections to the liar hypothesis and the lunatic hypothesis. The only alternative left is to call Jesus Lord. But the only objection to this is its initial shock and unexpectedness—which is exactly what we should expect from God.

The Quadrilemma: Lord, Liar, Lunatic or Myth?

The modern objector may hope to find a way out at this point by expanding the trilemma into a quadrilemma and embracing the new, fourth hypothesis. All three previous hypotheses—Lord, liar and lunatic—assumed that Jesus *claimed* divinity. Suppose he didn't. Suppose this claim is a myth (in the sense of fiction). Suppose the liar is not Jesus but the New Testament texts.

This supposition is by far the most widespread intellectual reason why

Christians have lost their faith in the twentieth century. For each one who thinks that the problem of evil or the progress of science has refuted religion, there are ten who think that textual scholarship, the "historical-critical method" and "higher criticism" have done so by reducing the New Testament texts to a mangled melange of myth and mysticism. Not the atheistic philosophers or skeptical scientists but the biblical theologians have performed the miracle of changing wine to water, faith to myth.

Why couldn't their position be true? Why couldn't Christ's divinity be neither a lie nor a lunacy but a myth, like the myths about Buddha being a god—myths that grew up after the historical Buddha, who claimed only to be a supremely enlightened man? Overdone hero-worship easily tends to divinize the hero; isn't this the simplest and most reasonable explanation for the data about Jesus?

No. The data itself makes the myth hypothesis impossible. Here's how.

1. If the same neutral, objective, scientific approach is used on the New Testament texts as is used on all other ancient documents, then the texts prove remarkably reliable. Complex, clever hypothesis after hypothesis follows another with bewildering rapidity and complexity in the desperate attempt to debunk, "demythologize" or demean the data—like declawing a lion. No book in history has been so attacked, cut up, reconstituted and stood on its head as the New Testament. Yet it still lives—like Christ himself.

2. The state of the manuscripts is very good. Compared with any and all other ancient documents, the New Testament stands up as ten times more sure. For instance, we have five hundred different copies earlier than A.D. 500. The next most reliable ancient text we have is the *Iliad,* for which we have only fifty copies that date from 500 years or less after its origin. We have only one very late manuscript of Tacitus's *Annals,* but no one is reluctant to treat that as authentic history. If the books of the New Testament did not contain accounts of miracles or make radical, uncomfortable claims on our lives, they would be accepted by every scholar in the world. In other words, it is not objective, neutral science but subjective prejudice or ideology that fuels skeptical Scripture scholarship.

The manuscripts that we have, in addition to being old, are also mutually reinforcing and consistent. There are very few discrepancies and *no* really important ones. And all later discoveries of manuscripts, such as the Dead Sea Scrolls, have confirmed rather than refuted previously existing manuscripts in every important case. There is simply no other ancient text in nearly as good a shape.

3. If Jesus' divinity is a myth invented by later generations ("the early

Christian community," often a code word for "the inventors of the myth"), then there must have been at least two or three generations between the original eyewitnesses of the historical Jesus and the universal belief in the new, mythic, divinized Jesus; otherwise, the myth could never have been believed as fact because it would have been refuted by eyewitnesses of the real Jesus. Both disciples and enemies would have had reasons to oppose this new myth.

However, we find no evidence at all of anyone ever opposing the so-called myth of the divine Jesus in the name of an earlier merely human Jesus. The early "demythologizers" explicitly claimed that the New Testament texts had to have been written after A.D. 150 for the myth to have taken hold. But no competent scholar today denies the first-century dating of virtually all of the New Testament—certainly Paul's letters, which clearly affirm and presuppose Jesus' divinity and the fact that this doctrine was already universal Christian orthodoxy.

4. If a mythic "layer" had been added later onto an originally merely human Jesus, we should find *some* evidence, at least indirectly and second-hand, of this earlier layer. We find instead an absolute and total absence of any such evidence anywhere, either internal (in the New Testament texts themselves) or external, anywhere else, in Christian, anti-Christian, or non-Christian sources.

5. The style of the Gospels is not the style of myth, but that of real, though unscientific, eyewitness description. Anyone sensitive to literary styles can compare the Gospels to any of the mythic religious literature of the time, and the differences will appear remarkable and unmistakable— for instance, the intertestamental apocalyptic literature of both Jews and Gentiles, or pagan mythic fantasies like Ovid's *Metamorphoses* or Flavius Philostratus's story of the wonder-worker Apollonius of Tyan (A.D. 220).

If the events recorded in the Gospels did not really happen, then these authors invented modern realistic fantasy nineteen centuries ago. The Gospels are full of little details, both of external observation and internal feelings, that are found only in eyewitness descriptions or modern realistic fiction. They also include dozens of little details of life in first-century Israel that could not have been known by someone not living in that time and place (see Jn 12:3, for instance). And there are *no* second-century anachronisms, either in language or content.

6. The claim of Jesus to be God makes sense of his trial and crucifixion. The Jewish sensitivity to blasphemy was unique; no one else would so fanatically insist on death as punishment for claiming divinity. Throughout the Roman world, the prevailing attitude toward the gods was "the more, the merrier."

Jesus had no political ambitions. His politics cannot explain his crucifixion. He disappointed the political expectations of both his friends and his enemies. The main reason why most Jews rejected his claim to be the Messiah was that he did not liberate them from Roman political oppression.

It was not easy for Jesus to be apolitical. In his day, religion and politics were closely interwoven. He was not afraid to touch political issues (e.g., calling King Herod "that fox" and saying "Give to Caesar the things that are Caesar's") but he would not be identified with any of the polarized political parties of his day. He went so far as to forbid his disciples to speak publicly of his miracles because the people wanted to make him a king.

Why then was he crucified? The political excuse that he was Caesar's rival was a lie trumped up to justify his execution, since Roman law did not recognize blasphemy as grounds for execution and the Jews had no legal power to enforce their own religious laws of capital punishment under Roman rule.

7. There are four Gospels, not just one. Matthew, Mark, Luke and John were written by four different writers, at four different times, probably for four different audiences and for four somewhat different purposes and emphases. So a lot of cross-checking is possible. By a textual trigonometry or triangulation, we can fix the facts with far greater assurance here than with any other ancient personage or series of events. The only inconsistencies are in chronology (only Luke's Gospel claims to be in order) and accidentals like numbers (e.g., did the women see one angel or two at the empty tomb?).

8. If the divine Jesus of the Gospels is a myth, who invented it? Whether it was his first disciples or some later generation, no possible motive can account for this invention. For until the Edict of Milan in A.D. 313, Christians were subject to persecution, often tortured and martyred, and hated and oppressed for their beliefs. No one invents an elaborate practical joke in order to be crucified, stoned or beheaded. And if they didn't know they would be persecuted for their "myth," they would certainly give it up as soon as they were. Yet no one ever confessed that they made it all up—even when martyred. Some refused martyrdom, rejecting Christ and worshiping the emperor, to save their lives; but not one of these ever said Christ was a myth that they had fabricated. They simply did what the emperor commanded them to do to save their lives.

9. First-century Jews and Christians were not prone to believe myths.

They were already more "demythologized" than any other people. The orthodox were adamantly, even cantankerously and intolerantly, opposed to the polytheistic myths of paganism and to any ecumenical syncretism. Nor would anyone be less likely to confuse myth and fact than a Jew. Peter explicitly makes the point that the Gospel story is historical fact, not "cleverly devised myths" (2 Pet 1:16).

10. Finally, if you read the Gospels with an open mind and heart, you may well conclude, along with Dostoyevsky and Kierkegaard, that no mere man could possibly have invented this story.

We have expanded the possible answers to the question of Jesus' identity to four: Lord, liar, lunatic or myth. We have eliminated the last three, including the reduction of the Gospels to myth, for the ten reasons above. Thus we are left, once again, with the Christian explanation of the data as the only rational one.

The Quintilemma: Lord, Liar, Lunatic, Myth or Guru?

One last possible escape-hatch opens up. Perhaps even though the Gospels tell the truth that Jesus claimed divinity, and even though he could not be a liar or a lunatic, and therefore the claim is true, yet he didn't mean it to be understood literally, but rather in a mystical way. According to this theory, we should interpret his claim to divinity not in a Western, Jewish or Christian, sense but in an Eastern, Hindu or Buddhist, sense. Yes, Jesus was God, and knew it, and claimed it—but we are all God. We unenlightened nonmystics just don't realize it. Jesus was an enlightened mystic, a guru, who realized his own inner divinity. There are thousands of people today, as in the past, who claim to be God but are neither liars nor lunatics. They are gurus, yogis, roshis, "spiritual masters," "enlightened" mystics. Why couldn't Jesus fit into this well-established and well-populated class?

For one very simple reason: because he was a Jew. No guru was ever a Jew and no Jew was ever a guru. The differences—more, the contradictions—between the religious Judaism of Jesus and the teaching of all the gurus, Hindu, Buddhist, Taoist or New Age, are so many, so great and so obvious that you have to be a dunce or a professor to miss them. It is utterly unhistorical, uprooted and deracinated to see Jesus as a Hindu and not a Jew; as a kind of generic, universal type of "enlightened consciousness." You cannot ignore his Jewishness.

If Jesus was in fact a guru or mystic who transcended and contradicted his Jewishness, then he utterly failed to get *any one* of the gurus' teachings across to *anybody, ever*, for almost two thousand years. He was the worst teacher in history if he misled all his followers on every one of the following essential points where Judaism and Eastern mysticism conflict. The Jews were extremely proud of these distinctive beliefs and held to them tenaciously against worldwide disagreement, against the whole pagan, polytheistic, pantheistic, mythical and mystical religious world of antiquity for nearly two millennia. Here are eight flat out contradictions between Jesus' Judaism and the universal teaching of all gurus. Together they make it utterly impossible to call Jesus a guru.

1. Judaism is an exoteric (public) religion of collective observance of a public law (Torah) and belief in a public book (the Scriptures). But the gurus and mystics of all cultures teach an esoteric (private), individual, inner experience that cannot be communicated in words.

When Jesus was on trial and under oath, questioned by the high priest he said: "I have spoken openly to the world; I have always taught in synagogues and in the temple, where all the Jews come together. I have said nothing in secret. Why do you ask me? Ask those who heard what I said to them; they know what I said" (Jn 18:20-21). That is not what a guru says; that is what a rabbi says.

2. The Eastern mystics or gurus believe in a pantheistic, immanent God. For them, "enlightenment" consists in the realization that we and everything else are all, ultimately, God. As the *Upanishads,* the holy books of Hinduism, say: "The idea 'one' is the source of all truth; the idea 'two' is the source of all error."

Judaism's distinctive doctrine of God is that God is distinct from the world. He created it out of nothing. There is an infinite gap between Creator and creature. To confuse or identify a creature with the Creator is idolatry, a terrible sin. The belief in the transcendence of God clearly distinguishes Judaism from the mystical religions, and Jesus from the gurus.

If a Hindu announced to his guru, "I just discovered that I am God," the response would be: "Congratulations. You finally found out." If a Jew had said that 2000 years ago, the response would have been stoning (Jn 8:31-59) or crucifixion (Jn 19:1-7).

3. For Jews, God is a *person.* The supreme revelation of God was to Moses in the burning bush when he told Moses his own true eternal name: "I AM." For Jews "I" is the name of Ultimate Reality—God.

For the gurus, "I" is the name of ultimate illusion. Individuality, personality, selfhood is the supreme illusion which must be seen through and dispelled if we are to attain the supreme truth of enlightenment.

Far from being the nature of ultimate reality in God, it is not even real in us.

4. For the mystics, time and history are also ultimately unreal, illusory, projections of unenlightened consciousness. Enlightenment consists of emancipation from time. Salvation is found in timelessness. Buddha forbade his disciples to perform miracles because that would have fostered the illusion that the temporal, material world was real and important. But for the Jews, time and matter (which are relative to each other) are real because God created them. For Judaism, God is known and loved and lived within time. Judaism is a historical religion; God has revealed himself in historical events.

For the mystic, salvation consists in going back beyond the birth of the ego to the simplicity of the womb. This is often done through breathing exercises, as in yoga and Taoism, where your breathing becomes like that of a baby, then almost that of an unborn baby, with inhaling and exhaling no longer distinguishable, so that ego and world are no longer distinguishable. The end sought is the realization of our primordial identity with all things. But for the Jews, salvation consists in God doing his thing ("the Day of the Lord") in the future, in time, in history, in the messianic age. Mystics look away from time or back; Jews look at time and forward.

5. Mystics believe God is unknowable, except wordlessly in mystical experience. Jews believe God made himself known publicly in deeds and words, divinely inspired writings. (Remember, the question is not which of these two opinions is right, but whether they are the same or opposite. If opposite, Jesus the Jew could not have been a guru.)

6. For the Jews, God is the active initiator. That is why he is always imaged as male—as king, husband, warrior. (Another reason is his transcendence; see the end of chap. 4.) Religion is not our search for God but God's search for us. Our search for God fails: the Tower of Babel; Job 1—37; the false, popular prophets; human expectations for the Messiah. God's search for us succeeds: the call of Abraham, Job 38—42, the true prophets, Jesus.

For the Eastern mystics, God is passive. We find him, not he us. He is timeless, we alone act in time (until we realize that we too are timeless, that we and he [or it] are identical). Thus the God of the mystics is asexual or bisexual, all-inclusive, not other. Only Judaism, of all ancient religions, insisted on exclusively masculine imagery for God (of course this is not to be understood literally; God has no body) because only Judaism knew God's full otherness and transcendence.

C. S. Lewis's *Miracles*, especially chapter eleven, "Christianity and 'Religion'," and particularly its last paragraph, is so powerful on this point that we cannot resist the temptation to quote it here.

Men are reluctant to pass over from the notion of an abstract and negative deity to the living God. I do not wonder. Here lies the deepest taproot of Pantheism and of the objection to traditional imagery. It was hated not, at bottom, because it pictured him as man but because it pictured him as king, or even as warrior. The pantheist's God does nothing, demands nothing. He is there if you wish for him, like a book on a shelf. He will not pursue you. There is no danger that at any time heaven and earth should flee away at his glance. If he were the truth, then we could really say that all the Christian images of kingship were a historical accident of which our religion ought to be cleansed. It is with a shock that we discover them to be indispensable. You have had a shock like that before, in connection with smaller matters—when the line pulls at your hand, when something breathes beside you in the darkness. So here: the shock comes when the thrill of *life* is communicated to us along the clue we have been following. It is always shocking to meet life where we thought we were alone. "Look out!" we cry, "it's *alive.*" And therefore this is the very point at which so many draw back—I would have done so myself if I could—and proceed no further with Christianity. An impersonal God—well and good. A subjective God of beauty, truth and goodness, inside our own heads—better still. A formless life-force, surging through us, a vast power which we can tap—best of all. But God himself, alive, pulling at the other end of the cord, perhaps approaching at an infinite speed, the hunter, king, husband—that is quite another matter. There comes a moment when the children who have been playing at burglars hush suddenly: was that a *real* footstep in the hall? There comes a moment when people who have been dabbling in religion ("Man's search for God"!) suddenly draw back. Suppose we really found him! We never meant it to come to *that!* Worse still, supposing he had found us?

7. The Jewish God is a moralist. He himself is moral, righteous, holy; and his command to us is: "Be holy, for I am holy." He gives commandments. He has a will. He discriminates. He hates evil and loves good.

The pantheistic God of the gurus has no will, no law, no preferences. He is totally nondiscriminating, like modern amoral Westerners. For the gurus, morality is at best a preliminary for enlightenment, a means to free the mind from passion (and love); at worst it is a dualistic illusion. It is our invention, not God's. Their God is "beyond good and evil."

8. Perhaps the major reason why Eastern religions are so popular among modern ex-Jews and ex-Christians is that they have no hell. There may be temporary purgatories—for example, reincarnations in this life and *bardos* in the next *(The Tibetan Book of the Dead)*—but everyone automatically gets to heaven eventually. The God of the gurus does not judge or punish sin. There is no sin, no separation from God, for God is the All.

Biblical and orthodox Judaism, like Christianity, teaches an eternal, ultimate justice and judgment. Not everyone is automatically guaranteed salvation. The existence of hell logically follows (as we shall see in chap. 12) from two other distinctively Judeo-Christian doctrines: the distinction between the Creator and the creature, and human free will. Pantheists cannot believe in hell because for them there is nothing but God, there can be no being apart from God. Determinists do not believe in hell because we are not free to choose it. Orthodox Jews and Christians believe in the possibility of hell (eternal separation from God) because we are not parts of God, and we are free to reject him. Which side is Jesus on? Jesus clearly, strongly and evidently believed in hell, and talked a lot about it.

So we have eight flat-out contradictions, all of them crucially important, between the teaching of Jesus as we have it in the New Testament and the teaching of the Eastern mystics and gurus. To classify Jesus as a guru is as accurate as classifying Marx as a capitalist.

But suppose everyone misunderstood him? Suppose he tried to teach the philosophy of the mystics, being one himself, but the Jews simply failed to understand him—both his friends and his enemies. That is the scenario you must believe if you take Jesus for a guru. In that case, Jesus was the worst teacher in history. On all eight of the above points he was understood to teach the distinctively Jewish, not mystical, doctrine—at all times, by everyone, until the twentieth century!

So if Jesus really was teaching mysticism, if Jesus was not a rabbi but an "enlightened master," then he was *not* an enlightened master. For he totally deluded everyone always about everything!

Jesus was a Jew; this simple fact refutes the guru hypothesis. He never told anyone to convert from Judaism. He said he came to fulfill the law and the prophets, not destroy them. He did not found a new religion; he fulfilled the old one. Despite the polemics between Jews and Christians that we see beginning already in the New Testament and which are still going on, there is not the slightest suggestion that these are two alternative religions or that the Old Testament teachings are false. Exactly the opposite;

they are always assumed to be true and quoted as divine authority.

Furthermore, Jesus had no way of learning Eastern religions. He never traveled from his native land. The stories of his doing so are myths that were started centuries later. No documents of any kind even suggest this for the first few centuries A.D. He would not have learned Oriental mysticism in Israel; the Jews were not open, tolerant or pluralistic. Jewish mysticism (e.g., that of the Essenes) was far more Western than Eastern on all eight of the above issues. If Hindus had learned of Judaism, they probably would have taken an "inclusive" attitude toward it, but if Jews had learned of Hinduism, they certainly would have taken an "exclusive" attitude toward it.

The ultimate philosophical reason for this is that the Jews believe in objective truth (this is one of the reasons they have frequently been in the forefront of science), while Hindus do not. This in turn is because Jews believe in the real distinction between human consciousness and its object, both its supernatural object (God) and its natural object (the material world); but Hindus believe these three things are fundamentally identical. We can hardly think of a more impossible synthesis than one between Judaism and Hinduism—the very synthesis proposed by the "Jesus as guru" theory.

Also, if the historical Jesus was fundamentally different from the Jesus of the Gospels—if the historical Jesus never claimed divinity, or if he meant it in the Eastern, pantheistic way—then we are back with the "two-layer" theory of the Gospels which we have already refuted (see pp. 162-63). There is no evidence whatsoever of an "earlier" layer different from the Gospels we have. There is also no motive for the arising of the new layer, the creation of traditional Christianity, if it was not from Jesus himself.

In fact, if it was not Jesus but the twelve apostles who invented orthodox Christianity with its divine Christ, then we need to multiply by twelve the misunderstanding and its motives. If the invention came from later generations, from "the early Christian community," its difficulty is multiplied 500 or 5000 or (by the second century) 500,000 times. The later the lie, or forgery, or misunderstanding, or myth, or hallucination—whatever alternative to the Gospels' account of a Christ who claimed divinity and meant it literally—the more impossible it is to explain.

Summary
The following outline summarizes all the logically possible alternatives.

I. Jesus claimed divinity
   A. He meant it literally
      1. It is true _____ Lord
      2. It is false
         a. He knew it was false _____ Liar
         b. He didn't know it was false _____ Lunatic
   B. He meant it nonliterally, mystically _____ Guru
II. Jesus never claimed divinity _____ Myth

The above argumentation has shown the inherent flaws of the last four options. Only one remains: Jesus is Lord.

Conclusions: Why Many Are Not Persuaded

On the one hand, all possible alternatives have been refuted. On the other hand, the Christian alternative has not. Instead, it has been shown to be the only explanation for the data:

1. It is intrinsically possible. It has no internal or external inconsistencies. Not one fact of history, science, philosophy, or common knowledge refutes it.

2. It is probable. God could well have done this. A good, wise, clever, loving God might well do just what the Gospels say he did in Christ: become human and die to save us.

3. It works. It has enlightened and transformed lives. It has created saints who lived and died for this "lie" or "lunacy" or "myth." It has been believed by the wise, lived by the holy and longed for by the skeptical. Even Freud saw it as wishful thinking, as fairy tale, that is, as desirable, as too good to be true. As Tolkien put it, "there has never been a tale which men more wished was true."

4. It gives the greatest hope and meaning and purpose ever proposed to human life. We are to become saints here and little Christs hereafter. What a destiny!

5. It is the only rational, honest alternative. Data and argument compel us to it.

Why, then, are many not compelled?

1. Not for rational reasons. No reason has ever been brought forth against Christianity which has not been refuted (see chap. 2). The vast majority of those who disbelieve in Christ's divinity disbelieve for other reasons, not because they have confronted the arguments.

2. Often, the thing hated and rejected is not Christ but Christians. Chesterton said, "the only good argument against Christianity is Christians."

3. Often, it is fear of the church and its teachings and authority that scares people away. The church is a concrete, visible, present institution that makes demands on our intellect to believe and on our will to practice a whole way of life that conflicts with our natural inclinations. Exactly like Jesus, who did the very same thing. The church doesn't wield a club, but it does wave a cross.

4. The reluctance is usually moral. To admit that Jesus is divine is to admit his absolute authority over your life, including your private life, including your sex life. Can a drug addict think clearly and objectively about moral truth when it comes to drugs? Why should a sex addict be different?

We are all addicts to something—to selfishness, at least. That is the meaning of sin, the very disease Jesus came to cure. *Of course* the cancer is going to fear the surgeon. That is exactly what you would expect. That is not a reason to disbelieve the surgeon's claim to be the specialist. Just the opposite.

The old self in us is no fool. It sees that Christ comes to kill it. It knows Christianity is not a harmless theory, but something alive and dangerous.

5. Some people are afraid of the supernatural because it is mysterious and uncontrollable. If there is a supernatural God, and if this God did such a strange thing as becoming a man, then reality vastly escapes the neat and comfortable little boxes that some of us like to stuff it into.

6. There may also be simple pride, refusal to loose control of the reins of our lives.

7. It is also not at all intellectually fashionable to believe in Christ as anything more than a human teacher. We Americans love peer acceptance, approval and support. We fear nonconformity, eccentricity, "weirdness," and being "out of it" even when "it" is a society that looks increasingly like garbage swirling down the drain.

8. Finally, Americans' deepest religion is often equality. The notion that Christ alone is God—superior, authoritative, supernatural—and that Christ's teaching and person is far greater than Buddha's, or Muhammad's, or Moses', no matter how much great and good wisdom may be contained in those others, is scandalous. The notion that all religions are *not* equal offends our real religion of equality, which makes no demands on us to discriminate and choose one and to justify that choice (see chap. 14).

None of these eight causes of unbelief is a reason, only a motive; that is, they are subjective, not objective; psychological, not logical.

If everything we have said so far is true, a surprising consequence necessarily follows. It is that there are only two things that are needed for anyone to be converted, for the whole world be converted, and to worship Christ as God. (Grace is also needed from God, of course, but God is willing to give his grace to anyone who is willing to seek and receive it.) These two things are intellectual honesty and the moral honesty that goes with it. This is exactly the attitude most unbelievers praise and claim to have: tough-minded, skeptical, scientific, logical honesty. Well, if they really have that, it will lead them to Christ.

It is exactly the opposite attitude that keeps unbelief alive, the attitude most unbelievers claim *Christians* have succumbed to—namely, wishful thinking, subjectivism, thinking not with the head but with the frightened heart or the quivering guts. For in light of all the above nonrefuted arguments, which of the two positions looks more like myth, fairy tale, wishful thinking, subjective projection, and human invention? And which looks like the cold, hard, objective truth?

Some Scriptural Data For Christ's Claim to Divinity

1. The early creedal formula "Jesus is Lord [*kyrios*]": 1 Cor 12:3; Phil 2:11.

2. The title "Son of God" ("Son of" implies "of the same nature as."): Mt 11:27; Mk 12:6; 13:32; 14:61-62; Lk 10:22; 22:70; Jn 10:30; 14:9.

3. The New Testament calls him "God": Tit 2:13; 1 Jn 5:20; Rom 9:5; Jn 1:1.

4. Absolutely, universally supreme: Col 1:15-20.

5. Eternally preexistent: Jn 1:1; Phil 2:6; Heb 13:8; Rev 22:13.

6. Omnipresent: Mt 18:20; 28:20.

7. Omnipotent: Mt 28:18; Heb 1:3; Rev 1:8.

8. Immutable: Heb 1:11-12; 13:8.

9. Creates (only God can create): Col 1:16-17; Jn 1:3; 1 Cor 8:6; Heb 1:10.

10. Sinless, perfect: Heb 7:26; Jn 8:46; 2 Cor 5:21.

11. Has authority to forgive sins: Mk 2:5-12; Lk 24:45-47; Acts 10:43; 1 Jn 1:5-9.

12. Rightly worshiped: Mt 2:11; 14:33; 28:9; Jn 20:28; Heb 1:5-9.

13. Speaks the unique, forbidden divine name: Jn 8:58.

14. Called "King of kings and Lord of lords": 1 Tim 6:15; Rev 17:14.

15. One with the Father: Jn 10:30; 12:45; 14:8-10.

16. Performs miracles: Jn 10:37-38; and throughout all four Gospels.

17. Sends the Holy Spirit: Jn 14:25-26; 16:7-15.

18. The Father testifies to him: Mt 3:17; 17:5; Jn 8:18; 1 Jn 5:9.

19. Gives eternal life: Jn 3:16; 5:39-40; 20:30-31.

20. Foreknows the future: Mk 8:31; Lk 9:21-22; 12:49-53; 22:35-37; 24:1-7; Jn 3:11-14; 6:63-64; 13:1-11; 14:27-29; 18:1-4; 19:26-30.

21. Is Lord over the Law: Lk 6:1-5.

Questions for Discussion

1. Since the entire chapter is one long, sustained, multifaceted argument for a single conclusion, it seems less fitting to list many different questions for this chapter, as we have for the others, than to ask the reader to reexamine the entire argument from the viewpoint of the rational unbeliever and ask how he or she would answer it. Are there obscurities or ambiguities in the terms? False premises? Logical fallacies? Non sequiturs?

2. Why do you suppose Christ raised the question in the minds of his contemporaries and of subsequent generations about *what* he is rather than just *who* he is?

3. What difference would it make whether or not Christ is divine to each of the other main points of Christianity, theological, moral and liturgical? (To answer this question you must first make a list of these fundamentals.)

4. Just how shocking is the claim of divinity? Compare it with other shocking claims or ideas, both true and false. If it is so shocking, why isn't the following argument valid? The improbability of Christ being God must be greater than the improbability of the arguments for his divinity containing errors. (This argument is parallel in structure to Hume's argument against miracles. See p. 111, objection 2. Compare the two arguments' validity and refutability.)

5. How should we assess the strength of such a "key and lock" argument as the one in the section on "clues"? (The doctrine of Christ's divinity, strange as it is, is like a key that unlocks and explains some similarly strange data.) Compare C. S. Lewis's argument in *Miracles* and George MacDonald's short story "The Golden Key." What are some other "key and lock" arguments in other fields? (E.g., the discovery of what is purportedly the missing part of a manuscript.) How do we evaluate such arguments?

6. What would be some of the consequences or corollaries of saying that (a) Jesus was not sane or (b) Jesus deliberately lied when he claimed to be divine?

7. How do modernist Scripture scholars answer the seven questions on pages 156-57 and the ten points on pages 162-65?

8. How might an Easternizer rehabilitate the "Jesus as guru" hypothesis by taking cognizance of and answering the objections (p. 166-69)?

9. Can you imagine a sixth hypothesis to escape the quintilemma?

10. Can you find (a) other reasons or (b) other motives, or psychological causes, for not being persuaded besides the eight motives mentioned here? (By the way, what is the difference between *reasons* and *causes*? Why do we use the same word ["because"] for both?)

Outline of Chapter 8
The Resurrection

1. The importance of the resurrection
2. The meaning of the resurrection: ten confusions
3. The strategy of the argument for the resurrection: five possible theories
4. Refutation of the swoon theory: nine arguments
5. Refutation of the conspiracy theory: seven arguments
6. Refutation of the hallucination theory: thirteen arguments
7. Refutation of the myth theory: six arguments
8. Conclusions: five more objections answered

CHAPTER 8
The Resurrection

E VERY SERMON PREACHED BY EVERY CHRISTIAN IN THE NEW TESTAMENT centers on the resurrection. The *gospel* or "good news" means essentially the news of Christ's resurrection. The message that flashed across the ancient world, set hearts on fire, changed lives and turned the world upside down was not "love your neighbor." Every morally sane person already knew that; it was not news. The news was that a man who claimed to be the Son of God and the Savior of the world had risen from the dead.

When Paul preached the gospel to the Stoic and Epicurean philosophers in Athens, they thought he was preaching two new gods, Jesus and Anastasis (Greek for "resurrection"; Acts 17:18)—that's how important the resurrection was. (And that's how muddled the philosophers and scholars were. Nothing changes.)

A reasonable challenge to the skeptic is this: If it can be proved that Jesus really rose from the dead, will you believe in him? For if he really rose, that validates his claim to be divine and not merely human, for resurrection from death is beyond human power; and his divinity validates the truth of everything else he said, for God cannot lie.

Rudolf Bultmann, "the father of demythologizing," said that "if the bones of the dead Jesus were discovered tomorrow in a Palestinian tomb, all the essentials of Christianity would remain unchanged." Paul disagreed. He said that "if Christ has not been raised, then

1. our proclamation has been in vain

2. and your faith has been in vain.

3. We are even found to be misrepresenting God, because we testified of God that he raised Christ—whom he did not raise if it is true that the dead are not raised. . . .

4. If Christ has not been raised, your faith is futile

5. and you are still in your sins.

6. Then those also who have died in Christ have perished.

7. If for this life only we have hoped in Christ, we are of all people most to be pitied." (1 Cor 15:14-19)

Now who is more likely to know what Christianity is, what its essentials are and whether these essentials would remain unchanged if Christ's corpse were to turn up tomorrow—the apostle or the skeptic? One of the religion's first-century founders or one of its twentieth-century subverters? A Jew who knew Christ or a German scholar who knew books?

The resurrection is of crucial practical importance because it completes our salvation. Jesus came to save us from sin and its consequence, death (Rom 6:23). (Thus points 5 and 6 in the above quotation.)

The resurrection also sharply distinguishes Jesus from all other religious founders. The bones of Abraham and Muhammad and Buddha and Confucius and Lao-tzu and Zoroaster are all still here on earth. Jesus' tomb is empty.

The existential consequences of the resurrection are incomparable. It is the concrete, factual, empirical proof that: life has hope and meaning; "love is stronger than death"; goodness and power are ultimately allies, not enemies; life wins in the end; God has touched us right here where we are and has defeated our last enemy; we are not cosmic orphans, as our modern secular worldview would make us. And these existential consequences of the resurrection can be seen by comparing the disciples before and after. Before, they ran away, denied their Master and huddled behind locked doors in fear and confusion. After, they were transformed from scared rabbits into confident saints, world-changing missionaries, courageous martyrs and joy-filled touring ambassadors for Christ.

The greatest importance of the resurrection is not in the past—"Christ rose"—but in the present—"Christ is risen." The angel at the tomb asked the women, "Why do you seek the living among the dead?" (Lk 24:5). The same question could be asked today to mere historians and scholars. If only we did not keep Christ mummified in a casket labeled "history" or "apologetics," he would set our lives and world afire as powerfully as he did two millennia ago; and our new pagan empire would sit up, take notice, rub its eyes, wonder and convert a second time. That is the existential import of the resurrection.

The Meaning of the Resurrection: Ten Confusions

What does it mean to believe that Jesus "rose from the dead"? For one thing, it means that those who follow him will do the same. The New Testament is clear on that. (See, e.g., 1 Cor 15:12-23.) "Existential import" again.

But what do the words mean? In one sense, they mean something very simple: Jesus rose "from the dead" (i.e., "from the corpses," the dead bodies). The words in the earliest creeds are *anastasis sarkos* and *anastasis nekrōn*, which mean "the standing up [*or* getting up] of the flesh" and "the standing up of the corpses"! Both expressions are as concrete as possible. *Anastasis* is a word for a bodily posture. *Sarkos* and *nekrōn* mean that the real concrete bodies of the dead will rise.

What kind of body this resurrection body will be, is not a simple question. Jesus' resurrection body evidently had something very strange about it, for his disciples and close friends did not recognize him at first, yet later they did. Paul's analogies in 1 Corinthians 15 do not remove the mystery. He says that our new bodies, like Christ's, are different from the old ones as sun from moon, animal from plant, plant from seed. They do not fit the old categories. But this is just what we should expect if they are new creation of God.

The best description we know of comes from C. S. Lewis:

The picture is not what we expected. . . . It is not the picture of an escape from any and every kind of Nature into some unconditioned and utterly transcendent life. It is the picture of a new human nature, and a new Nature in general, being brought into existence. . . . That is the picture—not of unmaking but of remaking. The old field of space, time, matter and the senses is to be weeded, dug, and sown for a new crop. We may be tired of that old field; God is not. . . . A new Nature is being not merely made but made out of an old one. We live amid all the anomalies, inconveniences, hopes, and excitements of a house that is being rebuilt. Something is being pulled down and something is going up in its place.

It is at this point that awe and trembling fall upon us as we read the records. If the story is false, it is at least a much stranger story than we expected, something for which philosophical "religion," psychical research, and popular superstition have all alike failed to prepare us. If the story is true, then a wholly new mode of being has arisen in the universe. (*Miracles*, chap. 16)

We also do not know exactly *how* Jesus rose. No one saw the act itself, only its consequences (the risen Jesus). No one knows what spiritual technology God used. In that sense we cannot define the resurrection. But we can distinguish it from ten alternatives with which it is sometimes confused.

1. First, the resurrected Christ is not a ghost. That was what the apostles first thought (Lk 24:36-43)—a notion Christ refuted by showing them his scarred hands and feet and by eating broiled fish. A ghost is a spirit without a body; the resurrected Jesus has a real body; therefore the resurrected Jesus is not a ghost.

2. The resurrection is also not just a resuscitation, like the resuscitation of Lazarus. The body Lazarus came out of his tomb with was the same old body with which he had gone into his tomb. He had his graveclothes on (Jn 11:44). Jesus' graveclothes were neatly laid aside and folded in his tomb (Jn 20:6-7). Lazarus had to die again—indeed, C. S. Lewis calls him the first martyr for this reason—Jesus did not (Rom 6:9). Lazarus was more like the millions of contemporary resuscitated patients who have "near-death experiences" or "out-of-body experiences." Whatever they are, they are temporary. Jesus' resurrection is permanent.

3. Resurrection is also not reincarnation. Reincarnation, like resuscitation (supposedly) only gives you another mortal body. Christ's resurrection body was immortal. It was both more old and more new than the body you (supposedly) get in reincarnation. It was more old in that it was recognizable by his friends, and more new in that it was immortal.

4. But resurrection must also be distinguished from simple immortality as a Platonist or Gnostic would expect it; that is, the freeing of the soul from its bodily prison. Once again, C. S. Lewis is the clearest about this:

> The Resurrection was not regarded simply or chiefly as evidence for the immortality of the soul. It is, of course, often so regarded today: I have heard a man maintain that "the importance of the Resurrection is that it proves *survival.*" Such a view cannot at any point be reconciled with the language of the New Testament. On such a view Christ would simply have done what all men do when they die; the only novelty would have been that in his case we were allowed to see it happening. But there is not in Scripture the faintest suggestion that the Resurrection was new evidence for something that had *in fact* been always happening. The New Testament writers speak as if Christ's achievement in rising from the dead was the first event of its kind in the whole history of the universe. He is the "first fruits," the "pioneer of life." He has forced open

a door that has been locked since the death of the first man. He has met, fought, and beaten the King of Death. Everything is different because He has done so. . . .

From the earliest times the Jews, like many other nations, had believed that man possessed a "soul" or *nephesh* separable from the body, which went at death into the shadowy world called *Sheol* . . . like the Hades of the Greeks. . . . In much more recent times there had arisen a more cheerful belief that the righteous passed at death to "heaven." Both doctrines are doctrines of "the immortality of the soul" as a Greek or a modern Englishman understands it; and both are quite irrelevant to the story of the Resurrection. The writers look on this event as an absolute novelty. (Lewis, *Miracles,* chap. 16)

5. Resurrection is also distinct from Enlightenment, or Nirvana, or *satori,* or *moksha*—the kind of thing a Hindu or Buddhist would hope for at death: a loss of personal individuality and a reabsorption into the One, the All (or, more accurately, a realization that one always was the One and not an individual at all). The risen Jesus is a very distinct individual, even an embodied one.

6. Resurrection is also distinct from translation or assumption into heaven. That is a Jewish notion; it happened to Enoch and Elijah, and perhaps to Moses. Catholics believe it also happened to Mary. But Jesus was not brought from earth to heaven by resurrection, but from the realm of the dead back to the earth, the "land of the living."

7. Resurrection is also distinct from a vision. Whether a vision is sent by God, by your own unconscious or by evil spirits, a vision remains purely spiritual and subjective: it is in your psyche. But Jesus' resurrection body was seen in public by many at the same time. He was touched. He ate.

8. Resurrection is also distinct from legend. Legends, however wise, are only fictions devised by mortal minds, not by God or by nature.

9. Resurrection is also not a myth. If we wish to distinguish myths from legends we may say that myths are symbolically true. For instance, the religions of the ancient Near East are full of grain gods and corn gods and vegetation gods who rise from death every spring. These gods do not exist, but the new life of vegetation does. So does the new life of Christ, which these myths, in the providence of God, seem to have confusedly foretold. But Christ's resurrection, unlike myths, is pinned down to a real, specific, concrete time and place in history, and certified by eyewitnesses. The New Testament explicitly distinguishes Christ's resurrection from myths and legends: "For we did not follow cleverly devised myths when we made

known to you the power and coming of our Lord Jesus Christ, but we had been eyewitnesses of his majesty" (2 Pet 1:16).

Modern demythologizers who say they believe the resurrection, but only as a myth, are altering the claim, fudging the data—as if one were to claim to be a Nazi and believe in Aryan racial superiority in some mythic sense while denying that the Aryan race is *really* superior. You're not a party member if you deny the essential planks in its platform.

The demythologizers try to get around this by distinguishing *heilsgeschichte* ("sacred history") from ordinary, secular history, saying that the resurrection really happened in the first, not the second. This seems to us either sheer obfuscation or downright deceit. This "sacred history"—did it ever happen or not? If not, don't call it "history" but fiction, like Santa Claus. If it did, then it happened just as crudely and literally as births or wars happen, and we don't need the distinction.

10. The resurrection of Christ must be clearly distinguished from what the modernists put in its place: a "resurrection of Easter faith" in the hearts and lives of the disciples. "Easter faith" without a real Easter is a self-contradiction or a self-deception. It is faith in what is not rather than faith in what is. And if it is a faith in faith, then we ask: faith in faith in what? Faith is like knowledge; it is essentially intentional. It needs an object other than itself. Otherwise, it is a hall of mirrors. Faith in faith is also perverse and unnatural. It is the attempt to get the taste of the meat without eating it, and is related to faith in facts as masturbation is related to copulation. It is spiritual auto-eroticism. There is no *other*. The disciples could never have experienced such a resurrection of faith and hope without a literal resurrection. If it wasn't the risen Jesus, then who transformed them and converted the world?

The Strategy of the Argument for the Resurrection: Five Possible Theories

We believe Christ's resurrection can be proved with at least as much certainty as any universally believed and well-documented event in ancient history. To prove this, we do not need to presuppose anything controversial (e.g., that miracles happen). But the skeptic must also not presuppose anything (e.g., that they do not). We do not need to presuppose that the New Testament is infallible, or divinely inspired or even true. We do not need to presuppose that there really was an empty tomb or postresurrection appearances, as recorded. We need to presuppose only two things, both of which are hard data, empirical data, which no one denies: the existence of the New Testament texts as we have them, and the existence (but not necessarily the truth) of the Christian religion as we find it today.

The question is this: Which theory about what really happened in Jerusalem on that first Easter Sunday can account for the data?

There are five possible theories: Christianity, hallucination, myth, conspiracy and swoon.

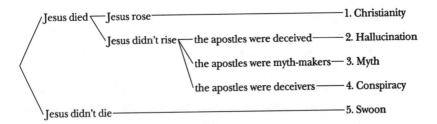

Theories 2 and 4 constitute a dilemma: if Jesus didn't rise, then the
apostles, who taught that he did, were either deceived (if they thought he
did) or deceivers (if they knew he didn't). The modernists could not escape
this dilemma until they came up with a middle category, myth. It is the most
popular alternative today.

Thus either (1) the resurrection really happened, (2) the apostles were
deceived by a hallucination, (3) the apostles created a myth, not meaning
it literally, (4) the apostles were deceivers who conspired to foist on the world
the most famous and successful lie in history, or (5) Jesus only swooned and
was resuscitated, not resurrected. All five possibilities are logically possible,
and therefore must be fairly investigated—even (1)! They are also the *only*
possibilities, unless we include really far-out ideas that responsible historians
have never taken seriously, such as that Jesus was really a Martian who came
in a flying saucer. Or that he never even existed; that the whole story was
the world's greatest fantasy novel, written by some simple fishermen; that he
was a literary character whom everyone in history mistook for a real person,
including all Christians *and* their enemies, until some scholar many centuries later got the real scoop from sources unnamed.

If we can refute all other theories (2-5), we will have proved the truth of
the resurrection (1). The form of the argument here is similar to that of
most of the arguments for the existence of God. Neither God nor the
resurrection are directly observable, but from data that *are* directly observable we can argue that the only possible adequate explanation of this data
is the Christian one.

We shall take the four nonbelieving theories in the following order: from the simplest, least popular and most easily refuted to the most confusing, most popular and most complexly refuted: first swoon, then conspiracy, then hallucination and finally myth.

Refutation of the Swoon Theory: Nine Arguments
Nine pieces of evidence refute the swoon theory:

1. Jesus could not have survived crucifixion. Roman procedures were very careful to eliminate that possibility. Roman law even laid the death penalty on any soldier who let a capital prisoner escape in any way, including bungling a crucifixion. It was never done.

2. The fact that the Roman soldier did not break Jesus' legs, as he did to the other two crucified criminals (Jn 19:31-33), means that the soldier was sure Jesus was dead. Breaking the legs hastened the death so that the corpse could be taken down before the sabbath (v. 31).

3. John, an eyewitness, certified that he saw blood and water come from Jesus' pierced heart (Jn 19:34-35). This shows that Jesus' lungs had collapsed and he had died of asphyxiation. Any medical expert can vouch for this.

4. The body was totally encased in winding sheets and entombed (Jn 19:38-42).

5. The postresurrection appearances convinced the disciples, even "doubting Thomas," that Jesus was gloriously alive (Jn 20:19-29). It is psychologically impossible for the disciples to have been so transformed and confident if Jesus had merely struggled out of a swoon, badly in need of a doctor. A half-dead, staggering sick man who has just had a narrow escape is not worshiped fearlessly as divine lord and conqueror of death.

6. How were the Roman guards at the tomb overpowered by a swooning corpse? Or by unarmed disciples? And if the disciples did it, they knowingly lied when they wrote the Gospels, and we are into the conspiracy theory, which we will refute shortly.

7. How could a swooning half-dead man have moved the great stone at the door of the tomb? Who moved the stone if not an angel? No one has ever answered that question. Neither the Jews nor the Romans would move it, for it was in both their interests to keep the tomb sealed; the Jews had the stone put there in the first place, and the Roman guards would be killed if they let the body "escape."

The story the Jewish authorities spread, that the guards fell asleep and the disciples stole the body (Mt 28:11-15), is unbelievable. Roman guards would not fall asleep on a job like that; if they did, they would lose their lives. And even if they did fall asleep, the crowd and the effort and the noise it would have taken to move an enormous boulder would have wakened them. Furthermore, we are again into the conspiracy theory, with all its unanswerable difficulties (see next section).

8. If Jesus awoke from a swoon, where did he go? Think this through: you have a living body to deal with now, not a dead one. Why did it disappear? There is absolutely no data, not even any false, fantastic, imagined data, about Jesus' life after his crucifixion, in any sources, friend or foe, at any time, early or late. A man like that, with a past like that, would have left traces.

9. Most simply, the swoon theory necessarily turns into the conspiracy theory or the hallucination theory, for the disciples testified that Jesus did not swoon but really died and really rose.

It may seem that these nine arguments have violated our initial principle about not presupposing the truth of the Gospel texts, since we have argued from data in the texts. But the swoon theory does not challenge the truths in the texts which we refer to as data; it uses them and explains them (by swoon rather than resurrection). Thus we use them too. We argue from our opponents' own premises.

Refutation of the Conspiracy Theory: Seven Arguments
Why couldn't the disciples have made up the whole story?

1. Pascal gives a simple, psychologically sound proof for why this is unthinkable:

The apostles were either deceived or deceivers. Either supposition is difficult, for it is not possible to imagine that a man has risen from the dead.

While Jesus was with them, he could sustain them; but afterwards, if he did not appear to them, who did make them act?

The hypothesis that the Apostles were knaves is quite absurd. Follow it out to the end, and imagine these twelve men meeting after Jesus' death and conspiring to say that he had risen from the dead. This means attacking all the powers that be. The human heart is singularly susceptible to fickleness, to change, to promises, to bribery. One of them had only to deny his story under these inducements, or still more because of possible imprisonment, tortures and death, and they would all have been lost. Follow that out. (Pascal, *Pensées* 322, 310)

The "cruncher" in this argument is the historical fact that no one, weak or strong, saint or sinner, Christian or heretic, ever confessed, freely or under pressure, bribe or even torture, that the whole story of the resurrection was a fake, a lie, a deliberate deception. Even when people broke under torture, denied Christ and worshiped Caesar, they never let *that* cat out of the bag, never revealed that the resurrection was their conspiracy. For that cat was never *in* that bag. No Christians believed the resurrection was a conspiracy; if they had, they wouldn't have become Christians.

2. If they made up the story, they were the most creative, clever, intelligent fantasists in history, far surpassing Shakespeare, or Dante or Tolkien. Fishermen's "fish stories" are never that elaborate, that convincing, that life-changing, and that enduring.

3. The disciples' character argues strongly against such a conspiracy on the part of all of them, with no dissenters. They were simple, honest, common peasants, not cunning, conniving liars. They weren't even lawyers! Their sincerity is proved by their words *and* deeds. They preached a resurrected Christ and they lived a resurrected Christ. They willingly died for their "conspiracy." Nothing proves sincerity like martyrdom.

The change in their lives from fear to faith, despair to confidence, confusion to certitude, runaway cowardice to steadfast boldness under threat and persecution, not only proves their sincerity but testifies to some powerful cause of it. Can a lie cause such a transformation? Are truth and goodness such enemies that the greatest good in history—sanctity—has come from the greatest lie?

Use your imagination and sense of perspective here. Imagine twelve poor, fearful, stupid (read the Gospels!) peasants changing the hard-nosed Roman world with a lie.

And not an easily digested, attractive lie either. Aquinas says:

In the midst of the tyranny of the persecutors, an innumerable throng of people, both simple and learned, flocked to the Christian faith. In this faith there are truths proclaimed that surpass every human intellect; the pleasures of the flesh are curbed; it is taught that the things of the world should be spurned. Now, for the minds of mortal men to assent to these things is the greatest of miracles. . . . This wonderful conversion of the world to the Christian faith is the clearest witness. . . . For it would be truly more wonderful than all signs if the world had been led by simple and humble men to believe such lofty truths, to accomplish such difficult actions, and to have such high hopes. (*Summa Contra Gentiles* I, 6)

4. There could be no possible motive for such a lie. Lies are always told for some selfish advantage. What advantage did the "conspirators" derive

from their "lie"? They were hated, scorned, persecuted, excommunicated, imprisoned, tortured, exiled, crucified, boiled alive, roasted, beheaded, disemboweled and fed to lions—hardly a catalog of perks!

5. If the resurrection was a lie, the Jews would have produced the corpse and nipped this feared superstition in the bud. All they had to do was go down to the tomb and get it. The Roman soldiers and their leaders were on their side, not the Christians'. And if the Jews couldn't get the body because the disciples stole it, how did they do that? The arguments against the swoon theory hold here too: unarmed peasants could not have overpowered Roman soldiers or rolled away a great stone while they slept on duty.

6. The disciples could not have gotten away with proclaiming the resurrection in Jerusalem—same time, same place, full of eyewitnesses—if it had been a lie. As William Craig says,

> The Gospels were written in such temporal and geographical proximity to the events they record that it would have been almost impossible to fabricate events. . . . The fact that the disciples were able to proclaim the resurrection in Jerusalem in the face of their enemies a few weeks after the crucifixion shows that what the proclaimed was true, for they could never have proclaimed the resurrection (and been believed) under such circumstances had it not occurred. (*Knowing the Truth About the Resurrection,* chap. 6)

7. "If there had been a conspiracy, it would certainly have been unearthed by the disciples' adversaries, who had both the interest and the power to expose any fraud. Common experience shows that such intrigues are inevitably exposed" (Craig, ibid.).

In conclusion, if the resurrection was a concocted, conspired lie, it violated all known historical and psychological laws of lying. It is, then, as unscientific, as unrepeatable, unique and untestable as the resurrection itself. But unlike the resurrection, it is also contradicted by things we do know (the above points).

Refutation of the Hallucination Theory: Thirteen Arguments

If you thought you saw a dead man walking and talking, wouldn't you think it more likely that you were hallucinating than that you were seeing correctly? Why then not think the same thing about Christ's resurrection?

1. There were too many witnesses. Hallucinations are private, individual, subjective. Christ appeared to Mary Magdalene, to the disciples minus Thomas, to the disciples including Thomas, to the two disciples at Emmaus, to the fisherman on the shore, to James (his "brother" or cousin), and even to five hundred people at once (1 Cor 15:3-8). Even three different witnesses are enough for a kind of psychological trigonometry; over five hundred is about as public as you can wish. And Paul says in this passage (v. 6) that most of the five hundred are still alive, inviting any reader to check the truth of the story by questioning the eyewitnesses—he could never have done this and gotten away with it, given the power, resources and numbers of his enemies, if it were not true.

2. The witnesses were qualified. They were simple, honest, moral people who had firsthand knowledge of the facts.

3. The five hundred saw Christ together, at the same time and place. This is even more remarkable than five hundred private "hallucinations" at different times and places of the same Jesus. Five hundred separate Elvis sightings may be dismissed, but if five hundred simple fishermen in Maine saw, touched and talked with him at once, in the same town, that would be a different matter. (The only other dead person we know of who is reported to have appeared to hundreds of qualified and skeptical eyewitnesses at once is Mary the mother of Jesus [at Fatima, to 70,000]. And that was not a claim of physical resurrection but of a vision.)

4. Hallucinations usually last a few seconds or minutes; rarely hours. This one hung around for forty days (Acts 1:3).

5. Hallucinations usually happen only once, except to the insane. This one returned many times, to ordinary people (Jn 20:19—21:14; Acts 1:3).

6. Hallucinations come from within, from what we already know, at least unconsciously. This one said and did surprising and unexpected things (Acts 1:4, 9)—like a real person and unlike a dream.

7. Not only did the disciples not expect this, they didn't even believe it at first—neither Peter, nor the women, nor Thomas, nor the eleven. They thought he was a ghost; he had to eat something to prove he was not (Lk 24:36-43).

8. Hallucinations do not eat. The resurrected Christ did, on at least two occasions (Lk 24:42-43; Jn 21:1-14).

9. The disciples touched him (Mt 28:9; Lk 24:39; Jn 20:27).

10. They also spoke with him, and he spoke back. Figments of your imagination do not hold profound, extended conversations with you, unless you have the kind of mental disorder that isolates you. But this "hallucination" conversed with at least eleven people at once, for forty days (Acts 1:3).

11. The apostles could not have believed in the "hallucination" if Jesus' corpse had still been in the tomb. This is a very simple and telling point;

for if it was a hallucination, where was the corpse? They would have checked for it; if it was there, they could not have believed.

12. If the apostles had hallucinated and then spread their hallucinogenic story, the Jews would have stopped it by producing the body—unless the disciples had stolen it, in which case we are back with the conspiracy theory and all its difficulties.

13. A hallucination would explain only the postresurrection appearances; it would not explain the empty tomb, the rolled-away stone, or the inability to produce the corpse. No theory can explain all these data except a real resurrection.

> Any theory of hallucination breaks down on the fact (and if it is invention [rather than fact], it is the oddest invention that ever entered the mind of man) that on three separate occasions this hallucination was not immediately recognized as Jesus (Lk 24:13-31; Jn 20:15; 21:4). Even granting that God sent a holy hallucination to teach truths already widely believed without it, and far more easily taught by other methods, and certain to be completely obscured by this, might we not at least hope that he would get the face of the hallucination *right?* Is he who made all faces such a bungler that he cannot even work up a recognizable likeness of the Man who was himself? (C. S. Lewis, *Miracles,* chap. 16)

Some of these arguments are as old as the church fathers. Most go back to the eighteenth century, especially William Paley. How do unbelievers try to answer them? Today, few even try to meet these arguments, although occasionally someone tries to refurbish one of the three theories of swoon, conspiracy or hallucination (e.g., Schonfield's conspiratorial *The Passover Plot*). But the counterattack today most often takes one of the two following forms.

1. Some dismiss the resurrection simply because it is miraculous, thus throwing the whole issue back to whether miracles are possible. They argue, as Hume did, that any other explanation is always more probable than a miracle. For a refutation of these arguments, see chapter five on miracles.

2. The other form of counterattack, by far the most popular, is to try to escape the traditional dilemma of "deceivers" (conspirators) or "deceived" (hallucinators) by interpreting the Gospels as myth—neither literally true nor literally false, but spiritually or symbolically true. This is the standard line of liberal theology departments in colleges, universities and seminaries throughout the Western world today.

Refutation of the Myth Theory: Six Arguments

1. The style of the Gospels is radically and clearly different from the style of all the myths. Any literary scholar who knows and appreciates myths can verify this. There are no overblown, spectacular, childishly exaggerated events. Nothing is arbitrary. Everything fits in. Everything is meaningful. The hand of a master is at work here.

Psychological depth is at a maximum. In myth it is at a minimum. In myth, such spectacular external events happen that it would be distracting to add much internal depth of character. That is why it is ordinary people like Alice who are the protagonists of extraordinary adventures like Wonderland. The character depth and development of everyone in the Gospels—especially, of course, Jesus himself—is remarkable. It is also done with an incredible economy of words. Myths are verbose; the Gospels are laconic.

There are also telltale marks of eyewitness description, like the little detail of Jesus writing in the sand when asked whether to stone the adulteress or not (Jn 8:6). No one knows why this is put in; nothing comes of it. The only explanation is that the writer saw it. If this detail and others like it throughout all four Gospels were invented, then a first-century tax collector (Matthew), a "young man" (Mark), a doctor (Luke), and a fisherman (John) all independently invented the new genre of realistic fantasy nineteen centuries before it was reinvented in the twentieth.

The stylistic point is argued so well by C. S. Lewis in "Modern Theology and Biblical Criticism" (in *Christian Reflections* and also in *Fern-Seed and Elephants)* that we strongly refer the reader to it as the best comprehensive antidemythologizing essay we have seen.

Let us be even more specific. Let us compare the Gospels with two particular mythic writings from around that time to see for ourselves the stylistic differences. The first is the so-called Gospel of Peter, a forgery from around A.D. 125 which Dominic Crossan, a current media darling among the doubters, insists is earlier than the four Gospels. As Craig puts it:

> In this account, the tomb is not only surrounded by Roman guards but also by all the Jewish Pharisees and elders as well as a great multitude from all the surrounding countryside who have come to watch the resurrection. Suddenly in the night there rings out a loud voice in heaven, and two men descend from heaven to the tomb. The stone over the door rolls back by itself, and they go into the tomb. The three men come out of the tomb, two of them holding up the third man. The heads of the two men reach up into the clouds, but the head of the third man reaches

beyond the clouds. Then a cross comes out of the tomb, and a voice from heaven asks, "Have you preached to them that sleep?" And the cross answers, "Yes." (*Apologetics*, p. 189)

Here is a second comparison, from Richard Purtill:

It may be worthwhile to take a quick look, for purposes of comparison, at the closest thing we have around the time of the Gospels to an attempt at a realistic fantasy. This is the story of Apollonius of Tyana, written about A.D. 220 by Flavius Philostratus. . . . There is some evidence that a neo-Pythagorean sage named Apollonius may really have lived, and thus Philostratus's work is a real example of what some have thought the Gospels to be: a fictionalized account of the life of a real sage and teacher, introducing miraculous elements to build up the prestige of the central figure. It thus gives us a good look at what a real example of a fictionalized biography would look like, written at a time and place not too far removed from those in which the Gospels were written.

The first thing we notice is the fairy-tale atmosphere. There is a rather nice little vampire story, which inspired a minor poem by Keats entitled *Lamia*. There are animal stories about, for instance, snakes in India big enough to drag off and eat an elephant. The sage wanders from country to country and wherever he goes he is likely to be entertained by the king or emperor, who holds long conversations with him and sends him on his way with camels and precious stones.

Here is a typical passage about healing miracles: "A woman who had had seven miscarriages was cured through the prayers of her husband, as follows. The Wise Man told the husband, when his wife was in labor, to bring a live rabbit under his cloak to the place where she was, walk around her and immediately release the rabbit; for she would lose her womb as well as her baby if the rabbit was not immediately driven away." [Bk 3, sec. 39]

The point is that this is what you get when the imagination goes to work. Once the boundaries of fact are crossed we wander into fairyland. And very nice, too, for amusement or recreation. But the Gospels are set firmly in the real Palestine of the first century, and the little details are not picturesque inventions but the real details that only an eyewitness or a skilled realistic novelist can give. (*Thinking About Religion*, pp. 75-76)

2. A second problem is that there was not enough time for myth to develop. The original demythologizers pinned their case onto a late second-century date for the writing of the Gospels; several generations have to pass before the added mythological elements can be mistakenly believed to be facts.

Eyewitnesses would be around before that to discredit the new, mythic versions. We know of other cases where myths and legends of miracles developed around a religious founder—for example, Buddha, Lao-tzu and Muhammad. In each case, many generations passed before the myth surfaced.

The dates for the writing of the Gospels have been pushed back by every empirical manuscript discovery; only abstract hypothesizing pushes the date forward. Almost no knowledgeable scholar today holds what Bultmann said it was necessary to hold in order to believe the myth theory, namely, that there is no first-century textual evidence that Christianity began with a divine and resurrected Christ, not a human and dead one.

Some scholars still dispute the first-century date for the Gospels, especially John's. But no one disputes that Paul's letters were written within the lifetime of eyewitnesses to Christ. So let us argue from Paul's letters.

Either these letters contain myth or they do not. If so, there is lacking the several generations necessary to build up a commonly believed myth. There is not even *one* generation. If these letters are *not* myth, then the Gospels are not either, for Paul affirms all the main claims of the Gospels.

Julius Muller put the antimyth argument this way:

One cannot imagine how such a series of legends could arise in an historical age, obtain universal respect, and supplant the historical recollection of the true character [Jesus] . . . if eyewitnesses were still at hand who could be questioned respecting the truth of the recorded marvels. Hence, legendary fiction, as it likes not the clear present time but prefers the mysterious gloom of gray antiquity, is wont to seek a remoteness of age, along with that of space, and to remove its boldest and most rare and wonderful creations into a very remote and unknown land. (*The Theory of Myths in Its Application to the Gospel History Examined and Confuted* [London, 1844], p. 26)

Muller challenged his nineteenth-century contemporaries to produce a single example anywhere in history of a great myth or legend arising around a historical figure and being generally believed within thirty years after that figure's death. No one has ever answered him.

3. The myth theory has two layers. The first layer is the historical Jesus, who was not divine, did not claim divinity, performed no miracles, and did not rise from the dead. The second, later, mythologized layer is the Gospels as we have them, with a Jesus who claimed to be divine, performed miracles and rose from the dead. The problem with this theory is simply that there is not the slightest bit of any real evidence whatever for the existence of

any such first layer. The two-layer cake theory has the first layer made entirely of air—and hot air at that.

Augustine refutes the two-layer theory with his usual condensed power and simplicity.

> The speech of one Elpidius, who had spoken and disputed face to face against the Manichees, had already begun to affect me at Carthage, when he produced arguments from Scripture which were not easy to answer. And the answer they [the Manichees, who claimed to be the true Christians] gave seemed to me feeble—indeed they preferred not to give it in public but only among ourselves in private—the answer being that the Scriptures of the New Testament had been corrupted by some persons unknown . . . yet the Manicheans made no effort to produce uncorrupted copies. (*Confessions*, V, 11, Sheed translation.)

Note the sarcasm in the last sentence. It still applies today.

Craig summarizes the evidence—the *lack* of evidence:

> The Gospels are a miraculous story, and we have no other story handed down to us than that contained in the Gospels. . . . The letters of Barnabas and Clement refer to Jesus' miracles and resurrection. Polycarp mentions the resurrection of Christ, and Irenaeus relates that he had heard Polycarp tell of Jesus' miracles. Ignatius speaks of the resurrection. Puadratus reports that persons were still living who had been healed by Jesus. Justin Martyr mentions the miracles of Christ. No relic of a nonmiraculous story exists. That the original story should be lost and replaced by another goes beyond any known example of corruption of even oral tradition, not to speak of the experience of written transmissions. These facts show that the story in the Gospels was in substance the same story that Christians had at the beginning. This means . . . that the resurrection of Jesus was always a part of the story. (Craig, *Apologetics*, chap. 6)

4. A little detail, seldom noticed, is significant in distinguishing the Gospels from myth: the first witnesses of the resurrection were women. In first-century Judaism, women had low social status and no legal right to serve as witnesses. If the empty tomb were an invented legend, its inventors surely would not have had it discovered by women, whose testimony was considered worthless. If, on the other hand, the writers were simply reporting what they saw, they would have to tell the truth, however socially and legally inconvenient.

5. The New Testament could not be myth misinterpreted and confused with fact because it specifically distinguishes the two and repudiates the mythic interpretation (2 Pet 1:16). Since it explicitly says it is not myth, if it *is* myth it is a deliberate lie rather than myth. The dilemma still stands.

It is either truth or lie, whether deliberate (conspiracy) or nondeliberate (hallucination). There is no escape from the horns of this dilemma. Once a child asks whether Santa Claus is real, your yes becomes a lie, not myth, if he is not literally real. Once the New Testament distinguishes myth from fact, it becomes a lie if the resurrection is not fact.

6. Craig has summarized the traditional textual arguments with such clarity, condensation and power that we quote him here at length. The following arguments (rearranged and outlined from *Knowing the Truth About the Resurrection*) prove two things: first, that the Gospels were written by the disciples, not later myth-makers, and second, that the Gospels we have today are essentially the same as the originals.

A. Proof that the Gospels were written by eyewitnesses:

1. Internal evidence, from the Gospels themselves:

a. "The style of writing in the Gospels is simple and alive, what we would expect from their traditionally accepted authors."

b. "Moreover, since Luke was written before Acts, and since Acts was written prior to the death of Paul, Luke must have an early date, which speaks for its authenticity."

c. "The Gospels also show an intimate knowledge of Jerusalem prior to its destruction in A.D. 70. . . . The Gospels are full of proper names, dates, cultural details, historical events, and customs and opinions of that time."

d. "Jesus' prophecies of that event (the destruction of Jerusalem) must have been written prior to Jerusalem's fall, for otherwise the church would have separated out the apocalyptic element in the prophecies, which makes them appear to concern the end of the world. Since the end of the world did not come about when Jerusalem was destroyed, the so-called prophecies of its destruction that were really written after the city was destroyed would not have made that event appear so closely connected with the end of the world. Hence, the Gospels must have been written prior to A.D. 70."

e. "The stories of Jesus' human weaknesses and of the disciples' faults also bespeak the Gospels' accuracy."

f. "Furthermore, it would have been impossible for forgers to put together so consistent a narrative as that which we find in the Gospels. The Gospels do not try to suppress apparent discrepancies, which indicates their originality (written by eyewitnesses). There is no attempt at harmonization between the Gospels, such as we might expect from forgers."

g. "The Gospels do not contain anachronisms; the authors appear to
have been first-century Jews who were witnesses of the events."

We may conclude that "there is no more reason to doubt that the Gospels
come from the traditional authors than there is to doubt that the works of
Philo or Josephus are authentic, *except* that the Gospels contain supernatural events."

2. External evidence:

   a. "The disciples must have left *some* writings, engaged as they were
in giving lessons to and counseling believers who were geographi-
cally distant; and what could these writings be if not the Gospels
and epistles themselves? . . . Eventually the apostles would have
needed to publish accurate narratives of Jesus' history, so that any
spurious attempts would be discredited and the genuine Gospels
preserved."

   b. "There were many eyewitnesses who were still alive when the books
were written who could testify whether they came from their pur-
ported authors or not."

   c. "The extra-biblical testimony unanimously attributes the Gospels to
their traditional authors, . . . testimony from the Epistle of Barnabas,
the Epistle of Clement, the Shepherd of Hermas, all the way up to
Eusebius in A.D. 315. . . . Theophilus, Hippolytus, Origen, Quadratus,
Irenaeus, Melito, Polycarp, Justin Martyr, Dionysius, Tertullian, Cyp-
rian, Tatian, Caius, Athanasius, Cyril. . . . Even Christianity's opponents conceded this: Celsus, Porphyry, Emperor Julian."

   d. "With a single exception, no apocryphal gospel is ever even quoted
by any known author during the first three hundred years after
Christ. In fact there is no evidence that any inauthentic gospel
whatever existed in the first century, in which all four Gospels and
Acts were written."

B. Proof that the Gospels we have today are the same Gospels originally
written:

   1. "Because of the need for instruction and personal devotion, these
writings must have been copied many times, which increases the chances of preserving the original text."

   2. "In fact, no other ancient work is available in so many copies and
languages, and yet all these various versions agree in content."

   3. "The text has also remained unmarred by heretical additions. The
abundance of manuscripts over a wide geographical distribution dem-
onstrates that the text has been transmitted with only trifling discrep-

ancies. The differences that do exist are quite minor and are the result of unintentional mistakes."

4. "The quotations of the New Testament books in the early church Fathers all coincide."

5. "The Gospels could not have been corrupted without a great outcry on the part of all orthodox Christians."

6. "No one could have corrupted *all* the manuscripts."

7. "There is no precise time when the falsification could have occurred, since, as we have seen, the New Testament books are cited by the church Fathers in regular and close succession. The text could not have been falsified before all external testimony, since then the apostles were still alive and could repudiate such tampering."

8. "The text of the New Testament is every bit as good as the text of the classical works of antiquity. . . . To repudiate the textual parity of the Gospels would be to reverse all the rules of criticism and to reject all the works of antiquity, since the text of those works is less certain than that of the Gospels."

Purtill summarizes the textual case:

Many events which are regarded as firmly established historically have (1) far less documentary evidence than many biblical events, (2) and the documents on which historians rely for much secular history are written much longer after the event than many records of biblical events. (3) Furthermore, we have many more copies of biblical narratives than of secular histories, and (4) the surviving copies are much earlier than those on which our evidence for secular history is based. If the biblical narratives did not contain accounts of miraculous events . . . biblical history would probably be regarded as much more firmly established than most of the history of, say, classical Greece and Rome. (*Thinking About Religion*, pp. 84-85)

Conclusions: More Objections Answered

No alternative to a real resurrection has yet explained: the existence of the Gospels, the origin of the Christian faith, the failure of Christ's enemies to produce his corpse, the empty tomb, the rolled-away stone or the accounts of the postresurrection appearances. Swoon, conspiracy, hallucination and myth have been shown to be the only alternatives to a real resurrection, and each has been refuted.

What reasons could be given at this point for anyone who still would refuse to believe? At this point, general rather than specific objections are usually given. For instance:

Objection 1:

History is not an exact science. It does not yield absolute certainty like mathematics.
Reply: This is true, but why would you note that fact now and not when you speak of Caesar or Luther or George Washington? History is not exact, but it is sufficient. No one doubts that Caesar crossed the Rubicon; why do many doubt that Jesus rose from dead? The evidence for the latter is much better than that for the former.

Objection 2:

You can't trust documents. Paper proves nothing. Anything can be forged.
Reply: This is simply ignorance. Not trusting documents is like not trusting telescopes. Paper evidence suffices for most of what we believe; why should it suddenly become suspect here?

Objection 3:

Because the resurrection is miraculous. It's the content of the idea rather than the documentary evidence for it that makes it incredible.
Reply: Now we finally have a straightforward objection—not to the documentary evidence but to miracles. This is a philosophical question, not a scientific, historical or textual question. See chapter five for an answer.

Objection 4:

It's not only miracles in general but this miracle in particular that is objectionable. The resurrection of a corpse is crass, crude, vulgar, literalistic and materialistic. Religion should be more spiritual, inward, ethical.
Reply: If religion is what we invent, we can make it whatever we like. If it is what God invented, then we have to take it as we find it, just as we have to take the universe as we find it, rather than as we'd like it to be.

Death is crass, crude, vulgar, literal and material. The resurrection meets death where it is and conquers it, rather than merely spouting some harmless, vaporous abstractions about spirituality. The resurrection is as vulgar as the God who did it. He also made mud and bugs and toenails.

Objection 5:

But a literalistic interpretation of the resurrection ignores the profound dimensions of meaning found in the symbolic, spiritual and mythic realms that have been deeply explored by other religions. Why are Christians so narrow and exclusive? Why can't they see the profound symbolism in the idea of resurrection?
Reply: They can. It's not either-or. Christianity does not invalidate the

myths, it validates them, by incarnating them. It is "myth become fact," to use the title of a germane essay by C. S. Lewis (in *God in the Dock*).

Why prefer a one-layer cake to a two-layer cake? Why refuse either the literal-historical or the mythic-symbolic aspects of the resurrection? The fundamentalist refuses the mythic-symbolic aspects because he has seen what the modernist has done with it: used it to exclude the literal-historical aspects. Why have the modernists done that? What terrible fate awaits them if they follow the multifarious and weighty evidence and argument that naturally emerges from the data, as we have summarized it here in this chapter?

The answer is not obscure: traditional Christianity awaits them, complete with adoration of Christ as God, obedience to Christ as Lord, dependence on Christ as Savior, humble confession of sin and a serious effort to live Christ's life of self-sacrifice, detachment from the world, righteousness, holiness and purity of thought, word and deed. The historical evidence is massive enough to convince the open-minded inquirer. By analogy with any other historical event, the resurrection has eminently credible evidence behind it. To disbelieve it, you must deliberately make an exception to the rules you use everywhere else in history. Now why would someone want to do that?

Ask yourself that question if you dare, and take an honest look into your heart before you answer.

Questions for Discussion

1. Is the resurrection so important that if it is proved true, Christianity is proved true? If it is proved false, is Christianity proved false? What would Christianity be like without a resurrection? What would resurrection be like without the rest of Christianity?

2. Pascal wrote, "If Jesus did not rise, who made the apostles act as they did?" How much and what kind of evidence for a real resurrection is the remarkable turnaround of the apostles from confused cowards to world-changing martyrs?

3. Compare the existential importance of resurrection with that of reincarnation.

4. Can you gather together the biblical clues about Christ's resurrection body and put together some coherent picture of what kind of thing that body is?

5. What exactly is the relation between the ideas of resurrection and immortality?

6. Is the chapter unfair to the demythologizers? If so, how? Can there be a middle category *(heilsgeschichte)* between myth and history? Can there be a middle category ("Easter faith") between resurrection and no resurrection?

7. Is there a sixth theory in addition to the five mentioned here? Which of the four alternatives to real resurrection seems most reasonable to you? Where are the

weak points in our refutation of this reasonable alternative?

8. If you are familiar with the literature of (not about) myth, how would you compare it with the Gospels in literary form, style and effect on the reader?

9. If the apostles' sincerity and martyrdom is evidence for the Gospel they lived and died for, why can't the same be said for any fanatics? (e.g., Jim Jones's disciples)

10. Why isn't a real resurrection less likely than any of the four alternatives, as Hume argues about miracles?

11. Imagine a later writer claiming that Socrates, Buddha, Muhammad, Solomon, King Arthur, Rasputin or Michael Jordan claimed divinity. How would that be different from the case of Christ? What would happen if a mere man were ascribed divinity? How is this different in the contexts of (a) theism, (b) pantheism, (c) polytheism?

12. How clear, strong and valid is the literary style argument (p. 189)?

13. Are the demythologizer's arguments against (a) the historicity of the Gospels, (b) the resurrection and (c) the claim that Christ claimed divinity all in the same boat? Or are there some arguments that count for one but not the other two?

14. Evaluate the negative argument against the two-layer text theory (p. 191).

15. In light of argument 5 (p. 192), why is the myth theory still more popular than the conspiracy theory?

16. Since history is not an exact science, and therefore a historical resurrection cannot be proved like an axiom in math, does it follow that the Christian faith rests on a mere probability? Compare Kierkegaard on this (*Philosophical Fragments* and *Concluding Unscientific Postscript*).

17. How accurate and likely does the motivation attributed to the modernist demythologizer (pp. 195-96) seem to you?

Outline of Chapter 9
The Bible: Myth or History?

1. Connections among the Bible, miracles and the resurrection

2. The importance of the issue

Footnote on psychological motives for unbelief

3. The role of Scripture in apologetics

☐ The fundamentalist extreme

☐ The modernist extreme

4. Eight basic principles of biblical interpretation

☐ Use common standards, methods and approaches.

☐ Read for the author's intended meaning.

☐ Separate interpretation from belief.

☐ Interpret a book according to its genre.

☐ Know when to interpret the Bible literally versus symbolically.

☐ Know which stories are historical.

☐ Don't separate religious versus historical questions.

☐ Historical proximity increases historical reliability.

5. Contradictions in the Bible?

☐ Internal contradictions?

☐ External contradictions?

6. A personal postscript

CHAPTER 9
The Bible:
Myth or History?

T HE BIBLE, MIRACLES AND THE RESURRECTION, EACH OF WHICH TAKES up a chapter in this book, are closely linked in modern apologetics. They typically stand or fall together. Most of those who do not believe that Christ physically rose from the dead disbelieve for two reasons: ' (1) "miracles like that don't really happen," and (2) "the Bible is myth, not history."

There is probably no word that causes more confusion in biblical studies today than the word *myth*. That is because it is used in many different senses by different writers in different fields and genres, which often overlap. G. B. Caird, in *The Language and Imagery of the Bible*, has distinguished nine distinct senses of the word myth. For our more popular, less technical purposes it is sufficient to distinguish six.

1. The literal sense of myth, from the Greek *mythos*, is simply "sacred story." This says nothing about its truth or falsity, historicity or nonhistoricity—just that it is a story and that it is sacred, or about sacred things.

2. The popular sense is simply "something that didn't really happen," or "something that isn't real"—like Santa Claus. Here myth is contrasted with truth or fact. This is the sense in which most people are concerned about the stories in the Bible, especially the miracle stories: did they really happen, or are they only "myths," that is, mere fictional human inventions?

3. A more technical and narrow sense of myth that is often used to describe biblical stories, especially miracle stories, is that of a literary genre that includes fantasy, talking animals and stories of the gods. These are supernatural stories that are not literally true, nor are they meant by the storyteller to be taken as literally true, but as a way of explaining natural facts by supernatural (or natural) fictions. Both supernatural stories of gods and talking animals, and natural stories like Jesus' parables, fit in this category.

4. Another technical meaning, unusual outside professional circles, is that of a projection of human consciousness out onto reality. In this sense, Kant's theory of knowledge ("the Copernican revolution in philosophy," as he called it) is the claim that all human knowledge is myth. In a narrower sense, dreams are myths if while we are dreaming we take them for objective realities.

5. A much broader, but still technical and professional, use of myth is "any story meant to articulate a worldview." This sense would include both literally true and fictional stories, but it is usually used with the connotation of fiction.

6. A last sense, also quite broad and quite technical, used in literary more than biblical circles, is that of a Platonic archetype in story form, a universal truth about human life expressed in a story. The story is usually fiction, but not necessarily. Christ's resurrection, even if factual, would also be a myth in this sense, as the pattern for our resurrection.

When it comes to biblical studies, the major controversy is between the demythologizers and orthodox Christianity. Demythologizers claim that all or most of the miracle stories in the Bible are myths in all six of the above senses. Orthodox Christians often agree that the Bible contains myth in senses 1 (sacred story), 3 (parables), 5 (worldview) and 6 (archetype), but not senses 2 (unreal) or 4 (projection). The bottom line is miracles, especially the resurrection: did they really happen or not? This simple question is not the only legitimate question, and consideration of differently nuanced senses of myth is quite proper, but not if it obscures the primary, simple question.

It is important at the outset to clarify the logical order and relationship among the three issues of demythologizing, miracles and the resurrection, because this relationship is often put backwards by those who argue against a literal resurrection and against miracles on the grounds that the Bible is myth, not history. The logic goes the other way: if the resurrection really did happen, then the assumption that "miracles don't happen" is refuted; in that case, the miracle stories in the Bible can be history, not myth.

Let us put the logical point in a different way. To argue that the resurrection didn't really happen because the Bible is myth begs the question. For when unbelievers are asked why they think the Bible is myth rather than history, they say it is because it is full of unbelievable miracle stories like the resurrection. This is arguing in a circle. It is arguing that the resurrection is myth because the Bible is myth, and the Bible is myth because it contains obviously mythical miracle stories like the resurrection.

The Importance of the Issue

We know from our experience as professors that the demythologizers have very effectively undermined the faith of vast numbers of young Christians. For instance, we would estimate that nearly half the students who enter Catholic colleges as believers exit as unbelievers, if we define *belief* in New Testament terms. And this loss of faith is in some measure surely due to the influence of demythologizing teachers. These students typically go through three stages.

1. They enter with a thoughtless belief in the Bible and its miracles, notably the resurrection.

2. They take theology courses that debunk these miracle stories via the historical-critical method.

3. They are graduated as unbelievers, or believers in a religion without miracles, a real resurrection or scriptural authority—a religion of mere "sharing and caring."

Footnote on Psychological Motives for Unbelief

The most powerful psychological *motive* for unbelief, as distinct from the most effective *argument* to undermine belief, is a different matter. The answer to *that* question is almost always moral rather than intellectual. That answer is addiction to sin and selfishness, usually in one or more of the following areas:

1. Addiction to power in this world. How often have you heard about the value of detachment or otherworldliness lately? Yet all the saints extol this as indispensable.

2. Addiction to lust, our society's favorite pastime. A sex addict is hardly more capable of objectivity than a cocaine addict.

3. Addiction to greed, the sin Christ spoke against the most frequently, and the one our consumerist society relies on for its very survival.

4. Addiction to worldliness, that is, acceptance and popularity, *not* being distinctive, like the prophets or the martyrs.

5. Addiction to freedom, defined as "doing your own thing," "accepting yourself as you are," "self-assertiveness," "looking out for Number One"—in short, acting like a self-centered child and calling it the psychology of maturity.

This book is about rational, logical, objective apologetics, not about subjective psychological motivations. But it's important to know what is really going on in the soul of the person to whom apologetic arguments are addressed, and to know the irrational forces behind unbelief. We made the strong claim in chapter two that *all* arguments against *all* the doctrines of Christianity are rationally refutable. Having said that, the most important task remains still undone. Arguments destroy ignorance and irrationality, but the real enemy is sin. Sin can be destroyed only by sanctity, prayer, faith, hope, charity, the blood of Christ, and the power of the Holy Spirit.

The Role of Scripture in Apologetics

We want to avoid two extremes here: the fundamentalist extreme and the modernist extreme.

These two labels, like most labels, are slippery and often fail to stick tight. Yet they are constantly used, so we cannot ignore them. Theological modernism at least includes or overlaps with demythologizing, as defined above. Fundamentalism, which emerged early in the twentieth century as a reaction against modernism, properly means belief in the five "fundamentals" listed by B. B. Warfield: Christ's divinity, resurrection, virgin birth, real Second Coming, and the infallibility of Scripture. In this sense, all orthodox Christians, Catholics as well as Protestants, are fundamentalists. But the term is usually used in two looser, more popular senses: (1) not just biblical infallibility but also biblical literalism, and (2) a generally closed-minded, narrow-minded, anti-intellectual, even bigoted attitude—obviously something fundamentalists have no exclusive rights to. These two senses are not only incorrect, they are also imprecise; for both biblical literalism and narrow-mindedness exist on a spectrum of more or less, never all or nothing.

The Fundamentalist Extreme

Most fundamentalists, as well as many who do not call themselves fundamentalists but evangelicals, will do apologetics only from the starting point of the authority of Scripture. We think this is a tactical error. There are three points to their tactics that seem questionable.

1. They think that it is *necessary* to begin by convincing you of the authority of Scripture because they think that natural human reason alone, apart from Scripture, is not strong enough or good enough to direct unbelievers to belief.

2. They think that therefore the only right order in apologetics is first to prove the authority of Scripture, and then to move on to other apologetic questions with this all-important weapon in hand.

3. They think that special standards must be used to understand and interpret Scripture since, unlike all other books, it is not just man's words about God but God's word about man.

But remember: for many years early Christian apologists and church fathers argued quite effectively for Christianity without even *having* the New Testament Scriptures as authoritatively defined, since the canon was not established until generations later. And down through the centuries many people have in fact been led to belief—at least belief in a Creator God and in the *possibility* of salvation—through rational arguments not based on Scripture. (Of course, saving faith, as distinct from intellectual belief, is not the work of reason alone.)

Also, it is very difficult to prove the authority of Scripture *first* to the unbeliever. It is much easier to prove something like the existence of God (chap. 3), or even the divinity of Christ (chap. 7), where arguments can be simple, short and clear in a way that the arguments for the authority of Scripture can never be. Traditional apologetics, Protestant as well as Catholic, has more often used the opposite order, coming to the authority of Scripture later. Instead of

1. Scripture is infallible,

2. therefore Christ is infallible,

3. therefore Christ is divine,

the more convincing order is:

1. Scripture is *reliable* as historical record, as data;

2. Christ's claims to divinity are found in Scripture;

3. then comes the argument for the truth of these claims (chap. 7).

You don't need to prove scriptural infallibility first to confront someone with the claims of Christ.

The third difficulty is that the unbeliever will not accept the use of any special standards or assumptions or attitudes toward Scripture at the outset, since they clearly beg the question. You must first prove that Scripture *deserves* such special treatment as the Word of God, and you must prove this without presupposing it, without giving Scripture special treatment. Otherwise you argue in a circle, assuming what you need to prove.

The Modernist Extreme

Modernists make the opposite mistake from fundamentalists about Scripture. If fundamentalists worship it, modernists trash it. But strangely, the two extremes share a common mistake. Both sides use special standards to judge the Bible, standards that are not used to judge other books.

Fundamentalists interpret everything, or everything they possibly can, literally, and insist right from the start on a believing attitude toward the Bible. Modernists interpret everything, or at least everything miraculous or supernatural (or morally unpopular) nonliterally, and insist right from the start on an unbelieving, skeptical attitude toward the Bible.

The dozens of clever, complex attempts by modernist Scripture scholars to discredit the historical accuracy of the biblical texts, especially the Gospels, is a story that is long, tedious and still in progress. Essentially, the argument is that if we used the same critical standards on other ancient literature that modernists use on the Bible, we would doubt every single fact we know today about every single writer and event before the Middle Ages. If modernists applied to the Bible the same standards that historians and textual scholars apply to secular literature of ancient times, the biblical records would be accepted as some of the most reliable and credible of all ancient documents. As Richard Purtill puts it in *Thinking About Religion:*

> It is sometimes claimed that historians simply as historians regard Old and New Testament history as unreliable on some independent historical grounds. But . . . many events which are regarded as firmly established historically have far less documentary evidence than many biblical events, and the documents on which historians rely for much secular history are written much longer after the event than many records of biblical events. Furthermore, we have many more copies of biblical narratives than of secular histories; and the surviving copies are much earlier than those on which our evidence for secular history is based.

Why then do modernists doubt the biblical accounts?

> If the biblical narratives did not contain accounts of miraculous events or have reference to God, angels, etc., biblical history would probably be regarded as much more firmly established than most of the history of, say, classical Greece and Rome. But because the biblical accounts do mention miracles and do involve reference to God, angels and demons, etc., considerations other than purely historical ones come into the picture . . . [modernists] are convinced as part of their general worldview that miracles don't happen. . . . Those who wish to demythologize Scripture reject *particular* accounts of miracles in Scripture because they hold a *general* view about the meaning of miracle stories [as mere myth, not historical fact]. (Purtill, *Thinking About Religion*, chap. 6)

(For further details about this argument and about the history of biblical manuscripts, see F. F. Bruce's *The New Testament Documents—Are They Reliable?* Josh McDowell's *Evidence That Demands a Verdict* or Craig Blomberg's *The Historical Reliability of the Gospels.* See bibliography.)

Typical modernist Scripture scholarship is *not* objective or neutral historical and textual scholarship. It is *eisegesis* ("reading into") rather than *exegesis* ("reading out of"); it reads a particular modern worldview—naturalism, denial of the supernatural and miracles—into the texts, and judges the texts on the basis of that worldview. Indeed, modernists commit a graver version of the very error they accuse fundamentalists of, for fundamentalists only read into the text the same worldview it contains—supernaturalism—while modernists impose an alien and modern worldview on it. Fundamentalists do not add miracles to the textual data, modernists subtract them. This is fudging the data to conform to the theory—the fundamental fallacy of bad science. It is the modernist who is being unscientific here.

Why? What is their motivational strategy?

Modernists want to deny the authority of Scripture for an obvious reason: Scripture clearly contradicts modernist theology on at least five crucial points:

1. Do miracles happen? Is the supernatural world real? Are there angels and devils? Does God ever reach down and "interfere"?

2. Is there a supernaturally-given moral law? Did God, not just Moses, invent the Ten Commandments? Are there, then, any moral absolutes— objective, unyielding moral laws that do not change when our feelings or societies change?

3. Is Christ divine and thus infallible and absolutely authoritative in everything he says?

4. Is human life on earth a spiritual warfare? (This would follow from the first three points. Work it out.) Are the stakes in life infinite? Is there a real heaven or hell at the end? Do our choices matter very much?

5. Is there one objective and true way to heaven—Jesus himself—as he claims (e.g., Jn 14:6)? Or are all the religions of the world equal and thus are generic human sincerity and niceness the only requirements for salvation?

Scripture unequivocally and repeatedly answers yes to all these questions. The typical modern mind answers no. Modernists want to make peace between these two minds. They also wish Scripture would answer less loudly, less clearly, more subtly so that only a scholar could properly interpret it. That would make scholars feel very important.

Unbelievers say (1) that Christianity is what the New Testament teaches and (2) that Christianity is false. Christians say (1) that Christianity is what the New Testament teaches and (2) that Christianity is true. Modernist theologians want to make peace with both sides, so they say (1) that Christianity is *not* what the New Testament, at face value, teaches but instead is what modernists have selected out of the New Testament (the love ethic without the miracles) as something that will be acceptable to both unbelievers and believers and (2) that this redefined Christianity is true.

But will Scripture allow Christianity to be redefined? See Galatians 1:8 for an answer.

Eight Basic Principles of Biblical Interpretation

This topic may seem out of place in a book on apologetics, but in light of the situation described in the previous section, it cannot be ignored. The following remarks are very introductory and sketchy; they focus on the most controverted principles only, and are not to be taken as an adequate introduction to hermeneutics, the science of interpretation.

Use Common Standards, Methods and Approaches

Our first principle for interpreting the Bible is to use the same standards, methods and approaches to the Bible you would use for any other book. This is the only way of making contact with unbelievers (which fundamentalists find hard to do) without patronizing them by fudging your textual data to make it more acceptable or palatable to them (as modernists do).

Read for the Author's Intended Meaning

The most important positive principle for interpreting any book is to read the book in the same spirit or mind as its author wrote it. In other words, exegesis, not eisegesis. Don't try to understand the author's mind through the colored eyeglasses of your own worldview, assumptions, beliefs, categories, ideologies or prejudices. Just the reverse. Look at everything, including yourself and your views, through the author's eyes. He is trying to communicate something new to you, something you did not know before; your job is to receive it intact, as fairly and objectively as possible. That is, after all, the purpose of reading any book in the first place: to grow and learn something new, not just to reinforce something old or flatter your own prejudices. As C. S. Lewis says,

The first demand any work of art makes of us is surrender. Look. Listen. Receive. Get yourself out of the way. There is no good asking first whether the work before you deserves such a surrender, for until you have surrendered, you cannot possibly find out. (*An Experiment in Criticism*) Before we respond, actively and critically, to a book (or a person), we must first receive, docilely. It takes great mental activity and effort to be docile, that is, teachable.

Separate Interpretation from Belief

We must clearly separate interpretation from belief. Many people, professional exegetes and ordinary readers alike, make the basic mistake of practicing, and even preaching, the opposite: the idea that we should interpret a book "in light of our own sincerely held beliefs." Drop the words "sincerely held" and it is clear how absurd this is. Interpretation means finding out what the *other* person meant and believed, not what you mean or believe. It means interpreting the author's words and thoughts and mind, not yours, and therefore this must be done in light of *his* beliefs, not yours.

After interpretation comes the question of belief or unbelief; after you understand what the other person means, you can and should make up your own mind whether you agree or disagree with it. But until you know what the author's words mean to him, you cannot either agree or disagree with him, because there is as yet no "him" in your mind, only you.

This principle is easy to preach but hard to practice. We love to flatter our own prejudices by making others agree with us, and we find it hard to stretch and open our minds to new, startling or offensive ideas. The Bible is full of new, startling and offensive ideas, because it claims to be the record of the words and acts of a God whose ways and thoughts are as far above our own as heaven is above earth (Is 55:8-9). A God who only comforted and reinforced us, and never shocked and puzzled us, would be a false God, one made in our own image—a mirror, not a light.

Interpret a Book According to Its Genre

We should always interpret a book by the standards appropriate to its literary form or genre. Thus we should first find out what that form is. There are different principles which govern the interpretation of poetry versus law, parable versus biography, science versus religion, myth versus history.

The point is obviously valid but commonly violated—for example, by students of political philosophy, who attempt to contrast Plato's *Republic* with Machiavelli's *The Prince* as if they had the same literary form. They do not. Plato's *Republic* is not practical politics but ethics and metaphysics. The politics is only an analogy, a parable. Plato explicitly says that his "ideal state" could never exist on earth. Machiavelli, on the other hand, explicitly says that he is not writing ethics or metaphysics but merely reporting on what strategies, moral or immoral, have actually worked in history to get, keep and efficiently use political power. Comparing these two books is like comparing Aesop's fables with Mutual of Omaha's *Wild Kingdom*.

A more crucial example of this confusion is comparing Darwin and Moses, or whoever wrote Genesis. If Genesis were science, or if *On the Origin of Species* were religion, the two accounts would meet and perhaps conflict. But in order to conflict, they must meet, and they do not. Darwin does not ask *who* created species or *why* but only *how* they appeared. His answer is evolution by natural selection. Genesis tells us *who* created (God) and *why* (goodness) but not *how*. Oceans of ink have been spilled and wasted on this confusion. (See also chap. 5 on creation and evolution.)

Modernists often try to show that biblical miracle stories are myths by pointing to resemblances in form between these stories and myths. For instance, they point to (1) repeated stock events, (2) symbolic numbers and (3) similar kinds of miracles in pagan myths.

An example of repeated stock events is Moses' repeated returns to Pharaoh, asking him to let the Israelites go, Pharaoh's repeated refusals and his defeat by the ten plagues. However, the fact that events like these are often described in myths does not prove that they cannot also occur in history. Many other events described in myths, legends and fairy tales also occur in history, like repeated warnings, betrayals, romance, murders, travels, puzzles and punishments.

Some examples of the second kind of resemblance, symbolic numbers, are the three days that Jonah was inside the great fish and Jesus was in the tomb, the seven churches of Asia in Revelation, the ten plagues, the forty years the Israelites wandered in the wilderness and the forty days Jesus was in the desert. Three, seven, ten and forty are all symbolic numbers. Once again the parallel does not prove that the events described did not really happen. This is so for two reasons. First, sometimes real things do happen in threes, sevens, tens or forties. For instance, you can visit the actual ruins of the seven churches in Asia. Second, if God is in control of history, he might well providentially arrange for events to conform to symbolic number schemes precisely so that Jesus' three days would parallel Jonah's, and his forty days in the wilderness would parallel the forty years of Moses and the Jews.

Behind the textual dispute between modernists and orthodox Christians there lurks a philosophical dispute. Modernists assume that real things cannot also be signs and symbols; that symbols are only mental, not real. Orthodox Christians, on the other hand, assume that God, like any artist, makes things that are also signs and symbols. As Aquinas said, "The author of Holy Writ is God, in whose power it is to signify his meaning not by words only (as man also can do) but also by things themselves" (*Summa Theologiae* I, 1, 10).

Examples of the third resemblance, similar miracles in pagan myths, include multiplying food, turning water into wine, walking on water and raising the dead. These miracles also appear in much myth and fiction. These similarities do not prove that they do not also occur in reality, any more than the appearance of apples or battles in fiction proves that all apples or battles are fictitious.

If modernists reply at this point that the difference is that we find apples and battles in the real world but we do not find men walking on water or raising the dead, then they beg the question. According to the Bible and many other authorities, both written and personal, many people have seen real miracles, just as they have seen real battles. Why do modernists disbelieve all these reports? They cannot give textual reasons for their disbelief without begging the question (e.g., "the texts are myths only because they contain miracles"). They cannot give scientific reasons because science is agnostic about miracles; it can neither prove nor disprove them (see chap. 5).

The dispute between the modernist demythologizer and the traditional believer is neither a textual dispute nor a scientific dispute, but a philosophical and theological dispute. Modernists read their philosophy of naturalism into the text, not out of it. They read the miracles out of it not because the text tells them to but because their philosophy tells them to, and they tell the text what to say.

From a strictly textual point of view, some biblical narratives have the form of invented moral fable, like Jesus' parables and probably the book of Job; some have the form of eyewitness description, like the miracles in the Gospels; and some have the form of traditional, highly stylized and selective history, like 1 and 2 Chronicles. Finally, there seem to be some borderline cases, like Noah's ark and Jonah's fish, about which literary critics can intelligently disagree.

Know When to Interpret the Bible Literally vs. Symbolically
Modernists often interpret "turn the other cheek" literally and embrace

pacifism, but interpret the miracles symbolically and embrace naturalism. Why? Fundamentalists often interpret the "days" of creation literally and reject evolution, but interpret "This is my body" symbolically and reject the notion of the real presence in the Eucharist. Why? Are there any consistent and objective guidelines for literal versus symbolic interpretation?

The first and simplest answer is this: When the biblical author claims he saw something in the external world with his own eyes, or that someone else did and told him, then we are to interpret it literally. (Remember, we must distinguish *interpretation* from *belief*; to say we must interpret it literally is not to say we must believe it.) On the other hand, when a thing is not visible to the eye, we cannot interpret it literally. Here are three such cases.

1. Sometimes the object in question is by its nature invisible, like God or the soul.

2. Sometimes the author claims to have "seen" it only with the inner eye, in a vision or a dream.

3. And sometimes the author "made it up"; it is fiction, like a parable.

The line between literal and nonliteral is not simply the line between natural and supernatural, or miraculous. For one thing, miracles are visible, not invisible, at least in their effects, though not in their causes. For another thing, the natural-or-supernatural criterion is an external criterion taken from philosophy or theology, not an internal criterion taken from the form of the text itself.

We find important examples of symbolic language in the Bible's first and last books: the first three chapters of Genesis and the last eighteen chapters of Revelation. We find important examples of literal language in the miracle stories in both Old and New Testaments. But both fundamentalists and modernists seem prone to violate this simple guideline here, for theological rather than textual reasons. Fundamentalists have theological reasons for not wanting to interpret Genesis symbolically, and modernists have theological reasons for not wanting to interpret miracles literally. But these are both criteria of *belief*, not *interpretation*.

Another point both sides ignore or deny is that a given passage could be rightly interpreted *both* literally and symbolically. (See Aquinas's quotation on page 210.) For instance the church fathers often interpreted the exodus symbolically. The children of Israel symbolized the church, Moses symbolized Christ, the Red Sea symbolized death, the Promised Land symbolized heaven, the wilderness symbolized purgatory, Egypt symbolized the world, Pharaoh symbolized the Devil (Jesus calls him "the ruler of this world," in Jn 12:31; 14:30; and 16:11). But they also believed it really happened. They were signs, and a sign must first stand there in the real world, literally, in order for it to have a second meaning in what it points to beyond itself.

For some strange reason, both sides seem reluctant to see the dimensions of interpretation the other side sees. For instance, most fundamentalists (and also many traditionalists who do not call themselves fundamentalists) are reluctant to explore the rich symbolic parallels between Christ's resurrection and the many mythic symbols of dying and rising gods, life battling with death, life and death interpenetrating, and the like. Modernists, on the other hand, would be terrified to find out that the symbols they love really happened. Both sides see the symbolic-literal issue as either-or when in fact it can sometimes be both-and.

Language that is not literal can still be true, and accurate, and extremely important. It is an elementary but common mistake to confuse the nonliteral with the nontrue or the nonimportant. Some of the truest and most important things we ever say are nonliteral—for instance, "I was beside myself," "My heart bleeds for you," or "Mother has gone to her home in the sky."

Know Which Stories Are Historical

There are three possibilities here: literal history, nonliteral history or fiction (drama, parable, fable, myth—many forms). Modern history is usually literal. Traditional history is often nonliteral—for example, the speeches in Thucydides. Fictions are not historical at all.

Some biblical stories are literal history—for example, the court history of the kings of Israel. Some is nonliteral history—for example, the story of the Garden of Eden and the Fall in Genesis 3, and the creation story in Genesis 1 and 2. And some stories are literary fictions—for example, the parables, perhaps Jonah, probably Job.

Genesis 3 is the crucial example in the Old Testament. There are three reasons why the Fall can't be mere moral parable or fiction. First, if the Fall is not historical at all, then its effects—suffering and death—also are not historical. If sin is historical in its effects, it must be historical in its cause.

Second, if Adam's fall didn't really happen, then Christ's salvation need not have really happened either. Paul deliberately juxtaposes and parallels these two in Romans 6, calling Christ the New Man or Second Adam. If "the first Adam" was not historical, why must the second Adam be? If the disease is merely mythic, not historical, then the cure can be merely mythic, not historical.

Finally, if the Fall didn't really happen in history, then God rather than humanity is to blame for sin, for God must have created us as sinners rather than innocents. If there was never any real unfallen state, then we were sinners from the first moment of our creation, and God was wrong to declare everything he made "good."

So the story must be historical. But it need not be *literal*. The two trees, the talking snake and the magic fruit seem to be poetic symbols rather than literal, physical things.

The same is true of the creation poems in Genesis 1 and 2. Creation really happened; God really did design and create the universe and all its ordered species. But these chapters cannot possibly be literal eyewitness descriptions, for there were no eyes before there were humans. And God has no physical body or literal eyes. So this story must fit the middle category: historical but not literal.

It is not difficult to decide where most passages in the Bible are meant to fit. Until the modernists came along, nearly all readers, educated and uneducated alike, interpreted nearly all passages in nearly the same ways. God did not design the Bible to be a dark puzzle for bright scholars but to be a bright lamp for travelers through a dark world.

Historical vs. Religious Questions

Modernist theologians often make a point of sharply distinguishing religious questions from historical questions, and they claim that it is of no religious importance whether Moses really led Israel through the Red Sea or whether Jesus' body was really resurrected; the *religious* question is whether Israel saw God's hand in their history, and whether "Easter faith" was resurrected in the hearts of the disciples.

But this seems ridiculous and self-contradictory; it implies that God really led Israel by not really leading it, and that there was an "Easter faith" without an Easter. How could the disciples have experienced a "resurrection" of faith in Christ if there was no real resurrection of Christ? Their faith was not faith in faith, but faith in Christ. The point seems almost too obvious.

It is also misleading to suggest that historical questions are irrelevant to religion. This may be true for other religions, but not for orthodox Judaism or Christianity. Buddhism, for instance, is independent of the historical Buddha. Platonism is independent of Plato. But without a historical Christ there is no Christianity. There is no such thing as Christianism. There is no abstract theory which just happened to have been taught by a man named Jesus. The "theory" is essentially *about* him.

Rudolf Bultmann said that "if the bones of the dead Jesus were discovered tomorrow in a tomb in Palestine, all the essentials of Christianity would remain unchanged." He thought Christianity was essentially an ethic, a blueprint for a good life, rather than "good news." Paul, on the other hand, said that "if Christ has not been raised, then our preaching is in vain and your faith is in vain . . . and you are still in your sins" (1 Cor 15:14, 17).

Unlike all "isms," including Buddhism, Platonism and modernism, Christianity is not a set of timeless truths but a faith in a historical person and historical events, the most important of which were miraculous: God's creation, lawgiving and prophet-inspiring, and Christ's incarnation, death and resurrection.

For orthodox Jews, too, religious belief is tied to historical facts. If Moses didn't really receive the law from God and didn't really lead Israel out of Egypt, then God did not really show his wisdom and love to the Jews. Judaism is not an abstract philosophy of a God of wisdom and love, but a specific belief that God manifested himself in a specific way to a specific people.

Christian faith is even more pinned to history, for its object is not only the invisible Father but also the visible, incarnate Son. Subtract all the history and all that is left of Christianity is a general ethical concern—in other words, modernist theology—for example, Unitarianism, "the fatherhood of God, the brotherhood of man and the neighborhood of Boston."

In fact, there is little that is absolutely new or distinctive in Christian *ethics*. Most of the radical ethical sayings in the Sermon on the Mount can be found in the rabbinic tradition, Socrates, Buddha, Lao-tzu or Confucius. The main difference is that they are not connected with "the kingdom of God" as they are in Jesus' teaching. But this kingdom, though spiritual, is historical. It happens. Christ brings it about.

The distinctively Christian teachings are the beliefs about the historical Jesus. That is why the modernist is embarrassed by them: they stand in the way of a single world religion and an end to religious disagreement. This is a serious problem (see chap. 14), but we cannot fudge our data in order to solve a problem, however serious.

Historical Proximity

The closer a source is to the event it describes, the more likely it is to be reliable, all other things being equal. Modernists assume that the message of Jesus was misunderstood by his own disciples, by their disciples, by the church fathers and by nearly all Christians for so many centuries until contemporary scholars finally doped it out. It is exciting and flattering to think that you can decipher a puzzle which fooled centuries of the most profound, honest and passionate thinkers, but it is not likely—especially if your cultural assumptions, values, categories, and worldview are quite different from those of the people who wrote your data and are closest to it. Who is more likely to understand an ancient Etruscan?—another ancient Etruscan or a bookish twentieth-century museum curator?

There is an implicit but astonishing arrogance in the idea that all the apostles, all the church fathers and all the millions of ordinary Christians were fundamentally mistaken about Christ for nineteen centuries, and only a few theologians, sitting at their desks, in a very different culture, nineteen centuries later, finally understood him.

Contradictions in the Bible?

The most obvious and straightforward apologetical question about the Bible is this: Can we prove any parts of it false by showing either (1) that it contradicts itself or (2) that it contradicts some other known facts outside itself?

Pro- and anti-biblical controversialists have argued about thousands of examples for hundreds of years. We can only provide a few samples and summaries of this debate here.

Internal Contradictions?

Here are five diverse but typical examples of supposed self-contradictions, or internal contradictions, in the Bible.

1. In the Old Testament, the populations of peoples and armies are often estimated differently in different accounts of the same events.

2. One passage in Exodus says God parted the waters of the Red Sea, but another passage says a strong east wind did it by blowing all night.

3. The chronological order of events in the life of Jesus is not the same in any two of the four Gospels.

4. One account of the first Easter morning says the women who went to Jesus' empty tomb saw two angels, while another account says they saw one.

5. One account of Judas's death says he hanged himself; another says he fell down and his guts burst asunder.

Two things can be said in response to questions like these. First, a sense of perspective is needed. These are not contradictions in substance. The

Bible could well be infallible in all its teachings, its message, even while being fallible in incidental details like these. Second, even these minor contradictions can all be explained as only apparent. For instance:

1. Ancient histories rarely claimed exact numbers. Inexact estimates were common and expected. So were the use of symbolic numbers instead of literal numbers to describe real events.

2. First and second causes do not exclude each other: God parted the Red Sea by using a wind.

3. Only Luke, who was a Greek scientist (a doctor) claimed anything like exact chronological order (1:3).

4. Perhaps one woman saw one angel and the other saw two. "I saw two angels" is not contradicted by "I saw only one."

5. Perhaps Judas's noose broke!

Hundreds of other minor details like these can all be made to fit a consistent and trustworthy pattern. But we must not impose our modern standards of accuracy on material that was never intended to have it. It is bad literary criticism to exaggerate the importance of details for which the ancient author was in all likelihood unwilling to vouch.

Another, more serious and substantial, kind of supposed internal contradiction concerns the Bible's descriptions of God. For instance:

1. On the one hand, God is eternal and changeless. On the other hand, he acts and effects changes in time and history.

2. On the one hand, God is just and punishes the wicked. On the other hand, he is merciful and revokes the eternal punishment of those who repent of their wickedness.

3. On the one hand, God is absolutely one. On the other hand, Jesus the Son and the Holy Spirit are also called "God," so he is three.

4. On the one hand, God is awesome and terrifying. On the other hand, he is compassionate and comforting.

Philosophical theology addresses such apparent contradictions as these. (See also chap. 4 on God's nature.) Briefly:

1. God's essence is timeless but he effects changes in time. No creature can change another without itself being changed, but God can do this because he is purely active, not passively responding to the laws of creatures. Like a rower moving a boat through the water while remaining dry himself, God moves without being moved.

2. He does not compromise either his justice or his mercy. The two are reconciled on Calvary. Jesus gets the justice and we get the mercy.

3. He is one in being and essence, three in persons.

4. He is both awesome *and* loving. What is more awesome than love? The "fear" of awe and respect is quite compatible with mature love; and the other kind of fear, craven fear, is the response love can evoke in the soul of the immature. The same God of holy love can be comforting to a saint and threatening to a sinner.

This is a mere sample or surface-scratch of a plethora of similar issues that have arisen in nearly two millennia of philosophical theology. The intellectual credentials of biblical theology remain impressive and unrefuted.

External Contradictions?

Has archeology found nothing to invalidate the claims of the Bible? Nothing. In every single case where the two overlap, the results have been that some biblical claims have been proved, some rendered probable and none simply disproved by archeology. Claims have been made (e.g., that Jericho fell long before the Jews came) and then withdrawn (see B. G. Wood in *Biblical Archaeology Review,* March-April 1990; *The New York Times International,* February 2, 1990, A8). All claims of contradictions have suffered the fate of the walls of Jericho and come tumbling down. Problems remain. Why, for example, didn't the Jews leave any physical remains as evidence of the exodus? But these are unanswered questions, not disproofs.

In addition, no prophecy has ever been disproved, and many have been proved true by history. Jesus fulfilled at least thirty, perhaps as many as three hundred, specific and distinct Old Testament messianic prophecies. This was by chance?

The practice of modernist scholars of course is to date prophecies by their fulfillment. For instance, they argue that Isaiah must have been written after King Cyrus because Isaiah mentions Cyrus by name as the Gentile king who would release the captive Jews to return to Israel. Or that Matthew's Gospel must have been written after the destruction of Jerusalem (A.D. 70) because it predicts it in such detail (chap. 24). This is a typical case of reading a text in light of a prior theological assumption; namely, that miraculous prophecies cannot really occur, that we cannot know the future and that God cannot or will not tell us about it ahead of time. Worse, it implicitly assumes that the prophetic writers were liars and deceivers, for they clearly present their prophecies as predictive. If Jesus didn't really predict the destruction of Jerusalem forty years ahead of time, then Matthew is simply deceiving us when he says he did. Modernists are not usually plain spoken enough to say that.

One apparent external contradiction occurs in this same chapter, Matthew 24, in Jesus' apocalyptic prophecies in which he assures his disciples that "all these things" will come to pass in "this generation" (24:34). But the apocalypse, or end of the world, has not yet occurred.

Two explanations are possible. The first supposes that "this generation" is not meant biologically but spiritually and world-historically; that is, this era, this age. A second explanation is that the prophecies of the destruction of Jerusalem and the prophecies of the end of the world are mixed together in this chapter. Perhaps one is meant as a symbol and forewarning of the other; or perhaps Matthew or a later editor just juxtaposed two discourses. The destruction of Jerusalem in A.D. 70 *did* happen in the lifetime of Jesus' hearers.

The most familiar cases of apparent external contradictions are between the Bible and science. This can take three different forms:

1. A general, sweeping statement that "science contradicts religion." This is very vague and unscientific. Which science? Which idea? Is that idea a proven fact? What proves it? Which statement in the Bible does it contradict? Is the statement properly interpreted? Once these specific questions are asked, the general challenge dissipates like fog under sunlight.

2. The supposed contradiction between biblical miracles and science. This is dealt with in chapter five.

3. Specific contradictions such as:

a. Language about a flat earth. This is indeed unscientific, but so is our ordinary language—like "sunrise." When we say the sun "rose," we do not mean we subscribe to the pre-Copernican view that the sun revolves around the earth. Common sense should tell us not to interpret ordinary language as a claim to scientific accuracy.

b. Creation vs. evolution. Before comparing these two ideas we must distinguish three meanings that "evolution" can have.

First, it can mean simply a theory about *what* happened— more complex species appeared on earth—and *when*, as shown by the fossil record. Second, it can mean a theory about *how* this happened: by "natural selection," "the survival of the fittest." Third, it can mean the *absence* of a divine design, as distinct from God *using* natural selection. This third sense is not scientific at all, but philosophical and theological. One can accept evolution in sense 1 but not 2, or 1 and 2 but not 3. There is certainly a contradiction between the Bible and evolution in sense 3. But evolution in sense 3 is not a scientific theory at all.

There are serious scientific problems with evolution in sense 2 and even in sense 1, but neither sense need contradict the Bible. The scientific problems include an absence of transitional forms in the fossil record, the suddenness of the appearance of new species, and the total absence of any empirical evidence for the inheritance of environmentally acquired characteristics, except *within* a species (e.g., Darwin's finches). In other words, there is no convincing empirical evidence of one species' evolving into another. But even if they did, there seems to us to be no contradiction at all between this theory of evolution and the Bible.

Those who believe there are such contradictions usually point to the following two: (1) Were other species *created* supernaturally by God, or did they evolve *naturally* by natural selection? and (2) What about us? Are we made in the image of King Kong or King God? Was Adam the son of an ape or the son of God? Let's look briefly at these two "pressure points" of the creation-evolution controversy.

Concerning the first issue, there is no logical contradiction between the Bible's claim that "in the beginning God created the heavens and the earth" (Gen 1:1) and the claim that once the earth was here, species evolved by natural selection. Science is like the study of the inner ecology of a fishbowl; the Bible is like a letter from the person who set up the fishbowl. Far from being logically exclusive, the two ideas of creation and evolution easily include each other, or at least suggest each other. On the one hand, the Bible does not say that God "created" (*barā*') each species by a separate act, but that he said, "*Let the earth bring forth* living creatures" (Gen 1:24). On the other hand, a theory of evolution that confines itself to empirical science does not claim to know whether or not there is a divine Designer behind these natural forces. But surely such an elegant and ordered design strongly suggests a cosmic Designer.

As to the second concern, there is also no logical contradiction between the Bible's claim that the human soul (the "image of God") is "breathed" ("spirited") into us from God, and evolution's claim that our body evolved from lower forms. Genesis 2:7 even suggests just such a double origin.

Like the controversy between the old, Ptolemaic, geocentric astronomy and the new Copernican, heliocentric astronomy centuries ago, the current controversy in biology between the "special creationists" and "evolutionists" is one that poses no real threat to theologians. But like that earlier controversy, this one has spawned a double misunderstanding. On the one hand, many theologians have misused the Bible to try to establish or disestablish a scientific theory in a most unscientific way. On the other hand, many scientists have misused a theory in science to try to discredit the Bible in a most unphilosophical way. Both hold onto their extraterritorial theories with fanatical tenacity. Many evolutionists are just as "zealous" and "fundamentalistic" as any fundamentalist. See Phillip Johnson's *Darwin on Trial* for proof of that claim. (See also our chap. 5.)

All these are a mere sampling of supposed biblical contradictions, internal and external. For both, the prosecution has been unable to prove the prisoner on trial guilty of a single offense. What other book in history with one-tenth the vulnerable claims of the Bible can stand up as well?

A Personal Postscript

Some readers may wonder why so much space has been devoted to attacking modernism in a book on basic Christian apologetics. The reason is given in section 2 on the importance of the issue. Modernists have undermined faith far more effectively than atheists. The wolves in sheep's clothing have carried away many more sheep than the honest wolves.

The reason for attacking modernism more polemically than atheism is ultimately Jesus. Jesus had only gentle words for honest skeptics and doubters like Thomas, but horribly hard words for religious teachers who caused the little ones who believed in him to stumble—something about millstones . . .

For Jesus did not regard people as theological partisans, but as lambs for whom the Good Shepherd came to die. He was as cool as an Oxford debater when he was attacked by the Pharisees, but mad as a mother bear when he saw his children's souls hurt by them. We do not think it a safe bet that he has a more "mature," "nuanced" and "sophisticated" attitude today.

Questions for Discussion

1. Of the three issues distinguished—the Bible, miracles and the resurrection—which should logically come first? Why? Is any alternative order possible?

2. The chapter attacks the demythologizers on three grounds: logically, psychologically and textually. How are these three critiques connected? How fair are they? Why?

3. How could a fundamentalist answer the argument in section three against his position? How could a modernist?

4. Does our view that we ought not to begin with the authority, inspiration or infallibility of Scripture, or argue from it, necessarily entail a lower view of Scripture than that of fundamentalists? Why or why not?

5. Do you have any objection to any of the eight principles of scriptural interpretation (pp. 207-215)? Evaluate some examples of the practice of scriptural interpre-

tation that you are familiar with (from theology or biblical studies classes) by these eight principles.

6. What other apparent contradictions in the Bible do you know of besides the examples mentioned (p. 215)? How might they be explained?

7. Do you think an orthodox Christian can admit errors of a nonreligious kind in the Bible? Why or why not?

8. Evaluate this chapter's solution to the creation-evolution controversy.

9. Evaluate the attack on modernism (p. 220).

Part 5
GOD & GLORY

Outline of Chapter 10
Life After Death

Preliminary overview: six theories

Refutation of four objections against immortality

Basic assumptions about the human person

Twenty-five positive arguments for life after death

☐ Arguments from authority

    1. The argument from consensus

    2. The argument from the sages

    3. The argument from the authority of Jesus

☐ Arguments from reason

  contemplating nature

    4. The argument from the conservation of energy

    5. The argument from evolution

  contemplating itself

    6. Primitive man's argument from dead cow

    7. The argument from magic

    8. Plato's argument from the soul's survival of its diseases

    9. The argument from the soul's simplicity

    10. The argument from the soul's power to objectify the body

    10A. The argument from being vs. having

    11. The argument from two immaterial operations

    12. The antimaterialist self-contradiction argument

  contemplating God

    13. The argument from God's justice

    14. The argument from God's creativity

    15. The argument from God's love

☐ Arguments from experience

  ordinary experience

    16. The argument from ultimate justice

    17. The argument from "the meaning of life"

    18. Pascal's Wager

    19. The argument from *Sehnsucht* ("longing")

20. The argument from presence
21. The argument from love

extraordinary experience

22. The argument from postmortem presence
23. The argument from near-death experiences
24. The argument from mystical experience
25. The argument from Christ's resurrection

CHAPTER 10
Life
After Death

THE HUMAN RACE HAS COME UP WITH SIX BASIC THEORIES ABOUT WHAT happens to us when we die.

1. Materialism: Nothing survives. Death ends all of me. Seldom held before the eighteenth century, materialism is now a strong minority view in industrialized nations. It is the natural accompaniment of atheism.

2. Paganism: A vague, shadowy semiself or ghost survives and goes to the place of the dead, the dark, gloomy Underworld. This is the standard pagan belief. Traces of it can be found even in the Old Testament Jewish notion of *sheol.* The "ghost" that survives is less alive, less substantial, less real than the flesh and blood organism now living. It is something like a "ghost image" on a TV set: a pale copy of the lost original.

3. Reincarnation: The individual soul survives and is reincarnated into another body. Reincarnation is usually connected with the next belief, pantheism, by the notion of karma: that after the soul has fulfilled its destiny, and learned its lessons and become sufficiently enlightened, it reverts to a divine status or is absorbed into (or realizes its timeless identity with) the divine All.

4. Pantheism: Death changes nothing, for what survives death is the same as what was real before death: only the one, changeless, eternal, perfect, spiritual, divine, all-inclusive Reality, sometimes called by a name ("Brahman") and sometimes not (as in Buddhism). In this view—that of Eastern mysticism—all separateness, including time, is an illusion. Therefore, in this view, the very question of what happens after death is mistaken. The question is not solved but dissolved.

5. Immortality: The individual soul survives death, but not the body. This soul eventually reaches its eternal destiny of heaven or hell, perhaps through intermediate stages, perhaps through reincarnation. But what survives is an individual, bodiless spirit. This is Platonism, often confused with Christianity.

6. Resurrection: At death, the soul separates from the body and is reunited at the end of the world to its new, immortal, resurrected body by a divine miracle. This is the Christian view. This view, the supernatural resurrection of the body rather than the natural immortality of the soul alone, is the only version of life after death in Scripture. It is dimly prophesied and hoped for in the Old Testament, but clearly revealed in the New.

For both (5) and (6), the individual soul survives bodily death. That is the issue we shall argue here. We do not take the time to argue against paganism (2) or reincarnation (3) or pantheism (4) here, but only against modern materialism (1), since that is the source of most of the philosophical arguments against immortality in our culture. (But see also page 260 for a critique of reincarnation.)

We divide our argumentation into seven basic subdivisions, which are placed in an ascending order of compelling force. (See the chapter outline.) The refutation of objections merely makes life after death *possible.* The arguments from authority (i.e., secondhand) are weaker than arguments from reason (i.e., firsthand) because they have an extra link, the trustworthiness of the authority. Within arguments from reason, reason finds better reasons in itself than in nature and better reasons in God than in itself. Arguments from experience are even more convincing and direct than arguments from reason. And within experience, some classes of people have special experiences which give them special certainty.

Refutation of Four Objections Against Immortality
Some objections are frequently raised against the possibility of life after death. Meeting them does not by itself make the case *for* immortality, but it does show that the case *against* immortality has not been successfully made. And that can be helpful. These objections are often troubling and distracting; they can spoil our appreciation of the positive case for life after death. We therefore consider them here.

Objection 1:
If there is to be personal survival after death, then a personal self must live beyond the destruction of the body. But a surviving self has got to be in some way self-conscious, and without a brain there can be no self-consciousness. At death the brain

ceases to function and, in a very short time, ceases altogether to be. So there can be no survival of bodily death.

The premise "without a brain there can be no self-consciousness" is ambiguous. It can mean that there is a causal relation between the brain and the conscious self or that the two are in some way identical.

Suppose there is a causal relation between the brain and the conscious self. This relation can be of at least two kinds. (1) The self might *interact* with the brain in order to bring about the activities and experiences of self-consciousness, or (2) the material brain might, by its motions, *produce* the self and all its mental contents.

If (1) is true, it would not follow that nothing survives bodily death. What would not survive is the instrument by which the self gains access to the material world and builds up a wealth of human experience. That is no minor loss. But neither does it exclude the possibility of life after death. Therefore, in order for this first objection to work, it must assume the truth of materialism. Either the self is *identical* with the material brain and its motions, or the self is wholly *produced* by them (2).

Some think that the recent and spectacular successes of neuroscience show that materialism is obviously true. How, after all, do scientists investigate the mind except by investigating the brain? So materialism would seem to be favored, even demanded, by modern science.

But this is false. Neurobiology is an empirical science and therefore must deal with material reality. This means it must deal with the material factors involved in human intelligence. It must abstract from any factors not capable of empirical investigation. This does not mean that such factors do not exist; in other words, it does not mean that materialism is true. Mathematics is also a science. It abstracts from what cannot be quantitatively considered. But this does not mean that all things are quantities or are able to be quantified, or that qualities are not also real.

Granted, there are many neuroscientists who are also materialists, but their materialism is not an essential component of their science. When they profess materialism, they are really making the claim that in matters relating to thought and intellect there is nothing for their science to abstract from. That is a philosophical claim, not a scientific one. It also happens to be false for the following reasons.

1. Whatever is material is limited to this region of space and time. It is always here (or there) and now (or then). It can never be in many places at the same time, and can never come to be in one place without leaving another. It follows that if thought is just a motion of matter, it must have spatial and temporal limits—the spatial limits of the matter, the temporal limits of the movement. But the content of our thinking is not limited in this way. For example, we think certain universal notions like *equality* and *truth* which do not, and cannot, take up space and time; which exist in many minds at once; and which come to be thought by some minds without ceasing to be thought by others. This means that whatever our thinking is, it cannot be captured in terms proper to the description of material reality, and therefore, of the brain.

2. We spoke of "our" thinking, but what, according to materialist doctrine, are "we"? We are not mere series of discrete thoughts. A self-consciousness unites these thoughts and makes them all *mine*. We are aware of many things at once—many colors, several sounds, countless feelings. But this does not result in a heap of awarenesses. There is *an* awareness of many things at once: my own self-conscious awareness. How can materialism account for self-consciousness? For the uniting of many parts into a single unified experience? It seems impossible. For if materialism were true, the awareness of the self would be merely one more motion among the many countless ones making up the brain. Far from uniting the other motions of matter, it would seem to add to their number.

Nor does it help to argue that these motions are all motions of *my* brain. For if materialism is true, there is no self whose material brain this is. The self just *is* these countless bits of matter "we" (i.e., countless bits of matter) call the brain.

Some materialists have recognized this problem. They have said that self-consciousness is produced by a self-scanning mechanism in the brain. But the scanning is still a discrete motion. If the self is the scanning, there will be as many selves as acts of scanning. Yet the notion of scanning was brought forward to account in material terms for a single self.

Could the single scanning mechanism, and not its many acts of scanning, be the self? Not really. For the self would be composed of countless bits of matter, bits replaced by countless others many times over. The unity of the self would vanish once again.

Philosophers sometimes laugh at Descartes's suggestion that the pineal gland is the point of contact between the self-conscious subject and the material brain. But it is surely no less comically absurd to hold that a material thing *like* the pineal gland (the so-called self-scanning mechanism) *is* the self-conscious subject.

3. Materialists claim that their doctrine is *true*. They expect us to consider their arguments; they want us to agree with their conclusions. But the

system of nature their doctrine affirms is a closed one: a self-sufficient series of material causes and effects. Is there room in such a system for rational argument? It seems not.

Think of a question to be considered. That question, the consideration of it, and the judgment finally rendered, are all, if materialism is true, the necessary (and, perhaps, partly random) result of the play of material forces: forces stretching back to the beginning of the universe itself. Thus the judgment that something (e.g., materialism) is true, and the judgment that it is false are both the result of physical causes. Both of them are equally real; both of them equally *necessary*. The same holds for the reflection preceding those judgments and for the discussion which might follow that reflection. The same holds for all reflection, each discussion, every judgment. But this means that the conditions for rational judgment have been eliminated. To judge means to be *free* to consider or weigh the merits of the thing we judge; no judge in court, for example, can ever be part of the group of prisoners on trial. But if materialism is true, there can be no freedom to weigh or to consider, and therefore no real act of judgment.

Materialists want us to judge that their doctrine is true. And yet their doctrine eliminates the possibility of making any true judgments at all. In other words, if materialism is true, it cannot be judged to be true—by anyone, including materialists. But we *are* capable of making real judgments about the truth of things (you are weighing the arguments in this book, after all). Therefore materialism is false. (For further discussion, see argument 12 for immortality; and chapter 3, argument 10, for the existence of God.)

4. Some writers retreat from an extreme form of materialism. Thought, they say, is not itself a motion of the brain, but is wholly produced by it (position 2 above)—as the creak of rusty machinery is not itself the rust or the iron, but is produced by them. This suggestion, however, like the rusty machinery that illustrates it, will not work. It tries to make concessions to the lived experience of being a self. But since it admits that matter alone is the total cause of mind, it must deny that mind can influence matter. And yet mind's influencing matter is one of the most vivid parts of the lived experience that this doctrine (whose technical name is *epiphenomenalism*) was brought forward in the first place to salvage.

Objection 2:

Even if materialism is false, there may still be no possibility of surviving bodily death. For the self gains access to the world of experience through the brain. We use the brain for sensing; we also use it for thinking. These are basic human experiences.

But death, in robbing us of the brain, robs us of the means by which we experience.
Now we human persons are centers of self-conscious experience. If what survives
death can in no way experience, then "we" do not survive death.

Reply: There is much truth in this objection. You need no scientific exper-
tise to notice the connection between the functioning of the brain and the
quality of our experience. Sensation is part of the way we humans come
to know about things, to live our lives in this world. And without the body,
with its central nervous system, we could have no sensations. Therefore,
after bodily death, the means by which we experienced the material world
and acted in it is removed. All this we grant. Does it entail that what survives
death could in no way have self-conscious experiences? By no means.

1. During our lifetime, the body gives us access to the world of human
living. It is here that we develop morally and intellectually; here that we
make choices and set our will toward the good—or away from it. Persons
who have lived on this earth for a certain time, when they face death, have
very definite moral and intellectual qualities. What they have known and
done and desired—all these are part of what they are. Death robs us of the
means for continuing to have such experiences, but that does not mean we
must lack consciousness of the kind of self such experience helped to
shape—consciousness, in other words, of what we are. This sort of self-
presence would not be exactly like the kind of experience we had of ourselves here on earth, in the body. That goes without saying. But our question was: Is *all* self-conscious experience apart from the body impossible?
This has not been shown.

2. Christians believe in a special connection between themselves and
their bodies. Without their bodies they are not really complete. Christians
believe also that God made them to live with him forever, not as disembodied souls, but in the glorified body raised up in the resurrection on the
last day. We have something to say elsewhere about the resurrection, but
here we should note that what you believe about life after death depends
very much on what you believe about God. If God exists, and if God has
destined us for eternal life, then there is really no problem about the means
for self-conscious experience. God will provide them. At the death of the
body and before the general resurrection, God is fully capable of providing
the means by which we enjoy his presence. No doubt, as we have said
before, this will be very unlike the way we now experience. We may even
find it frightening to think about. But this is beside the point. What is
strange and unfamiliar is not for that reason impossible. Thus this second
objection fails.

Objection 3:

What we mean by "person" involves embodiment. So no person can survive bodily death.

Reply: If "we" is shorthand for "we materialists," then the objection begs the question. After all, some of us believe in a personal God and in angels. What "we" mean by "person," therefore, does not always involve embodiment.

But narrow the focus a little. For "person" write "human person." Do we human persons mean by "human person" something that involves embodiment? Many would answer yes, in a sense, but not in a sense which excludes the possibility of life (or a different embodiment) after death. Many believe that for any human being there was or is a time when life was lived in the body. That does not seem controversial. Christians (and some others) believe that there will again be such a time. What "we" mean by human person allows for this possibility and cannot therefore be a reason to declare it impossible.

Objection 4:

If life after death is to have real personal meaning, each disembodied soul must have its own identity. There must be some way in which any two souls can be distinguished. But we use bodily criteria to identify (and so to distinguish) human persons, and these criteria cannot apply to a disembodied soul. Therefore we have no means of distinguishing one disembodied soul from another. Now if disembodied souls cannot be distinguished, they cannot be identified. Since personal identity is essential to life after death, the question is: Can there be such a life? The problem of identifying disembodied souls casts serious doubt on its possibility.

Reply: Granted, here on earth we identify other living human persons by means of bodily criteria—the style of their hair, for example, or the cut of their clothing. And granted, these criteria could not be used to identify disembodied souls. But what follows from this? Merely that we cannot identify disembodied souls as we now identify living human beings. It does not follow that these souls cannot be identified or that they have no identity. The objection seems to demand that we provide bodily criteria to identify or distinguish disembodied souls. The demand is absurdly unfair. The criteria by which we have habitually identified living human persons could not be applied in altered circumstances—for example, after the death of the body. Everyone admits that. But are these criteria the only ones possible? If the objection assumes this, then it sorely begs the question. It must demonstrate that no others are possible. And of course it cannot show this, for even now, while we live on earth, criteria other than bodily ones are involved in identifying persons.

Think of your own case. You have a certain height and weight. You can identify yourself in a photograph or a mirror, but you would never confuse these ways of identifying yourself—or the material conditions they require—with your own personal identity. You are not your height or weight, or the shape of your nose, or the color and style of your hair. These things can change drastically, but you would remain the same person—how else could you recognize that some change had occurred? "I don't recognize myself!" you might say, when a mirror is held up before you, though you know very well you are the same person whose appearance, just a short time ago, was so different. How do you know this? Not because of any sensible attributes. These, we are now imagining, have been radically altered.

How do you know that this radically altered appearance belongs to you? Surely because of a self-consciousness that retains its identity throughout these bodily changes, which makes memory possible, which holds together the varied fabric of sensible experience and makes it all one, makes it *yours*. Here is the most radical center of personal identity. It cannot be understood in bodily or material terms, but it is very real. Without it, we could make no use of bodily criteria to identify anyone or anything; for without it, there could be no acts of knowledge and, therefore, no acts of recognition. That much is clear. It is not clear how souls are individuated, how God identifies them, or how they can identify and communicate with each other. But we have no need to know these things. We know that we are just the persons we are. We know that the self-identity allowing this knowledge is not describable in material terms and therefore cannot be understood that way. We know, in other words, enough to refute the present objection.

Basic Assumptions About the Human Person

Peeking out from behind our criticisms of the arguments against immortality were certain assumptions about what it means to be a human person. We think it important, before continuing our discussion of the soul, to be more explicit about them. We do not want to mislead anyone about the point of the positive arguments for immortality. Some might take them to imply that human beings are essentially immaterial souls or disembodied spirits. But while a good pagan may hold that view, a good (i.e., orthodox) Christian certainly cannot.

Christians believe that the human person is a mysterious unity of matter and spirit. There is a part of us that is extended in three dimensions and takes up space; this we call "matter." But there is another facet of the unity we are which cannot be thought of in that way; this is the part of us we call "spirit." Scripture says that God breathed life into lifeless matter, and that image of breath and life is most appropriate to the nature of spiritual being. The human spirit animates matter, gives it vital energy and gathers it into a living organic unity. That is what God created it to do. Thus Christians believe that a human spirit exists for a body; it was made to exist in matter as its life-giving principle. This means that all those parts of human life that seem most essentially spiritual, like knowing and choosing, also involve the body; the spirit experiences *through* the body. And so human life involves a most intimate relation between these two sides of our being: matter needs spirit to bind it into a functioning unity; spirit needs matter to release its potential for pursuing and enjoying all the goods, moral and intellectual, proper to a human life.

That is why Christians look forward to the resurrection of the body. It is part of their belief that the soul without the body is incomplete; that the full and complete person is present on the last day when matter and spirit, transformed and redeemed, are joined together in the resurrection of the just.

Twenty-five Positive Arguments for Life After Death
Arguments from Authority
Arguments from authority (1-3) are the weakest kind of arguments, according to a maxim of medieval philosophers. Nevertheless they *are* arguments, and we all use them more frequently than any other kind. Nine out of ten things we believe, we believe because we trust the authority that assured us of their truth: textbooks, parents, teachers, "experts," "society." When the authority is only human, and therefore fallible, the argument can only amount to a probability or a clue, not a certainty or a proof.

1. The Argument from Consensus
The argument from consensus consults authority quantitatively—what G. K. Chesterton called "the democracy of the dead," extending the franchise to all who have ever lived. Nearly all cultures and the vast majority of all individuals who have ever lived have voted for life after death, have believed in life after death. Children naturally and spontaneously believe it unless conditioned out of it; they do not have to be conditioned into it. This at least puts the onus of proof on the minority of doubters. For although it is not true that "forty million Frenchmen can't be wrong," it is less likely than forty Frenchmen being wrong.

The formal argument is:

1. What the vast majority believe is probably true.
2. The vast majority believe in life after death.
3. Therefore life after death is probably true.

A slightly different version of the argument challenges the doubter to explain the origin of the nearly universal consensus in favor of life after death. How could a mere mortal come up with the idea of immortality? Answers, of course, are given: fear, wishful thinking, social conditioning, religious indoctrination. But each of these answers could be criticized as having fatal weaknesses. For instance, the "social indoctrination" answer merely passes the buck back a step without answering the question where the belief originated. And if fear prevented us from believing in final annihilation, why did it not prevent us from believing in something much more fearsome, namely hell?

2. The Argument from the Sages

This second argument, though also only probable, is stronger than the first because it appeals to quality rather than quantity: nearly all the sages, the wise, have believed in life after death.

We must not, of course, answer the challenge "How do you know they were wise?" by saying, "Because they believed in life after death"; that would be begging the question pure and simple. But thinkers considered wise for other reasons have also believed in life after death. It seems unlikely that this one belief should be the exception to their wisdom.

When we put together the authority of Moses (cf. Mt 17:3), Job (19:25-27), Socrates, Plato, Aristotle, Plotinus, Zoroaster, Akhenaton, *Gilgamesh*, Lao-tzu, Confucius, Buddha, Ramanuja, Krishna, Muhammad, Maimonides, Avicenna, Augustine, Aquinas and Jesus, we have a pretty impressive team—certainly to be favored over the likes of Epicurus, Lucretius, Machiavelli, Hobbes, LaMettrie, Voltaire, Comte, Marx, Sartre and Bertrand Russell.

The formal argument goes like this:

1. What the sages believe is probably true.
2. The sages believe in life after death.
3. Therefore life after death is probably true.

3. The Argument from the Authority of Jesus

This argument does not assume Jesus' divinity or infallibility, only that he was a wise, great and reliable human teacher. Jesus' belief in life after death was central and crucial to all his teaching—if the remarkably well-preserved first-century records are to be trusted more than the remarkably groundless speculations of twentieth-century revisionists. The Sermon on the Mount, for example, and especially the Beatitudes, refer repeatedly to "the kingdom of heaven" as the justification, reason and foundation for Jesus' norms and counsels about how to live in this world.

For the sake of variety, we could formulate this argument disjunctively:

1. Either life after death exists or Jesus was fundamentally and foolishly mistaken.

2. It is very unlikely that Jesus was fundamentally and foolishly mistaken.

3. Therefore it is very likely that life after death exists.

The argument is stronger than 2 for the same reason 2 is stronger than 1. The first appeals to mere quantity, the second to a mixture of quantity and quality *("nearly all* the sages have believed"), and the third to pure quality, to one preeminent sage.

Arguments from Reason
4. The Argument from the Conservation of Energy
Arguments from reason (4-15) are stronger than arguments from human authority. But the arguments from reason contemplating nature are the weakest of the arguments from reason because nature offers only clues and probabilities, not certainty, about life after death.

The principle of the conservation of energy states that physical energy is never created or destroyed. (This does not prove that energy *cannot* be created or destroyed, only that it is never observed to be created or destroyed.) Now the immortality of the soul seems to be the spiritual equivalent of the conservation of energy. If even matter is immortal, why not *(a fortiori)* spirit?

Here is the formal argument:

1. Matter is never destroyed, only transformed.

2. It is more likely that spirit is not destroyed than that matter is not.

3. Therefore it is very likely that spirit is not destroyed.

The weakness of the argument is that it does not provide evidence for *individual* immortality. For the argument is based on an analogy with matter, and individual material things are not immortal, only matter in general. Yet the argument does seem to be at least probable evidence against simple annihilation. It may not be evidence for theories 4 or 5 (pp. 227-28) but it is evidence against theory 1.

5. The Argument from Evolution

Like the previous arguments, this is not a proof, but a strong clue, with much potential for instinctive, intuitive appeal.

It seems to us ironic that evolution has usually been seen as a threat to Christianity rather than a reinforcement, for the fossil record strongly suggests a design and purposive direction in nature, with the same order we find in the Genesis account—progress from simple to complex. Of this progress human consciousness is the vanguard, or front line, or point. Even though it is only a theory, not a fact, and even though the theory is saddled with serious difficulties (see p. 219), its general outline of a planetary progress from less to more conscious and complex organisms remains clear and strong.

Now if death ends all for us, then human consciousness is Mother Nature's cosmic abortion. If this intuitive argument were put into a logical structure, making clear its assumptions, it would look something like this:

1. Evolution reveals a natural design and purpose in the cosmos, the point of which is the attainment of human consciousness. (This is intuitively obvious to minds without materialistic premises.)

2. But natural designs and purposes are not in vain. (Another intuitively obvious premise, though challenged extensively by modern philosophers.)

3. Therefore human consciousness is not in vain.

4. But if consciousness dies forever, it is in vain (the "cosmic abortion"). Why would Nature go to all that trouble to conceive us only to kill us?

5. Therefore that consciousness does not die forever. Death is not the last word.

6. Primitive Man's Argument from Dead Cow

This is the first and weakest of a group of arguments whose data come not from reason contemplating nature but from reason contemplating itself. Surely this is the most obvious place for reason to look for evidence. But the looking requires not just reasoning plus sensation, but insight. Sheer empiricists, who rely only on out-sight, not in-sight—that is, materialists—cut themselves off from access to the relevant data a priori. Hardly an open-minded, rational, scientific thing to do!

Let us imagine a likely scenario about how the primitive mind would reason. Remember, *primitive* does not necessarily mean *stupid*, only *early*—unless you tell the truth by the clock or the calendar.

Data: Primitive Man has two cows. One dies.

Question: What is the difference now between Dead Cow and Live Cow?

The difference is so great that Primitive Man needs two different words now to designate these two different cows—*live* and *dead*. *Dead*, of course, means lacking what *live has;* but what is that? What makes Live Cow alive?

Method: Primitive Man hits upon a brilliantly simple method for finding the answer, one that probably would not have occurred to a philosopher: he looks at his data! There appears to be no material difference (e.g., in size or weight or color, between the two cows). Yet something is clearly missing. What is it? What is "life"?

Empirical aspect of the answer: The answer is obvious to any observer whose head is not yet in the clouds of competing theories: Life is what makes Live Cow *breathe*. (The word for "life," or "soul," is the same word for "breath" in many ancient languages.) This does not mean that life is air, but the power to move it through the lungs. There is still air in Dead Cow's lungs, but not breath. Life comes to the body from the soul, "the breath of life."

Clarification of terms: The term *soul* can mean at least three different but related things: (1) the principle or source of life for a living body, (2) the principle of consciousness or (3) the principle of self-consciousness, or personality. This argument uses soul in the first, simplest sense. In this sense, humans, animals, even plants have some sort of soul.

Corollary: Primitive Man has discovered that life is not a material thing, like an organ. It is the life *of* the organs, the life of the body. It is not something that lives but something *by* which we live.

Inference: If life (soul) is not something that lives, then it also cannot die, at least not as bodies die. Bodies die by the removal of life (soul); but soul cannot die by the removal of soul. Soul cannot lose soul. Bodies die because they have life on loan. Soul does not have life on loan. Soul does not *have* life, soul *is* life, or at least *gives* life, while body *gets* it. (This is essentially Plato's argument in the *Phaedo*, which is a more abstract and sophisticated version of Primitive Man's Argument from Dead Cow.)

In evaluating this argument, we must point to two serious weaknesses:

1. If it proves the soul's immortality, it proves either too much or too little. Too much if every individual soul is immortal, for every animal and plant has a soul in sense 1 (life). Too little if it is only soul in general rather than individual soul that survives Dead Cow's death, for the same may then apply to human death: no individual immortality, but only general immortality.

2. Even if the soul cannot die as the body dies, it may die in another way. If the body has life on loan from the soul, the soul may, in turn, have it on loan from another, higher source, and thus be able to lose it. This is in fact the biblical view—that God alone is by nature immortal (1 Tim 1:17; 6:16), and that human souls can die (spiritually in hell: Mt 10:28; Rev 2:11).

Of what apologetic use, then, is the argument? For one thing, it shows how natural and obvious a nonmaterialistic worldview is. And once materialism is disposed of, the way is open for stronger arguments for immortality. For another thing, the argument does validly reach its conclusions, weak as they may be for purposes of demonstrating *human* immortality. It is a clue to higher things. We must not despise such arguments; we learn to crawl before we learn to walk or run.

7. The Argument from Magic

The conclusion of this argument is that there exists in us an immaterial soul which, since it is not made of matter, need not be subject to the laws of matter, including mortality. The evidence for this conclusion is so pervasive and obvious that we miss it by taking it for granted. It is the daily and hourly experience of real magic, the power of mind over matter. For instance, we can levitate. That is, we can command our bodies to rise up into the air contrary to the laws of physics—the law of gravity—by sheer thought and will power. We also have magic wands which can levitate other heavy objects if we touch them with our wand and will them to levitate. The self-levitation is called jumping and the magic wands are called arms.

This is no trick. If there were no mind or will behind my legs and arms, my muscles and nerves, I would not be able to jump or lift things. When my body dies, its limbs can no longer move, even though the muscles and nerves remain. When I die, my body reverts to obedience to merely physical laws, like a sword dropped by a mortally wounded swordsman.

The evidence is so obvious that one wonders who the real "primitive" is: the savage who believes in spirits or the modern materialist who does not, and who cannot understand the difference between mind and brain, spirit and matter, active programmer and passive program, mover and moved.

The formal argument is this:

1. We can do real magic.
2. What can do real magic is more than matter.
3. What is more than matter is impervious to bodily death.
4. Therefore something in us is impervious to bodily death.

8. Plato's Argument from the Soul's Survival of Its Diseases

We have chosen to merely edit and rearrange Plato's own words, from book 10 of the *Republic*, as follows:

Preliminary definitions:

1. Evil: "all that which destroys and corrupts."

2. Proper or intrinsic or natural evil: "Each thing has its evil . . . for instance ophthalmia for the eye, and disease for the whole body, mildew for corn and for wood, rust for iron."

3. The effects of evil: "The natural evil of each thing . . . destroys it."

4. Corollary of (3): "and if this does not destroy it, nothing else can,

    a. for I don't suppose good can ever destroy anything,

    b. nor can what is neither good nor evil,

    c. and it is certainly unreasonable . . . that the evil of something else would destroy anything when its own evil does not."

Major Premise: "Then if we find something in existence which has its own evil but which can only do it harm yet cannot dissolve or destroy it, we shall know at once that there is no destruction for such a nature."

Minor Premise: "The soul has something which makes it evil . . . injustice, intemperance, cowardice, ignorance. Now does any one of these dissolve and destroy it?"

Conclusion: "Then, since it is not destroyed by any evil at all, neither its own evil nor foreign evil, it is clear that the soul must of necessity be . . . immortal."

In other words,

1. If the soul is destructible, it must be destroyed either by:

    a. its own intrinsic evils, or

    b. the evils of another thing, or

    c. something that is not evil.

2. But the soul is not destroyed either by:

    a. its own intrinsic evils (intellectual and moral vices), or

    b. *a fortiori,* the evils of something other than itself (the body), or

    c. something that is not evil at all; for only evil destroys.

3. Therefore the soul is not destructible.

This argument appears roundabout and complex at first, but a careful reading will probably reveal its intuitive point. It is for that point that we have included it, despite its rational weakness.

That weakness consists largely in the inconclusiveness of its conclusion. For even if souls cannot be destroyed by bodily evils, they may be destroyed by other things, either external (God or evil spirits) or internal (soul-diseases other than vice and ignorance, if there are such things). The argument does show, however, that it is unreasonable to think that the soul is destroyed by the evil of something other and less than itself. And if, as most people believe, the body is something other than and less than the soul, then this argument shows that the soul does not die just because the body dies.

9. The Argument from the Soul's Simplicity

Major premise: What is not composed cannot be decomposed. Whatever is composed of parts can be decomposed into its parts: a molecule into atoms, a cell into molecules, an organ into cells, a body into organs, a person into body and soul. What is not composed of parts cannot be taken apart.

Minor premise: The soul is not composed of parts. It has no countable, quantifiable parts as the body does. You can cut a body in half but not a soul; you can't have half a soul. You don't cut an inch off your soul when you get a haircut.

Conclusion: Therefore the soul is not decomposable.

Now there are only two ways of being destroyed: by being decomposed into parts, as the body is, or by being annihilated as a whole. But we know of nothing that is ever annihilated as a whole. Nothing simply pops out of existence. If the soul dies neither in parts (by decomposition) nor as a whole (by annihilation), then the soul does not die.

Formal argument:

1. If souls die, they must die either by decomposition or by annihilation.
2. But what is not composed cannot decompose.
3. And souls are not composed.
4. Therefore souls cannot decompose.
5. And nothing is annihilated as a whole.
6. Therefore souls are not annihilated as a whole.
7. Thus souls do not die either by decomposition or annihilation.
8. Thus souls do not die.

10. The Argument from the Soul's Power to Objectify the Body

Major premise: If there is a power of the soul which cannot come from the body, this indicates that the soul is not a part or a function of the body. That, in turn, indicates that it is not subject to the laws of the body, including mortality.

Minor premise: Such a power of the soul exists which could not come from the body. It is the power to objectify the body. The body cannot objectify itself, be its own object of knowledge, or know itself.

Conclusion: Therefore the soul is not subject to the body's mortality.

To objectify X, I must be more than X. I can know a stone as an object only because I am not merely a stone as object. The projecting machine can project images on the screen only because it is not merely one more image. I can remember my past only because I am more than my past, I am a present knower. (My present is alive, my past is dead.) I can know my body as object only because I am more than my body. The knowing subject must be more than the known object.

A surprising corollary of this argument seems to be that I can never know my soul, as an object, at least completely, for I do not transcend it. If I do, if I am really some "soul *of* my soul," then I cannot know *that* as object. My senses can know the world, my mind can know my senses, but only Another can know my mind, my soul, my I, my self, my subject—as his object. A God who is pure subject, "I AM WHO I AM," could know everything as object.

10A. The Argument from Being vs. Having

Another version of the same argument proceeds from the distinction in our language and our experience between and *being* and *having*. I *have* my shoes, my friends, my feelings and my body. But I *am* myself. There is a gap, or distinction, between haver and had, possessor and possession; and my body is "had" as a possession; thus my body can be "un-had" or lost in death. But not my soul, my self. There is no "death spot" in me, as the *Tao Te Ching* puts it, no place for death to insert itself between me and my soul as there is between me and my body.

But I also speak of "my" soul, don't I? And doesn't this indicate a gap between I, self or subject, and my soul as objectifiable? Yes. I "have" thoughts and feelings in my soul, I can know them as objects, and I may lose them in death, at least temporarily. These are only part of *what* I am. But I am also a *who*, an I, a subject. Nature gave me my *what*, through heredity and environment, and takes it away in death; but nature did not give me my *who* and cannot take it away in death. C. S. Lewis, in reflecting on his dead wife's immortality, put it this way: "If she is not now, then she never was. I mistook a cloud of atoms for a person" (*A Grief Observed*). If I am not immortal, I am not an I; if I am an I, I am immortal.

The argument is essentially an insight into the meaning of "I," the most mysterious word in the language. It is the one nonobjectifiable word, for my "I" is not your "I" but your "you"; the person who is subject to me is object to you, and the person who is object to me is subject to you. "I" is mysterious ultimately because it is the image of God, whose self-revealed name and essence is "I AM" (Ex 3:14).

11. The Argument from Two Immaterial Operations

Major premise: If I perform operations in which the body plays no intrinsic or essential role, operations which are not operations of the body, then I am more than my body, I am also an immaterial soul (which need not die when the body dies).

Minor premise: Two such operations are (1) thinking, as distinct from external sensing or internal sensing (imagining), and (2) deliberate, rational, responsible willing, as distinct from instinctive liking, desiring or feeling.

Conclusion: I am an immaterial and immortal soul.

Proof of (1): We can know by introspection that our thought is not limited to images, like pyramids, but can also understand abstract, immaterial, universal essences and principles, like triangularity and trigonometry. We cannot imagine the difference between a 103-sided figure and a 104-sided figure, as we can imagine the difference between a 3-sided figure and a 4-sided figure; but we can understand the difference between a 103-sided figure and a 104-sided figure, even though we cannot imagine it. Therefore our understanding transcends our imagining.

Proof of (2): If willing is only instinctive desiring, two absurd conclusions follow. (a) None of us would be free and in control of our willing, therefore none of us would be responsible for our choices, thus all praise and blame and responsibility would be illusion. (b) If there were only instinct in us and not will, then the strongest instinct would always win. But this is not the case, for I can and sometimes do choose contrary to my strongest instinct (e.g., when I choose to follow the weaker instinct of compassion rather than the stronger instinct of fear and self-preservation in going to the aid of a victim who is drowning or being mugged).

12. The Antimaterialist Self-Contradiction Argument

A computer is not reliable if it has been programmed by chance rather than by rational design (e.g., by hailstones falling at random on its keyboard).

The human brain and nervous system are a computer. They may be much more, but they are not less than a computer. So the human brain is not reliable if it has been programmed by mere chance.

But if materialism is true, if the soul is only the brain, if there is no spirit, no human soul and no God, then the brain has been programmed by mere chance. All the programming our brains have received, through heredity (genetics) and environment (society), is ultimately only unintelligent, undesigned, random chance, brute facts, physical *causes,* not logical *reasons.*

Therefore materialism cannot be true. It refutes itself. It destroys its own credentials. If the brain is nothing but blind atoms, we have no reason to trust it when it tells us about anything, including itself and atoms. Thus, if there is nothing but atoms, we have no reason to believe there is nothing but atoms.

If materialism is not true, this means there is immaterial reality too. And that immaterial reality—usually called spirit, or soul—need not be subject to the laws of material reality, including the law of mortality. (For a more extended and adequate treatment of this argument, see C. S. Lewis, *Miracles*, chap. 3. We said more along these lines in chap. 3, argument 10, and in this chapter's refutation of objections against immortality, pages 230-31.)

13. The Argument from God's Justice

We now turn to a stronger class of arguments: not from the nature of humanity but the nature of God. These arguments do not say "Because of what *I* am, I must be immortal," but "Because of what *God* is, I am immortal." These are stronger arguments because they give the real, objective reason or cause why we are immortal: because God wills it. They are demonstrations from cause to effect rather than from effect to cause.

These arguments are weak from a practical point of view, however, because they seldom convince anyone who is not already convinced, since they presuppose the existence of God, and those who admit God usually also admit life after death already, while those who deny life after death usually also deny God. Thus they deny the necessary premise of these arguments.

The argument is as follows:

1. God is just.

2. Therefore his dealings with us must reflect that attribute, for all God's attributes are unchanging and ubiquitous, permeating all his acts.

3. But there is great injustice in the short run, in this life. Here, the wicked flourish and the righteous suffer.

4. Therefore "here" cannot be all there is. The "short run" cannot be identical with the "long run." In other words, there must be justice after death to redress and compensate for injustice before death (cf. Lk 16:19-31, esp. v. 25).

5. For this to be true, there must be life after death.

14. The Argument from God's Creativity

God is creative. He loves to create. Just look at the size of the universe he created, and the variety of things in it. Look at all the bugs! God is also persistent, patient and unchanging. He continues to will the plenitude of being that he created, and he continues to uphold it in being, for his creative act is not in time, in the past, but originates in eternity and permeates all time, all present moments. Both these attributes, creativity and unchangingness, can be arrived at by reason, as well as by revelation. For creativity and unchangingness are perfections, are more perfect than their opposites (for they indicate what is fully actual and not potential). And God is whatever it is more perfect to be than not to be.

The argument is a fortiori: If even human "creators" (artists, parents, etc.) want their "creations" to last, how much more must God? Human works and children do not last, because their makers lack the power to implement their will. God does not lack the creating will or the preserving power. Therefore some work of God's, at least, must last. What could this be but the soul of man, God's image?

How long does it last? God is unchanging. God wills forever. Therefore we last forever.

But doesn't this argument prove too much—the immortality of every creature? In "the new heaven and the new earth" perhaps this is true. Or perhaps human immortality *is* the immortality of all God's creatures, since we are the mirrors in which all creation is reflected and preserved. We are creation's priests and God's ministers.

15. The Argument from God's Love

The argument from God's love is stronger than the argument from God's justice or creativity because it reveals the ultimate cause of our immortality. Love is God's very essence, while justice and creativity are two of his essential proper attributes, two of love's essential attributes.

Major premise: If you love someone, you do not kill them. "You shall not kill" means "love does not kill," for "love is the fulfillment of the law."

Minor premise: "God is love" (1 Jn 4:8).

Conclusion: Therefore God does not kill us, but gives us life.

It is an *a fortiori* argument: if *we* want human life to triumph over death in the end because we love, how much more must God? If we want our children to live, how much more must God want us to live? Is God less loving than we are? Is he a divine hypocrite, not practicing what he preaches? Only if God does not love us, and wills our destruction, or if God is powerless to do what he wills, do we die forever. Only if God is wicked or weak, that is, only if God is not God, can death be the last word.

Objection: But we do die.

Reply: Only because of our own sin, fault and choice (Deut 30:15-18). God did not make death, but life (2 Tim 1:10). And even after we brought death into the world by sin (Gen 3:2), God still wills our life, and arranges for our death to be nonfinal, by means of the resurrection.

Arguments from Experience

We now come to the strongest arguments, the arguments from experience (16-25). In a sense, all arguments are arguments from experience of some sort. Even the arguments from authority are arguments from others' experience, and arguments from reason begin with data from experience—like a diving board—before they jump from it through the air of reason into the pool of the conclusion. The remaining arguments swim in the pool. To vary the image slightly, arguments from authority (1-3) are like a road map to the sea; arguments from reason (4-15) are like driving there; and arguments from experience (16-25) are like swimming in the water.

16. The Argument from Ultimate Justice

This argument is similar to the argument from God's justice (13), except that it does not presuppose the existence of God, only the existence of the human moral instinct that demands justice at least in the long run. Since justice is often not done in the short run in human life on earth, either (1) justice *is* done in the long run—in which case there must *be* a "long run," a life after death—or else (2) this absolute demand we make for moral meaning and ultimate justice is not met by reality, but is a mere subjective quirk of the human psyche—in which case there is no foundation in reality for our deepest moral instincts, no objective validity or justification for justice. The statement "I want justice" only tells something about us, like "I feel sick," not about objective reality, what really is or what really ought to be.

Few people believe there is no objective justification for justice. Few believe morality is a mere subjective quirk. Those who do believe this moral nihilism—almost always uprooted "professionals" and overeducated "experts," not ordinary people—find no force in this argument; but everyone else does. For the argument shows the connection between what they already believe—real, objective justice—and what they may doubt—life after death.

The argument does not prove life after death simply and absolutely, but it shows what price must be paid to deny it: the price of moral seriousness. Once we stop believing that morality has a basis in objective reality, once we start believing that morality is nothing more than subjective feelings and wishes, once we reduce justice from a cosmic law to a private preference, we no longer see it as binding or fear to disobey it when it is inconvenient. As Dostoyevsky notes, "if there is no immortality, everything is permitted."

17. The Argument from "The Meaning of Life"

We all experience the instinct and absolute demand that human life must have an adequate meaning, purpose, point, goal, good or end—what Aristotle called a "final cause" or *telos*. Viktor Frankl, in *Man's Search for Meaning*, calls this our primary need. Even pleasure, power, peace and freedom can be, and have been, sacrificed—if only there is a reason, a meaning, an adequate purpose for the sacrifice.

Two qualifications for such an adequate purpose are (1) that it be objectively true and real, not just a subjective, artificial, invented game or fantasy and (2) that it be an end worth striving for for its own sake, not a means worth striving for only for the sake of some other end beyond it.

The first qualification is obvious. Ends less than the self are not adequate for the self to believe in and live for. But invented, subjective ends are less than the self. Therefore such ends are not adequate to live for.

The second qualification depends on the fact that in any order (kind) of causality, "second" (caused, dependent) causes depend on a "first" (uncaused, independent) cause. In the order of *efficient* causality (agents or movers; causes of existence or change), this is the temporally first agent. In the order of *final* causality (reasons, end, purposes), it is the last end, ultimate purpose or supreme good *(summum bonum)*, the thing worth striving after for its own sake. If there is no such final end, then there is no adequate motivation for the means to it, for *means* refers to "means *to the end*." "The end justifies the means" indeed, though a good end does not justify a bad means. We do not lift our little finger unless moved, however unconsciously, by the belief that there is in the long run something worth moving it *for*.

We are now ready to formulate our argument.

Major premise: If life ends in final annihilation, then life does not have an end worth living for.

Minor premise: Life must have an end worth living for.

Conclusion: Therefore life does not end in final annihilation.

Explanation of the major premise: If "the whole temple of man's achievements is destined to be buried beneath the debris of a universe in ruins," and "no thought, no heroism can sustain an individual life beyond the grave" (Bertrand Russell, *A Free Man's Worship*), then we must build our lives on what Russell calls "the firm foundation of unyielding despair." But this is psychologically impossible and logically contradictory; despair is not a "firm foundation" but precisely the lack of one.

The argument is not a theoretical proof that life after death does in fact exist, but a practical proof that we need to believe it exists. The argument is a practical *ad hominem* and *reductio ad absurdum* to those who strive for a goal without believing in a final goal, or who believe in a final goal which nevertheless ends in death.

18. Pascal's Wager

The Wager was for Pascal an argument for believing in God. It can also be used as an argument for believing in life after death. It is similar to the previous argument (17) in that it is based on our experience of needing and wanting something. In the previous argument, the need or want was meaning; in this one, it is happiness. Both necessitate life after death, but the difference is that the previous argument was based on our knowledge, while this one is more securely based: it is based on our ignorance.

For skeptically inclined people, arguments based on the fact that we do not know something—arguments from ignorance—are more convincing than arguments based on supposed knowledge, which the skeptic can question. For instance, the argument against abortion from the fact that you can't be sure that the fetus is not a human being is a stronger argument for such a skeptic than the argument from the premise that we know for sure that the fetus is a human being.

The argument does not prove that life after death exists, only that it is foolish not to believe in it. Similarly, Pascal's Wager for the existence of God does not prove that God exists, only that it is foolish not to believe in him— or at least not to *want* to believe in him (since our only chance of happiness is there).

If the Christian claim is true, the only chance for gaining eternal happiness is by believing. "The one who does not believe will be condemned" (Mk 16:16). Perhaps that is false—but perhaps it is true. How foolish to ignore the second possibility. "For what does it profit a man to gain the whole world and lose his own soul?" (Mk 8:36). If it is reasonable to bet a small sum of money on a fifty percent chance of winning an enormous fortune, it is all the more reasonable to "bet" on eternal life, infinite happiness, by believing what may well be true: that it exists. God and immortality are a package deal, offered free; the "bet" is simply saying yes.

19. The Argument from Sehnsucht (Longing)

To most people, this is the most moving and fascinating of all the arguments for life after death. In order to exhibit its logical structure, we have stripped it of its emotional detail and appeal, which the reader is invited to restore and explore by reading C. S. Lewis's *Surprised by Joy, The Pilgrim's Regress,* the "Heaven" chapter in *The Problem of Pain,* the "Hope" chapter in *Mere Christianity,* and especially his sermon "The Weight of Glory." See also *Heaven: The Heart's Deepest Longing* by Peter Kreeft for a book-length treatment of this argument.

Major premise: Every natural, innate desire in us—as distinct from artificial and conditioned desires—corresponds to a real object which can satisfy that desire. If there is hunger, there is food; if thirst, drink; if eros, sex; if curiosity, knowledge; if loneliness, society. It would be surpassing strange if we found creatures falling in love in a sexless world.

Minor premise: There exists in us one desire that nothing in this life can satisfy, a mysterious longing *(Sehnsucht)* that differs from all others in two ways: (1) its object is undefinable and unattainable in this life; and (2) the mere presence of this desire in the soul is felt to be more precious and joyful than any other satisfaction.

However inadequately we may understand what we want, we all want paradise, heaven, eternity, the divine life. Augustine said "Our hearts are restless until they find their rest in Thee"—even if we don't know who or what "Thee" is. Something deep in our souls is not satisfied with this whole world of time and mortality. Even the atheist Sartre admitted that "there comes a time when we ask, even of Shakespeare, even of Beethoven, 'Is that all there is?' "

Conclusion: Therefore this "more"—eternal life—exists.

Complaint about anything shows that there must be an alternative, something more and better. We do not complain about being, or about 2 + 2 making 4. But we complain about pain and ignorance and poverty. We also complain about time; there is never enough of it—even now, much less when we are dying. Therefore there must be more than time; there must be eternity. We complain about this world. It is never good enough. Therefore there must be another world that *is* good enough. We may not attain it, just as we may die of starvation. But the innate hunger for it proves that it exists, just as the innate hunger for food proves that food exists. (For further discussion, see chap. 3, argument 16.)

20. The Argument from Presence

Only persons are present. Persons are "here"; things are "there." Persons are present to other persons. The presence of a person is not the mere presence of an object: if I knock you down bodily in a crowd without recognizing you, we are not present to each other. So presence is not merely physical. But neither is it merely mental: the idea in your mind of a friend who is absent is not the same as his real presence. Nor is presence both physical and mental together: if I accidentally knock you down in a crowd while I happen to be thinking of you, but do not recognize your presence, we are still not present to each other.

Since the presence of a person to a person, I to Thou, is not identical with the presence of an object to a subject, therefore that presence need not be removed when the presence of the objective physical body is removed by death. In other words, the *I* detects the presence of a *Thou* not subject to the death of an *It.*

When this presence is experienced before death, we have an argument from ordinary experience, argument 20. When it is experienced after death, we have an argument from extraordinary experience, argument 22.

The formal argument goes like this:

1. If the presence of a subject transcends that of an object, the subject is not doomed to death when the object is removed.

2. The presence of a subject does transcend that of an object.

3. Therefore the subject is not doomed to death.

21. The Argument from Love

This argument, inspired by Gabriel Marcel, is less tight but more deep than most others; it depends more on a "seeing" than on strict logical compulsion. Yet it can be formulated logically as follows. (See *Two Arguments from the Heart for Immortality* by Peter Kreeft [Eerdmans, Stob Lectures, 1989] for a longer version.)

1. Love here means *agapē*, not *eros*; gift-love, not need-love; love of the other, not love of enjoyment.

2. This love is not blind. It has eyes. "The heart has its reasons." We all instinctively know this; for if we were asked who loves us best, someone less bright who loves us more or someone more bright who loves us less, we all know that the one who loves us best, understands us best. *Eros* may be blind, but *agapē* is just the opposite of blind. How could *agapē* be blind if God is *agapē*? God is not blind!

3. What love sees is the intrinsic value of the beloved. If I do not love you, I see you as one of the many objects in my world—something replaceable, like a ballplayer or an actor. Your value there is your ability to perform certain functions, which others could also perform; therefore you are not indispensable. But the one thing no one else can ever do is be you. I value *that,* and see your indispensability, only if I love you for your own sake, not for my sake or for your function's sake. If I do not love you, I see you as a mere object in the world; if I love you, I see you as the center of a world—your world—as indispensable as I see myself.

4. On this basis, I can now argue that it is morally intolerable that the indispensable be dispensed with, the irreplaceable replaced.

5. Why couldn't this morally intolerable situation be real? Because if it were, then reality—ultimate, universal, cosmic reality—would do to all persons in the end what is morally intolerable, what we should never do; in that case our values would have no ground in reality. They would be no longer binding then, but mere subjective desires, instincts, facts about our subjective consciousness, not objectively real "oughts."

6. Therefore, either moral values are groundless or persons are not dispensed with, but live forever. The eye of death seems to see the eclipse of love, but the eye of love sees the eclipse of death. Thus C. S. Lewis could write the following remarkable epitaph on the death of his friend Charles Williams: "No event has so corroborated my belief in the next life as Charles Williams did simply by dying. For when the idea of death and the idea of Williams thus met in my mind, it was the idea of death that was changed."

The same epitaph, in effect, was given by Plato to Socrates in the *Phaedo.* The strongest evidence for immortality is not what Socrates *said* but what he *did* and what he *was* and how he died. Death did not change the meaning of Socrates; Socrates changed the meaning of death.

The supreme example of this change, of course, is Jesus. In that case, the changed meaning of death flowed over, so to speak, into a changed body and a changed appearance too by the resurrection. What had appeared to the eyes of the heart also appeared to the eyes of the flesh; when the Word became flesh, Truth became fact. But it was the same truth.

The weakness of this argument is the weakness of love itself: it is free, not a compulsion. If you do not choose to love, you will not see. But if you really want to know, you can perform the relevant experiment. The road to certainty about immortality can be an active experiment, not just a thought, and this can be more, not less, convincing than any theoretical argument. As Dostoyevsky's Father Zossima says in *Brothers Karamazov* to the "lady of little faith" who wonders how to regain her lost faith in immortality, "insofar as you advance in love, you will grow surer of the reality of God and of the immortality of the soul. This has been tried. This is certain." The way is offered to all sincere seekers with the promise that if they really travel it, they will surely see.

22. The Argument from Postmortem Presence

We have no statistics on how frequently people experience the presence of the dead, but we estimate, on the basis of talking to thousands of people over dozens of years, that between ten and forty percent of the living have had some experience of the real presence of the dead, usually a family member.

The experience is occasionally physical, something seen with the eyes or heard with the ears. More often it is not physical; yet it is not merely subjective and mental either, but objective and real. It is not a memory or an image of a person, but a real *person* that is present. The presence is always sudden and unexpected, and usually in a specific, limited place and time: "Grandma was in my bedroom last night."

The experience almost always seems to occur between two people who had been personally close while both were alive. The spiritual link between the two, mediated through the flesh when both were enfleshed, now persists in a new and unfleshly form—like a speaker still speaking even when the microphone goes dead. Those with good ears, in the front row, continue to hear him.

Even those who are by nature skeptical and well aware of the self-deceptive power of the mind rarely doubt the veracity of the experience when they themselves have it. In any field, deception works in only one direction: the unauthentic deceives by being confused with the authentic, but not vice versa. The authentic authenticates itself.

23. The Argument from Near-Death Experiences

Near-Death Experiences (NDEs) and Out-of-Body Experiences (OBEs) are now well known, because of the work of Kübler-Ross, Moody, Ring and many others. Twenty million Americans claim to have had them. The experience may be occasioned by the anticipation of death (as in a narrowly averted auto accident or a fall) or by a medical crisis during which heart death and even brain death seem to occur but are reversed, most commonly by CPR. Whether the patient experiences only a few or many of the features commonly found in the experience (Moody lists fifteen), one feature is always present: certainty about life after death and the eradication of the fear of death being final after the patients return to ordinary consciousness.

They cannot doubt because they claim to have seen, or experienced first-hand, life outside the mortal body.

The likelihood of this being a subjective hallucination caused chemically or psychologically seems very small. Consider (1) that the experience usually occurs while the subjects are free from all drugs; (2) that the frequent reports of things seen while "out of the body," when later checked, prove true (e.g., the location of lost objects); (3) the remarkable unanimity of the experience for all different kinds of people; and (4) the fact that the subjects do not experience what they had expected (e.g., golden streets, angels, haloes). It is at least a very powerful clue or piece of evidence to open-minded investigators.

The problem is that unusual or ecstatic experiences *could* be deceptive, just as ordinary experiences can—perhaps more so, since their force compels us to believe them, unlike ordinary experiences where the doubting ego is still active. Furthermore, none of these people actually died. Death is irreversible, barring a miracle, and all these people lived to tell about it. Therefore they were only near-death experiences, not death experiences. Also, the truth or message usually derived from near-death experiences by their subjects seems to contradict Christian doctrine, for even when they meet the "being of light," there is no fear, no sin, and no repentance or perceived need for repentance. The philosophy taught by the experience seems suspiciously identical with pop psychology.

So we have serious reservations. Yet we also seem to have serious data and impressive testimonies, often from otherwise reliable, wise, even holy people, including orthodox Christians. The jury is still out on this one.

24. The Argument from Mystical Experience

Near-death experiences (23) are widespread and common to all kinds of people. True mystical experiences, however, are rare and proper to only certain kinds of people, namely, mystics, saints, contemplatives, and the morally and mentally pure.

The relation between these two arguments is similar to the relation between the first two arguments from authority: quantitative versus qualitative. The mystics constitute the qualitative class. Most are very saintly and trustworthy, so their testimony is not easy to dismiss as lies or hallucinations. And what they say is sometimes that they actually see the life of heaven, or life after death. The clarity, detail and certainty of their experiences is usually even greater than that of the NDE patients.

The problem is that the mystics do not all say the same thing. Americans desperately want to believe they do, for that would be evidence that all religions are one and the same at their core if mystical experience is their core. But there is a further problem with that premise, for Eastern religions claim that mystical experience is the core of religion, but Western religions (Judaism, Christianity and Islam) do not. Thus this modern mystical idea is not really egalitarian at all; it is decisively Eastern and not Western.

Eastern mystics usually claim to experience the truth of their theology, pantheism. Western mystics usually claim to experience the truth of *their* theology, theism—a personal, transcendent God. In the case of Christian mystics, it is sometimes an explicitly trinitarian God.

All mystics, however, agree that the part of us that has mystical experience, whether they call it the individual soul or "cosmic consciousness," does not die when the body dies.

25. The Argument from Christ's Resurrection

What would be the most convincing evidence for life after death? Skeptics would probably reply: Only if we could put our hands into the wounds of a dead man who had risen again and showed himself to us, could we be absolutely sure. Only then would have a "sure and certain hope of the resurrection" (in the words of the old Christian Burial Service). Even this evidence, however, will not convince one whose will is set and whose mind is made up (cf. Lk 16, esp. v. 31).

A dead man did rise and appear to many on this earth. The risen Christ was seen and touched (1 Jn 1:1-3). Christians are assured of life after death not through argument first of all, but through witnesses. The church is that body of witnesses, the chain of witnesses beginning with the apostolic eyewitnesses to the resurrection. The Catholic doctrine of "apostolic succession" means first of all that chain of testimony (cf. Lk 1:1-4; Jn 21:24).

Thus the Christian's answer to the most skeptical question of all, "What do you really know about life after death, anyway? Have you ever been there? Have you come back to tell us?" is "No, but I have a very good Friend who has." For the detailed proof of Christ's resurrection, see chapter eight.

Questions for Discussion

1. Can you imagine a seventh theory of what happens at death, in addition to the six mentioned?

2. How might a believer in each of the five non-Christian theories of death try to prove it?

3. Are there any other arguments against life after death that you can think of that are not mentioned here? If so, how might they be answered?

4. What evidence might there be for the possibility or impossibility of self-consciousness apart from a physical brain?

5. How can we conceptualize the self, or "I," whose thoughts and physical actions we are aware of when we speak of "my" body, "my" thoughts, "my" mind, "my" soul? What else are you besides body and soul?

6. How can a theoretical materialist explain what truth means without confusing reasons with causes? What *is* that distinction? (See C. S. Lewis, chap. 3 of *Miracles*.)

7. How might we identify disembodied souls?

8. Describe the relationship between the body and the soul. Why is this such a difficult question, even (especially?) for philosophers?

9. Compare the argument from consensus for life after death with the "common consent" argument for the existence of God. Are they equally strong or weak?

10. How legitimate is it to argue from human authority? Why?

11. Can there be a legitimate argument from the world of matter (e.g., from evolution, or from the conservation of energy) for a conclusion about something immaterial (the soul)? Why or why not? Are there any legitimate similarly-structured arguments in other fields?

12. Why do you think materialism is a recent and minority view? Why is materialism more "primitive" than belief in magic?

13. Evaluate argument 9.

14. Evaluate the surprising corollary of argument 10. Compare 10A.

15. Compare the moral argument for life after death (16) with the moral argument for God. What people would be more convinced by these two arguments? What kind would not?

16. What sort of people would be influenced by argument 17? What would an existentialist nihilist like Sartre do with it?

17. Is Pascal's Wager equally strong or weak for God and for life after death?

18. In general, how are most of the arguments for life after death discussed in this chapter different from most of the arguments for the existence of God?

19. How do you personally evaluate reports of near-death experiences? Why?

20. Is Christ the strongest argument for the existence of God just as he (his resurrection) is the strongest argument for life after death? Explain.

Outline of Chapter 11
Heaven

- [ ] The definition of heaven
- [ ] Seven alternative theories of life after death
- [ ] Ten refutations of reincarnation
- [ ] Earthly analogies for heaven
- [ ] Twenty-nine objections to heaven answered
    1. Prescientific superstition
    2. No scientific evidence
    3. Wishful thinking
    4. Mythic
    5. Escapist
    6. Diversion
    7. Irrelevant
    8. Bribery
    9. Too dogmatic
    10. Too egotistical
    11. Too selfish
    12. Too unselfish
    13. Too earthly
    14. Too unearthly
    15. Pantheism or imitation?
    16. Boring
    17. Not happy if loved ones are in hell
    18. No work
    19. No future
    20. Anthropomorphic
    21. No freedom to sin
    22. No individuality
    23. Too much individuality
    24. No equality
    25. No privacy
    26. No sex

27. Disloyal to earth
28. Earth is preferable
29. Alien

CHAPTER 11
Heaven

N EXT TO THE IDEA OF GOD, THE IDEA OF HEAVEN IS THE GREATEST IDEA
that has ever occurred to the human mind. If it is denied and attacked more today than in the past, then the apologist had better explain and defend it better today than in the past, and certainly not water
it down or ignore it.

The focus of this chapter is to answer the objections of unbelievers
against heaven. It is not a theology of heaven, nor is it designed to be for
inspiration or personal edification. Much, much more remains to be said
after the objections have been answered.

To answer the objections against heaven, we must begin with some kind
of definition of heaven, so that we know what we are talking about. But
heaven cannot properly be defined. Scripture describes it negatively: "What
no eye has seen, nor ear heard, nor the human heart conceived, what God
has prepared for those who love him" (1 Cor 2:9).

We cannot define heaven as we can define earthly things (1) because of
a lack of experience and a paucity of data, and (2) because heaven is
unique, *sui generis*, not one of many instances of a genus. In that sense it
is like God. But we can (a) distinguish it from everything else, and we can
(b) describe it at least analogically, just as we can distinguish God from idols
and talk about him analogically. We can say what he is *not* and what he
is *like*.

Seven Alternative Theories of Life After Death

There are essentially seven non-Christian notions of what happens after death. These seven notions naturally occur to the human mind in many different times and places and cultures. The Christian notion differs from all of them.

1. Atheistic materialism: Since there is no God, there is no image of God, or soul. Therefore we are only material organisms, and when our bodies die, all of us dies and stays dead, forever.

2. God but no life after death: It is unusual, but possible, to believe in this. Such a God either does not love us enough to save us from final death or lacks the power to do it.

3. Skepticism: No one can ever know what happens after death.

4. Ancient paganism: After we die we become pale, hardly living copies of the living things we were: ghosts, inhabiting a gloomy, dark underworld.

5. Platonism: The immortality of the soul alone: The body dies forever, and the spirit or soul lives forever. This is often confused with Christianity.

6. Pantheism: We are drops of the cosmic ocean, pieces of God-stuff. At death the drop returns to the sea. There is no real individuality.

7. Reincarnation: After our body dies, our soul gets another earthly, mortal body. The soul is to the body like a traveling salesman to a motel room. (Reincarnation is usually combined with either pantheism or Platonism. After enough reincarnations to "enlighten" the soul, it is freed from its alien series of bodily prisons forever.)

Ten Refutations of Reincarnation
Christianity rejects reincarnation for ten reasons.

1. It is contradicted by Scripture (Heb 9:27).

2. It is contradicted by orthodox tradition in all churches.

3. It would reduce the Incarnation to a mere appearance, the crucifixion to an accident, and Christ to one among many philosophers or avatars. It would also confuse what Christ did with what creatures do: incarnation with reincarnation.

4. It implies that God made a mistake in designing our souls to live in bodies, that we are really pure spirits in prison or angels in costume.

5. It is contradicted by psychology and common sense, for its view of souls as imprisoned in alien bodies denies the natural psychosomatic unity.

6. It entails a very low view of the body, as a prison, a punishment.

7. It usually blames sin on the body and the body's power to confuse and darken the mind. This is passing the buck from soul to body, as well as from will to mind, and a confusion of sin with ignorance.

8. The idea that we are reincarnated in order to learn lessons we failed to learn in a past earthly life is contrary to both common sense and basic educational psychology. I cannot learn something if there is no continuity of memory. I can learn from my mistakes only if I remember them. People do not usually remember these past "reincarnations."

9. The supposed evidence for reincarnation, rememberings from past lives that come out under hypnosis or "past life regression" can be explained—if they truly occur at all—as mental telepathy from other living beings, from the souls of dead humans in purgatory or hell, or from demons. The real possibility of the latter should make us extremely skittish about opening our souls to "past life regressions."

10. Reincarnation cannot account for itself. *Why* are our souls imprisoned in bodies? Is it the just punishment for evils we committed in past reincarnations? But why were those past reincarnations necessary? For the same reason. But the beginning of the process that justly imprisoned our souls in bodies in the first place—this must have antedated the series of bodies. How could we have committed evil in the state of perfect, pure, heavenly spirituality? Further, if we sinned in that paradise, it is not paradisical after all. Yet that is the state that reincarnation is supposed to lead us back to after all our embodied yearnings are over.

If the answer is given that our bodies are not penalties for sin but illusions of individuality, the pantheistic One becoming many in human consciousness, no reason can possibly be given for this. Indeed, Hinduism calls it simply *lila*, divine play. What a stupid game for God to play! If Oneness is perfection, why would perfection play the game of imperfection? All the world's sins and sufferings are reduced to a meaningless, inexplicable game.

And if evil is itself only illusory (the answer given by many mystics) then the existence of this illusion is itself a real and not just illusory evil. Augustine makes this telling point.

Where then is evil, and what is its source, and how has it crept into the creation? What is its root, what is its seed? Can it be that it is wholly without being? But why should we fear and be on guard against what is not? Or if our fear of it is groundless, then our very fear is itself an evil thing. For by it the heart is driven and tormented for no cause; and that evil is all the worse, if there is nothing to fear yet we do fear. Thus either there is evil which we fear, or the fact that we fear is evil. (*Confessions*, VII, 5)

(See also Justin Martyr, *Dialog with Trypho* [ca. A.D. 180], and Albrecht, *Reincarnation*, for extended Christian critiques of this idea.)

Earthly Analogies for Heaven

In stark contrast to all seven alternatives, the Christian concept of life after death is a surprise because it comes from divine revelation, not human speculation or experience. It is "the resurrection of the body." After death, the whole self, including the purified, perfected soul and a new, immortal body given by God's supernatural power, is destined to live forever.

What might this life be like?

Perhaps the only way we can conceive of the nature of heaven is by earthly analogies. What does not appear in our experience (yet) cannot be defined, only related to what *does* appear in our experience by analogy. For instance, a suburban house in Long Island is to a slum in Calcutta what a castle in Switzerland is to a suburban house on Long Island. Even if you have never lived in a castle in Switzerland, you know something about it by this analogy.

The problem is that we do not have a proper proportion with heaven as we do with Switzerland. If Calcutta is 2, Long Island 6, and Switzerland 18, heaven is not 54 but infinity. We must factor in the principle of transformation. Thus a better analogy would be that heaven is to earth as the butterfly is to the caterpillar, or the adult to the fetus.

We must (1) begin with earthly analogies, (2) then correct them, (3) then note that the reason for the correction and negation of the earthly analogy is not that heaven lacks anything earthly, but that it is far more. These three progressions of thought correspond to the three traditional steps in thinking about God that come down to us from Dionysius the Areopagite and became standard throughout the Middle Ages: (1) positive theology, (2) negative theology and (3) superlative theology. (For further discussion, see chap. 4, section 4—"Mystery and Revelation.")

Positive theology gives positive analogies (e.g., God is a Father, God is good). If we want to speak positively of God or of heaven we must use analogies rather than literal, univocal words. Then we must correct the literal interpretation of the analogy by negative theology: "For my thoughts are not your thoughts, nor are your ways my ways, says the LORD. For as the heavens are higher than the earth, so are my ways higher than your ways and my thoughts than your thoughts" (Is 55:8-9), and "What no eye has seen, nor ear heard, nor the human heart conceived, what God has prepared for those who love him" (1 Cor 2:9). If you want to speak positively, you must settle for analogies. If you want to speak literally, you must settle for negations. Finally, "superlative theology" explains that the negations are limitations of our mind, not of its object. God and heaven cannot be put into words not because they are too vague, thin and wispy, but because they are too definite and specific, too real for words. It is our language and concepts that are too vague, thin and wispy.

Granted, then, that all positive language about heaven must be analogical, is there anything we do on earth that continues in heaven, in however higher and different a form? Evidently there will be no need at all for money, cars, lawyers, doctors, electricity, locks, guns. What do you take with you?

The best answer we have seen to this is suggested by Richard Purtill in *Thinking About Religion* (chap. 10) and developed in Peter Kreeft's *Everything You Ever Wanted to Know About Heaven* (chap. 3). There are six earthly activities that continue in heaven. These six things are the reason we are here on earth in the first place. They are our fundamental task, the meaning of life. And they are rarely if ever perfected or completed here, so they must be perfected and completed there. Why these six? Because there are two distinctively human activities, knowing and loving, that flow from the soul, not the body, and distinguish humans from animals; and there are three objects for each of these two activities that are infinitely precious and eternal: God, neighbor and self. Thus the meaning of life, on earth and in heaven, is:

1. To understand God
2. To love God
3. To understand others
4. To love others
5. To understand yourself
6. To love yourself

The understanding and the loving will probably be done in heaven by means whereof all earthly expressions of knowing and loving are pale and distant foreshadowings. All earthly art, love, poetry, philosophy, theology, music, liturgy, and loving deeds probably resemble their heavenly fruit about as much as a watermelon seed resembles a watermelon.

Twenty-nine Objections to Heaven Answered
Objection 1:
The idea of heaven is prescientific superstition.

Reply A: That *objection* is unscientific. The scientific way to refute an idea is by evidence, not name-calling.

Reply B: Plenty of "prescientific" ideas are valid, true and important, not superstitious—for example, birth, death, life, good, evil, beauty, ugliness, pleasure, pain, earth, air, fire, water, love, hate, happiness.

Objection 2:
There is no scientific evidence for heaven.
Reply A: Nor for many other ideas that everyone admits are valid, even the scientist. When the scientist closes his laboratory and goes home and kisses his wife, he does not believe there is nothing there but hormones and neurons and molecules.
Reply B: There is no scientific evidence for the notion that nothing exists except what is proved by scientific evidence. The objector assumes that whatever there is no scientific evidence for, does not exist (e.g., there is no scientific evidence for heaven, therefore heaven does not exist). But there is no scientific evidence for that assumption; it cannot be proved by the scientific method. It is simply an assumption—in fact, it is an arbitrary decision and desire to narrow the bounds of reality to the bounds of the scientific method. It is a decision of the *will*, not the intellect.

Objection:
Heaven is obviously wishful thinking. If there were no heaven, we would have to invent it. It is a "necessary dream."
Reply A: The heaven of the Bible does not correspond to our dreams or wishful thinking. It is selfless, self-forgetful love and saintliness, not the gratification of selfish desires; the death of egotism rather than its ratification; holiness rather than indulgence; adoration and self-forgetful worship of God rather than self-caressing autoeroticism; spiritual love rather than physical love.
Reply B: Even the physical details or symbols of heaven do not correspond to the popular picture. Whether we consider the details in the Bible or the details in the experiences of the saints, mystics or contemporary resuscitated patients who have had near-death experiences, in all cases the experience of heaven is a surprise and a shock.
Reply C: Even if there is a correspondence between our innate wishes and the idea of heaven, that correspondence could equally well be explained by God's having designed us for heaven rather than by our having designed heaven for ourselves. The glove could have been made for the hand, *or* the hand could have been made for the glove.
Reply D: The objector's reasoning is fallacious. It argues: If there were no heaven, we would have to believe in one (because we need and want it so much); and we do (have to) believe in one; therefore there is no heaven. This is an example of the fallacy of affirming the consequent. It is like arguing that if there were no earth, we would still have to believe in it

(because it appears to our senses); and we do (have to) believe in it; therefore there is no earth.

Reply E: If an effect cannot exceed its cause, how can the idea of heaven, perfect and beautiful as it is, be caused only by our fallen, foolish, fallible, finite minds?

Objection 4:

The very form, or structure, of the idea of heaven is mythic or legendary. The golden streets are just another version of the "happy hunting grounds" or the Elysian Fields.

Reply A: Distinguish the imagery from the substance. The biblical imagery is not literal. To disbelieve in the substance because you mistook the imagery for literal description is as foolish as disbelieving in the moon because you mistook the "man in the moon" for a literal man.

Reply B: The fact that all religions and cultures have some version of heaven or paradise is evidence *for*, not against, its reality. If everyone (or nearly everyone) believes a story, only snobbery would conclude from that fact alone that the story is likely to be false rather than true. (See the argument from common consent in chap. 3.)

Reply C: The biblical version of heaven differs from that of popular and pagan religions in that it does *not* appeal to natural, worldly, selfish desires.

Objection 5:

Believing in heaven is escapist.

Reply A: The most pointed answer to the charge of escapism is C. S. Lewis's simple question: "Who talks the most against 'escapism'? Jailers." Think about it.

Reply B: Is it escapist for an unborn baby to wonder about life after birth? Is it escapist for a pilgrim to wonder about his holy destination? Is it escapist for the shipwrecked sailor on a raft to dream of landfall? Is it escapist for the seed to dream of the flower? The caterpillar of the butterfly? Juliet of Romeo? Heaven is not escapist because it is the fulfillment of all good earthly desires.

Reply C: Heaven is not escapist, because it is real. The idea is "escapist" only if it is a lie. To call the idea of heaven escapist is to presuppose atheism but not to have the clarity or courage to say so. If heaven is real, it is escapist *not* to think about it. It is realistic to do so.

The first question about any idea cannot be whether it is escapist but whether it is true. Even if an idea is escapist, that does not make it false. The idea that there is a tunnel under the prison is certainly an escapist idea, but that does not mean it is not true.

Just as the only honest reason for believing any idea is that it is true, so the only honest reason for disbelieving any idea is that it is false, not that it is escapist. The label "escapist" is itself escapist; the labeler is trying to escape his or her primary obligation to prove the idea false.

Objection 6:

Heaven is a diversion. Whether true or false, it distracts us from our present tasks.

Reply A: Not if heaven is real. If it is, and if it is our ultimate destination, then our present tasks more often distract us from our primary task. That is why we have to be reminded to "strive first for the kingdom of God" (Mt 6:33) and not to have our minds "set on earthly things," because "our citizenship [home] is in heaven" (Phil 3:19-20).

Reply B: Concern for heavenly things does not devalue or demean concern for earthly things for the same reason a pregnant woman's concern for her baby's future does not devalue, detract, or distract from her concern for her baby's present. If she believed her baby was going to be born dead, or if she wanted her baby dead (i.e., wanted an abortion), *then* the baby's life would be demeaned and devalued, and she would cease to care for it. If we believe that this life ends with death, like a cosmic abortion, then we will care for it not more but less than if we believe that it is a pregnancy that will bear eternity.

The early roads that led to California and the gold mines were well paved and cared for. The roads that led to ghost towns were abandoned. If earth is the road to heaven, we will care for it. If it leads nowhere but to the ghost town of the grave, we will not.

Samuel Beckett, in *Waiting for Godot,* compresses the naturalistic worldview into one arresting image: "They give birth astride a grave." If that is the truth, and we believe it, will we love the thing that just falls from womb to tomb *more,* or will we love it less?

Reply C: Throughout history, it has been those who believed most strongly in heaven who made the greatest difference to earth, including Jesus himself. For if you believe in the fatherland, you care for its colonies. The stereotype of the wild-eyed religious fanatic preaching gloom and doom and waiting around for the world to end and everyone to die exists largely in the propaganda of the antireligious fanatic, not in ordinary believers' lives.

Objection 7:

Heaven is irrelevant to the here and now. You can love or hate this world whether you believe in a next one or not.

Reply: Heaven is more than just relevant to the present; it actually *begins* in the present. The joy of heaven begins now for the believer because that joy is essentially Christ's presence, and that begins now, just as he promised (Mt 28:20; Jn 15:9-11). Even if we are far from fully appreciating that joy, it is here; the life of heaven is not an abstract "lifestyle" but the actual life-blood, like the sap of a vine that flows into its branches (Jn 15:4-5).

In fact, if heaven's life is not in us now, it will not be in us forever, for heaven is where God is. God determines where heaven is, not vice versa. God "contains" heaven somewhat as a play "contains" its setting. Heaven does not contain God. If God is in our souls now, through faith, then the very life of heaven is here and now in us, tiny and invisible though that heavenly seed is (Mt 13:31-32). This is the very thing Jesus preached most about, centered on, and told dozens of parables about—"the kingdom of heaven." That is "the pearl of great value" (Mt 13:45-46), the thing for which the whole world is far too small a price to pay (Mk 8:36). And it's free! (Rev 22:17). What could be more "relevant" or make a bigger difference than that? For a Christian to preach about heaven is like one starving beggar telling another where there's free food.

Objection 8:

Heaven is a bribe. It makes religion selfish. You work for your heavenly reward, not for pure love. It's mercenary.

Reply: Is it mercenary for Romeo to want to marry Juliet? For a team that has worked hard to want victory? For a student of a foreign language to want to read and speak it fluently? Some rewards are not mercenary but natural and right. They are not artificially tacked on to the activity they reward, like a grade in a course, but are that activity itself in its perfected state. Such is heaven. It is not some reward externally added to love of God and neighbor, but that love itself perfected.

Objection 9:

Heaven is too dogmatic. How can we know anything about heaven, anyway? If "no eye has seen, nor ear heard, nor the human heart conceived," then it has not entered into our hearts yet. It can be only faith or speculation, not knowledge.

Reply A: Analogical and negative knowledge is knowledge. Knowing what a thing is like or what a thing is not is knowledge.

Reply B: "Only faith or speculation"? But faith is not fantasy; faith is knowledge. Faith is accepting divinely revealed data. And speculation can be knowledge too, if it is responsible and correct. Philosophical reasoning can lead to some truth, surely—unless you are a skeptic.

Objection 10:
Heaven is too egotistical. What arrogance to think you are destined to be spiritually married to God!
Reply: God said it, not us. It is indeed amazing. God is amazing.

Objection 11:
Heaven is too selfish. It is the idea of infinite and eternal happiness. What makes you think your little ego is so important, or that it can carry such a heavenly load of happiness?
Reply: Heaven is wholly unselfish and self-forgetful—so much so that the mystics often use language that seems to say the self is an illusion or something to be destroyed. This is a misunderstanding or an exaggeration—it is egotism, not the ego, that is folly and illusion and is to be totally destroyed. But the misunderstanding is the misunderstanding of a profound truth: that in heaven everyone will be mentally standing outside themselves in unselfconscious ecstasy ("ecstasy" comes from the Greek *ek-stasis,* "standing outside yourself"). They will be so in love with God and each other that they will not notice themselves.

Objection 12:
Heaven is too unselfish, in that case; too spiritual, too mystical for ordinary human tastes.
Reply: The other half of the great paradox answers this objection. The paradox is that "those who lose their life for my sake will find it." In other words, self-forgetful love is our supreme joy. This is true of us because we are made in the image of the God whose very essence is self-giving love. The reply to objection 11 was that heaven's self-fulfillment comes only through self-abandonment; the reply to objection 12 is that heaven's self-abandonment brings the greatest self-fulfillment. This strangest of all paradoxes is the most easily tested at any time, at any place, throughout life.

Objection 13:
Heaven is too earthly. Golden streets and jewelry and city gates and a sea of crystal—

this is obviously a mere projection and extension of some of the earthly things valued by a past culture.

Reply: The objection confuses the culturally relative imagery with the not culturally-relative substance or essence of heaven. Images are mere analogies, pointers. (See C. S. Lewis's "The Weight of Glory" for a profound interpretation of some of these problematic pointers.)

Objection 14:

Heaven is too unearthly, too spiritual. How can we be human and happy without sex, food, clothing—even some frustrations and challenges? Perfection would be terrible for us.

Reply: How do you know what will be "too spiritual" for the changed beings we will be after death? Why set limits on human growth? The objection is too limited in imagination and too bound to present worldly goods as if there are no higher possibilities for joy, but we know there are even in this life.

Both of the last two objections fail to understand the principle of transformation. Heaven's transformation of earth (the "new earth," Rev 21:1) and the new humanity (the "spiritual body," 1 Cor 15:44) neither simply extends and perfects, nor simply transcends and abolishes, the present earth and the present humanity, but transforms it, as caterpillar to butterfly, or tadpole to frog or frog to prince. God goes around the earth kissing frogs (us) to turn them into princes. Truth is stranger than fairy tales.

The principle of transformation is the answer to each of the many questions of the form: Will we have X (some earthly thing) in heaven? Take emotions as an example. Will we have emotions in heaven? Yes and no. Yes because emotions are part of our human nature as designed by God. They will no more be abolished than our nature. But no, they will not be the same as they are now, just as our nature will not be the same. We will not be emotionless computers or disembodied intellects, but our emotions will not drive us or control us. Here, they come mainly from the body into the soul; there, they will come mainly from the soul into the body. They will be raised from the unconscious to the conscious. They will be less passive, but more passionate.

For instance, take joy. Augustine said that in heaven the love we receive from God into our souls will overflow into our new, resurrection bodies in a "torrent of joyful pleasure" *(torrens voluptatis)*. Emotions are stronger, not weaker, in the saint. Aquinas believed that sexual pleasure was much greater, not less, before the Fall, because sin always harms and never helps any good, God-designed thing.

Objection 15:
Do we become parts of God in heaven or not? If so, this is pantheism, not Christianity. If not, if we only approximate and approach and imitate him from without; this is not enough, for we still have something more (God himself) to aspire to and desire. Such a heaven would not be complete fulfillment.

Reply: We do not *become* God, but we do more than just *imitate* or approximate him: We share his own inner life. But we do this only by grace (gift), not by nature. God pours himself into us as the sun pours sunbeams on the sunbather.

The objection assumes we will not be completely happy unless we become God. This sounds like the worst of sins—pride—and the most foolish of sins—envy—the only sin that never brings any pleasure at all. In heaven everyone will be wise and content with what they are. We will remain finite creatures, yet we will share, "participate," in God's divine nature (2 Pet 1:4), be filled to overflowing with his love. It is not at all clear just *how* this is done, but is clear *that* it is between the two horns of the objection's dilemma.

Objection 16:
Heaven will be boring. Nothing to do but worship—an unending church service. Not many people can be happy that way. And even if that did make you happy, sheer happiness without unhappiness is boring. We appreciate everything only by contrast with its opposite. We need darkness to set off light, some pain to appreciate pleasure. If heaven has no pain, we won't appreciate its pleasure.

Reply A: The last point in the objection assumes that earthly limitations and foolishness will extend to heaven. The wiser you are, the less you need pain to appreciate pleasure. God does not need any negatives, and he will teach us his "trick" of appreciating good apart from evil once we get there.

Reply B: Boredom is a specifically earthly and fallen emotion. Even more, it is especially modern; a word for boredom in general does not exist in any premodern language. We will not be bored in heaven because we will be good and wise. Even here on earth, it is the most foolish and spoiled and jaded among us that are the most bored. Saints are never bored.

Reply C: The picture of a heavenly church service is symbolic, not literal. Revelation says there is no temple in heaven (Rev 21:22) because God is fully present himself. Church can be boring, but God cannot be boring.

Reply D: Heaven will not be boring because it will not be merely the satisfaction and lulling of desire. It will not be merely contentment, which gets boring, but joy, which does not. Joy is as passionate and dynamic and stimulating as desire itself. (See chap. 4 of *Heaven, the Heart's Deepest Longing* and chap. 14 of *Everything You Ever Wanted to Know About Heaven.*)

Reply E: Heaven is not boring because it is perfect love and work. Even Freud knew that the two things everyone needs to make life worth living are love and work. The two are really one, for love is a work, not just a feeling, and good work must be a work of love.

What love-work will heaven be? The six love-works mentioned earlier: knowing and loving God, others and yourself. Even on earth these are the six things that are inexhaustible and nonboring. They are our dress rehearsal for heaven.

They are inexhaustible because persons are inexhaustible. Persons are inexhaustible because they are free subjects, not determined objects; open, not closed; *I*'s, not *It*'s. They are like magic cows that give fresh milk every morning.

Objection 17:

How can we be happy in heaven if any of our loved ones are in hell? If we stop loving them, we are not good; if we keep loving them, we are not happy.

Reply A: Let us begin with the data that we do know and try to proceed from there to find out what we do not know. We know that there will be no sadness in heaven, though we may not know *how* God manages this. God "will wipe away every tear from their eyes. Death will be no more; mourning and crying and pain will be no more" (Rev 21:4).

Reply B: In whatever way God manages not to be sad, even though people he created and loves are in hell—however he manages to do this, we will learn from and share in this way. Somehow or other God manages it. God is infinite love and infinite joy, even though some go to hell. It *can* be done, because it *is* done: God does it. If God does it, he will teach us how to do it.

Reply C: Some clues to how God does this are in Jesus' parable of the sheep and the goats (Mt 25:31-46) and his response to some who called him "Lord": at the end, he says to the damned, "I never knew you" (Mt 7:23). He does not know and see and worry about the damned. This sounds like ignorance or self-deception; but these cannot find any place in Omniscience. What then does it mean?

It is not falsity, it is truth. In a sense the damned have lost their true reality. Though they *exist*, they are in the "outer darkness," not in heaven. But heaven is the standard of reality; it is not only the standard of all joy and all goodness, it is also the standard of all realness. The closer you are to heaven, the more real you are; the farther from heaven, the less real. The damned are like ashes, not like wood. They have lost their true reality. The blessed in heaven, like God, do not mourn over what the damned once were—real wood, real men and women—because they do not live in the past.

If human beings were alive in hell, and heaven were parallel to hell in time as Earth and Mars are parallel worlds, then there would seem to be no answer to the objection. But hell is a place of eternal death, not eternal life; and what goes to hell is what was once a human being, but is now "remains" (see C. S. Lewis, *The Problem of Pain*, chap. 9). Nor are heaven and hell parallel—you can't go from one to the other (Lk 16:26). Nor are they in time. So all the implicit assumptions of the objection are false.

Reply D: Even if all these answers are totally inadequate, the best one still remains. It is not a theoretical solution but a practical one. If there are people you love and identify with so deeply that you simply cannot see how you could possibly be happy forever without them—as if they were a very part of you—then one of the jobs God may have put you on earth for is to do everything you can for their salvation as well as your own. If it is God's providence that has arranged this love and closeness between you, then God will honor the prayer from the heart that tells him that he just *has* to arrange your friends' salvation, as he has providentially arranged yours, because your friends are a real part of you, and God saves people as wholes, not parts. Be sure it is not a wheedling or blackmailing prayer, just a presentation of the facts, like Mary's "They have no wine" (Jn 2:3). Let God do his thing. His way is always more loving, more wise, and more powerful than ours—far better than we can imagine or desire (1 Cor 2:9). Trust him to use your earthly love as a channel of grace for your friends. Perhaps your concern is a clue to its answer: perhaps God has put that burden on your heart for you to work with him to lift it, to solve it.

Objection 18:

Heaven is eternal. But eternity seems inhuman because without time there is no progress, no change, no work. Passive, changeless adoration perhaps seems fit for angels, but not for us.

Reply: Who says there is no time and work and change in heaven? Probably eternity includes all time rather than excluding it. Perhaps instead of only a tiny bit of time being present (what we now call "the present"), *all* of time is accessible in heaven's present. As to work, there is work in heaven, and that work is to love. Love is a work. Before the Fall, work was also a love. Only after the Fall did work become onerous (Gen 3:17-19). Heaven will restore and surpass all the good in paradise (Eden) including all the good in work, change and time.

Objection 19:

If all time is present at once in heaven, there can be nothing future, only present, and thus nothing left for which to hope. But we cannot live without hope. "It is better to travel hopefully than to arrive."

Reply: C. S. Lewis destroys that cliché very logically: "If that were true, and known to be true, how could anyone travel hopefully? There would be nothing to hope for." If "arriving" is threatening, boring or less joyful than hoping, we do *not* hope to arrive. Would the objector really prefer hunger to eating? Courting to marrying? Curiosity and ignorance to knowledge and understanding? There is no hope in heaven and no hope in hell. Something far better than hope awaits those in heaven: fulfillment, consummation.

Objection 20:

The "resurrection body" and the "new earth" seem impossible, mythological and anthropomorphic.

Reply A: They are not impossible, for the God who could bang out the Big Bang and create a whole universe out of nothing, including this earth, can surely make a new earth. And if he can make a whole new earth, he can surely make a whole new body. (See 1 Cor 15.)

Reply B: They are not mythological, but the truth of which the myths are confused foreshadowings. (See "Man and Mythologies" in G. K. Chesterton's *The Everlasting Man* and "Myth Become Fact" in C. S. Lewis's *God in the Dock.*)

Reply C: The new earth and new body are just the opposite of anthropomorphic; they are not reduced in size to present human proportions, but beyond our present power to comprehend. They are not like the old ones but as new and as surprising to us in our present state as the body of an adult would be to an unborn baby.

Objection 21:

Are we free to sin in heaven? If not, we are unfree robots, not free-willed humans. If so, heaven is dangerous, like earth. And if anyone chooses to sin, it's Eden and the Fall and earth all over again.

Reply: "Free to sin" is like "healthy disease." It means "freedom of enslave-ment."

Free will, or free choice, is the means to a higher freedom, or liberty. The lower freedom, the means, is freedom from compulsion. The higher free-dom, the end, is the freedom from evil.

In heaven no one will sin because no one will want to. All will freely choose never to sin. Though they have the power to sin, they do not have the motive. A great singer does not make elementary mistakes and sing off key, even though she has the power to do so if she wanted. Why would she want to? Why would anyone want to sin, or be tempted to sin, in heaven? There, we will all see the beauty and joy and attractiveness of God and goodness, and the ugliness and joylessness and stupidity of sin, so clearly that there will be no possible motive to sin.

Now we are enslaved by ignorance. Every sin comes partly from ignorance; for we sin only if we see sin as somehow attractive (which it is not) and see goodness as somehow unattractive (which it is not). That is ignorance. It is an ignorance for which we are responsible and to blame, but it is indeed ignorance, and without that ignorance we would not sin. In heaven, there will not be that ignorance, therefore there will not be sin. The "Beatific Vision" of God face to face will dispel that ignorance like the sun dispelling fog.

Objection 22:

If we will all be perfect saints in heaven, where will individuality be? Billions of carbon copies of God seems dull.

Reply A: Copies of each other are dull; copies of God are infinitely inter-esting. God is like a diamond with infinitely diverse facets. Each of the blessed reflects a different facet.

Reply B: Even now, the saints are the truest individuals. "How drearily alike are the great tyrants and sinners; how gloriously different the saints!" (C. S. Lewis).

Reply C: Lewis also explains *how* this comes about. Sanctity, letting God rule your soul and life, is like salt: it brings out the individual flavor of each of the different foods it flavors. It makes fish fishier, steak steakier and eggs eggier. It makes Augustine more Augustinian and Thomas more Thomistic, Teresa more Teresian and Mary more Marian.

Reply D: Revelation 2:17 says: "To everyone who conquers . . . I will give a white stone, and on the white stone is written a new name that no one knows except the one who receives it." Our heavenly individuality is so real that only God knows its secret. Quoting Lewis again:

What can be more a man's own than this new name which even in eternity remains a secret between God and him? And what shall we take this secrecy to mean? Surely, that each of the redeemed shall forever know and praise some one aspect of the Divine beauty better than any other creature can. Why else were individuals created? . . . If he had no use for all these differences, I do not see why he should have created more souls than one. . . . Your soul has a curious shape because it is a hollow made to fit a particular swelling in the infinite contours of the Divine substance, or a key to unlock one of the doors in the house with many mansions. . . . Your place in heaven will seem to be made for you and you alone, because you were made for it—made for it stitch by stitch as a glove is made for a hand. (*The Problem of Pain*, chap. 10)

Objection 23:

Then heaven sounds so individualistic that it is egotistical.

Reply: Again, C. S. Lewis is helpful:

This may seem a perilously private and subjective notion of the pearl of great price, but it is not. . . . Always it has summoned you out of yourself. . . . Even the desire for the thing lives only if you abandon it. This is the ultimate law—the seed dies to live, the bread must be cast upon the waters, he that loses his soul will save it. . . . For in self-giving, if anywhere, we touch a rhythm not only of all creation but of all being. For the Eternal Word also gives himself in sacrifice; and that not only on Calvary. For when he was crucified, he "did that in the wild weather of his outlying provinces which he had done at home in glory and gladness" (George MacD). From before the foundation of the world he surrenders begotten Deity back to begetting Deity in obedience. And as the Son glorifies the Father, so also the Father glorifies the Son (Jn 17:1, 4, 5). . . . From the highest to the lowest, self exists to be abdicated and, by the abdication, becomes the more truly self, to be thereupon yet the more abdicated, and so forever. This is not a heavenly law which we can escape by remaining earthly, nor an earthly law which we can escape by being saved. What is outside the system of self-giving is not earth, nor nature, nor "ordinary life," but solely and simply hell. (*The Problem of Pain*, chap. 10)

Objection 24:

Will we all be equal in heaven? The traditional picture is one of inequality: a hierarchy of greater and lesser rewards. But this seems to make God an elitist, a snob, an aristocrat.

Reply A: Judging God by human political categories is like judging a great symphony on which stanza of "Mary Had a Little Lamb" it most resembles.
Reply B: The traditional, hierarchical picture follows necessarily from the essence of justice, which is not simply equality, but equal treatment of equals *and unequal treatment of unequals.* The modern obsession with equality comes from a passing ideological aberration, not natural justice. (That this is indeed an obsession is evident from the fact that of the hundreds of issues about heaven this one—a very minor one—is always the one our students fixate on the most.)
Reply C: We will all be equal in heaven in the same sense that we are all equal now: equal in worth and dignity as possessing human nature, the image of God, and equal in being loved totally by God with nothing held back. But this does not mean we will be (or are) equal in the sense of *the same.* We will all be totally filled with the presence and love of God, but some vessels will be able to hold more than others. Is a totally full gallon jug more full than a totally full pint glass?
Reply D: One of the chief joys of this life and the next is sharing differences and experiencing the pleasure of humility, that is, looking up to and admiring and learning from someone who is better than you in some way. The resentment expressed in the common saying "I'm just as good as you" is not heavenly but hellish. (By the way, that is one sentence that *always* means exactly the opposite of what it says. If you believed that, you would never say it. The only reason you say it is because you *don't* believe it.)

Objection 25:
If God's light and truth permeate heaven, there will be no privacy. That will be intolerable.
Reply: Privacy is needed now only because of sin—like clothes, locks and police officers. We hide from others because (a) we feel shame and (b) we fear others will misunderstand or reject us. In heaven there is no shame (for all sin is gone) and no misunderstanding or rejection by God or his saints. We will enjoy there the intimacy we fear (and yet long for) here.

Objection 26:
Is there sex in heaven? If not, most people today will not want to go there. If so, it seems too earthly, too anthropomorphic.
Reply A: That many will not want to go there says nothing against heaven, only against the nongoers.
Reply B: Of course there is sexuality in heaven. Sexuality, or sexual identity,

is part of our divinely-designed humanity, and is not abolished but transformed. We will be "like the angels" (Mt 22:30) not by being neutered but in not marrying.

Sex is first of all something we *are*, not something we *do*. If the question is whether we can "do it" (i.e., copulate) in heaven, the answer is probably the same as the answer to a six-year-old boy who asks whether he can play with his model airplanes while he makes love when he grows up.

Since we will have real bodies, it will be *possible*, just as it will be possible to eat—Christ did that in his resurrection body. But we will probably never give it a thought—not because it will seem shameful or silly or vulgar but because there will be infinitely more ecstatic pleasures at hand. Perhaps these pleasures will include some kind of total union with other souls of which physical intercourse is now a clumsy and confused foreshadowing. Don't lovers seek a total intimacy and oneness and always attain only a partial and temporary one? (See also "Sex in Heaven," chap. 8 of *Everything You Ever Wanted to Know About Heaven.*)

Objection 27:
To love heaven is to be a traitor to earth, leaving it behind like a rat leaving a sinking ship. It is disloyal.
Reply A: Unless the Bible lies, earth is not our home; heaven is. Disloyalty to *heaven* is the fault, not disloyalty to earth.
Reply B: Earth is only the setting of the play. It is dear primarily because of the play and the characters. Remove its people, and the earth is no longer dear to us. But these people are not left behind forever; they will join us in heaven when their time comes, God willing. We are not disloyal to *them.*
Reply C: Perhaps we do not even leave them behind as we think. Perhaps the blessed dead are present but invisible observers of us the living. This seems to be meant by "a great cloud of witnesses" in Hebrews 12:1: not only those who witnessed to their faith on earth as martyrs, but also those who are now witnessing our struggles from their heavenly stadium seats. After all, the verse says "we are [now] surrounded by so great a cloud of witnesses," not just that they already witnessed (in the past). Compare Luke 20:38.

Would such interest in us on earth somehow pollute the perfection of the blessed in heaven? If you were in heaven, wouldn't you want to see how your family was faring on earth? Wouldn't you pray for them? Would this be displeasing to God?

Earth and heaven are not cut off from each other. Death is not stronger than "the communion of saints" (one of the twelve articles of the Apostles' Creed). "Love is strong as death" (Song 8:6). Death is not an iron door with no chinks and no windows.

Objection 28:

Given a choice, most people would prefer earth to heaven.
Reply A: That says something about most people, not about heaven.
Reply B: The objection implicitly thinks of earth and heaven as rivals, as in the previous objection, or at least as alternatives, like baseball or church services. But earth is really related to heaven as shadow to substance, seed to plant, courtship to consummation, sign to thing signified, traveling to arriving, pilgrimage to home, pregnancy to birth, hope to fruition.
Reply C: After a thousand years on earth, you would no longer prefer earth to heaven. You would be bored. Our time on earth is like an egg: if we don't hatch, we eventually go rotten. Heaven is like the sky in which we baby birds are designed to fly. Earth is our nest.

Objection 29:

Heaven sounds so alien, far, other, threatening, "unfit for human habitation." Like trying on a weird outfit of clothes and saying, "It's just not me."
Reply: The one thing you will certainly feel in heaven is that this is your home, this is what you were designed and made for. God is a good tailor; he fits the heavenly clothes perfectly to each of his customers. A place is set at the heavenly banquet table with your name on it. Your Father has been waiting for a long time, and when it is time and he calls you, you will gladly put away your toys and go home.

Questions for Discussion

1. Which of the eight alternative theories of what happens after death is the *least* natural and popular, so that it was not even mentioned in the parallel passage at the beginning of chapter ten? Once paganism was the most popular position; today it is the least popular, even less popular than this unusual position. Why is this? Is the human heart so subject to fashion?

2. In light of the ten refutations of reincarnation, why is it so popular, even among some Christians?

3. How could a believer in reincarnation try to answer each of these ten arguments?

4. What is meant by saying that God and heaven are "too definite and specific for words" (pp. 262-63)? Doesn't calling God "specific" deny his infinity? Compare

C. S. Lewis, *Miracles*, chap. 11.

5. Can you think of anything else as important as the six things mentioned on p. 263?

6. Does reply B to objection 2 (p. 264) mean that scientism is self-contradictory? If so, why is it so popular? Can the same be said about skepticism?

7. In light of the responses to objection 3, evaluate Freud's argument that Christianity corresponds so well to what we would have to believe in order to stay sane and endure life if there were no God and no heaven, that this fit between our psychological needs and the belief in God and heaven makes it very likely that the beliefs are wish-fulfillment dreams, projections of desperate and needy consciousness. Which of the five replies address this argument?

8. What is meant by "diversion" (objection 6)? What did Pascal mean by it?

9. Why is it so popular to think that heaven is a diversion from earth? Do Christians often think this too? Give evidence for your answer.

10. How, in practice and in history, did God solve objection 8 (p. 267)?

11. If "this strangest of all paradoxes is the most easily tested" (p. 268, reply to objection 12), why do so many disbelieve it and not test it? Why don't we all do it, if it always works and makes us happy, which is what all of us want? Are we all insane?

12. How can you test the answer to objection 16 (p. 270) here and now?

13. How important do you find objection 17? What does that fact tell about you? Answer the same question for objection 26.

14. If all time is present to us in heaven (objection 19), how are we different from God with respect to time and eternity?

15. (Regarding objection 21) Plato believed that all evil was due to ignorance (and thus was involuntary), for if we really knew the good and knew that the moral good (virtue) was always also the psychological good (happiness), it would be psychologically impossible for us to choose evil or vice, since we always seek happiness. How does the reply to objection 21 (p. 274) implicitly explain what is right and what is wrong in this view, what Plato saw and what he failed to see?

16. Why do you think moderns fixate on equality (objection 24)?

17. Can you imagine happiness without privacy (objection 25)?

18. *Is* there sex in heaven (objection 26)? If so, isn't that crude, earthly and unimaginative? If not, is that why moderns don't want to believe in heaven?

19. How does the author know that heaven will feel like home, not alien (objection 29)?

20. Can you think of any other objections against heaven?

Outline of Chapter 12
Hell

☐ The difficult question of hell

☐ Ten issues at stake in the doctrine of hell:

1. The trustworthiness of Scripture and the church
2. The trustworthiness of Jesus
3. The existence of propositional data
4. The infinite importance of earthly choices
5. The freedom of the will
6. The objectivity of good and evil
7. The reason for a savior
8. The consequence of indifference
9. The need for Christ's sacrifice
10. The basis for believing in God's love

☐ Defining the doctrine of hell

Fourteen things hell is not:

1. Unreal
2. Earthly
3. Purgatory
4. Annihilation
5. Reincarnation
6. Temporary
7. Unpopulated
8. Limbo
9. Divine hate
10. Forced on the damned
11. A place for humans
12. Necessary
13. Justice over love
14. A double predestination

Three things hell is:

1. Punishment
2. Pain

    3. Privation

☐ Demonstrating the doctrine of hell: seven reasons for believing in hell:

    1. The Bible

    2. Christ

    3. The church

    4. Justice

    5. God's exclusivity

    6. Free will

    7. The argument from fear

☐ Defending the doctrine of hell: thirteen objections answered:

    1. Contrary to God's love

    2. Contrary to justice

    3. Contrary to omnipotence

    4. Contrary to human freedom

    5. Contrary to human sanity

    6. Contrary to the morality of Jesus

    7. Effects are fear, despair and hatred

    8. Prevents the joy of heaven

    9. Vastly overpopulated

    10. Makes evil eternal

    11. Thwarts God's purpose

    12. Unendurable by human nature

    13. Instinctively monstrous and intolerable

☐ The proper use and misuse of the doctrine of hell

CHAPTER 12
Hell

O F ALL THE DOCTRINES IN CHRISTIANITY, HELL IS PROBABLY THE MOST difficult to defend, the most burdensome to believe and the first to be abandoned. The critic's case against it seems very strong, and the believer's duty to believe it seems unbearable.

The relatively large amount of space devoted to hell in this book does not reflect the relative importance of this doctrine in Christianity. Heaven is far more important than hell, we know much more about it, and it is meant to occupy our mind much more centrally.

But in battle an army must rush to defend that part of the line which is most attacked or which seems the weakest. Though other doctrines are more important than this one, this one is not unimportant or dispensable. In fact, it is important enough to make a tremendous difference. This is the first point we must prove to justify a whole chapter on hell.

Ten Issues at Stake in the Doctrine of Hell
William James rightly reminds us that the first question we should ask about any idea is whether it is important, that is, whether it makes a difference. If not, he refuses to call it "true" in any practical sense of the word. So why is hell important? What difference does it make? What happens if we drop it?

Obviously, the difference between heaven and hell is by definition infinite. And the difference between a world in which there is no heaven or hell, and a world in which there is, is enormous. But what is the difference between a world in which there is only a heaven but no hell, and a world in which there is also a hell?

Disbelief in hell involves three presuppositions and entails seven consequences that destroy the whole Christian faith. In other words, removing hell is not like removing one stone from a pile and leaving all the others untouched. It is like removing a vital organ from a body; all the others are affected and eventually killed.

First, the three totally destructive presuppositions.

1. To believe there is no hell presupposes that both Scripture and the church lie, for both clearly teach the reality of hell. They are our authorities, our reasons, our premises for believing in hell. If they are wrong about hell, they could be wrong about anything and everything else.

2. If Scripture and the church do not lie about what Jesus said about hell, then it presupposes that *Jesus* is the liar. For he was far more explicit and adamant about hell than anyone else in Scripture. If there is no hell, the fundamental reason why Christians believe anything—the authority of Christ—is denied.

3. If we drop hell because it is unbearable to us, that presupposes the principle that we can change whatever doctrines we find unbearable or unacceptable; in other words, that doctrine is negotiable. Christianity then becomes a human ideology, not a divine revelation; a set of humanly chosen ideas and ideals rather than propositional *data*. There is then nothing new or surprising to learn. Doctrine becomes a nose of wax to be twisted into any shape we choose. Try this principle out in any other branch of knowledge and see whether it makes a difference.

In addition to these three presuppositions, there are also seven disastrous consequences of dropping the belief in hell.

1. If there is no hell, life's choices no longer make an infinite difference. The height of the mountain and the depth of the valley, the importance of winning and the importance of losing a war or a game—these two things are relative to each other and measure each other. Drop hell, and heaven becomes a bland, automatic anything and everything for anyone and everyone. The razor-edge drama of life is blunted into a flat, safe plain.

We can see the difference hell makes by comparing Hindu or Buddhist cultures. In these Eastern religions there is no eternal hell, only temporary purgatories or reincarnations. The difference this makes to life here on earth is striking. Drama, especially tragedy, is something the West has specialized in and excelled at because it has theological roots in the doctrine of hell. C. S. Lewis said he never met a person who had a lively belief in heaven who did not also have a lively belief in hell. "If a game is to be taken seriously, it must be possible to lose it."

2. If salvation is universal and automatic, then ultimately there is no free will. We may still be free to choose between one road to heaven and another, but we are not free to choose destinations or directions on the road—forward versus backward, up versus down, good versus evil. It is no accident that those Eastern religions that do not teach hell also do not teach free will. Free will and hell go together; scratch the idea of free will and you will find underneath it the necessity of hell.

3. The same Eastern religions that teach there is no hell also teach there is no absolute morality, no real and objective opposition between good and evil. Morality becomes then only this-worldly and pragmatic—at most a means for purifying the mind from desire so that we can attain the enlightenment of seeing the truth of pantheism. A real, objective opposition between good and evil is incompatible with pantheism. If everything is God, there can be nothing else, nothing anti-God.

4. If there is no hell to be saved from, then Jesus is not our Savior, but only our teacher, prophet, guru or model.

5. If there is no hell, a religious indifference follows. If faith in Christ as Savior is not necessary, we should recall all the missionaries and apologize for all the martyrs. What a waste of passion and energy and time and life! If there is no such thing as fire, fire departments are a distraction and a waste.

6. If salvation is automatic, Christ's sacrificial death was not what Christ himself said it was: necessary, planned, the culmination of his whole earthly life and his reason for coming from heaven to earth. Instead, it was a stupid mistake, a tragic accident. (This idea is devastatingly satirized in C. S. Lewis's *The Great Divorce*, chap. 5.)

7. If there is no reason for believing in the detested doctrine of hell, there is also no reason to believe in the most beloved doctrine in Christianity: that God is love. The beloved doctrine is the reason critics most frequently give for disbelieving the detested doctrine; yet the two stand on exactly the same foundation.

Why do we believe that God is love? Not by philosophical reasoning. What logic can prove that the perfect, self-contained, independent Reality, who has no needs, nevertheless loves these superfluous creatures of his so much that he became one of them to suffer and die for them?

How do we know that God is love? Not by observation of nature, any more than by philosophical reasoning; "nature red in tooth and claw" does not manifest love.

Not by science. No experiment has ever verified divine love, or measured or weighed it or even observed it.

Not by conscience, for conscience is "hard as nails." Conscience tells us what is right and wrong and tells us we are absolutely obliged to do right and not wrong, but it does not tell us we are *forgiven*. The King's laws imprinted on the walls of our conscience do not excuse, but accuse, the lawbreakers. Only the King himself forgives.

Not by history either. History does not move by universal love but by universal selfishness. In fact, history began to move only after universal love was dethroned in Eden. Before the Fall, what happened? Adam and Eve loved each other and God. Hardly headlines. To us fallen creatures, evil and its conflict with good is necessary for anything dramatic and interesting.

There is one and only one reason anyone ever came to the idea that God is love, mercy and forgiveness—and only one good proof that this idea is true. That reason is the character of God revealed in the Bible, culminating in Jesus Christ. *The exact same authority which is our only authority for believing God is love also assures us that there is a hell.* Either we accept both on the same ground or reject both on the same ground, for they stand on the same ground.

Defining the Doctrine of Hell

Before reaching a verdict, we need to cross-examine the defendant. Before deciding whether the doctrine of hell is guilty of being a monstrous myth, or is innocent and true, we need to know just what it is, what it means.

Divine revelation gives us much less information about hell than about heaven. This is what we should reasonably expect, for at least two reasons.

First, hell is essentially the absence of heaven, "the outer darkness." Darkness is defined only negatively, as the absence of light. Light is not the absence of darkness. Evil is the privation of good, good is not the privation of evil. If you believe good and evil are each relative to the other, then you cannot believe in the God of the Bible, for this God is perfectly good and independent of all evil.

Second, we were designed for heaven, not for hell. The travel agent tells you more about the beach resort you are supposed to go to than about the swamp by the side of the highway that you are not supposed to fall into.

Fourteen Things Hell Is Not

Even though we can know only a little about hell, we can know enough to distinguish it from fourteen things with which it is sometimes confused, fourteen popular substitutes for hell. Before we can intelligently argue whether hell exists or not, we must know what it *means*. The first eight confusions are usually found toward the theologically left end of the spectrum, and the last six toward the right.

1. The most obvious alternative to hell is universalism, or universal salvation. Universalism was believed, or at least strongly suggested, by a number of otherwise very orthodox Christians, for example, Julian of Norwich, George MacDonald and Hans Urs von Balthasar. But it seems clearly contradicted by Jesus' frequent teachings about hell's reality.

2. There is also the popular notion that hell exists but only in this life. However, what Jesus warns us against is not merely Pharisees, lawyers, theologians or Roman soldiers, but Satan and eternal death. The pains of this life end at death; what Jesus warns us against has no end (Mk 9:44-48).

Perhaps it could be said that hell begins in this life in the same sense that heaven does: its seed is planted here. Perhaps when we reach eternity we will look back and see this life as the beginning of our eternity; thus the blessed will say they have always been in heaven and the damned will say they have always been in hell. That is not extending this life into the next but extending the next into this; not mitigating hell's horrors by "earthifying" them but magnifying earth's sins by "hellifying" them.

3. Most orthodox Protestants believe in hell but not in purgatory; some unorthodox Catholics believe in purgatory but not in hell. They interpret Scripture's references to hell as references to purgatory. Purgatory seems to them to do all that hell is supposed to do (punish sin), but not eternally. This seems to satisfy both their sense of justice *and* the purpose of purgatory, which is reeducation, or purification; and also their sense of ultimate optimism (everyone in purgatory eventually graduates to heaven).

But the difference between hell and purgatory is clear. By definition, purgatory is good; it purges and purifies. By definition, hell is evil. Demons live and work in hell; angels work in purgatory. (We are merely comparing the definitions of these two things here, not assuming that either one exists or doesn't exist.)

Christ says nothing explicitly about purgatory, but he says explicitly that hell is eternal, and this is enough to distinguish it clearly from purgatory. Dante was right in his *Inferno* to have the sign over hell's gate read: "Abandon all hope, ye who enter here"; and Sartre was right to call his play about hell *No Exit.*

4. Some think the eternity of hell can be preserved without conceiving it as horrible pain but instead as the annihilation of souls. The effect of annihilation would be eternal, thus hell would still be an eternal punishment.

There are three problems with annihilationism. First, it seems contrary to the plain words of Christ. Second, it would make hell to have an end, like purgatory; once you are annihilated, all pain ends. Thus it makes hell temporal and only its *effects* eternal. Third, souls seem to be intrinsically immortal, immortal by their essence, so that it would be as self-contradictory to have a soul cease to exist as to have a circle become square.

Yet something *like* annihilationism was suggested even by that paragon of orthodoxy, C. S. Lewis.

> In all our experience . . . the destruction of one thing means the emergence of something else. Burn a log, and you have gases, heat and ash. To *have been* a log means now being those three things. If souls can be destroyed, must there not be a state of *having been a human soul?* And is not that, perhaps, the state which is equally well described as torment, destruction, and privation? You will remember that in the parable, the saved go to a place prepared for *them,* while the damned go to a place never made for men at all (Mt 25:34, 41). To enter heaven is to become more human than you ever succeeded being on earth; to enter hell is to be banished from humanity. What is cast (or casts itself) into hell is not a man; it is "remains." To be a complete man means to have the passions obedient to the will and the will offered to God; to *have been* a man—to be an ex-man or "damned ghost"—would presumably mean to consist of a will utterly centered in its self and passions utterly uncontrolled by the will . . . a loose congeries of mutually antagonistic sins rather than a sinner. *(The Problem of Pain,* chap. 8, "Hell")

5. Reincarnation is also a popular substitute for hell. The two ideas are far from the same. In Eastern religions, reincarnation is punishment and undesirable, and in that sense functions as hell does in Christianity; but it is not eternal and hopeless. It is like a universal purgatory. To believe in reincarnation is to believe that everyone necessarily gets to heaven (or rather "enlightenment") in the end. There is no hell in Eastern religions.

Reincarnation denies not only hell but also free will. Eventual enlightenment is fated for you; you have no choice.

It also denies individuality, for according to the Hindu scriptures, "Brahman is the only reincarnator" (Brahman does not create individual souls), and according to Buddhism there is *anatta,* or "no soul," in the first place. Thus reincarnation denies what hell affirms (eternity) or presupposes (free will and individuality).

6. Some believe in a *temporary* hell. One version of the medieval story of "The Harrowing of Hell" has Christ clear out hell at the end of the world. (The orthodox version merely has him show himself to the dead on Holy Saturday, as suggested by 1 Pet 3:18-20.)

The word *hell* is sometimes used, misleadingly, to translate two different notions in Scripture: (a) *gehenna,* eternal fire, and (b) *sheol,* the realm of the dead (as in the clause in the Apostles' Creed, "he descended into hell"). If Christ empties *gehenna* and not just *sheol,* this contradicts his own words that hell is eternal. It also seems to contradict free will. What if a soul *will* not choose heaven?

7. Some teach that hell exists but is empty. They rightly distinguish what Jesus teaches and we must believe—that hell exists and we must beware it—from what he does not teach and we need not believe—that any certain number of people are in it. Since this is apparently the most orthodox and biblical way to mitigate the horrors of hell, we must look more carefully at this promising idea. In defense of the possibility that hell may be unpopulated, one could point out that when his disciples asked, "Lord, will only a few be saved?" he did not reply "Yes" but "Strive to enter" (Lk 13:23-24). And even though on other occasions he described the saved as "few" and the damned as "many," we must remember that Jesus is not a census taker or a statistician but the Good Shepherd. In the parable of the ninety-nine sheep (Mt 18:10-14), the Shepherd thought ninety-nine percent safe and saved was too few and just one lost was too many. If a loving parent of twenty children sees just one die in a tragic accident, that one is too many and the nineteen left are too few.

In the past, many Christians misinterpreted this "many" and "few" so as to think they could be certain that most people went to hell. But it is equally a misinterpretation to think we know that few or none go to hell. We simply do not know. Jesus refuses to tell us. Instead of satisfying our theoretical curiosity he tells us what we need to know practically: "Strive to enter."

However, if no one went to hell, we would not have to strive. And if we have to strive in order to enter heaven, then those who refuse to strive do not enter heaven. Thus "strive" implies that some go to hell.

But Jesus also says that "it is not the will of my Father who is in heaven that one of these little ones should perish" (Mt 18:14). Is God's will thwarted?

The fact that it is not God's will that any perish does not mean that none perish. It is not God's will that any sin either, but we do sin. This verse does not refute hell; it refutes a double predestination, a God-willed reprobation, a God who *wants* some to go to hell. Jesus' remark about Judas, that "it would have been better for that one not to have been born" (Mt 26:24), seems to indicate that Judas, at least, is in hell, not heaven. Could Judas be history's one and only exception?

The point is not that some commit more or worse sins than Judas, but that many refuse to repent, as he refused. An infinitely loving God would forgive any sin that is repented, but would respect our free will to refuse repentance if we chose that. How uncommon is that refusal? Scripture speaks of a sin that "will not be forgiven" (Lk 12:10); this is usually interpreted to be the final refusal to repent, the refusal to accept the forgiveness God freely offers to all. If we are free, this is possible. Thus if we are free, hell is possible. (The argument deducing hell from free will is explored more carefully later.)

8. Hell is occasionally confused with limbo. Limbo was invented by some Catholic theologians to solve the problem of unbaptized infants, who have original sin (and thus cannot enter heaven) but have not actually committed sins (thus do not deserve hell). Limbo was pictured as a pleasant sort of nursery for spiritual infants. The doctrine was never officially defined or declared, and most Catholic theologians today do not believe it. Whether there is a limbo or not, it is not hell, for limbo is pleasant and hell is terrible. A nursery and fire are two images that obviously symbolize opposite things.

These first eight confusions all mitigate hell. The next six make it worse, more horrible than it needs to be.

9. Many have believed, and some still believe, that since there is a hell, God must be a God of wrath and vengeance and hate. But this conclusion does not follow from the premise of hell. It may be that the very love of God for the sinner constitutes the sinner's torture in hell. That love would threaten and torture the egotism that the damned sinners insist on and cling to. A small child in a fit of rage, sulking and hating his parents, may feel their hugs and kisses at that moment as torture. By the same psychological principle, the massive beauty of an opera may be torture to someone blindly jealous of its composer. So the fires of hell may be made of the very love of God, or rather by the damned's hatred of that love.

"The wrath of God" is a scriptural expression. But (a) it is probably a metaphor, an anthropomorphic image, like "God's strong right hand" or God changing his mind. It is not literal. And (b) if it is not a metaphor but literal wrath (hate), it is a projection of our own hate onto God rather than a hate within God himself. And (c) if it is an objective fact in God rather than a subjective projection from us, then it refers to God's holiness and justice, not a smoldering resentment; it is his wrath against sin, not against sinners. God practices what he preaches to us: love sinners, hate sins. For surgeons to love their patients, they must hate their patients' cancers. The damned are those who refuse to dissociate themselves from their sins by repenting. Every sin must meet its necessary fate: exclusion from heaven. Only if we glue ourselves to our sins do we glue ourselves to that fate.

The point (b) about God's wrath being our projection is implied by Julian of Norwich, who was disturbed by scriptural language about God's wrath and asked God to show her this wrath. He did, and she wrote: "I saw no wrath but on man's part."

10. Some have taught or implied that hell is forced on the damned, that they are thrown into hell against their will. This would go contrary to the fundamental reason for hell's existence: our free choice and God respecting it.

The damned in hell do not *enjoy* hell, but they do *will* it, by willing egotism instead of love, self instead of God, sin instead of repentance. There can be no heaven without self-giving love. The thing the damned wish for—happiness on their own selfish terms—is impossible even for God to give. It does not exist. It cannot exist.

If hell is chosen freely, the problem then becomes not one of reconciling hell with God's love, but reconciling hell with human sanity. Who would freely prefer hell to heaven unless they were insane?

The answer is that all of us do at one time or another. Every sin reflects that preference. The skeptic objects that if we freely choose hell over heaven, we must be insane; the Christian replies that that is precisely what sin is: insanity, the deliberate refusal of joy and of truth. (See Charles Williams's terrifying novel *Descent into Hell* for a profound instance of this. It is terrifying because it shows how ordinary people like us can go to hell!) Perhaps the most shocking teaching in all of Christianity is this: not so much the doctrine of hell as the doctrine of sin. It means the human race is spiritually insane.

11. The popular, literalistic picture of hell imagines a place populated by creatures like ourselves as we are now. It thus creates the apparently insoluble problem of how the blessed in heaven can have eternal joy if they know that friends they loved on earth are in hell.

We probably should not think of the damned in hell as *persons* any more (see the Lewis quotation above in point 4), but as ghosts—rather like the ghost images on a TV show that appear briefly on the screen after you turn the set off. What is in hell is not a person any more, just as the ashes of a burned painting are not a painting any more. It *was* a painting, and the damned *were* persons.

But it is right for us to mourn over the ashes of a burned painting, because they were once a great painting and are no more. Something great has been lost, and this causes us sorrow. Why will we not have a similar sorrow in heaven over the damned? Perhaps because the blessed live in the present, not the past; and because it is not possible for those who live in the eternal present to regret and mourn the dead past. Regret presupposes a kind of time which is probably exclusively earthly.

In heaven, space is probably transformed, as well as time, in a similar way. We should not think of heaven and hell as parallel places, like Malibu and Alcatraz. C. S. Lewis symbolizes this in *The Great Divorce* by making hell a tiny crack in the ground of heaven. The point of the symbolism is that just as heaven is far more solid and substantial than earth, hell is less so. Even on earth, one place is more "real" than another—for example, compare an island with a parking lot.

Thus, since hell is not a "place" like earth, and since the blessed in heaven do not live in the past, and since the damned are not like paintings but like ashes, the blessed in heaven do not see, love and mourn them. The heaven-cleansed eyes of the blessed will see forever as Jesus' disciples saw for a moment on the Mount of Transfiguration—that is, they will see reality as it really is, unclouded by earthly shadows. And in this vision they will see nothing in hell that can blackmail the joy of heaven.

If this speculative picture is not convincing, the following argument should be. In heaven, we will be more like God. Can one damned soul in hell destroy God's joy for eternity? Can we blackmail God? If not, then *however* this is done, it *is* done: the divine joy, which we shall imitate, or in which we shall participate, will not be disturbed by hell. And this cannot be because of ignorance or lack of love, since God is all-knowing and all-loving. These are the data. If no hypothesis satisfactorily reconciles all the data, let us at least not abandon our data. We may not know *how* God solves this problem, but we know *that* he does. And we will too; for our heaven takes its cue from him, not from our present limitations.

12. Some think that hell is a structural necessity in the great scheme of things; that if there is a heaven there must be a hell, for the height of the mountain is measured only by the depth of the valley. This is true only for us fallen, spoiled creatures. For us, appreciation of good depends on contrast and on our experience of evil. But in Eden there was, and in heaven there will be, joy without sorrow, pleasure without pain, beauty without ugliness, as there cannot be here. This present limitation is not due to God's creation but to our fall. There did not ever need to be a hell. If angels and humans had all obeyed God's will there would never have existed any such thing. Hell is due to freedom, not necessity.

13. Some think that if there is a hell, justice has the last word, not love or mercy, which is one of love's works. We naturally think of mercy as the relaxation and compromising of justice, and justice as prior. But in God, love is more primordial than justice. Justice is simply a form that love takes. The very act of creation is pure love, for no creature was even there to justly deserve anything, not even existence, before it was created. Scripture never says "God is justice," but it does say that "God is love" (1 Jn 4:8). Love is God's essence, justice is one of its works, and mercy is another. Justice is the structure of love. Justice is like the skeleton, love is like the person.

Hell is due more to love than to justice. Love created free persons who could choose hell. Love continues to beat upon the damned like sunlight on an albino slug, and constitutes their torture, as we have seen. The fires of hell are made of the love of God.

14. Perhaps the worst exaggeration of hell is the Calvinistic doctrine (not even held by all Calvinists) of a double predestination. According to this doctrine, God decrees and designs some souls for hell before they are born; God *wills* their damnation. This is contradicted both by Scripture (Mt 18:14) and by moral sanity—how could one love such a monster God?

There is indeed a predestination to heaven, like a AAA road map plotting the right road for your happy vacation. The words *destined* and *predestination* are right there in Scripture (Rom 8:29-30; Eph 1:5, 11). We think the *pre* has to be interpreted nonliterally, since God is not in time. But the crucial point is what kind of God God is. We must not think that just because there is a hell God acts like a divine concentration camp commander who capriciously sends some to the gas chambers and spares others. Christians believe God himself has told them how to think of him, and they always bear in mind his images of love—father, good shepherd and mother hen (Mt 23:37).

Three Things Hell Is

Having spent considerable space on what hell is *not*, we can describe more quickly what hell *is*. Christian theologians have traditionally described hell under three aspects: punishment, pain and privation.

1. The word *punishment* can be interpreted in two different ways: as "positive law" or as "natural law." A "positive law" is a law that is "posited" or made by a will that chose to make it and could have chosen differently. The punishments of positive law are not necessary but rather chosen by the punisher. They may be right and reasonable, but they are not necessary; they are changeable. "If you steal that cookie, I'll slap your hand"; "If you drive ninety miles an hour, we will take away your license"—this is positive law. This is not, we think, the right way to conceive of the punishment of hell: as something God chose but could have chosen differently.

The punishments of "natural law" are intrinsic rather than extrinsic, necessary rather than chosen. "If you eat that cookie before supper, you will spoil your appetite"; "If you drive ninety miles an hour, you will endanger your life"; "If you jump off a cliff, you will die"; "If you are a promiscuous, sexually active homosexual, you are likely to get AIDS"—these are the punishments of natural law.

Take as an example God's command to Adam and Eve not to eat the forbidden fruit. If this is a positive law, it is like a mother threatening to slap her child's hand if he takes a cookie. If it is a natural law, it means that if we eat the forbidden fruit of disobedience to God's will, divorcing our will and spirit from God's, then the inevitable result will be disaster and death, for God is the source of all joy and life.

In a natural law ethic, virtue is its own reward and vice is its own punishment. Virtue is to the soul what health is to the body. It has its own intrinsic, necessary and unchangeable structures, such that all good deeds help the doer as well as the recipient and all evil deeds harm the doer as well as the victim.

The punishment of hell is inevitable, by natural law. Any human soul that freely refuses the one Source of all life and joy *must* find death and misery as its inevitable punishment. Once again, C. S. Lewis makes the point most clearly:

Though Our Lord often speaks of hell as a sentence inflicted by a tribunal, he also says elsewhere that the judgment consists in the very fact that men prefer darkness to light, and that not he, but his "word" judges men (Jn 3:19; 12:48). We are therefore at liberty—since the two conceptions, in the long run, mean the same thing—to think of this bad man's perdition not as a sentence imposed on him but as the mere fact of being himself. The characteristic of lost souls is "their rejection of everything that is not simply themselves." Our imaginary egoist has tried to turn everything into a province or appendage of the self. The taste for the *other*, that is, the very capacity for enjoying good, is quenched in him except in so far as his body still draws him into some rudimentary contact with an outer world. Death removes this last contact. He has his wish—to live wholly in the self and to make the best of what he finds there. And what he finds there is hell. *(The Problem of Pain,* chap. 8, "Hell")

In the famous painting of Jesus with a lamp knocking on a door (= your soul), there is no knob on the outside of the door. Only from the inside can the door of the soul be opened, freely, to goodness and truth and joy. And only from the inside can it be locked. If we lock that door, our folly and crime is its own punishment.

2. Since the God to whom we choose to open and love and obey is the sole source of all the joy in reality, our refusal of this God must necessarily be joyless and painful. Thus hell must have the aspect of pain as well as punishment. If God is joy, hell must be pain.

Somewhat as with punishment, the pain can be thought of either externally or internally. The internal pain would be far worse than external pain, just as internal and spiritual joys far exceed any physical, external pleasures. Therefore the old question of whether there is physical fire in hell is a moot and pointless point.

When our soul is in pain (e.g., despair), we may hit our head against the wall. Why? Because physical pain is not as bad as spiritual pain, and it distracts us from the worse pain, the spiritual. It was probably because she realized this principle that Catherine of Genoa said that she thought there were no physical fires in hell because if there were, that would not be the worst hell conceivable, since fire is a good and a creature of God. Thus, if we wish to deny the crude, old picture of hell as a physical torture chamber, we may be left not with a gentler hell but with a far more horrible and unbearable one.

The only premise we need to prove the conclusion that hell is supremely painful is the premise that the supreme joy is love, and thus the supreme pain is lovelessness. Dostoyevsky says that "hell is the suffering of being unable to love." There can be no greater pain than that because there is no greater joy than loving. Loving is even greater joy than being loved, for "It is more blessed [happy, joyful] to give than to receive" (Acts 20:35). Anyone who does not know that is still a spiritual infant.

Satan's primary lie that deceives humanity, keeps it in spiritual infancy and causes more suffering than anything else, is the lie that selfishness is fun and unselfishness is not. The origin of sin and suffering is faith in Satan's lie (which began in Genesis 3) that life and joy come from disobedience to God, from "my will be done." At the far end of that lie lies hell

3. The third aspect of hell is privation, or deprivation of God. This does not mean that God shuts us out, but that we shut him out, and thus are deprived of God by our own choice.

This aspect of hell is the cause of the other two. Only because hell is the *privation* of God—the source of all joy—is hell *painful.* And only because hell is the deprivation of God, the only God, the true God, "the only game in town," is hell's alternative to God the inevitable and just *punishment* for the folly of refusing this only game in town. The desire to be happy without God is doomed to failure, pain and inevitable punishment because God is not one among many sources of joy but the only ultimate source of all joy. Deprivation of the ultimate cause must mean deprivation of all its effects.

It is not a very popular idea—that God is "the only game in town." Yet it necessarily follows from the much more popular idea that God is Creator. If everything is either God or a creature of God, then there cannot be any source of good or joy that is not God or sourced in God. Everything in the world that gives us joy is like a sunbeam from the divine sun. However perverse or perverted, however turned or twisted, all joys are reflections of God. Therefore the privation of God is the privation not just of some joy but all joy. Of all hell's aspects, this is the most terrible. You see it on the faces of the damned in Gustave Doré's illustrations of Dante's *Inferno.* You can imagine it when pondering this quotation: "All your life an unattainable ecstasy has hovered just beyond the grasp of your consciousness. The day is coming when you will wake to find, beyond all hope, that you have attained it; or else, that it was within your grasp and you have lost it forever" (C. S. Lewis, *The Problem of Pain,* chap. 10, "Heaven").

Seven Reasons for Believing in Hell

Can we prove that hell exists? There are at least seven good reasons to believe it does. The first three are arguments from authority, the other four from philosophical reasoning. While arguments from human authority are the weakest of all arguments, arguments from divine authority, which can neither deceive nor be deceived, are the strongest.

1. The Bible assures us that there is a hell. If the Bible is God's word, then to disbelieve in hell is to disbelieve God. To call the message a lie is to call its author a liar.

The usual way out of this argument is to interpret the Bible—or rather those parts of it that you do not want to believe—nonliterally. The problem with this, besides the obvious dishonesty in foisting your own wants onto the data, is that although the scriptural *imagery* is not meant literally, the *reality* of the hell that is thus imaged clearly is.

2. Most unanswerably of all, we have the authority of Christ himself. If you do not believe in hell, you deny the Incarnation, the divinity of Christ. For only a man can lie, not God.

3. The church has always taught, and dogmatically defined, hell. Even a traditional Protestant, who would appeal to Scripture alone, would be disturbed if such a central part of the church's message were a lie. A Catholic should be scandalized. If the church is deceived or deceiving about this, why not about anything else—like heaven or salvation?

A Christian who does not believe in hell is a contradiction in terms, because a Christian is one who believes in Christ, and Christ is one who believes in hell. The only way to believe in Christ without believing in hell is to reconstruct Christ according to your own desires. (*He* wants to reconstruct you according to *his* desires!) Then the game begins: Christ the Marxist, Christ the capitalist, Christ the Democrat, Christ the Republican, Christ the environmentalist, Christ the magician, Christ the homosexual, even Christ the Nazi. Why not? *Why* not? Hitler's propagandists created such a Christ. They subtracted his Jewishness to suit their ideology, just as the modernists subtract Christ's otherworldliness to suit theirs. The fact that modernist ideology is "nicer" than Nazi ideology does not justify the principle that you can fudge your data to suit your ideology. If the modernist can use that principle, why can't the Nazi? The logic of the argument is indifferent to niceness or nastiness.

If there is no hell, Christ is not only a deceptive teacher but a wicked one, for he terrifies us needlessly, falsely and harmfully. Everyone knows the horrible abuses that have come from believing this doctrine—the private fears and the public manipulation of those fears. Unless there is a hell and the other-worldly consequences of not believing in hell outweigh the very considerable this-worldly consequences of believing in it, it is a terribly harmful doctrine and its teacher is terribly at fault for laying this terrible and unnecessary burden on our shoulders.

In fact, the kindest, gentlest, most loving and compassionate man who ever opened his mouth has warned us with the greatest seriousness, strenuousness and sternness about hell. That is the irrefutable argument for it.

4. Justice demands punishment for evil. Justice means moral discrimination between good and evil, reward and punishment. Justice is not a human creation, and thus we cannot destroy it. It is as unchangeable as mathematics, because it is an attribute of God. Divine justice does not prevent God

from forgiving, but it prevents him from treating final impenitence as if it were repentance. Mercy may go infinitely beyond justice, but it cannot destroy it or contradict it.

Justice must discriminate between the repentant and the unrepentant, between those who accept the gift of mercy and those who do not, between those who freely choose heaven and those who do not. Not to do so would be like giving the Nobel Peace Prize to Stalin. God cannot tell such lies.

5. Hell follows from the exclusivity of God. If we were pagans, the god we worshiped could be dispensed with and exchanged for another. If you don't like the Furies, choose the Olympians; if you don't like Zeus, worship Apollo instead. But if God is the sole source of all life, light and joy, then to avoid him is necessarily to avoid life, light and joy forever. Those who deny hell fail to see this simple point: that God is the only God, and his heaven is the only heaven.

6. The simplest of all arguments for hell is human free will. If we are really free to choose to respond to God's marriage proposal to our souls, if God is not a rapist but a gentleman, then we must be free to turn him down. And if our souls at death enter eternity in that state, after there is no more time for change and repentance, then we must endure the identity we have chosen eternally.

Even if there were time for second chances or reincarnations after death, what if one still refuses? If we are free, we can always refuse. If ever it becomes *necessary* that we accept God, that acceptance becomes unfree. In other words, if we say that enough second chances or reincarnations will infallibly guarantee that everyone chooses for God, then we say that after a sufficient amount of time, free choice turns into unfree necessity and determinism. But this is impossible; it is to say that, given enough time, a thing can lose its own essence.

If the happiness of a creature lies in (free) self-surrender, no one can make that surrender but himself, though many can help him to make it, and he may refuse. I would pay any price to be able to say truthfully, "All will be saved." But my reason retorts, "Without their will, or with it?" If I say, "Without their will," I at once perceive a contradiction: how can the supreme voluntary act of self-surrender be involuntary? If I say "With their will," my reason replies "How if they *will not* give in?"

In the long run the answer to all those who object to the doctrine of hell is itself a question: "What are you asking God to do?" To wipe out their past sins and, at all costs, to give them a fresh start, smoothing every difficulty and offering every miraculous help? But he has done so, on Calvary. To forgive them? They *will* not be forgiven. To leave them alone? Alas, I am afraid that is what he does. (C. S. Lewis, *The Problem of Pain*, chap. 8, "Hell")

7. A final argument for hell is the argument from fear. It is parallel to the argument from desire for the existence of heaven (see p. 250). Both arguments use the same major premise: that a universal, innate, natural desire always corresponds to a real object. Since fear is correlative to desire (we fear to lose whatever we desire to have, and we desire to lose whatever we fear to have), the same premise can be used substituting "fear" for "desire." Thus every innate fear corresponds to something real. Then the minor premise reports that we have an innate desire for heaven. Correlative to this is our innate fear of hell. The conclusion is that heaven and hell must both be real.

The innate desire for heaven is inchoate and does not specify much of the content of heaven, just something more and better than anyone ever gets on earth. Similarly, the innate fear of hell does not specify much about the nature of hell, just that it is worse than the worst things anyone ever experiences on earth. (That's bad enough!)

The only attackable part of the argument seems to be the minor premise: is there really an innate fear of hell? The evidence for it is both external and internal. Externally, we find the fear expressed in many different times, places, cultures and religions, not just accepted on Christian authority. Internally, we can only appeal to deep honesty: Is it not true that the deepest reason why we fear death is that something in us is not quite certain that there is no hell and that we could not possibly go there?

Defending the Doctrine: Thirteen Objections Answered

The arguments *against* believing in hell seem very strong and simple. Yet each can be answered.

Objection 1:

Most obviously, hell seems clean contrary to the love of God. How could a God of total love make or even tolerate such a torture chamber? The stark contrast between the character of God taught and exemplified by Jesus—love, kindness, mercy and forgiveness—and the character of a God who presides over a creation that includes a hell is too obvious for argument. Only by not thinking these two ideas at the same time could anyone believe both of them.

Reply A: Of *course* hell is contrary to the God of love. That is its very essence. But its existence does not refute God's existence. For love wants the beloved to be free, like itself. Love created freedom, love appeals to freedom, love respects freedom. It is this freedom that chooses hell.

Reply B: True, God is perfect mercy and forgiveness. But let us be clear about what that means. Forgiveness appeals to freedom; it must be freely given *and freely accepted,* like any gift. If we do not repent and ask for God's forgiveness, we do not receive it—not because God holds it back but because we hold ourselves back.

Reply C: God's love is also truthful. Love is *not* blind; love is accurate. God is love, and God is not blind but accurate. God's love is not a subjective feeling but is utterly realistic. In fact, it is reality itself. In a sense there *is* nothing else. The room you are sitting in is God's love in the form and limits of a room, and you are God's love in the form of a created image of himself. Thus, all who refuse that love refuse reality, and there is no alternative to reality except "outer darkness."

Reply D: Hell does not refute God's love because the very fires of hell may be of God's love (see point 9, p. 289). The damned hate this love, and it tortures them, but it is unavoidable. God can't stop loving any more than the sun can stop shining or water can stop being wet.

Imagine a person who commits suicide seeking death, not life, and is horrified when he finds that, after he has died, his soul is immortal and can never die; he can never escape himself. God and himself are the only two realities he can never escape. If *these* are hated and become misery to him, rather than loved and become joy, then he is in eternal and inescapable misery.

This is not to say that all suicides are damned. Probably most suicides are not wholly sane or responsible. God will see and grant whatever deep desire lies in their hearts, hidden from us but not from him. (For a convincing case for a saved suicide, see Charles Williams's novel *Descent into Hell.*)

Objection 2:

Hell seems contrary to justice as well as love. For the punishment does not seem to fit the crime here, either in quantity or quality. What is the relation or proportion between hell's unthinkable, infinite, eternal torments and earth's thinkable, finite, temporal sins? The same sort of relationship as fifty years of torture to a three-year-old's theft of a cookie. How can finite sin justly merit infinite punishment? How can temporal sin merit eternal punishment?

Reply: There are three charges here: (a) temporal crimes do not merit eternal punishments, (b) finite crimes do not merit infinite punishments, and (c) mild crimes do not merit such intense punishments.

a. Eternity is not quantitative. It is not more time, or even endless time. It is another *dimension* than time, just as time is another dimension than space. Whatever we make of ourselves in time is destined to be "fleshed out" into the dimension of eternity. To use a crude image, if we make squares of ourselves in time, we are cubes eternally; temporally blueprinted triangles go to the sculptor to become eternal pyramids. The relation between earthly choices and eternal rewards or punishments is not like the relation between crimes and prison sentences, but like the relation between a foundation and a building. It is not external but internal. In a sense, heaven or hell is the same thing as earth; the same life, the same person, only with another dimension—somewhat as life after birth is the same life, the same person, but with more dimensions. Souls in time are like boats on a river, all destined for the ocean of eternity. It is a structural internal necessity, not an imposed external reward or punishment.

b. Hell's punishments are *eternal,* but not *infinite.* Only God is infinite. Souls, sin and punishment are all finite. Just as one saint is more saintly, more great-hearted, more loving, and therefore more able to contain God's joy in heaven than another, and in this sense is naturally "higher" in heaven than another, so one sinner is "lower" in hell than another (i.e., more deep-set in despair and pride and hate). There are limits.

c. The intense images of physical torture are meant to suggest something beyond themselves: the privation of God, source of all joy and meaning. The unimaginable thing suggested by the imaginative images of fire is more awful, not less, than the literal misinterpretation of the images. Physical pain comes in degrees of intensity; the privation of God is total.

Hell's punishment fits sin's crime because sin is divorce from God. The punishment fits the crime because the punishment *is* the crime. Saying no to God means no God. The point is really very simple. Those who object to hell's overseverity do not see what sin really is. They probably look at sin externally, sociologically, legalistically, as "behaving badly." They fail to see the real horror of sin and the real greatness and goodness and joy of the God who is refused in every sin. We all fail to appreciate this. Who of us fully appreciates God's beauty? The corollary immediately follows: who of us fully appreciates sin's ugly horror?

Hell shocks our human minds. To believe in hell is to allow the divine mind to instruct and correct our human minds of their little illusions, to measure our thoughts by God's. To refuse to believe is to measure God's thoughts by ours.

Objection 3:

Not only does hell seem to contradict God's love and his justice, but also God's power. The God who created the whole universe out of nothing is omnipotent, all-powerful. If his power has no limit, why does he not destroy hell or arrange for no one to go there?

The argument can be put in the form of a dilemma. Does God will everyone to be saved or not? If not, he is not all-loving. If so, and not all are saved, then his will is thwarted and he is not all-powerful.

If God is all-good and all-powerful, he must have created the best of all possible worlds, for to prefer a worse world to a better one is not to be all-good. But a world in which no one goes to hell, or a world in which there is no hell, is a better world than a world in which some go to hell. Therefore, if there is a hell, God deliberately created a bad world, and he is not all-good. Or else he tried to create a wholly good world, one without a hell, but failed. In this case, he is not all-powerful. If God is both all-good and all-powerful, there cannot be a hell.

A world without a hell seems to be a conceivable and possible world, even granted human free will. For all God would have to do is foresee whether the person about to be conceived was going to hell or to heaven; if to hell, God would arrange, whether by natural providence or supernatural miracle, for that person not to be conceived. Omnipotence could surely do that.

Reply: To reconcile God's omnipotence with hell, we must first be sure we have a true concept of omnipotence. Omnipotence is limited by nothing outside itself, but God's power does not extend to contradicting his own essential nature. God is consistent. The logical laws of consistency (identity and noncontradiction) are reflections of the very nature of God. God cannot do meaningless and self-contradictory things (see pp. 138-39). One such intrinsically impossible, self-contradictory and meaningless thing would be to have a world with free creatures and no possibility of hell.

There are three ways one might think God could do this: destroy hell, annihilate the souls in hell, or arrange for no hell-bound persons to be conceived. To destroy hell means to destroy free choice by destroying one of its two options. If there is no hell, no separation from God, then all *must* choose God, and this is not a free choice. To annihilate the souls in hell would be to destroy something God created to be intrinsically and essentially immortal and indestructible—this is another self-contradiction. To arrange for only heaven-bound souls to be conceived would be in effect to destroy free choice again: to destroy free choice of evil before it happens rather than after.

The objection claims that a world with no hell is possible and asks why

God did not create it. He did! God did not create separation from himself. God did not create hell. We did. God created a perfect world, but in creating humans (and angels) with free will, he left it up to us whether this actual world—the one without hell—would *continue* to be, or whether another possible world—one with hell—would *begin* to be.

Of course this is not "the best of all possible worlds" or even a world as good as it *might* be. But that's not God's fault, it's ours. What the objection comes down to is resentment at God for creating free will at all.

What is the answer to the dilemma about God's will? Is it thwarted or not? It is. God clearly wills all to be saved (2 Pet 3:9). But this is not a contradiction to his omnipotence; it is the greatest mark of his omnipotence, that he can create free children, not just robots or holograms.

It is objected that the ultimate loss of a single soul means the defeat of omnipotence. And so it does. In creating beings with free will, omnipotence from the outset submits to the possibility of such defeat. What you call defeat, I call miracle; for to make things which are not Itself, and thus to become, in a sense, capable of being resisted by its own handiwork, is the most astonishing and unimaginable of all the feats we attribute to the Deity. (C. S. Lewis, *The Problem of Pain*, chap. 8, "Hell")

If the objector replies that that is not what he means by omnipotence, we retort that that's what *God* means by omnipotence! The objector's model of omnipotence is a divine puppeteer, robot-maker or tyrant rather than a divine Father.

Objection 4:

Hell also seems contrary to human freedom, for no one would freely choose hell over heaven if given a free and open choice. Thus, hell would have to be imposed upon us, since no one loves punishment, pain or privation of joy, which is what hell is.

Hell would render religious and moral choice unfree, just as the threat of torture renders a forced confession unfree. "Repent, believe and be good, or you'll fry" means that your repentance, belief and goodness are forced, not free. Fry and free are opposites.

Reply: Distinguish, as Augustine does, the freedom of liberty from the freedom of choice (*libertas* vs. *liberum arbitrium*). Hell is contrary to liberty but not to free choice. Free choice is a means to the end of higher freedom, liberty from sin. Those who fail to attain heaven's liberty reached their eternal destination by the same means as those who attained that liberty: by their free will.

We do, and therefore can, freely choose hell over heaven. We do this in principle in every sin. We do not want or explicitly choose sin's "wages," sin's inevitable punishment—banishment from the paradise of God's presence—but we do choose the sin and hope to escape the punishment.

Does the fear of hell remove free choice? Does *fry* contradict *free?* No more than the fear of falling off a cliff removes the free choice to skate close to the edge or to avoid it. If the threat "repent or you'll fry" removed free will, then all would repent. But this is not so; the threat is issued, but some respond and some do not. So in fact the threat does *not* remove free choice.

Objection 5:

Even if hell is not contrary to human freedom, it seems contrary to human sanity. For only someone insane would freely choose hell over heaven. But insanity is a good excuse. We do not punish criminals if we find that they are insane. Is God less just or merciful than we? What an incredible insult it is to humanity to imply that all who do not believe and are saved are insane!

Reply: We do not know how anyone could freely prefer hell to heaven, misery to joy, but it happens. It happens in every sin. We *are* spiritually insane! That is what the doctrine of original sin implies.

We know this from our own experience. Think of all the times you turn to God in love and obedience, and find peace and joy. Then think of all the times you turn away from God in sin, and find no peace and no joy. We know by millions of repeated experiences and experiments, all yielding the same results: "the wages of sin is death," the death of joy, and yet we sin. We are insane. Only the insane prefer misery to joy.

If sin exists, hell can exist; for hell is only sin eternalized. Hell is not so much an external punishment added to sin, as it is sin come to full fruition. Similarly, heaven is not an external reward added to faith and love; it is that very state of soul made perfect.

Sin does not mean just disobeying a law. That is only its formula. Sin means separating yourself from God, knowing God's will and yet "no-ing" it instead of "yes-ing" it. That is also the essence of hell.

But if we are insane, isn't that an excuse? If it comes to me against my will, yes; but if I choose it, no. In sinning, I *choose* to go insane. If someone else force-feeds me drugs, I am not responsible for the crimes I commit under their influence; but if I choose to take them, I am responsible. Sin is the ultimate drug.

Objection 6:

Hell seems contrary to the morality of Jesus. The famous atheist philosopher Bertrand Russell argued, in "Why I Am Not a Christian," that any teacher who believed and taught hell could not be a truly moral teacher. He thought the God of Christianity to be a cosmic hypocrite, preaching forgiveness but practicing vengeance, preaching kindness but practicing cruelty, preaching love but practicing torture.

We can distinguish four elements of this criticism of hell as immoral: (a) vengeance, (b) cruelty, (c) mercilessness and (d) retributive punishment itself. Didn't the ethic of Jesus substitute nonjudgmental forgiveness for retributive punishment? How can the morality we are supposed to practice be higher than its divine Source?

Reply: What the critic means by "the morality of Jesus" is quite different from the actual morality of the real Jesus, the only Jesus we have any objective evidence for, that is, the Jesus of the New Testament. That Jesus taught both mercy and justice, love and judgment, heaven and hell.

To say that anyone who teaches and warns about hell is immoral is like saying that any mother who warns her children not to play with fire is immoral. It is just plain silly.

The cause of hell is not divine vengeance or cruelty or mercilessness. The cause of hell is our free choice to refuse God's forgiveness and kindness and mercy.

Jesus did not substitute mercy for justice. He told many parables about justice and judgment and punishment. We are told to "judge not"—not because God does not judge, but because he does. God alone can judge human hearts. We shouldn't try, because we can't. We can judge only deeds.

The critic seems to be confusing *forgiving* with *condoning*. Condoning sin means pretending it isn't sin, pretending that "there's nothing to forgive." There is. God is not ignorant or dishonest. Omniscience cannot hide its head in the sand like an ostrich; it must deal with sin, and deal justly. His mercy does not destroy his justice; both are elements of his goodness, and both are inescapable. But his mercy separates our sins from ourselves, and gives our sins their just punishment in Christ, not in us. He pays our debt. We go free. Still, the debt must be paid. Justice cannot be ignored.

Objection 7:

The effect of believing in hell is the opposite of what the God of the Bible wants from us. God wants faith, hope and love. But if we believe in hell, we naturally feel fear, despair and hatred.

Reply: Sometimes belief in hell has produced these terrible effects, but this is due to bad teaching. The doctrine *has* been abused. But *abusus non tollit usus:* the abuse does not annul the proper use.

When the doctrine of hell is abused, that abuse serves the very purposes of hell (fear, despair and hatred) instead of the purposes of heaven (faith, hope and love).

On the other hand, fear is sometimes good and necessary. "The fear of the Lord is the beginning of wisdom" (Prov 1:7), though it is not the end. (Love is that.) George MacDonald said, "When there are wild beasts about, it is better to feel afraid than to feel secure." Fear is reasonable and useful even in little things; what is more reasonably feared than hell, if it exists? The critic is presupposing that it doesn't exist, not proving that it doesn't. A person can't say that the reason hell does not exist is that it is bad to fear it, and also that the reason it is bad to fear it is that it doesn't exist. That's begging the question and arguing in a circle.

Belief in hell does not produce despair and hatred; hell itself produces despair and hate. If you believe that there are two roads ahead, one of which leads home and one of which leads over a cliff, you do not despair—especially if the two roads are clearly marked by signs, as are the roads to heaven and hell. Only after the wrong choice is made and you have fallen over the cliff does despair take over. Dante had the sign over hell's gate read: "Abandon All Hope, Ye Who Enter Here."

Belief in hell should not produce hatred of God, for God did not invent hell or sin. We did. He invented salvation.

Objection 8:

If hell exists, no loving soul in heaven can be happy for all eternity. Suppose your spouse or parent or child goes to hell and you go to heaven. Either you know your beloved is in hell or not. If not, your heavenly happiness is founded on ignorance. If so, this knowledge must disturb your heavenly happiness. If it doesn't, you are selfish, cold and unloving. Thus, if hell exists, then heaven is either ignorant, unhappy or unloving. Heaven cannot be any of these things. Therefore hell cannot exist.

In addition to the answers given above (point 17, p. 271), the most practical answer to the objection is this. If you cannot imagine how you can be happy in heaven if X goes to hell, then pray for X's salvation: "God, I know you want me to be happy with you forever, and it seems to me that I can't be happy without X; so you are going to have to save X for my sake." We think God would not refuse that prayer, for even if its theology may be a little out of place, its heart is not.

Objection 9:

If hell exists, it is vastly overpopulated. It may be tolerable and right for a few irredeemable monsters like Mao and the Marquis de Sade and TV executives, but not for masses of ordinary people such as we meet every day. But if there are no masses in hell, Jesus overdid its danger and spoke too much about it.

Most Christians in the past believed that the majority of humans who have ever lived end up in hell and only a minority in heaven. Jesus even said that the way to hell is "wide" and "many" find it, while the way to heaven is "narrow" and "few" find it (Mt 7:13-14). But this would be a divine defeat: more points (souls) lost than won. It would have been better for God not to have created us at all if he foresaw that he would lose more than he won.

If he failed to foresee this, he is not all-wise. If he foresaw it but was compelled to create this hell-bound world, he is not all-powerful. If he foresaw it and freely created it, he is not all-good. Thus, if there is a hell, God is either not all-wise or not all-powerful or not all-good.

Reply: How can we judge when hell is "overpopulated"? How can such a line be drawn? It is like the problem of evil: how much evil is too much to be compatible with an all-good God (p. 123)? The only two possible answers are (a) any evil, and any damned soul, even one, refutes God; or (b) no amount of evil and no amount of the damned refutes God. No reason can be given for drawing a line of refusal at some finite point between these two.

The popular past assumption that most go to hell is no more valid than the popular modern assumption that most go to heaven. We simply do not know. When his disciples asked Jesus whether the saved would be few or many, he answered: "Strive to enter" (Lk 13:24). The doctrine of hell is addressed to our will and practical living, not to our detached curiosity, not to the statistician in us. (See point 7 above.)

The objection assumes—falsely—that if more than fifty percent of humanity is damned, God was wrong to have created us. We do not claim to prove that even if most are damned God is still right to create. Our point is simply that the question is unsolvable and unmeasurable by any standards we know. It is the objector, not the defender, of the doctrine of hell, who appeals to this unprovable premise. Life is not a game played between God and the Devil in which the one who ends up with the most souls wins.

Objection 10:

An eternal hell seems to mean that God is not totally or finally victorious over evil.

Heaven and hell seem coeternal forever. But this is Manichaean dualism, where good and evil exist as equal and opposite warring ultimates. In that case God is not omnipotent.

This contradicts both Scripture and reason. It contradicts Scripture because Scripture says God will, in the end, be totally victorious over evil, and will be "all in all" (1 Cor 15:12-28, 54-57). It contradicts reason because it is inherent in the nature of evil to be self-destructive, not to last forever.

Reply: This objection, like objection 8, wrongly assumes that hell implies an eternal coexistence of good (heaven) and evil (hell). But coexistence implies a common field of some kind of time and/or place in which to coexist. But neither heaven nor hell are in time, in history. They are at the end of history. A parallel: another person's death can occur in my life's time, but my own death cannot. My own death ends my life's time. Whatever eternity is, it is not time, not even endless time.

Scripture is quite clear both that hell is eternal and that there is no eternal Manichaean dualism, no stalemate between good and evil, only God's final triumph. *How* both these doctrines can be true may not be clear from Scripture, but *that* they are both true is clear. This is given as our data, just as both divine predestination *and* human free will and responsibility are both given as data, but not how the two are to be reconciled. In both cases, our limited understanding of time and eternity prevents us from seeing the answer clearly.

Objection 11:

The God of the Bible is a God not only of knowledge and love and justice and power, but also a God of purpose. Everything in his creation serves a purpose. What purpose does hell serve? If it is eternal, it is not for reeducation and rehabilitation. What purpose could God have for sustaining in existence the souls of those in an eternal hell from which there is no hope of escape?

Reply: Hell does not serve a good purpose, because it is not good, but evil. Only good serves a purpose; evil attacks purpose.

Also, hell is not in time. But purposes are served in time. The purpose of pregnancy is birth; the purpose of courtship is marriage. Even merely apparent goods, which are not really good but evil, have purposes in time: for example, the purpose of suicide is death. But hell is not in time, hell does not have a purpose, and hell was not made by God at all.

God does not sustain in existence the souls of the damned by any supernaturally willed act. Rather, his sustaining of souls forever is built into the *nature* of souls. In the act of creating eternal souls in the first place, God sustains them forever. God is not in time; his sustaining does not come *after* his creating, for him.

Objection 12:

Hell must be annihilation rather than eternal existence, because human nature could not hold up under eternal alienation from God. The law of diminishing returns would set in. A point is reached at which the creature in hell is no longer a person but (as we supposed above) "remains." How can "remains" be tortured or punished?

Reply: Hell is indeed annihilation—of goodness, hope, joy, even the unifying power of the personality, the *I*. We see the seeds of hell in the demon-possessed man in Luke 8:26-30. Jesus asked him his name and he replied, "Legion," for many demons had entered him. He had lost his unifying self, his I. Yet *something* remained there. He was not simply annihilated. C. S. Lewis points out that "in all our experience, the destruction of one thing means the emergence of other things. Burn a log and you get ashes and gases." What burns in hell are the soul's putrid, hate-filled remains.

Objection 13:

The simplest and strongest objection is instinctual. All these arguments are superfluous; our deepest heart finds hell intolerable and incredible. The doctrine can be accepted only by idiots, moral monsters or professors who look at abstract arguments but do not hold the doctrine up steadily before their eyes and look candidly into it. It simply cannot be done.

Reply: Our instinctive denial of hell proves nothing, just as our instinctive denial of our own death proves nothing. If you went to the doctor feeling fine and were told you had six weeks to live, your natural reaction would be denial, but denial is not disproof.

Our instinctive denial of this doctrine comes partly from our confusing the doctrine with the imagery—fiery pitchforks gleefully inserted by demons in red tights into human posteriors. This is not even scriptural imagery, but bears all the marks of human invention. The doctrine does not.

The same is true of heaven: the doctrine is not tied to the popular imagery of harps and haloes, or even to the scriptural imagery of jewelry and city gates. Imagery is not meant to be taken literally, but it *is* meant to be taken seriously. When we cannot find words, we point to analogies. We do not find truth with the imagination, the image-making faculty. We find truth with reason and faith. Both assure us that hell exists.

Instinct is often a way of finding truth. But our instincts are not infallible.

Nor is our reasoning. We may well have made mistakes in our reasoning in this chapter, but God cannot lie. If we cannot trust God's Word, we can trust nothing. Christians do not believe in hell because they *want* to (what a horrible thought!) but because God has instructed them to believe it.

The Proper Use and Misuse of the Doctrine of Hell

Most passionate objections to the doctrine of hell are really objections to those religious teachers who have misused it. (This seems especially prevalent among American fundamentalists and Irish Catholics.) The objection comes down to this: Hell was probably invented out of hate and fear and the desire to control and dominate people, since that is the fruit the doctrine produces.

The same objection, however, can be lodged against the doctrine of heaven: that it is misused, produces an irresponsible lack of concern for this world, and manipulates people like a carrot on a stick. In fact, *any* idea, true or false, can be misused and abused. This tells us nothing about its truth or a falsity.

Those who have been hurt by the misuse of this doctrine often seem to think that those who believe in hell:

1. want hell to exist (as if doctrines were not facts but desires);

2. want humans to go there (as if Christians could want what the Devil wants!);

3. self-righteously exclude themselves from its dangers (as if Christians were Pharisees instead of saved sinners); and

4. coolly and detachedly discuss this ultimate holocaust and horror (as if missionaries were making maps of the ocean instead of throwing out the life boat).

All four assumptions are false, of course—in fact, hellish distortions. If Christians follow Christ, they will give anything to save humanity from hell, because that is what Christ did.

The third cavil above is the most devastating, if true—but it is not. Christian teachers have repeatedly made the point C. S. Lewis makes to conclude his chapter on hell in *The Problem of Pain:* "In all our discussions of hell we should keep steadily before our eyes the possible damnation, not of our enemies nor our friends . . . but of ourselves. This chapter is not about your wife or son, nor about Nero or Judas Iscariot; it is about you and me." That is the proper use of the doctrine of hell.

We began this chapter with a justification for its inclusion and length. We conclude with another, for many readers may still wonder: Why must we believe in and teach hell? First, for the only good reason to believe or teach anything: because it is true, because it is there. In other words, out of honesty. Second, out of love, out of compassion, out of the fear that love generates that any loved and precious soul end up there by disbelieving the warning signs, like children drowning because the ice seemed thick enough and the warning signs were ignored. When there is real war, the *least* loving thing we can do is to cry "peace, peace when there is no peace" (Jer 8:11).

Those who preach this truth will be hated and feared, mocked and maligned, as fools, sadists or manipulators. So be it. Christians today are often more terrified of sharing their Lord's holy unpopularity than of hell itself. (You don't nail a man to a cross for telling you things you like to hear!) To be called a nasty name is a small price to pay for the privilege of possibly contributing one strand to the rope that saves an infinitely precious little one for whom Christ died.

Questions for Discussion

1. Is there any other teaching in Christianity that is more unpopular than hell today?

2. Is it possible to abandon the doctrine of hell without abandoning each of the ten more central Christian teachings (pp. 283-84)? If so, how might someone answer the ten arguments? If not, why do so many intelligent Christians think they have done just that? Have they?

3. Why are the first three points so unpopular—especially point 3 (p. 283)?

4. Suppose God revealed to you (and you could not doubt) that you would certainly escape hell and go to heaven. What would be the consequences in your life and thought and feeling? How and why would they be any different from the consequences of believing there was no hell for anyone at all?

5. Concerning point 5 (p. 284), don't Aristotle and Aquinas teach that we are free only to choose the means, not the end, since all necessarily seek happiness? If this is true, doesn't it contradict the assumption in point 5 that we are "free to choose destinations"?

6. Concerning point 6, can there be an absolute morality without a hell? Why or why not? If so, why historically is there such a strong connection between the two ideas, so few examples of one without the other? (Are there any?)

7. What would be meant by Jesus' name ("Savior") if there were no hell to be saved from?

8. Is there any passion stronger than fear of hell?

9. Is fear of hell morally or spiritually bad? If so, why does Christ appeal to it? If not, why do many think it is?

10. Could one somehow justify belief in the love of God on some other secure

ground than the authority of the revelation of Christ, Scripture and the church, which also teach the reality of hell?

11. How can orthodox, believing theologians, like MacDonald and von Balthasar, hope for universal salvation?

12. How can they believe in annihilationism? How would they escape the three problems in point 4? What is the difference between C. S. Lewis's position (p. 287) and annihilationism, if any?

13. Do you think heaven and hell can begin in this life? Why or why not? What then is the relation between this life and the next?

14. What are the reasons for and against belief in purgatory?

15. Do we have any information at all, even clues or probabilities, about the comparative size of the populations of heaven and hell?

16. Concerning point 7 (p. 288), might hell be empty because God has warned us against it? Drowning is a real possibility, but it is possible that all the swimmers avoid it. Might the same be true of hell? Why or why not?

17. Is there an alternative to limbo (point 8) that solves the problem it was designed to solve?

18. What do you think Scripture means by "the wrath of God"? Why? Are the three points on pages 289-90 mutually exclusive or inclusive?

19. How is it possible for the damned to freely prefer misery (hell) to happiness (heaven) if the will always seeks happiness? Is the only answer to this question one that implies that we are spiritually insane?

20. How can some be predestined to salvation without others being predestined to damnation?

21. How *do* double-predestination Calvinists love a God who predestines many to hell?

22. If "God is the only game in town" (p. 295), does it necessarily follow that all worshipers of other gods and all believers in false religions are inevitably damned? (See chap. 13.)

23. Could someone who believes in the Bible but not in hell interpret the Bible's teaching about the existence of hell nonliterally? How can nonliteral interpretation apply to the existence as well as the nature of a thing? Are there any other examples of this?

24. If "justice demands punishment for evil" (p. 297), how can forgiveness not be unjust? How can Paul call it "the justice of God" (Romans 1:17)?

25. If "justice must discriminate" (p. 297), how can anyone indiscriminately criticize all "discrimination" in the name of justice? What do those who say this mean?

26. Why is the doctrine of God's exclusivity (p. 297) so unpopular today?

27. How might a believer in free will but not in hell reply to the argument in point 6?

28. Do you think there is an innate fear of hell (p. 298)? Do you think that that is the deepest reason for our fear of death? Why or why not?

29. Which of the thirteen objections to hell might be rehabilitated in the face of the answers given to them? How?

30. How do you think a suicide might be saved? How damned?

31. What are the objections many modern people, both Christians and non-Christians, have to the idea of a hierarchy or levels of rewards and punishments in heaven and hell?

32. Objection 3 (p. 301) is quite complex; do you find the reply sufficient? If not, what more is needed? Theologians have traditionally made distinctions such as that between God's "revealed will" and his "secret will," or between his temporal and eternal will. Do these distinctions add or detract from the solution? Why?

33. If threats do not remove free choice (objection 4, p. 303), why do we think they do?

34. If "sin is the ultimate drug" (objection 5, p. 304), does this mean that drugs are (at least an image of) the ultimate sin?

35. If fear is good (p. 305), why do most religious educators today never appeal to it and even explicitly attack it and try to extirpate it?

36. Is it true that numbers don't count (reply to objection 9, p. 306)? If forty billion people were damned and only four hundred saved, wouldn't that defeat God or mean that God should not have created humanity at all? Why or why not?

37. If American fundamentalists and Irish Catholics are so similar (p. 309), why do they fear each other so much?

38. Why is it so hard to use the doctrine of hell properly, as defined on page 309?

Outline of Chapter 13
Salvation

1. Six investigative questions
2. The importance of the question
3. The *when* and *where* of salvation
4. *What* is salvation?
   - ☐ Different scriptural images and terms
   - ☐ The "two roads"
   - ☐ Eternal happiness
   - ☐ Faith and works
5. *How* are we saved? Four objections and replies
   - ☐ Salvation seems arbitrary
   - ☐ Salvation seems unjust
   - ☐ Sincerity alone seems sufficient
   - ☐ Christianity seems unfair to pagans
6. *Who* saves? Christ alone?
   - ☐ The dilemma
   - ☐ The distinction between objective salvation and subjective knowledge of it
   - ☐ Could Socrates have had faith in Christ?
   - ☐ The objection to the salvation of pagans
7. Who then is saved?
8. Objections to our answer
   - ☐ Four objections from the right
     1. God is too liberal
     2. Salvation of pagans is contrary to Scripture
     3. Salvation of pagans leads to indifference
     4. Salvation of pagans leads to universalism
   - ☐ Seven objections from the left
     1. Contradiction between Christ's narrow theology and broad love
     2. No need for a historical Christ if the preincarnate Logos can save
     3. "Christ alone" is judgmental
     4. "Christ alone" is narrow-minded
     5. "Christ alone" is un-Godlike

CHAPTER 13
Salvation

L IKE INVESTIGATIVE REPORTERS, WE NEED TO ASK SIX QUESTIONS ABOUT
our topic: why, when, where, what, how and who.

1. Why should we worry about salvation? Why is it important?

2. When and *where* does salvation begin? Here and now or there and then? Does heaven begin on earth?

3. What is salvation? Just eternal fire insurance? Does it include sanctification or just justification? Good works or just faith? Is it a new reality in us or just a new relationship with God?

4. Most important of all, *how* are we saved? (This question is not the difficult, technical and speculative question of how the atonement "works," how God manages the spiritual technology, so to speak. That is a question for theology, not apologetics. The "hot" question for apologetics is the apparent arbitrariness, narrowness and even injustice of the "only one way to heaven" doctrine.)

5. The *how* question turns into the *who* question: Is Jesus the only savior? If so, does that mean that no non-Christians can be saved? (The "who" question is thus two questions: Who saves? and Who is saved?)

The Importance of the Question
One of the most unforgettable bishops in New York's history electrified the large audience in the Bronx at his inaugural speech half a century ago. He had been preceded by a typical "brick and mortar" administrator, fundraiser, organizer and "nice guy." But the new bishop announced, "I am here

for one reason and one only. Everything I do for you will have one single aim: to save your souls." Unfortunately, most of the people had never heard anyone say that before.

The only justification for every dollar raised, every Bible or hymnbook printed, every speck of dust swept up from under every pew, is salvation. That is the business the church is in.

The church also seems to be in the social service business, the counseling business, the fundraising business, the daycare business—dozens of the same worthy businesses the secular world is also in. Why? What justifies these things? The church's ultimate end for all these things is different from the world's end; it is salvation. This is its distinctive "product."

Why put out a product that is just the same as other companies' products already on the market? Why would anyone expect such a product to sell? That's why modernist or liberal Christianity, charitable as its services are, is simply not selling. The only reason for any of the church's activities, the only reason for the very existence of the church at all, is exactly the same as the reason Jesus came to earth: to save poor and lost humanity. The church, after all, is in the same business as its Head. When the body runs in a different direction from its Head, it is like a chicken with its head cut off: it goes nowhere and quickly dies.

Jesus did not come to be a philosopher or a doctor. If he did that, he failed. He didn't solve most of the philosophers' problems. He healed some people, but left most of the world just as sick as before. He healed some bodies to show that he could heal all souls.

Not only is salvation the reason for the church's existence, it is also the ultimate reason for your existence: your end, goal, point, purpose, hope, final cause, *summum bonum*, meaning. The difference between success and failure at life's first task—becoming who you were meant to be—is not the difference between riches and poverty, fame and obscurity, health and sickness, pleasure and pain, even niceness and nastiness, but between salvation and damnation. Leon Bloy wrote, "There is only one tragedy: not to have been a saint." Jesus said, "What does it profit a man if he gains the whole world but loses his soul?" No one in history ever asked a more practical question than that one. In other words, don't get all A's but flunk life.

That is why ordinary people, as distinct from scholars, always ask questions about salvation whenever they think about religion. And that's why a book on apologetics must address this topic: it's what religion is *for*.

Literally everything is at stake here. It's a matter of eternal life or death.

How could anyone who is sane rank any question before the question "What must I do to be saved?" Salvation was the reason for the Incarnation, the reason Jesus came an infinite distance, from heaven to earth, and even to hell, from the highest life to the lowest death. It was the reason for your conception, the end God had in view from the beginning. It was the reason for the very creation of the universe. The universe is a saint-making machine. Galaxies are for souls, not souls for galaxies. Life is a play, and God was setting up the stage and the scenery for billions of years before arranging for the players to enter it. The point and consummation of his play is salvation.

In chapter eleven we explored some apologetically important questions about that end, heaven. Here we explore the way to that end.

The When and Where of Salvation

One of the most well-known jibes against Christianity is that it offers "pie in the sky bye and bye." Two answers must be made to this. First, as C. S. Lewis said, "either there is 'pie in the sky bye and bye' or not. If there is, then this fact, like any other, must be faced, whether it is useful at political meetings or not." In other words, simple honesty demands that the first question is not whether an idea is useful or relevant but whether it is *true*. Second, it is not only "in the sky bye and bye." "The kingdom of heaven," or "the kingdom of God," or "eternal life," or "grace," or "being born again," or "regeneration," or "life in the Spirit," or "the state of grace" (these all refer to the same thing) begins *before* death, not after. To prove that, just get a concordance and read every New Testament passage that uses the above phrases. Notice the context each time.

The kingdom of heaven begins now as a seed; it flourishes after death as a full-grown plant. It begins now as a spiritual fetus and at death it is born into a bigger world. Like a fetus, it is already there, already conceived, already a member of the species, already in the family, but it is not yet able to exercise most of the functions and actions that will characterize its mature stages of life. Yet it does exercise some. It rehearses. Even before birth, a fetus practices kicking, swallowing and groping. Life is a series of spiritual fetal rehearsals, as pregnancy is a series of physical fetal rehearsals. (The metaphor is not original; it comes from Scripture: see Jn 16:21 and Rom 8:22.)

A foolish fetus might be skeptical of the idea of life after birth, and life in the womb as preparation or rehearsal for it, calling such an idea "pie in the sky bye and bye." The skeptic is a foolish fetus.

What Is Salvation?

Salvation is (1) the single reality behind many different and often confusing phrases, (2) one of two opposite possible destinies, (3) eternal happiness and (4) both "justification" and "sanctification."

Different Scriptural Images and Terms

As we have seen above, there are many different images and phrases for salvation, some in Scripture, some not. (Jesus used literally dozens of images for salvation in his parables, which he called "the kingdom of heaven.") Different traditions use different terminology. Fundamentalists say you must be born again. (So did Jesus.) Many mainline Protestant theologians use the term *regeneration*. Catholic theology's technical term is *sanctifying grace*. Salvation by any other name would smell as sweet. Interdenominational squabbles over terminology are about as reasonable as arguments between the Navy and the Coast Guard over whether to say "life jacket" or "flotation device" while thousands are drowning.

The Two Roads

One common point behind all the different terms and images is that two totally opposite eternal destinies await us at the end of two opposite life-roads. Psalm 1 summarizes this biblical vision succinctly. One road leads to God and to blessedness; the other leads away from God and to "perishing." In the physical world, all roads do not lead to the same place. You simply cannot walk to Boston from Chicago by going west, only east, no matter how hard, or how sincerely, you try. The roads in the world of the mind are similarly objective. You can't get five from two plus two no matter what you say or do. You can get to the conclusion that all A is C from the premise that all A is B and all B is C; you can't get another true conclusion from those premises. Morally, too, there are objective roads. You can't get to the destination of justice or rightness by the road of theft, nor can you get to the destination of dishonesty by the road of always obeying your conscience.

The physical world, the intellectual world and the moral world all have an objective structure of their own, with hard edges, so to speak, which we did not design or create but discover. If we conform to right roads, we succeed; if we do not, we fail. Why should the same not be true in religion? If there is a real God (and if not, religion is a lie and a sham) there must be a real road that leads to him and a real road that leads away. So the immensely popular image of all roads converging at the top of the mountain is simply false. No, not *simply* false, *disastrously* false. It is a lie that costs souls. Some roads go down, not up.

The most influential book, next to the Bible, that teaches this traditional doctrine of two roads is Augustine's *City of God.* Augustine saw all of human history under the image of two "cities," or spiritual communities:

Two loves have made two cities. Love of self to the despising of God has made the City of the World; love of God to the despising of self has made the City of God. Let a man consult himself to see what he loves, and he will find which city he belongs to.

C. S. Lewis also used the "two roads" principle in *The Great Divorce:* "There are only two kinds of people, in the end: those who say to God, 'Thy will be done,' and those to whom God says, in the end, '*Thy* will be done.' " For "we are not living in a world in which all roads, if pursued long enough, eventually join and meet at the center; rather, in a world where every road, after a while, forks in two, and then in two again; and at each fork you must make a decision." That is as true of spirit as it is of matter.

A dualistic *world*view (two roads running through the world) means a dualistic *life*view (life as choice between good and evil, God and anti-God, heaven and hell). Life-view follows from worldview. The reason our free-will choices determine our eternal destiny is because of the nature of the real spiritual world in which we live. Like the physical world, the spiritual world has roads that can be traveled in opposite directions. Salvation and damnation are those opposite directions.

All orthodox Christians believe in "double destination," though not "double predestination" (see p. 292). Christianity shares this teaching with nearly all premodern religions and moralities. Today this doctrine of the objective reality of the two roads and their two opposite final destinations (heaven and hell) is widely challenged, and therefore Christian apologetics must defend it. (The most difficult part of that defense is the case for hell: see chap. 12.)

Eternal Happiness

Everyone who has ever observed widely and thought deeply about human behavior, from Aristotle to Freud, has noted that we act for ends, goals and purposes; and also that the one end, goal or purpose that motivates everyone all the time is happiness. The reason why salvation is of primary importance is that it equals true happiness, eternal happiness.

Happiness here should not be taken merely in the shallow, subjectivistic and relativistic modern sense—essentially, "whatever turns you on"—but in the older sense of "blessedness": real, objective completion, human perfection, true success, health of soul. Blessedness is the right satisfaction of right desires, not just the satisfaction of whatever desires you happen to have, or the feeling of subjective satisfaction. In this older, deeper sense of happiness, salvation equals eternal happiness.

Faith and Works

The issue of salvation sparked the Protestant Reformation and split the church. It seemed to both sides at the time that Protestants and Catholics taught two radically different gospels, two religions, two answers to the most basic of all questions: What must I do to be saved? Catholics said you must both believe *and* practice good works to be saved. Luther, Calvin, Wycliffe and Knox insisted that faith alone saves you. Unfortunately, both sides have been talking past each other for 450 years. But there is strong evidence that it was essentially a misunderstanding and that it is beginning to be cleared up.

Both sides used key terms, *faith* and *salvation*, but in different senses.

1. Catholics used the term *salvation* to refer to the whole process, from its beginning in faith, through the whole Christian life of the works of love on earth, to its completion in heaven. When Luther spoke of *salvation* he meant the initial step—like getting into Noah's ark of salvation—not the whole journey.

2. By *faith* Catholics meant only one of the three needed "theological virtues" (faith, hope and love), faith being intellectual belief. To Luther, *faith* meant accepting Christ with your whole heart and soul.

Thus, since Catholics were using *salvation* in a bigger sense and *faith* in a smaller sense, and Luther was using *salvation* in a smaller sense and *faith* in a bigger sense, Catholics rightly denied and Luther rightly affirmed that we were saved by faith alone.

Catholics taught that salvation included more than faith, just as a plant includes more than its roots. It needs its stem (hope) and its fruits (love) as well as its root (faith). Luther taught that good works can't buy salvation, that all you need to do and all you *can* do to be saved is to accept it, accept the Savior, by faith.

Both sides spoke the truth. Since truth cannot contradict truth, the two sides really did not contradict each other on this most important of all questions. That assessment may sound unduly optimistic, but it is essentially what Catholic and Lutheran theologians said publicly in their "Joint Statement on Justification" a few years ago. Pope John Paul II said the same thing publicly to the German Lutheran bishops. It both astonished and delighted them.

Such real agreement in substance beneath apparent disagreement in words should not be surprising, for both Catholics and Protestants accept the same data, the New Testament. The New Testament teaches both points: both the "Protestant" point that salvation is a free gift, not earned by works of obedience to the law; and the "Catholic" point that faith is only the beginning of the Christian life of good works, that "justification" (being made right with God) must, if it is real, lead to "sanctification" (being made holy, saintly, good), that "faith without works is dead."

Regarding that last point, the Scottish Presbyterian preacher George Mac-Donald wrote, "The notion that the salvation of Jesus is a salvation from *punishment* for our sins is a mean, selfish, low notion. He was called Savior because he would save us from our *sins.*"

The official teaching of Catholicism (as distinct from the popular misconception) is that salvation is a totally free gift that we can do nothing to "buy" or produce. The Council of Trent's "Decree on Justification" is as insistent on the gratuitous nature of grace as Luther or Calvin. So is Aquinas in the Treatise on Grace in the *Summa Theologiae,* the bottom line of which is that we can do *nothing* without God's grace—not be saved, not deserve grace, not even ask for grace.

It would be as absurd for Catholics and Protestants to disagree about this fundamental point of how to be saved as for two astronomers to disagree about whether stars exist. The answer is not in doubt because it is not in our theories but in our data, in Scripture.

Scripture clearly says both that salvation is a free gift to be accepted by faith (Romans and Galatians) *and* that "faith without works is dead" (James). "Works" means "love," and "love" means "the works of love," for Christian love *(agapē)* is not a feeling, like worldly love *(eros, storgē, philia)*; if it were, it could not be commanded.

How Are We Saved? Four Objections and Replies

Once it is clearly seen that salvation is a free gift to be accepted by faith, rather than something we make or buy with our good works, four objections naturally tend to occur to the unbeliever.

Objection 1:

Salvation then is apparently arbitrary: "If you believe, you will be saved; if you do not believe, you will be damned." That is the clear and repeated scriptural formula.

But that seems as arbitrary as a father saying to his son: "If you believe that I am three thousand years old, have green blood and come from Mars, I will give you ten expensive cars." There seems to be no more of a meaningful, reasonable or just connection between believing the right things about Jesus and being rewarded with eternal happiness than there is between believing equally strange things about your father and getting ten cars.

Reply: The objection fails to understand both terms of the formula "faith $\longrightarrow$ salvation." Faith is not just intellectual belief, and salvation is not just future rewards. Faith is *letting* God into your soul; and salvation, or eternal life, is *having* God in your soul. The connection is natural and necessary, not external and arbitrary.

That explains why salvation is not a matter of degree: enough good works, enough sincerity, enough orthodoxy. There is no sliding scale with some arbitrary cutoff point, as on a school exam. Salvation is like pregnancy; you can't be partly pregnant. Either you have the new life or you don't.

A totally loving and generous God would not parcel out this gift of eternal life grudgingly only after we had performed "enough" steps. He would give it out with reckless abandon, shining his Son on the just and the unjust alike. Only one thing could possibly prevent our receiving this gift: our refusal. Faith is not just *believing* but also *receiving* (Jn 1:12). Faith is not like signing a contract or passing a test, but more like getting pregnant.

Objection 2:
It seems unjust that eternal rewards and punishments follow from temporal choices. How can a finite cause produce an infinite effect?

Reply A: In the same way that opening a faucet can produce water, or opening a small crack in a dam can produce a flood; or opening the windows and drawing back the blinds can let fresh air into a room. Faith only lets in the God who is already there "outside" the soul.

Reply B: We can use either of two spatial metaphors for salvation (as long as we remember that they are only metaphors): we can speak of "going to" heaven or "entering" heaven, or we can speak of heaven (or eternal life, or the life of God) as "entering" our soul. The New Testament uses both: we are "in" Christ and Christ is "in" us. Sometimes the second way illuminates something that the first does not. Perhaps that is so here. Salvation is not like entering a stadium by buying a ticket if you have enough money (=justice); it is like letting a guest into your house by trusting him (=faith) and opening the door.

Reply C: Salvation is like marriage. Marriage is a permanent commitment, with no prearranged end or limited time span. Yet it is entered in time, through a choice that takes only a little time. Why shouldn't our eternal marriage to God also follow from a temporal choice to accept his proposal? **Reply D:** Though our time is finite, the One whom we accept by faith or reject by sin is infinite. Acceptance of infinite love and forgiveness naturally leads to infinite riches, and rejection of infinite love and forgiveness leads to infinite deprivation.

Objection 3:

Why should God demand faith in Jesus in order to be saved? Nearly everyone seems to feel very deeply that sincerity alone should be enough. It is intolerable that A, a sincere unbeliever, should deserve hell while B, a less sincere believer, should deserve heaven. What more does God want than a sincere heart? That's all a good man or woman should want. Why does God have a different morality, a different will, a different set of demands, than we do?

Reply: No one accepts sincerity alone as sufficient in any other field than religion. Sincerity may be *necessary* but it is not *sufficient.* Is it sufficient that your surgeon, your accountant or your travel agent be sincere? Is sincerity alone enough to save you from cancer, bankruptcy, accident or death? It is not. Why then do you think it should be enough to save you from hell?

The assumption behind this objection comes from the single most important change in religious thought in the last 1,900 years. Whereas nearly all the ancients (not just the Christians) believed that religion is about objective truth, just as medicine or economics or geography are about objective truth, most typical moderns do not. (See chap. 16 on objective truth.)

Moderns typically see religion in four radically different ways from nearly all premoderns.

1. Moderns see religion as subjective rather than objective; as something in us and our consciousness rather than as something which we and our consciousness are in. Modern religious educators talk less about God than about our religious experience and practice.

2. Moderns see religion as only practical rather than theoretical, only good rather than true, only moral rather than theological, only a pattern for living rather than a map of reality. Thus it became pragmatic and relativistic: if it works for you, use it.

3. Moderns see religion as something man-made rather than God-made; something we create rather than discover; our road to God rather than God's road to us.

4. Moderns see religion as an addition rather than subtraction; as self-growth rather than self-death; as exercise rather than as surgery. For the typically modern mind does not believe in the disease called sin.

This is why most moderns say sincerity alone is enough to save you. But:

1. Subjective sincerity alone is not enough if we are dealing with objective reality. Two things are necessary whenever we deal with objective reality: we need to be sincere in seeking the truth, but we also have to really find it!

2. Sincerity alone also is not enough to make a map true, and if a map is not true, it is not useful either.

3. Sincerity alone can't find the road someone else made, though it may be enough to remind you of the road you made.

4. And sincerity alone is not enough to take away sin, any more than it is enough to take away cancer. You need a real doctor. You can't do it yourself. Your hand shakes; how can you be the surgeon on your own hand? You've fallen into quicksand and have no solid place to stand for leverage to get yourself out. You've sold yourself into slavery and you are no longer free or rich enough to buy your own freedom back. You need more than sincerity; you need a Savior. Sincerity is *necessary* for salvation—only those who sincerely seek, find—but it is not *sufficient*.

Objection 4:

It seems unfair to good pagans to make salvation dependent on faith in Jesus. Surely Socrates deserves heaven more than Torquemada?

Reply A: How do you know who does and does not deserve heaven? Are you God? Is heaven your gift to give? Is life a game whose rules you invented?

Reply B: How do you *know* that Socrates is not in heaven, or that Torquemada is?

Reply C: The objection rejects the data in the name of a theory, rejects the known in the name of the unknown. We do not know *who* is saved—we have not been told this—but we do know *how* to be saved—we have been told this. We also know that God is just. He may be obscure, but he is just. His justice is bound to appear obscure to us because we are in time and see "through a glass, darkly." Only the view from eternity is total and clear.

Who Saves? Christ Alone?

Whether we answer yes or no, we seem to be in a dilemma. If we answer yes, the objection fairly leaps out: Then all non-Christians go to hell, even a good pagan like Socrates. It wasn't his fault that he didn't live in the right time or place to meet Jesus or a Christian missionary. How unfair and unloving of God to consign most of the world to hell! If we reply that non-Christians like Socrates can be saved, then the question naturally arises: Why then become a Christian? If whatever Socrates had is enough to get to heaven, why add the narrow claim about Jesus being the only way? In other words, if Socrates is not in heaven, God is not just, and if Socrates is in heaven, then Jesus is not the only way there.

Objective Salvation vs. Subjective Knowledge of Salvation

The dilemma is not just a tricky, technical, theological problem, nor is it only about Socrates. It is about the most important of all questions and about everyone. To answer it, we need to make a crucial distinction between the objective and the subjective dimensions of the question. The New Testament gives a clear, uncompromising and narrow answer to the objective question, but not to the subjective question.

Objectively, the New Testament insists that Christ is the only Savior: "There is no other name under heaven given among mortals by which we must be saved" (Acts 4:12). Jesus himself insisted: "I am *the* way. . . . No one comes to the Father except through me" (Jn 14:6). Christians believe Jesus is the only Savior because he said so. If this is not true, he is no Savior at all, but a liar, a blasphemer and an incredibly egotistical fool.

Subjectively, what do we need to be saved? The New Testament says we need faith in him to be saved, but what does this mean? What kind of faith? There cannot be different kinds of Jesus, but there *may* be different kinds of faith. The line between Jesus and all others is clearly drawn: the line between the God-man and mere men. The line between the certain faith of Peter and the possible faith of Socrates is not so clear.

What might it mean to say Socrates could have had faith in Christ? To have faith in Christ, you must somehow know Christ. How could Socrates have known Christ? In the same way everyone can: as "the true light, which enlightens everyone" (Jn 1:9). As the preincarnate Logos, the divine Word or Light or Reason.

No one can know God except through Christ (Jn 1:18; Lk 10:22). But pagans know God (Acts 17:28; Rom 1:19-20; 2:11-16). Therefore pagans know Christ.

For Christ is not just a six-foot-high, thirty-three-year-old Jewish carpenter. He is the second person of the eternal Trinity, the full expression, or revelation, or Logos, of the Father (Col 1:15,19; Jn 14:9). He is to the Father as sunlight is to the sun. As such he is "light, which enlightens everyone" through reason and conscience. Thus, the doctrine of Christ's divinity—classified as "conservative" or "traditionalist" by liberals—is the very foundation of the liberals' hope that pagans may be saved.

So objectively, it is only Christ who can save pagans. But subjectively, what kind of faith is it that might save pagans, or Hindus or agnostics? Is it: (1) a vague, generalized honesty and sincerity; (2) a total commitment to the Truth not as something diffuse but as something absolute, implicitly a divine attribute; (3) seeking not just the Truth but also Goodness, true morality, a fundamental option for good rather than evil, in general; (4) love of Goodness not as something diffuse and general but as an absolute, a divine attribute; (5) repentance for sin, however unclear may be the concept of the God to whom the pagan repents; (6) faith in God, the God of natural revelation, the intelligent Designer of nature and the holy Source of the voice of conscience; (7) a deliberate, free and conscious response to divine grace, however dimly understood? The Bible seems to point to all seven as being necessary.

But explicit knowledge of the incarnate Jesus is not necessary for salvation. Abraham, Moses and Elijah, for instance, had no such knowledge, yet they were saved. (We know that from Mt 17:3 and Lk 16:22-23.) The same person—the second person of the Trinity—is both the preincarnate Logos who "enlightens everyone" *and* the incarnate Jesus who was seen only by some. *Those who know either one, know the other too, because both are the same person.*

If you were to ask Abraham, "Do you believe in Jesus as your Savior?" Abraham would not be able to answer yes. His yes was only implicit in its *knowledge*, but it was a *real contact* with the real Christ. Yet Abraham did say yes to Christ implicitly, and so was saved. Therefore, the inability to answer with an explicit yes to that question does not automatically condemn you. Therefore Socrates is not automatically damned. Whether and how Socrates had real contact with Christ as Logos is the remaining question. The mere abstract, intellectual pursuit of truth is not sufficient to save you. But neither are intellectual mistakes sufficient to damn you.

God does not give you a theology exam when you die, as an entrance test to heaven. If he did, we'd all flunk parts of it. And there would be the problem of the arbitrary cutoff point. What then could the faith of a Socrates be that which would save him? What would it mean for him to believe in Christ the Logos? What can he do to be saved?

Let us consult our data again, namely, Scripture. There are three answers in Scripture: you must *seek* God, *repent* of your sin and *believe* (i.e., accept by faith, and thus receive, God's grace). Let's see whether we can define some of the parameters of these three universal requirements for salvation.

1. Seeking the Truth as a divine Absolute can be seeking God because God is Truth. Truth is what God is "made of," so to speak, as the sun is made of light and energy. This truth is more than mere mental correctness. Truth-seeking is motivated by the will. It is the free choice of the will, of the heart—the *love* of Truth—that makes one seek it. And seeking is already a kind of faith. It is faith directed to the future, that is, it is really hope. Hope is a "theological virtue," something that connects us to God. We are promised that all who seek (him), find (him) (Mt 7:7-8).

To seek God shows the presence of divine grace already in the seeking soul. Augustine imagined God saying to him, "Take heart, child. You would not be seeking me unless I had already found you." And an old hymn says: "I sought the Lord, and afterward I knew / He moved my soul to seek him, seeking me. / It was not I that found, O Savior true; / No, I was found of Thee."

Pascal says there are only three kinds of people in the world: those who have sought God and found him, those who are seeking him and have not yet found him, and those who neither seek him nor find him. Pascal called the first class "reasonable (wise) and happy"—reasonable because they seek and happy because they find. He calls the second class "reasonable and unhappy"—reasonable because they seek and unhappy because they have not yet found. He called the third class "unreasonable and unhappy"—unreasonable because they do not seek and unhappy because they do not find.

The greatest difference is not between those who have found God and those who have not. This is only a temporary difference, for all in the second class will get into the first; all seekers will find. The greatest difference is between seekers and nonseekers, for that is an eternal difference. And there is no fourth class, those who do *not* seek and nevertheless find.

2. Isaiah couples repentance—a second requirement—with seeking.
[1] Seek the LORD while he may be found,
   call upon him while he is near;
[2] let the wicked forsake their way,
   and the unrighteous their thoughts;
let them return [repent] to the LORD, that he may have mercy on them,
   and to our God, for he will abundantly pardon. (Is 55:6-7)
So seeking must be supplemented by repenting. All can repent, for all know the moral law (Rom 1—2) and thereby their own sin. Merely seeking truth

and even goodness is not enough, for the motive may be pride and self-righteousness, to be good with my own goodness, not God's. Will I surrender to God if I meet him?—that is the crucial question.

3. The third requirement is faith, that is, believing and thus receiving God, his grace and life. But how can we believe and receive God if we don't know him? We can't. But we all do know him (Rom 1). How can we know him without Christ? We can't. We all do know Christ the Logos (Jn 1:9).

How *much* knowledge of God must we have to have faith and be saved? The amount cannot be quantified, like statistical facts. However, we know (Rom 1—2) that we all have enough knowledge of God to make us responsible before him. Even if you only know the God of AA, "a Higher Power" or God "as you conceive him," you know enough to make you responsible before God.

The question of just what knowledge of God we must have to be able to choose to believe or disbelieve, is answered more easily in other languages than English. Most other languages have two words for *know* where English has one. One means knowing facts, the other means knowing persons. The first is knowing by objective description, the second by personal acquaintance (e.g., *wissen* vs. *kennen* in German, *savoir* vs. *connaître* in French). Knowing facts can be quantified. You know so many facts. But either you know a person or you don't, no matter how many facts you know *about* him. All know God, though they do not know much *about* him (see Rom 1 and Acts 17).

To summarize our solution: Socrates (or any other pagan) could seek God, could repent of his sins, and could obscurely believe in and accept the God he knew partially and obscurely, and therefore he could be saved—or damned, if he refused to seek, repent and believe. There is enough light and enough opportunity, enough knowledge and enough free choice, to make everyone responsible before God. God is just. And a just God judges justly, not unjustly; that is, he judges according to the knowledge each individual has, not according to a knowledge they do not have (see Jas 3:1).

The Objection to the Salvation of Pagans

Conservatives often object that this position, which allows the possibility for pagans to be saved, undercuts the motivation for mission work. Why spend your life, why risk your life, to tell the world about Jesus if people can be saved without that knowledge? It is a good question. It deserves a good answer.

There are three possible reasons for mission work, that is, for telling others the gospel, the "good news" of Jesus. (By the way, all Christians are commanded to be missionaries; the Great Commission [Mt 28:18-20] did not come with a "clergy only" tag.) First, there is the reason given by many fundamentalists: We know that the world is going to hell unless they accept Christ as their Savior. Second, there is the reason given by many modernists: We just want to love our neighbor and share whatever we have with them, do a sort of super social work. We don't believe in hell, and if we did, we wouldn't think anyone went there, and if they did, we'd think it was only a Hitler or a Stalin. We are not in the salvation business, we are in the social service business. Third, there is the traditional reason: We do *not* know exactly who is on the way to hell, that's why we risk all to save some. A mother doesn't need to know that her children are going to fall through the thin ice and drown before she is motivated to shout "Get off the ice!" All she needs to know is that she *doesn't* know that they *won't* drown—that they *may* drown. We know that anyone *may* go to hell, because Jesus said so. So we are not modernists. But we do not know exactly *which* children are going to be lost, because Jesus didn't tell us. So we shout the warning and throw out the life preserver just as insistently as the fundamentalists.

There is a parallel here with abortion. There are three possible attitudes to abortion, parallel to the three reasons given above for mission work, distinguished by what you claim to know. Some claim to know that the soul enters the body at conception, making the fetus a person, and therefore that abortion is murder. Some claim to know that this is *not* true, and therefore that abortion is *not* murder. And some do not claim to know when the soul enters the body, when the fetus becomes a person. Though this skeptical claim is most often found among prochoice people, it is a compelling reason for being prolife. If you don't know for sure that an unborn baby is not a person and has no soul, how horribly callous and irresponsible to risk the possibility of murder! It's like shooting a gun into a busy city street, or running over a human-shaped pile of clothes with a truck.

Ignorance and risk can be as compelling reasons for action as knowledge and certainty. If you think your child *may* be dying, you will rush to the doctor at the same speed as if you *know* your child is dying. Thus, the open-minded skepticism of the liberal and the passionate total commitment of the fundamentalist are perfectly compatible.

There is something more to be said about the motivation for mission work that is more important than all this calculation and possibility. Our motive for preaching the gospel is not only to increase the population of heaven and decrease the population of hell, but also to invite others to a deeper spiritual life in *this* world: intimate knowledge and love of Christ that brings deep faith, hope, love, joy and peace. Without an explicit knowledge of Christ it is probably impossible to have these. And without them, though salvation may be possible, the *assurance* of salvation is not.

Who Then Is Saved?

We have argued that the answer to the question "Who saves?" is Christ alone. We have also argued that this does not necessarily entail the conclusion that pagans like Socrates cannot be saved. We now ask the question: *Is* Socrates saved? And if he is, how exceptional is he? How many are saved?

The obvious answer is that we simply do not know. We are not to judge that which we cannot judge.

But didn't Jesus say that only a few would be saved and that the road to eternal life was narrow while the road to destruction was wide (Mt 7:13-14)?

Yes, but "few" and "many" here are not mathematical percentages. Jesus is a lover, not a mathematician; a shepherd, not a statistician. The Good Shepherd feels about his sheep the way good parents feel about their children: even *one* lost is too "many," and even ninety-nine out of one hundred saved is too "few." When the disciples asked Jesus about comparatively heavenly and hellish population statistics ("Lord, will only a few be saved?"), his answer was not "Yes" *or* "No" but "Strive to enter through the narrow door" (Lk 13:23-24). In other words, "Mind your own business!" Speculating about others is as worthless, even harmful, as speculating about the exact date of the end of the world—another subject God wisely did not tell us about (Mt 24:36).

So we cannot know. But we can work. Christ does not answer our theoretical question, but gives us a practical task. We have our marching orders: Preach the gospel to every creature. Apologetics is part of that task, clearing away the intellectual mine fields, the obstacles to faith.

The most effective way to implement our orders is through sanctity. Sanctity testifies to the reality of the gospel. "Everyone loves a lover." Jesus won souls with his love, not his "theology." He never won a soul with his books, for he wrote none.

Fortunately, his disciples did, and those books (the New Testament) give a clear answer to the question of who is saved in general, but not in particular. It is like the problem of evil: We know the answer in general (God allows evil for a greater good—Rom 8:28) but not in particular (why does God let *this* evil, now, happen to me?).

The answer to "Who is saved?" is clear: "Anyone who desires" (Rev 22:17). Heaven's door is always open (Rev 21:25; 3:7-8; 4:1), and hell's doors are locked from the inside. It stands to reason that if God is pure love, salvation is pure gift. If salvation is a free gift, then all get it except those who refuse it. God refuses no one but those who refuse him.

Objections to Our Answer

The position staked out here will seem too much like liberalism to fundamentalists and too much like fundamentalism to liberals. In this section we try to refute both misperceptions. Each side, each mind, right and left, is very clear-eyed about the defects of the other side but blind to its own defects. If this were not so, the two would meet and marry and live happily ever after.

Objections from the Right
Objection 1:
Such a God is too liberal.
Reply: That's impossible. You can't be too liberal-hearted. God is indeed a "bleeding-heart liberal." He is also hard-headed. He is love *and* he is truth—*both* infinitely and uncompromisingly.

Objection 2:
It's contrary to Scripture to say pagans can be saved without becoming Christians.
Reply: Pagans can't be saved by paganism, only by Christ. If "to become a Christian" means to receive the real, objective Christ, then the only way to be saved is to become a Christian. But nothing in Scripture proves that Socrates was not a Christian in this sense. If on the other hand "to become a Christian" means knowingly to profess the orthodox faith in Christ, then you do not need to be a Christian to be saved, or else Abraham is unsaved, and so are all who believe unorthodox ideas. *How* unorthodox do your ideas have to be to send you to hell? Where is the dividing line? Does God give you a theology exam?

Objection 3:
Saying pagans can be saved leads to indifference.
Reply: Not necessarily. See page 329 for the three reasons for mission work.

Objection 4:
If God saves Socrates, why not everyone? Where does he stop? Where's the dividing line? It's not clear. But Christ is clear.

Reply: He stops at nothing. He wants to save everyone. But not everyone wants to be saved. The objective dividing line is clear; it is Christ. The subjective dividing line is not clear: How explicit, how complete, does one's faith have to be? Why should that be clear to us? God alone sees hearts.

Objections from the Left
Objection 1:

There seems to be a contradiction between two teachings of orthodox Christianity: between the rigidity, hardness, narrowness and judgmentalism of the Christian theology of hell—with its "one way to heaven," divine wrath and threats—and the open-hearted love, mercy, generosity, forgiveness and nonjudgmentalism of Christian morality. In the name of the progressive morality we must correct the regressive theology.

Reply: No, in the name of the morality of love, Christians do not *correct* but *interpret* the theology of judgment. It is God's love that is at the root of his judgment and even his wrath. Wrath is what love feels like to us when we hate it. We are projecting our own wrath onto our divine Lover. (See chap. 12.) Such an interpretation is legitimate, but it is not legitimate to deny half of our data for the other half. Rather, we must find a vision that encompasses, reconciles, validates and illuminates *all* the data.

The rhetoric about "progressive" and "regressive" hardly deserves comment. Those who tell truth by the clock or the calendar are practicing chronological snobbery.

Christians need hard heads as well as soft hearts. Who is compelled by soft heads or hard hearts? Christ tells us to be both wise as serpents and innocent as doves (Mt 10:16). Two things are necessary: seeking God and finding God; the first is done with our hearts and the second with our heads. The first is the desire to know God, the second is the knowledge. The first is subjective, the second is objective. The first is love, the second is truth. Both are absolutes because love and truth are what God is.

The theological right emphasizes the objective, the doctrinal truth, the hardness of head; the left emphasizes the subjective, the love, the softness of heart. Both are needed. For *salvation*, both are needed! Orthodoxy will not save you if your heart is full of hate. And love will not save you if you are not honest and do not care about truth, for then your love will not be *true* love.

Objection 2:

Why bother preaching about the historical Jesus if anyone can be saved through knowledge of the preincarnate Logos? If you can get to heaven through the back door, why bother so much about the front door?

Reply: First, the Logos is not a back door. Heaven has no back doors. There is only one door, one way: the One who said he was it. The eternal Logos *is* the Jesus of history. He is the Truth all honest unbelievers are seeking; how could we who know this withhold from those who seek this the very thing they seek?

Second, we preach Jesus and everyone should believe Jesus because Jesus is true. That is the only honest reason why anyone should ever preach or believe anything.

Third, the knowledge of the historical Jesus gives people *a better chance* to be saved than the vague knowledge they already have by natural reason and conscience alone. That's one reason why he came: "to testify to the truth" (Jn 18:37) much more clearly than human reason can. Your neighbor probably has some vague knowledge of how to deliver your baby, but wouldn't you prefer an obstetrician?

Fourth, to love God is to want to know him better. Anyone who is indifferent to knowledge is indifferent to love. Love always wants to grow, and the way it grows is through knowledge and communication. The same principle holds true for loving God or loving neighbor. Mental indifference is really moral lovelessness, and that puts salvation itself at risk.

Objection 3:

The doctrine that Jesus is the only Savior is judgmental.

Reply A: It is Jesus who said this, not us.

Reply B: It is judgmental to sins, but forgiving to sinners. Jesus judges sins and forgives sinners. We are supposed to make the same distinction, and love sinners while hating sin. (After all, God preaches to us only what he practices himself; he is not a cosmic hypocrite!) If we identify ourselves with our sins, refuse to repent and glue ourselves to our spiritual garbage, then when God's garbage truck carts our garbage off to the incinerator, we get burned too.

If there was only one thing in the world that could dissolve the glue between ourselves and our sins, would that be "judgmental"? That's just the nature of the world. If we don't like it, we are quarreling not with an ideology but with reality itself.

Reply C: Would you really want God to be totally "nonjudgmental" and not judge sins at all? Would you want salvation to mean only salvation from punishment and not from sin? Would we want God to tolerate sin in heaven too? Would you want everyone to cart all their earthly garbage to heaven, everything from war to adultery to rape? Would you really prefer a heaven that needed lawyers and cops?

The Inquisition confused sin with sinners and judged both. Liberals make the same mistake and judge neither. But if you don't judge the sin, you don't care about the sinner. If you don't hate the cancer, you don't love the patient.

The key distinction, between objective and subjective, head and heart, truth and love, justifies hardheaded judgmentalism objectively without succumbing to hardness of heart subjectively. There is no more contradiction between Christianity's hardnosed doctrines and its softhearted love than there is between the hard objective truths of anatomy and the surgeon's compassion for the patient.

Objection 4:
"Jesus only" is terribly narrow.
Reply: Yes it is. Reality is terribly narrow. There is only one operation that can save you, only one road out of the forest, only one answer to the equation, only one place a body can be at one time, only one living spouse to be married to. There's only one correct formula for Pepsi; other formulas give you other things. Other roads lead to other places. Other saviors save from things other than sin—if they save at all.

Objection 5:
The "narrow way" doctrine is un-Godlike, unholy. God's character is not narrow but broad.
Reply: How do you know the character of God? A Christian must answer: through Christ. He is the full revelation of the Father (Jn 14:9; Col 1:15, 19). This Christ tells us that God's heart is both infinitely wide (Mt 18:14; cf. 2 Pet 3:9) and that the way to life is narrow (Mt 7:14), like the birth canal. We know what God is much more surely through his own revelation than through our own fallen, socially conditioned assumptions.

Objection 6:
God forgives everyone, therefore everyone is forgiven and saved.
Reply: God is *willing* to forgive everyone; he *offers* forgiveness as a free gift to everyone; but a gift must be freely received as well as freely given. What if we do not trust him and do not believe in the gift?

Objection 7:
Perhaps religion is only subjective. Science has taken over the whole extent of our objective knowledge of the world; what other area is left for religion except our subjective souls? And subjectively, sincerity alone is enough.
Reply A: If religion is only subjective, then Christianity is not a religion, because Christianity contains objective truth-claims.
Reply B: Science has *not* taken over the whole field of objective knowledge. Science knows only a bright but narrow swath of objective reality, like a searchlight or a laser beam.
Reply C: Science does not refute, displace or devalue religion in any way. (See chaps. 2 and 5.)
Reply D: The God described in the Bible is constantly surprising us, in countless ways. Subjectivity does not surprise us, since it simply *is* us.
Reply E: We strongly recommend that anyone who is not wholly clear and wholly convinced on this point read chapter eleven of C. S. Lewis's *Miracles*, "Christianity and Religion," especially the last long paragraph.

Postscript
It is important to make clear that we are *not* claiming here to know that Socrates has been saved, or that any, many or most pagans will be saved. We ask fundamentalists or evangelicals who find this position too "liberal" to first be sure exactly what our position is. We have said repeatedly that we simply do not know who or how many will be saved.

On the other hand, we ask liberals who are impatient with all this kow-towing to fundamentalists to consider how "liberal" their impatience really is, and to reexamine their own motives for rejecting the clear and repeated teaching of the only Christ we know. A love of believers in other religions and an appreciation for whatever true and good things there may be in these other religions should not blind us to their errors and defects. If Christ is the only Savior and all the other religions of the world deny this, then logically and necessarily all the other religions are dead wrong about this crucial point. It does not follow from this that non-Christians must be condemned, but that they must be told the truth, out of love for them *and* for the truth.

Questions for Discussion
1. Should salvation be the only final aim of all religious activity, even social services? Isn't this false pretenses, like a spy's cover? Shouldn't we feed the hungry to save them from hunger, not hell? If, on the other hand, salvation is only one

of many ends, is this not a chaos of ends? Mustn't there be *one* ultimate end or *summum bonum* ("supreme good")? And if not salvation, what?

2. Does the point that "galaxies are for souls" mean that humans and the earth are the center of the universe (spiritually if not physically)?

3. Do you agree with the "tough-minded" premise that truth is an absolute and that the only honest reason to believe or preach anything is because it is true? What would the "tender-minded" say? How can the two argue, if they have different fundamental ends? (What are these different ends?)

4. Does the section on the when and where of salvation answer the earlier question about heaven and hell, namely, what is the connection between this life and the next? What are alternative answers to this question? What is the most popular answer? Why?

5. Is there any substantive point behind the different theologies' different terminologies for salvation?

6. Is the parallel valid (p. 318) among physical, intellectual, moral and spiritual roads or ways? If not, why not? If so, why do most intellectuals today not admit this?

7. Is Augustine's point of the "two cities" the necessary Christian key to a philosophy of history? How has it been criticized by some modern Christians? What alternatives might supplant it? Evaluate them.

8. If Lewis's image is correct (p. 319), why is the opposite image of many roads up the same mountain the overwhelmingly most popular one today?

9. Is the dualistic worldview, and thus the reality of hell, the necessary background for the moral dualism of a real distinction between good and evil? If so, why do more believe the second than the first?

10. Does the section on faith and works resolve the essence of the Reformation divide between Catholicism and Protestantism, at least on this one point? Is this point the most essential one dividing the two? Why or why not?

11. Is the definition of love as a *work* true? If so, why do so few see it? What is the most popular alternative concept of love? Why is it so popular?

12. If you believe that the difference between salvation and damnation is the difference between being good and evil, how do you answer the question about the "cutoff point" (p. 322)? Just how good do you have to be to be saved? Why not just a little bit less?

13. Why do so many good and wise people feel that sincerity alone is enough for salvation?

14. Which of the reasons in the reply to objection 3 (p. 324) is the most determinative one? Why?

15. Why isn't the distinction that is made between the objective and subjective dimensions of salvation (p. 325) the same as saying that subjective sincerity alone is enough to save you?

16. How would those conservatives who do not agree that a pagan like Socrates could possibly be saved refute the arguments given (as distinct from simply giving

other arguments)?

17. How likely do you think it is that the average pagan, without an explicit knowledge of Christ, will seek God, repent and have faith?

18. If it is true that a liberal skepticism about who is saved can motivate mission work as passionately as fundamentalist dogmatic certainty about all pagans going to hell, then why hasn't it been borne out in history?

19. Why are we so naturally tempted to answer the question of who is saved in some other way than "we simply do not know"?

20. If there are objections to the position staked out here other than the ones listed, what are they?

21. Isn't the position that Christ alone saves deeply threatening, insulting and offensive to all Hindus, Muslims and those of other religions?

22. If both truth and love are absolutes, why do we all tend to emphasize either the head or the heart and deemphasize the other?

23. If the third answer to objection 2 (p. 333) is true, does it necessarily follow that a higher percentage of professed Christians must be in heaven than Jews, Hindus, Buddhists, Muslims?

24. How would liberals reply to the charge that they make the same mistake as the Inquisition (p. 334)?

25. Why do we hate narrowness if truth and reality are narrow?

Part 6
CONCLUSIONS

Outline of Chapter 14
Christianity & Other Religions

1. The charge of "exclusivism"
2. The importance of the issue
3. Defining the issues
   - ☐ Are other religions *true?*
   - ☐ Are they *good?*
   - ☐ Are they *salvific?*
   - ☐ Are they *educative* to Christians?
   - ☐ Are they *useful* to Christians?
4. Defining the genus *religion*
   - ☐ A subjective attitude?
   - ☐ Indefinable?
   - ☐ Equivocal between East and West?
   - ☐ Exclusive of Christianity?
   - ☐ Sociological description: creed, code and cult
5. Defining differences within religion: six fundamental theological choices
6. Ten answers to the question of comparative religions
7. Ten answers reduced to three
8. Three answers reduced to one
9. Two postscripts

CHAPTER 14
Christianity
& Other Religions

THIS CHAPTER DOES NOT SET OUT TO BE AN INTRODUCTION TO THE RELIG-
ions of the world, or to the science of comparative religions (an enterprise Ronald Knox called the best way he knew to make someone
comparatively religious). You will not learn here in detail what other religions teach, and which of these teachings are or are not acceptable to
Christians. Our purpose in this chapter is to explore the relation between
Christianity and other religions from an apologetic point of view. We concentrate on answering the very common charge against Christianity that it
is exclusivistic, intolerant, narrow-minded, elitist, snobbish, self-assured,
self-righteous, bigoted. Everyone has heard charges like these, explicitly or
implicitly, especially from our secular media. We need to sit back and look
at the issue and the charges from a logical viewpoint instead of an emotional one.

For a generally fair, clear and sympathetic summary of the data, that is,
the central teachings of the major religions of the world, emphasizing why
they are important, attractive and influential to millions, we recommend
Huston Smith's *The World's Religions* as the best such book by a non-Christian that we know.

The Importance of the Issue
In teaching apologetics and philosophy of religion for many years, we have
found that students worry more and are more embarrassed by Christianity's
"un-American" exclusivist claims than about any other aspect of their religion. In an age of toleration and pluralism, the most popular argument

against the Christian religion seems to be simply that it is only one of many religions. The world is a big place, "different strokes for different folks," "live and let live," "don't impose your values on others."

A Georgetown University professor polled hundreds of his Catholic students and found that the overwhelming majority said they thought of themselves as Americans who happened to be Catholic rather than Catholics who happened to be American. We suspect the percentage would be at least as high among mainline Protestants, since Protestantism has been at the center of American "civil religion" for two centuries.

The real religion of most Americans is equality; that is their absolute, self-evident value. God *must* be an American, an equal-opportunity employer. All religious roads, if only followed sincerely, *must* equally lead to God.

This way of thinking is very comfortable and seems very enlightened—until someone starts to think logically and ask obvious, hard questions like: Does that include Jim Jones's road to Jonestown? Satanism? Where do you draw the line?

One of the most necessary apologetic tasks today is some hard, clear thinking about this most popular objection to the claims of Christ, the church, the Bible and the creeds. Once these claims are known (and many people, both Christians and non-Christians, simply do not know them), they strike the modern mind as meriting the very worst insult that mind can possibly imagine, an insult far worse than "wicked" (a word now used by teenagers to mean "great") or "sinful" (chuckle, chuckle), worse than "false" (how abstract!) or even worse than "irrelevant" or "out of it"—namely, "fanatical." A fanatic is the most un-American thing you can be, especially a "religious fanatic."

How dare Christians claim that their religion just happens to be the only true religion! This claim seems to most Americans so self-evidently narrow-minded, prejudicial and just plain idiotic that the topic is unarguable—and it remains unargued. We need to argue it here.

Defining the Issues

We must distinguish at least five different questions about the Christian position regarding other religions:

1. Are they true?

2. Are they good (moral)?

3. Are they salvific? (Can they save you?)

4. Are they educative ? (Can Christians learn from them?)

5. Are they useful? (Should Christians practice things in them?)

Christians have traditionally been divided into three tendencies: the liberal tendency is to answer yes as much as possible to these questions; the conservative, especially fundamentalist, tendency, is to answer no; and the mainline tradition has tended to answer partly yes and partly no. These positions, and their labels, are not sharp and clearly defined, but *tendencies.* We shall be defending mainly the traditional mainline position here, with a more conservative than liberal slant.

Are Other Religions True?

We cannot address this question until we agree on what is meant by "true." (See chap. 16.) If we use the definition that is commonsensical in the West, namely, correspondence with objective reality, then the correct answer seems to be: Partly. (But as we shall see in a moment, other religions, especially Eastern religions, have a different definition of truth.)

We could say, for instance, that Vedanta Hinduism is true in being monotheistic and false in being pantheistic, or that Islam's insistence on prayer and justice are true, but its denial that God can have a Son is false.

But the very meaning of "truth" changes when you move East. For a pantheist the difference between truth and falsity cannot be the difference between conformity and nonconformity between subjective (mind, ideas) and objective reality. For reality to a pantheist is one, not two; truth is not an idea's *conformity* but its *size,* so to speak. Only the idea of Oneness or Brahman or Nirvana is totally "true"; all lesser ideas are partly true and partly false, partial manifestations of the Whole.

(Pantheism is not the only Eastern option, and the very word is Western, and thus perhaps unfair; but it is *typically* Eastern. We shall use "Eastern" and "Western" here in an oversimplified way in order to make our main point as simple as possible.)

This makes argument between East (Hinduism, Buddhism, Taoism) and West (Judaism, Christianity, Islam) extremely difficult. For the West claims that the East is wrong on some points, and the East claims that there is no such thing as being wrong. A Hindu can believe everything, including Christianity, as a partial truth, or a stage along the way to total truth. Even contradictory ideas can be accepted as true; the stumbling block of East-West dialogue is the law of noncontradiction.

The East's argument is that its notion of truth includes the West's, but not vice versa; that the East is inclusive, the West exclusive. This is probably the main reason for the great popularity of Eastern religions in the West today, especially on an informal, unofficial level. Not many Americans are

Hindus, but most prefer the Hindu notion of truth to the Western one, at least in religion.

The real situation is just the opposite: the traditional West includes the East, not vice versa. The West already understands the Eastern insight that there is such a thing as degrees of truth (i.e., degrees of understanding, insight, depth, adequacy, wisdom). But the West adds that there is also such a thing as the law of noncontradiction. Contradictory propositions cannot both be true in the same sense at the same time. The East does not admit this.

For instance, suppose there are many degrees of depth in understanding the meaning of the word "God." Even so, either God has a will and wills a moral law, as the West believes, or else not, as the East believes. It can't be both. It is the East that fails to see the West's insight here, that truth is more than just the degree of understanding of a term's meaning; it is also the either/or matter of a proposition's being correct or incorrect.

Using this Western meaning of truth, our answer to the question "Are other religions true?" is: Certainly, in part. Even Satan has to speak some truth in order to sell his lies. Satanism tells Satanists some truths (e.g., that Satan is real and powerful and wants us to commit crimes like the ritual sacrifice of babies). How much more, then, will we find many truths in wise and humane and enlightened teachers like Buddha, Confucius and Muhammad. It remains to be seen, however, how their truths compare with Christianity's, and how and whether they are mixed with falsehoods.

The only "other" religion Christians accept as *wholly* true is biblical Judaism, for the simple reason that this is not an "other" religion at all but the foundation of Christianity. Christ said, "Do not think that I have come to abolish the law or the prophets. I have come not to abolish but to fulfill" (Mt 5:17). Christians believe everything Jews believe and more, just as Catholics believe everything orthodox, biblical Protestants believe and more. Modern Jews fault Christians for believing too many things, just as Protestants fault Catholics for believing too many things.

Are Other Religions Good?

What of the ethics, the morality of other religions? With the exception of Satanic religion(s), every religion in the world has not only some but a lot of true morality. The moral codes of the world's great religions are not nearly as different as their theologies. You can even find many of the values Jesus taught in the Sermon on the Mount in Plato, Confucius or Buddha, though not in the same context of a historical "kingdom of God."

There are some significant ethical contradictions between religions, however, based on their different theological beliefs. For instance, suppose you were an orthodox Hindu. You would believe that (a) this body is ultimately only an appearance; (b) we must all work out our karma, or moral fate; and (c) after death everyone except a fully enlightened mystic must go through many more reincarnations. For these reasons, you would not be swift to rescue a dying derelict from the gutter. For (a) bodily death is not very important; (b) you may be interfering with the person's karma, or fated learning experience through this suffering and dying; and (c) death is not terribly tragic because it is not final—we go round again and may get other chances through reincarnation.

If, on the other hand, you were a Christian or a Jew or a Muslim, you would act like the good Samaritan because you believe that (a) the body is real and good and important; (b) we are not fated but free (or both fated and free); and (c) we live only once, so life is incalculably precious.

However, such moral disagreements as these are unusual. More often there is not only agreement but remarkable agreement. Moral codes can be classified into three levels: codes for pragmatic survival, codes of objective justice and codes of selflessness. All three tell us not to bash each other's brains out, but for three different reasons: not to get bashed back; because it's not fair; and because we should be unselfish like God, or the Ultimate Reality. Everyone knows level one, and most civilized people know level two, but level three is high and rare. Yet all the great religions of the world teach level three morality.

This fact makes it tempting to identify religion with morality and minimize theological differences, thus uniting all the religions of the world. The modernists' reduction of Christianity to its morality, and their willingness to relativize or negotiate away theological doctrines, comes largely from this source.

Orthodox Christians should not be afraid to learn something from modernists here. Although it is either stupid or dishonest to negotiate away Christian doctrines (like Christ's divinity and resurrection) to win popular acceptance, it is nevertheless true and important that there already is a great amount of agreement among world religions on morality; this fact could be better taught and used in many ways for practical cooperation. For instance, Muslims and Christians can cooperate in urban antidrug programs. Only religious antidrug programs seem to work well, but any religious program seems to work well if its faith and devotion are strong.

Are Other Religions Salvific?

Can other religions save you? So far, our answers have been rather liberal: there is much truth and much moral goodness in other religions. Now we will begin to sound very conservative. Christianity cannot get rid of its founder's claim to be the only Savior.

However, as we have seen in chapter thirteen, the doctrine that Christ is the only Savior does not necessarily entail the conclusion that consciously professing Christians are the only ones saved. Passages like Romans 1 and John 1:9 tell us that God shines light into everyone's mind, and speaks to all people through conscience—God's inner microphone. Christians do not claim to know how many people respond to this knowledge of God in such a way as to be saved; but they do claim to know (because Jesus has told them) that if and when and however anyone is saved, it must be by Jesus, the one and only Savior. (See chap. 13.)

In other words, Christian exclusivism is not a *demographic* claim about heavenly and hellish population statistics. It is also not a *psychological* claim about exactly what has to go on inside the mind and feelings, or the conscious or unconscious levels of the soul, to be saved; about how clear, conscious and explicit saving faith must be. It is also not a theological claim about how much information you have to have about the true God to be saved. Rather, it is the claim that Jesus is the only objectively real Savior. So if and when a Jew, Hindu, pagan or atheist is saved, it is not by Judaism, Hinduism, paganism or atheism but by Christ.

Christ's claim is different from others' claims. He claims to save from sin and its wages, eternal death. Others claim to save from ignorance of morality or lack of mystical enlightenment or social disaster.

Only two reactions are logically possible to Christ's distinctive claim. If it is believed, he cannot be lowered to just one among many human teachers. If it is not believed, he cannot be raised to the level of Buddha or Muhammad, for he claims much more than they do: to save from sin and hell, and to be the only one who does. If this is not true, it is an intolerably arrogant lie. (See chap. 7 on Christ's divinity for a more thorough treatment of this dilemma.)

Christianity's exclusive claims are not for Christianity but for Christ. Christians, by definition, believe Christ to be God-made-man, God-in-the-flesh. His claims cannot be amended, watered down, relativized, negotiated away or nuanced into acceptability.

But this exclusivism is not an exclusivism of Christian culture, of Christian ethics or of Christians as the only candidates for heaven. Attacks on

Christian exclusivism often ignorantly or maliciously confuse these three indefensible exclusivisms with the real one, which is almost never squarely faced. (How often have you heard any non-Christian face the central question of whether Jesus' claims for himself are true or false?)

To the charge that they are being stubborn and arrogant about their position, Christians reply that it is Jesus' teachings, not theirs, that they are being stubborn about; and that this is not arrogant, for they do not arrogate to themselves the power to change them. Christians simply do not have the authority to do that, because "authority" means author's rights, and Christians are not the authors, nor even the editors, but only the mail carriers, of God's words. What would be arrogant indeed would be to correct Almighty God for the sake of ecumenism.

Are Other Religions Educative?

Can Christians learn any wisdom from other religions? Certainly! Our own Scriptures tell us that the God who spoke in many and various ways to our Jewish fathers (Heb 1:1) has not left himself without a witness among the Gentile nations (Rom 1:19-20; Acts 17:22-28).

There are at least three good reasons for Christians to study other religions.

First, to appreciate our own religion better by contrast. We fallen creatures need contrast to appreciate anything. We appreciate life by death, pleasure by pain, light by darkness, dogs by cats, cats by dogs, men by women, women by men, and perfect religion by imperfect religion.

Second, to reinforce and deepen our understanding of similar aspects of our own religion. For instance, Confucius can teach us much about practical social, moral and cosmic harmony; Lao-tzu about God's quiet, invisible, yielding power in nature; Buddha about the importance of silence and meditation; and, above all, Muhammad, about submission *(islam)* to God and his will. However, great caution and discernment are needed, especially if these teachings are not just studied from without but integrated into one's life from within.

Third, simply to seek and find truth wherever it may be. All truth is God's truth. We do not know where truth is until we look. So we should look everywhere, if we value truth, like a parent in search of precious children.

Are Other Religions Useful?

Should a Christian use some Zen Buddhist meditation techniques? Should Chinese Christians use Confucius as their teacher of social ethics? Should

Christian pacifists learn from Gandhi's methods? Should Jewish Christians celebrate the Jewish holidays?

Such questions should be addressed with great care, for religion is the active, actual service of God, gods, spirits or demons. Before Christians use a mantra from a Transcendental Meditation teacher, they should be sure it is not the name of a demon, camouflaged—because *it usually is!* Before opening up their spirit to meditation, they should be sure it opens up to God, not to nothingness—because in Zen there is no difference! Discernment is needed, on a case-by-case basis. Indiscriminate inclusion or indiscriminate exclusion are equally unthinking.

On the one hand, Christians believe Christ has already given us everything necessary, so nothing *need* be added. And there is truth in the old adage "Better safe than sorry." On the other hand, just as Christian theologians found Aristotle's logic very useful and fruitful, divorced from some elements in his pagan worldview, so Christians may *in principle* be able to use techniques from other religions that are in fact only simple, human, natural, universal, without any specific religious baggage.

On the one hand, there is a rich and orthodox tradition of Christian mysticism, so why look across the world for diamonds when your own back yard is full of them? On the other hand, we can learn something from everything.

On the one hand, we must remember that Eastern methods have been developed as means to non-Christian ends; and there is an organic connection between means and ends. The Eastern end is mysticism; sanctity is only a means. The Christian (and Jewish and Muslim) end is sanctity; mysticism is only a means to or a result of this higher end. For a Hindu or Buddhist, sanctity only purifies the individual soul so that it can see through itself as an illusion. For Christians, mysticism is only a reward of sanctity or a motor for more sanctity.

Christ tells us to love God; Hindus tell us we *are* God. Christ tells us to love our neighbor; Buddha tells us we *are* our neighbor. The Eastern goal is to see through the illusions of ego, soul, body, self, other, matter, space, time, world, good, evil, true, false, beautiful, ugly, this and that. The Christian goal is to know, love, please, serve, marry and enjoy God in this life and the next.

On the other hand, while the Bible tells us a lot about the second half of its own command to "be still and know that I am God," it tells us very little about how to do the first. In principle, some natural and neutral Eastern techniques might be separated from Eastern ends and enlisted in the service of that Christian end.

It is the saints, not the theologians, who will be our leaders in discernment here.

Defining the Genus *Religion*

To compare two or more things, you need first a common genus and then a specific difference. Thus we have two preliminary logical problems in comparing Christianity with other religions: first to define the genus *religion* and second to specify how Christianity essentially and specifically differs from all other religions.

First the genus. What is *religion?*

To define a term, like *religion,* or a class of things, like *religions,* we must remember the most basic rule of all definition: The definition must be coextensive with the thing defined, not too broad and not too narrow. For instance, the definition of humans as two-legged animals is too broad, since it also includes ducks. (Even if it is narrowed to two-legged animals without feathers, it still includes plucked ducks.) But the definition of humans as male rational animals is too narrow, since it fails to include females. But "rational animals" is just right.

When we try to find some definition of religion that is neither too narrow nor too broad, we are stumped. "The worship of God" is too narrow, for it does not include such religions as Buddhism and Confucianism, which do not even mention God. But "an ultimate concern" or "the meaning of life" are too broad, since they include such nonreligious philosophies as Marxism or Platonism.

We know of five attempts to solve this problem, none of them completely satisfactory.

1. A common attempt is to subjectivize and psychologize the term *religion* by defining it merely as an attitude one can take toward anything: an attitude that is passionate, irrational, fanatical, unscientific or naively credulous.

This assumes that religion is not true; in fact, that it is deceptive and unintelligent. It confuses a definition with an evaluation. Also, it is too broad, for one can take such an attitude toward anything. The term has no objective content left. Thus the definer has just adopted an unscientific, nonobjective, irrational attitude toward religion in confusing religion with an unscientific, nonobjective, irrational attitude!

2. Wilfred Cantwell Smith, in *The Meaning and End of Religion,* makes the unusual and challenging suggestion that we simply drop the term *religion* instead of defining it, since it arose not from within any religion, indigenously, but only from the accidental and external demand to compare religions, to "sell" one religion by showing prospective customers that it was better than others on the market. Thus some generic term was needed to show that one "thing" was a better "thing" than other "things." No founder of a world religion said he was founding a "religion."

But the term has a long history, however mixed up, like a nation, or a grandparent. We cannot commit linguistic euthanasia just because our patient is sick and confused. We must take language as it is used and define it, not recreate it. It is part of the philosopher's data.

3. Another suggestion is that the term is simply equivocal; or at least that Eastern and Western religions are essentially different. Religion in the West is the belief in (and worship of) a supernatural God, a life after death and a moral law from this God. Eastern religion is essentially a transformation of consciousness or a vision of ultimate oneness. (But even this does not apply to Confucianism.)

But the fact that all sorts of people have used the same word, usefully and meaningfully, to cover pagan myths, Christianity, Judaism, Islam, Hinduism, Buddhism, Taoism, Confucianism, Shinto and many other things means that the mind intuits some kind of unity there, not pure equivocation. But we have not yet defined what that is.

4. Some Christians have said that the universal essence of religion is man's search for God, and that Christianity is not a religion because it is God's search for man.

This may be true, even profoundly true. But Buddhism and Confucianism would not describe themselves as searches for God. And religions other than Christianity—notably Judaism and Islam—also claim to be God's search for man, divine revelations. Even Hinduism claims divine revelation, though in an experiential, mystical, private and nonpropositional way.

This Christian definition of real religion as God's search for man presupposes the superior truth of Christianity. The claim may be true—in fact, we believe it *is* true—but it cannot come at the very beginning of discussion. Definitions should be noncontroversial because they are like the level playing field, or like the universal ground rules, for the game or battle or debate to come. Both sides must play by the same rules in order to communicate.

5. The sociologist may try to supply a universal definition of religion by observing three aspects to religious behavior everywhere: beliefs, morality and liturgy; or creed, code and cult; or words, works and worship.

This may be useful empirical *description*, like St. Paul's fifteen-part description of *agapē* in 1 Corinthians 13; but it is not a *definition*. It may help us to recognize the thing when we find it; but it does not define its essence by genus and specific difference.

Besides, each of these three elements presents the same problem as the original term *religion.*

We have no sixth and better answer. We know no clear, common, universal definition of *religion.*

Fortunately, that does not prevent us from proceeding. Implicit knowledge sometimes supplies for the lack of explicit knowledge. For instance, we may not be able to define *time* either, but we can go ahead and theorize about it on a very high level. People have said all sorts of true and useful things about terms like *religion* without being able to define them.

Defining Differences Within *Religion:* Six Fundamental Theological Choices

If we do not know the genus, we cannot narrow that genus down by giving a specific difference that distinguishes our subject from all other members of that genus. What we can do, however, is to *subdivide* the still-undefined term: to give not the specific difference *of* religion but the specific differences *within* religion; or, in other words, the basic options, the kinds of religion there are.

At least, we can do this with reference to the first of the sociologist's three ingredients: belief, especially belief about God or some sort of God-object or Godlike object.

These fundamental belief options can be set out in disjunctive outline as follows:

1. Agnosticism ("I don't know") vs. belief ("I claim to know something");

2. Within belief, atheism (no gods) vs. theism (some kind of God or gods);

3. Within theism in this most vague and general sense, polytheism (many gods) vs. monotheism (one God);

(Note: when polytheism and monotheism are combined, as in Hinduism, the many gods are only inferior, apparent, projected or mythological manifestations of the one and only supreme, real, ultimate God.)

4. Within monotheism, pantheism (God = everything, and everything = God; God is immanent but not transcendent) vs. theism proper, or supernaturalism (a transcendent God);

5. Within theism proper, deism (God is real but remote; he has not revealed himself) vs. revealed theism (God is present and has made himself known);

6. Within revealed theism, unitarianism (only one person in God) vs.

trinitarianism (three persons in God).

Thus we have six *kinds* of non-Christian religious options: (1) agnosticism, (2) atheism, (3) polytheism, (4) pantheism, (5) deism and (6) unitarianism.

How does Christianity compare with all these? The question is not the easy-to-answer question of what doctrines of Christianity are unique and taught by no other religion. That is a factual, empirical question. The controversial apologetical question is to compare Christianity with other religions in terms of truth, value or adequacy.

Ten Answers to the Question of Comparative Religions

Christians have given at least ten distinguishable answers to this question:

1. That only Christians can be saved. Since other religions are false religions, all non-Christians will go to hell.

This is certainly a powerful "sales pitch" and motivation for missionaries. More importantly, it seems to follow from some exclusivist statements in Scripture. But as we saw earlier (chap. 13), these claims are made not for *Christianity* but for *Christ*.

2. That although we cannot judge that every non-Christian is unsaved, we can judge that every non-Christian religion is simply false and that only Christianity is true.

Again, this goes beyond scripture, which does not speak of other religions except Old Testament polytheism. And, as we have seen, it is impossible to call *every* part of the whole of a religion untrue.

3. That other religions may have some truth, perhaps much truth, perhaps even some very profound truths, but that Christianity alone has pure, infallible *truth*. Other religions mix truth with errors.

4. That other religions have some truth, perhaps much truth, but Christianity alone has the *full* truth, or fullness of truth.

Answers 3 and 4 often go together. Logically, the problem with 3 is that agnosticism also can claim to be infallible and free of error because it makes no truth claims at all. Infallibility cannot be the *specific* and essential mark of Christianity. The problem with 4 logically is that Christianity does *not* claim to teach every truth (e.g., astronomy); its borders remain to be defined. Nor does it claim to teach every truth about God, for that would take an infinity of time.

5. That other religions have profound but confused foreshadowings of Christianity, especially in their myths; that Christianity clarifies and makes historical and thus fulfills the truths that are gropingly set forth in myth and mystery and mysticism; it is "myth become fact" (C. S. Lewis).

This is true, but it does not define the difference between Christianity and *all* other religions, especially those that arose *after* it (Islam).

6. That each religion teaches different and incomparable truths; that we simply have a quilt of pluralism; that each religion is better than any other at *something;* that you simply can't compare religions overall as better or worse. They are just different, like cats and dogs.

This is generous but inaccurate, for religions can be compared on many specific teachings where they contradict each other. "Jesus is the Messiah" and "Jesus is not," or "God has a will" and "God does not," are quite comparable. One of the two beliefs must be true and the other false.

7. That all religions are essentially one at their hidden esoteric, mystical, nonverbal core. They only seem to contradict each other when you take too seriously and too literally their public, exoteric, popular, verbal teachings.

This is an extremely popular view in academic circles, best represented by Fritjof Schuon's *The Transcendent Unity of Religions* and by popular writers such as Aldous Huxley and Alan Watts. The problem is that it Easternizes religion. One of the major differences between East and West is on just this issue. The West does not believe the East's two-layer theory of religion: exoteric teachings for the masses and esoteric teachings for the mystics. And there is no evidence of another, esoteric Christianity different from the only data we have, the actual words of the Gospels—except heresies constantly defined as such by the church, especially Gnosticism.

8. That religion is wholly subjective, and therefore religions cannot be compared any more than feelings or appetites can: "Whatever works for you."

This is simply inaccurate. Every religion insists we get *out* of our immediate subjectivity and know or unite with Reality. The solution here reduces religion to pop psychology.

9. That religion is evolutionary and progressive, like everything else. Thus Christianity is more highly evolved than Judaism, but not as highly evolved as Modernism or Bah'ai.

The problem here is telling truth with a clock or calendar, confusing "true" with "new." By this standard, Marxism is one of the most progressive religions. If, on the other hand, we use a standard other than simply happening later in time to judge evolutionary advancement, this brings us back to a nonevolutionary criterion. Which?

10. That Christianity is in fact the worst, or one of the worst, of all religions because of its intolerance and exclusivism.

This view at least has the guts to meet the problem head on.

Ten Answers Reduced to Three

These ten answers naturally tend to group themselves into three tendencies or schools of thought. This is true both systematically, by their own structure, and historically, by consensus. Today's politicized journalism would call these three positions the right, the center and the left. The ten answers have been arranged along this spectrum from "right" (low numbers) to "left" (high numbers), or from "fundamentalistic" to "liberal" or "modernist."

The church, both officially and unofficially, in its greatest saints and theologians, has tended to the middle position, that is, answers 3-5 (often combined; they are not mutually exclusive), with occasional experiments with 2 or 6.

The extreme position, 1, may seem the most orthodox to outsiders, but it is not. Those who hold it have over and over again, in different centuries, been censured and even excommunicated by the church: for example, Tatian in the second century, Tertullian in the fourth, Father Feeny in the twentieth.

The other extremes, 7-10, are definitely heterodox and deny, ignore or make mincemeat of Jesus' claim to be the only Son of God and the only Savior.

Why don't orthodox Christians buy into the popular liberal answers? (Answers 6-8 are the most popular.) The reason is not that they insist that within the genus *religion* their *religion* is the only good or true one. It is the insistence that there is *no* genus for Jesus, that he is the only Son of God and the only Savior.

The only logical alternative to that position is the position that when he made those claims he was *not* speaking the truth; and in that case, he is either a fool (if he sincerely thought they were true) or a liar (if he knew they were not). Those are the only two logical possibilities. (See chap. 7.)

Orthodox Christians can admit profound parallels in the theologies of other religions, though not exact equivalences: for example, a vague notion of the Trinity in the Hindu *sat, chit* and *ananda*. They can admit profound parallels in morality: for example, Buddha's *Dhammapada* or Lao-tzu's *Tao Te Ching* teaching something very like the radical nonviolence of the Sermon on the Mount. But there is not even any other *claimant* to Christ's titles, no other sane man in the history of the world who seriously claimed to be the Creator-God incarnate.

And there is no other empty tomb. (See chap. 8.)

Three Answers Reduced to One

We may look at the problem of comparative religions teleologically (i.e., with respect to an end sought) and ask what would be the ideal solution to the problem, what would be the best of all possible future worlds with regard to comparative religions. The answer to this question should also be the primary goal we should then work for.

Three possible answers appear.

1. Conversion of the whole world to Christ. This is the simplest and most direct and obvious answer, and has the "advantage" that it is the answer Christ himself gave in authorizing missionary work (Mt 28:18-20; Acts 1:8). Its "disadvantage" is that it seems too simple for scholars and too idealistic and unattainable for mere human power. (Of course no conversion comes about by mere human power.)

2. Perpetual *pluralism* with tolerance. Hindus remain Hindus, but respect and understand and tolerate Christianity. Christians, in turn, respect and understand and tolerate Hinduism. The advantage here seems to be the relative ease: we need not find or even seek *truth*, only decide to tolerate other's opinions. And most people already accept this ideal in theory. The "disadvantage" is that it seems like indifferentism. We *tolerate* things we do not deeply care about, like different fashions in clothes, but not things we care most about, like fascism or racism or superstition in science.

3. World religious *unification*, not by conversion but by universal agreement. There are only two ways this can be done: exoterically or esoterically.

a. Exoterically, in terms of public teachings of different world religions, the contradictions would have to be ignored and the agreements (especially in morality) highlighted. Thus a sort of "lowest common denominator" religion would be created.

The "advantage" of this scheme is again that it is easy. Any scholar can go through the different scriptures and find the agreements. The disadvantage is that it would satisfy only weak believers, not strong believers, in every religion. What each religion is proudest of, and considers its essence, is usually the very thing or things that make it distinctive.

b. Unification could be seen esoterically, in terms of a hidden, unwritten, mystical "common core" supposedly equally present in all world religions. For this unification to take place, everyone would have to become a mystic and see through the illusion that religions contradict each other (which they do on the exoteric, public, verbal level), or else believe the mystics who do.

The "advantage" of this solution is that if there is such a "common core," and it is *true*, we had better know it. The "disadvantage" is that it may not be true. Generally, Easterners and Westerners disagree about precisely this point: is the true essence of religion esoteric and mystical, or not? Western religions believe God revealed his deepest secrets publicly to all, not through unusual private mystical experiences. So this solution is really imperialistic; it *annexes* Western religions.

If Christianity is true, solution 1 seems to be the valid and only solution. If solution 2 or 3 is preferable, then the claims of Christianity cannot be true. If it is better for a Hindu not to know Christ than to know Christ, then Christ is not what he claimed to be: everyone's Savior. He is only a local option, like a tribal chief.

And really, when it comes down to it, what is the objection to solution 1 if not that the claims of Christ are not true? That Christian missionaries have been imperialistic and insisted on cultural as well as religious conversion? That was a mistake and a perversion. That the attempt to convert everyone to Christ is loveless and lacks compassion? It is precisely love and compassion that motivates missionaries to risk martyrdom. It is love and compassion that once converted the world and can do it again.

Two Postscripts
Postscript 1
In comparing Christianity with others religions, the relation between Christianity and Judaism is in a class by itself. For Christians accept everything in traditional (biblical) Judaism, and regard it as not only true but divinely revealed.

Nevertheless, ironically, this makes Jews and Christians disagree, more clearly and adamantly than any other two kinds of believer can, over the center of Christianity, Christ. For debate between any two other religions can hope to overcome misunderstandings caused by radically different cultural backgrounds, languages, philosophical traditions, assumptions, and world-views. But Christians understand and accept all these things from Judaism. When Christians and Hindus disagree about God, they mean different things by "God." But when Jews and Christians disagree about whether Jesus is God, they mean the same "God."

Thus the only two logically possible ways for a Christian and a Jew to agree would be for a Jew to become a Jewish Christian and accept Christ, or for the Christian to become an apostate and reject him.

This is not to say that mutual hatred and suspicion is inevitable, that the wounds of history do not need healing, or that Jews and Christians cannot respect and even love each other. We assume every reader is intelligent enough to see through the absurd propaganda that confuses ideas with persons, and either rejects persons or refuses to reject ideas.

Postscript 2

We caution beginners that the field of comparative religions is like a mine field. Much dangerous nonsense has been written here, for it is a relatively new and unmarked field; and the desire, in itself laudable, to overcome the scandal of religious conflict and contradiction frequently overcomes the reason.

The most enlightening single chapter we have ever read about the difference between Christianity and its most popular rival, pantheism, whether in its traditional Eastern form or in its currently popularized New Age form, is chapter 11 of C. S. Lewis's *Miracles*, "Christianity and 'Religion.' "

The most enlightening single book we have ever read on the subject of comparative religions and the uniqueness of Christ is the book that, more than any other, converted C. S. Lewis, namely G. K. Chesterton's *The Everlasting Man*. It defends position 5 on our spectrum, and paints a picture of the history of religions that is uniquely brilliant, poetic and exciting.

Questions for Discussion

1. Why is the charge that the claims of Christianity are "bigoted" a charge that was almost unknown until relatively recently and has dramatically escalated as modernity wears on?

2. Which Christians are more worried about the charge of exclusivism than about any other charge or objection against Christianity?

3. Why is the real religion of Americans equality? How can the idea of equality arouse religious passion? If we were to symbolize ideas by colors, God may be colorless, goodness white, sin black, hell red, heaven blue, wonder purple, hope green, comfort tan, and happiness yellow; but equality would be gray, all colors blended equally together. Why don't Americans find this dull?

4. Why do people want very much to believe that all religious roads lead to God? Do you? In what other fields do people want to believe in such equality, and in what other fields do they not? Compare, for example, romance, sports, finances, surgery, morality, art, technology, cosmology. What general principle emerges from these examples?

5. Why are some people fanatical only against fanatics? What motivates such a unique passion? Compare, for example, Merseault in Camus's *The Stranger*.

6. On the face of it, it would seem that the claim that one religion is true and that others, insofar as they contradict it, are therefore false, is reasonable and natural, whether that claim is in fact true or false. Why do most Americans not only disagree with it but find it so self-evidently absurd that they feel no need to give

any arguments to disprove it?

7. Are there other important questions about other religions than the five distinguished (pp. 343-44)?

8. Can the essential philosophy of most of the East, namely monism or pantheism, be refuted simply by pointing out that (a) it entails denial of the correspondence theory of truth (pp. 344-45) and (b) that denial is self-contradictory, for it claims to really correspond to the way things are? In other words, it entails the conclusion that no one is wrong and no idea is false, only less right or less true; but this seems self-contradictory for it claims that the denial of this position is wrong. How would a sophisticated Hindu philosopher respond to this argument, do you think?

9. Can both theism and pantheism be equally true? If not, can Hinduism and Christianity be equally true? If not, can they be equally false? Why?

10. How would a monist or pantheist reply to the argument that their notion of truth (which is only the largeness or adequacy or depth of the idea) deals only with the products of the first act of the mind, concepts, and fails to take into account the products of the second act of the mind, judgments or propositions, while the Western notion (truth in propositions) includes the Eastern notion (degrees of truth in concepts) (pp. 344-45)?

11. Can morality be separated from religion? Why or why not? Can it be separated from metaphysics, or a worldview? Why or why not? What are the arguments on the other side of this controversial question and how do you answer them?

12. Why do you think it is that different religions agree more on ethics than theology?

13. What do you think the result would be if believers in different religions worked together against the common enemy of secularism and moral evil in society, like drugs or promiscuity? Would it make a difference whether the common enemy were something secularists also saw as an enemy (like drugs) or something most of them did not (like promiscuity)? What do you think the different results would be in each of the following cases of such cooperation: (a) Protestant-Catholic, (b) Christian-Jew, (c) Christian-Jew-Muslim and (d) Eastern-Western religions?

14. Is there any way one can be an orthodox Christian yet give a more "liberal" answer to question 3? Why or why not?

15. Why do conservatives have a reputation of being more arrogant than liberals?

16. Why is the answer given to question 5 (pp. 348-50), though carefully nuanced, likely to offend many conservatives *and* liberals?

17. Must we define religion first to answer the main question of this chapter?

18. Which of the five answers to the problem of defining religion without being too broad or too narrow do you think is best? Why? How do you answer the criticism of this answer that is given in its last paragraph? Can you come up with a sixth and better answer?

19. Does the six-point classification of religions on page 352 leave out anything essential?

20. Which of the ten answers to the question of comparative religions do you prefer? Why?

21. Do you see the irony, humor and self-contradiction in the positions of Tatian, Tertullian and Father Feeny (p. 355)? (Fr. Feeny was a Catholic priest who was excommunicated for teaching that the church's teaching that "outside the church there is no salvation" referred to the visible Roman Catholic Church only.)

22. What is the distinction, made a number of times in this chapter, between Christ and Christianity? Is it the distinction between individual and institutional religion? Private and public? Invisible and visible? Spirit and letter? Piety and theology? Why doesn't the chapter identify it with any one of these?

23. Are there other special difficulties in the relation between Christians and Jews besides the ones mentioned in postscript 1?

24. Why is it so hard for many to make the distinction in the last paragraph of postscript 1?

Outline of Chapter 15
Objective Truth

1. **The importance of the issue**
2. **Definitions**
   - ☐ Objective
   - ☐ Truth
   - Alternative theories of truth
   - ☐ Pragmatic
   - ☐ Empiricist
   - ☐ Rationalist
   - ☐ Coherence theory
   - ☐ Emotivist
3. **Four possible attacks on apologetics**
   - ☐ Universal skepticism
   - ☐ Universal subjectivism
   - ☐ Religious skepticism
   - ☐ Religious subjectivism
4. **Refutation of five arguments for universal skepticism**
5. **Refutation of religious skepticism**
6. **Refutation of subjectivism**
   - ☐ Kant's "Copernican revolution"
   - ☐ Hegelian historicism
   - ☐ Pantheism
7. **Refutation of moral subjectivism: answers to eight objections**
   - ☐ Values are culturally relative
   - ☐ Society only conditions our values
   - ☐ Subjectivism produces tolerance
   - ☐ Morality is relative to situations
   - ☐ Good subjective motives alone suffice to make one moral
   - ☐ We must be free to create values
   - ☐ Moral values are not discoverable by science
   - ☐ Morality can be reduced to "natural selection"
8. **Refutation of religious subjectivism**
9. **The origin of subjectivism**

CHAPTER 15
Objective Truth

T HIS CHAPTER HAS DELIBERATELY BEEN KEPT BACK UNTIL THE END BE-
cause it is the most philosophical and abstract. But it is also the most
fundamental and the necessary foundation of all the other chapters—
in fact, of all honest argument about anything.

The Importance of the Issue

1. From a practical point of view, the question of whether we can know
objective truth is one of the most important questions in apologetics,
because today most arguments between Christians and non-Christians
eventually come down to this point. What usually happens is this: After
the Christian has won the substantive argument, the non-Christian, unable
to refute the Christian's argument, retreats to this ubiquitous line of defense: "What you say may be true for you, but not for me. Truth is relative.
What right do you have to impose your beliefs on me? You're being judgmental."

Christian apologetic strategy must be ready to cope with this move. We
must be prepared to show our opponents (i.e., our friends) that they take
refuge in this relativism and subjectivism only after they have lost the argument, never after they have won it, or think they have won it.

2. Not only is the subjectivist defense against Christian apologetics the
most popular one today, it is also universal: it undercuts all arguments for
all doctrines, and makes impossible the whole enterprise of apologetics—
for that matter, it makes impossible all reasoning about anything. If reasons
cannot be proofs of objective truths, but only personal rationalizations,

feelings and prejudices, then it is futile to "give a reason for the faith that is in you"—except to your psychoanalyst.

3. The consequences of a subjectivism and relativism of truth are destructive not only to apologetics but also to intellectual honesty and to life. For

> if Truth is objective, if we live in a world we did not create and cannot change merely by thinking, if the world is not really a dream of our own, then the most destructive belief we could possibly believe would be the denial of this primary fact. It would be like closing your eyes while driving, or blissfully ignoring the doctor's warnings. (C. S. Lewis, "The Poison of Subjectivism" in *Christian Reflections*)

Of all the symptoms of decay in our decadent civilization, subjectivism is the most disastrous of all. A mistake can possibly be discovered and amended if and only if truth exists and can be known and is loved and searched for. If you close your eyes to the light in the operating room, there is no chance at all that the operation will work and that the patient will be saved. But prophetic warnings by themselves are not enough; we need careful definitions and analyses. And to that more modest intellectual task we now turn.

Definitions

Before proving the objectivity of truth and disproving subjectivism, we must define our terms, in order to know clearly what we are talking about and to be sure we are not talking past each other rather than to each other. We think much subjectivism begins here, at the beginning, with a misunderstanding of the meaning of the terms *objective* and *truth.*

Objective

1. The word *objective* in the phrase "objective truth" does not refer to an unemotional, detached or impersonal attitude. Truth is not an attitude. Truth is not *how* we know, truth is *what* we know.

2. Objective does not mean "known by all" or "believed by all." Even if everyone believes a lie, a lie is still a lie. "You don't find truth by counting noses."

3. Objective does not mean "publicly proved." An objective truth could be privately known—for example, the location of a hidden treasure. It could also be *known* without being *proved*; to know is one thing, to give good proofs or reasons for your knowledge is another.

What *objective* means in "objective truth" is "independent of the knower and his consciousness." "I itch" is a subjective truth; "Plato wrote the *Republic*" is an objective truth. "I don't want to be unselfish" is a subjective truth; "I ought to be unselfish whether I want to or not" is an objective truth.

Truth

In a sense, the whole issue between the subjectivist and the objectivist is the definition of truth. The definition we offer here is commonsensical; it is what most people and cultures in all times and places mean by "truth." But the subjectivist would not agree with our definition. The definition itself is an "objectivist" one. So the issue is right here in the definition. We shall therefore compare and evaluate five alternative definitions of truth after giving the true one.

Aristotle, the master of common sense in philosophy, defined what ordinary people mean by truth as "saying of what is that it is and of what is not that it is not." Truth means the correspondence of what you know or say to what is. Truth means "telling it like it is."

(Here is a technical point which unphilosophical readers can skip. Although we used the term "correspondence" for the Western, as versus the Eastern, meaning of truth in chapter fourteen, Aristotle's definition of truth does not involve what philosophers call "the correspondence theory of truth," as held, for example, by John Locke—that is, a correspondence between our ideas [or mental images] and things in the real world. Instead, Aristotle [and Aquinas] held an *identity* theory of truth—that is, the mind actually [but mentally rather than physically] *becomes* the object, or the form [nature] of the object, that is known. The very same form, or nature, or essence, that exists in the objective world as the form of a concrete material thing [e.g., the treeness of a tree] reexists in the world of the mind abstracted from material things. The problem with the correspondence theory of truth is this: if true ideas are pictures or copies of real things, and what we have in our mind and immediately know are only those pictures, and not the things themselves, or their real forms or essences, then we can never know whether or not those pictures correspond to real objects. If all we can directly see is photos and not real persons, we can never be sure whether the photos are accurate likenesses.)

Alternative Theories of Truth

1. The Pragmatic Theory of Truth: "Truth is what works."

Since "what works" is subjective and relative (what you *think* works, or what works *for you*), pragmatism is a form of subjectivism and relativism. G. E. Moore proved (in his essay "William James's Pragmatism") that the pragmatic theory of truth is based on a linguistic confusion. There is a perfectly good word in the language for "what works." That word is "efficient" or "effective" or "practical." If we reduce truth to "what works," we lose a different, distinctive, independent meaning of truth as "saying what *is*." Moore shows quite simply and conclusively that truth cannot mean "what works" or "what is practical," because what is true is not always practical (e.g., death) and what is practical is not always true (e.g., a "successful" lie).

Chesterton refuted pragmatism by saying that "man's most pragmatic need is to be something more than a pragmatist." For without an end, no one will work for any practical means. "Means" *means* "means-to-an-end." Without a more-than-pragmatic end, no one can be pragmatic. Pragmatism doesn't work, it isn't practical.

2. The Empiricist Theory of Truth: "Truth is what we can sense."

Not all empiricists are subjectivists and relativists, but they should be; for if truth is empirical, and what is empirical is determined by my subjective experience, then truth is subjective and relative. The orange tastes sweet to you, bitter to me.

Empiricism is also built on a linguistic confusion, between what is "sensible" and what is "true." Some things we sense are not true (e.g., mirages or hypnotic images) and some things that we all know are true are not sensed (e.g., the fact that 13 x 13 = 169, or the fact that you are thinking about the nature of thought right now).

Empiricism as a theory of truth seems designed a priori, from the beginning, rather than empirically and from experience, to eliminate soul, spirit, God, heaven and objective moral law from the realm of objective truths.

Empiricism itself is not an empirical, experimental, experiential report on how we do in fact use words (like "spirit"); instead, it is a rationalistic, a priori ideological doctrine. Empiricism is not empirical enough.

3. The Rationalist Theory of Truth: "Truth is what can be clearly and distinctly understood by reason" or "truth is what can be proved by reason."

Just as pragmatism is unpragmatic and empiricism is not empirical, rationalism is irrational. You can't *prove* that truth is only what can be proved. And it's not perfectly clear that all truth is perfectly clear. In fact, many truths *cannot* be proved: for instance, the law of noncontradiction (X does not equal non-X). This is presupposed in all proofs, so that trying to prove it always begs the question; it assumes what you claim to prove. Many important truths also are not clear: for instance, the truth that most people are both good and bad, mysteriously mixed; or that "life is worth living."

4. The Coherence Theory of Truth: "Truth is not a relationship of correspondence between an idea and its external object, but the coherence or oneness or harmony among a set of ideas." Truth is a consistency, wholeness or totality of ideas.

This theory is usually found among monists and pantheists, like Spinoza and Hegel, who reject dualism, including the subject-object, knower-known dualism.

Once again, this is a linguistic confusion. We already have words for coherence, consistency, wholeness and totality, and we do not need another one—truth—especially when that other one already has a distinct and useful meaning.

Furthermore, the coherence theory *presupposes* the truth of something like the correspondence theory. For it claims it is *true*, that is, that this theory (coherence) really tells what is—or corresponds to the facts, the real situation, the way it really is—and that the other theory (correspondence) does not. Thus it contradicts itself. The coherence theory is incoherent.

5. The Emotivist Theory of Truth: "Truth is what I feel." This is held by many teenagers but few philosophers. It is also a linguistic confusion between two distinct notions: feeling and knowing truth.

These two notions may coincide. Sometimes feelings may be perceptions of objective truth: for instance, when a saint feels love for an ugly person and perceives the intrinsic value of the person through this feeling. Love is more than a feeling, but it can include feeling, and this feeling can perceive truth.

But to *identify* truth with feeling is absurd. For many feelings are false—for example, irrational fears or infatuations—and many truths are not felt emotionally at all—for example, "there are four paper clips in the wastebasket."

All theories of truth, once they are expressed clearly and simply, presuppose the commonsensical notion of truth that is enshrined in the wisdom of language and the tradition of usage, namely the correspondence (or identity) theory. For each theory claims that it is really true, that is, that it corresponds to reality, and that the others are really false, that is, that they fail to correspond to reality.

Four Possible Attacks on Apologetics
Four different theories about truth make apologetics impossible. They are

universal skepticism, universal subjectivism, religious skepticism and religious subjectivism. They must be answered in different ways.

Universal Skepticism

Universal skepticism maintains that no truth is knowable. This is immediately self-contradictory, for it claims to know that it is true that no one can know truth. If it is modified to mean only that no truth is knowable *with certainty*, only probability, the same problem occurs: is the theory itself only probable or certain? If certain, it contradicts itself. If probable, is *that* certain or only probable? Et cetera ad infinitum. In that case no statement is made because no statement is finished: probablism is saying that it is probable that it is probable that it is probable that . . .

Universal Subjectivism

Universal subjectivism claims that all truth is subjective, that is, "in" or dependent on the knower. This is also self-contradictory, but the self-contradiction is not as obvious as that of skepticism. The contradiction lies in the fact that the subjectivist claims that truth really, objectively, *is* subjective. If they claimed only that the subjectivity of truth is a subjective truth, a mere personal opinion or feeling in the mind of the subjectivist, then they would not be claiming that the subjectivist theory was really correct and the objectivist theory incorrect. In that case they would not really be disagreeing with their opponents at all.

Religious Skepticism

Religious skepticism claims that although we may know objective truth in nonreligious fields, especially the sciences, we can't know objective truth in religion. When this theory functions as an excuse not to look at apologetic arguments, it begs the question. For apologetics claims to prove that at least some religious claims are *demonstrably* true. One cannot exempt oneself from refuting those proofs by merely claiming at the outset that no truth can be known in religion.

Of course, no reasonable and intelligent religious believer claims that God and the things of God are completely or adequately understood by human reason. But that is not skepticism. It is instead the notion of mystery, which sees these things as *opaque*, reflecting some light from the surface to the eye but not revealing or reflecting what is beneath the surface. Skepticism sees these things as dark and empty, as holes reflecting no light at all. The third possible position would be a rationalism which sees things as *transparent*, clear through and through. In the Middle Ages some religious philosophers drifted close to rationalism (e.g., Ramon Lull, who invented a theological computer). Today the skeptical extreme is far more popular.

Religious Subjectivism

Religious subjectivism is the most popular position today. It sees religion as "true for you but not for me." This really means that it sees religious truth as feeling, as a mode of sensibility, something to help us cope and live more successfully, a set of ideals and values, rather than as a creed, as statements that are either true or false because they claim to reveal facts, like "Christ has died; Christ is risen; Christ will come again."

Religion does include all these other dimensions, but it also claims to include fact-claims (e.g., that one all-powerful, all-good and all-knowing God exists; that he created the universe; that he became a man and died and rose; that there is a real, objective moral law; and that there is a real judgment, a real heaven and a real hell). These claims may be true or they may be false, but they are not claims about things inside our consciousness but about things outside it. They are about objective truth, not subjective truth; about beings, not just consciousness; about laws, not just values; about the resurrection of a real man of flesh and blood, not about the mere arising of "Easter faith" in people's minds.

Refutation of Five Arguments for Universal Skepticism

The strongest arguments for skepticism are also the simplest and clearest. (Other, more technical philosophical arguments are not as influential.) Each of these arguments can be refuted:

Objection 1:
We do err. We are fallible. We are also fallible about when we are fallible; when we err, we do not think we are erring. How then do we know in any given case of apparent knowledge of truth whether we are erring or not? In other words, if we can err, we can err about whether we are erring now. If we err sometimes, we can err at any time, and if we can err at any time, we can be in error this time.
Reply: Error does not prove skepticism, it refutes it. Josiah Royce's essay "The Possibility of Error" (in *The Religious Aspect of Philosophy*) proved that the possibility of error is necessarily grounded in, and logically presupposes, the knowability of objective truth.

To simplify the argument: We do indeed err, as the skeptic says. But we are also sometimes aware of our error; we can judge our errors as errors and correct them. The only way we could ever do this is by using a standard to measure the error as erroneous, as failing to come up to the standard. That standard cannot also be in error, otherwise we could never know that the original error is in error; for it is only by the authority of the standard that we can judge the original error to be an error. Thus the very concept of "error" presupposes some certain knowledge of truth.

Objection 2:

Certainty comes only by adding a reason, a proof, to an idea. But every proof depends on its premises being true. These premises, in turn, are certain only if proved by other premises, et cetera ad infinitum. Thus nothing can be absolutely certain.

Reply: The argument that all arguments must have an infinite regress of premises was answered long ago by Aristotle. He said that the chain of premises does not stretch back infinitely because it ends at "first principles," or "self-evident truths," which need not be proved by prior premises because they prove themselves, so to speak. For the predicate arises necessarily from reflection on the meaning of the subject. For instance, "Good ought to be done, and evil ought to be avoided"; "Everything that begins must have a cause for its beginning"; and "A whole is greater than any of its parts."

These principles are not mere tautologies, or empty repetitions, like "X = X," as modern analytic philosophy has contended, because they give us real insight into reality. This insight is not a knowledge of empirical facts, which might have been different (like "the sky is blue") but understanding of necessary and unchangeable principles which state the relations between some of the essences or natures of things. (Analytic philosophy does not believe there *are* "essences.") From such first principles alone we cannot deduce the rest of knowledge, as we can deduce conclusions from the postulates of geometry. But arguments can "reduce" to (or back up to) first principles. For instance, if we can show that murder is evil, we prove it ought not to be done. If we can prove that a miraculous event is either caused by something supernatural or by nothing at all, we prove that it is caused by something supernatural. And if we can prove that the common good is a whole and that the private good is a part of it, we prove that the common good is greater than the private good.

Even if such "first principles" were empty tautologies, or if arguments which "reduce to first principles" were somehow mistaken, there is a second way to stop the infinite regress: things we know by experience. Reasoning has two starting points: abstract first principles and concrete experience.

Objection 3:
The burden of proof should be on the believer in certain knowledge, not on the skeptical unbeliever. In the absence of any compelling proof for the existence of certainty, we should remain skeptical. For the most reliable method we have of attaining certainty, the scientific method, demands that we begin not in belief but in universal methodic doubt. Ideas, unlike people, should be treated as guilty until proven innocent.

Reply A: If the burden of proof is always on the one who believes any idea, then that principle should also apply to the belief in the idea of skepticism.

Reply B: There is no scientific method for proving that only the scientific method proves truth. "Accept nothing except what the scientific method proves" is thus self-contradictory.

Reply C: The burden of proof is on the one who says that the burden of proof is always on the believer. Common sense says that the burden of proof is sometimes on the believer and sometimes on the skeptic; that sometimes methodic faith is more reasonable than methodic doubt (e.g., trusting a previously reliable friend, or traditions, or your senses); and that the burden of proof is then on the innovator and on the minority. And skepticism is largely a modern innovation and a minority view.

Objection 4:
We can always be shown in practice that we do not believe we have absolutely certain knowledge about anything. For would you consent to be tortured if you were mistaken about something you felt absolutely certain about? Take "the sky is blue," for instance, or "the earth is round." When you discover that the sky is really colorless and that the earth is really oval-shaped, you realize you had only certitude, not certainty; only the subjective feeling of confidence, not certain knowledge of objective truth.

Reply: Fear of torture does not make us rational but irrational. Fear changes our feelings, but not our knowledge; it takes away our certitude (which is a feeling) but not our certainty (which is a knowing). We can be certain without feeling certain just as we can feel certain without being certain.

Objection 5:
Freud has shown that our reasoning depends on our desires rather than vice versa,

as Plato and the ancients thought. Reasoning is really rationalizing. Thus it loses its claim to certainty.

Reply: Freud says, on the last page of his most philosophical book, *Civilization and Its Discontents,* that the only thing he knows for certain is that all reasoning is rationalizing ("the attempt to support illusions with arguments"). This "one thing he knows for certain" is in fact the one thing we can know for certain is false because it is self-contradictory. If all reasoning is rationalizing and thus self-invalidating, then so is that bit of reasoning. It commits mental suicide. It invalidates itself.

All forms of skepticism are self-contradictory, in the last analysis. They all amount to saying that it is true that there is no truth, or we can know that we cannot know, or we can be certain that we cannot be certain, or it is a universal truth that there are no universal truths, or you can be quite dogmatic about the fact that you can't be dogmatic, or it is an absolute that there are no absolutes, or it is an objective truth that there is no objective truth.

Refutation of Religious Skepticism

A much more modest form of skepticism is skepticism only about religious knowledge, not all knowledge. This is not immediately self-contradictory, but it is refutable.

For religious knowledge is (broadly) knowledge of God. Now if the religious skeptic is right, we can know nothing about God. And if we can know nothing about God, how can we know God so well that we can know that he cannot be known? How can we know that God cannot and did not reveal himself—perhaps even through human reason? What right does this so-skeptical, so-limited human mind have to limit God in this way? Skepticism seems humble but it is really arrogant.

Religious skepticism is an a priori dogmatism, a prejudice. We must be open-minded and look to see whether or not there is religious knowledge by fairly and carefully examining the evidence, the claims to religious truth (such as the Christian religion). Most who investigate this claim open-mindedly and objectively come to believe it. Most unbelievers never bother to look, or look with minds already made up.

Of course, we can know God only very inadequately. This is not skepticism—*no* knowledge, *no* truth, *no* certainty at all. It is instead the notion of mystery. We can be certain that "God is One" without totally understanding any one of the three profoundly mysterious words in that little sentence.

Refutation of Subjectivism

The skeptic says we cannot know truth. The subjectivist says we all know it. The skeptic says there is truth for nobody. The subjectivist says there is truth for everybody. The skeptic denies truth; the subjectivist denies error. To a subjectivist, everything is true "for" somebody; for *truth* means "true *for* me" but not necessarily "true *for* you," because the link between "true for me" and "true for you," namely universal objective truth, is missing.

Universal subjectivism is refutable quite quickly, in the same way that universal skepticism is. If truth is only subjective, only true for me but not for you, then that truth too—the "truth" of subjectivism—is not true, but only "true for me," (i.e., true for the subjectivist). So the subjectivist is not saying that subjectivism is really true and objectivism really false, or that the objectivist is mistaken at all. He is not challenging his opponent, not arguing, not debating, only "sharing his feelings." "I feel well" does not contradict or refute your statement "But I feel sick." Subjectivism is not an "ism," not a philosophy. It does not rise to the level of deserving our attention or refutation. Its claim is like "I itch," not "I know."

Yet influential modern philosophies have espoused forms of subjectivism, and the apologist should have at least an elementary, unsophisticated knowledge of these sophisticated philosophies and be able to refute them. Space limitations require us to confine ourselves to brief treatments of just three (quite different) of the most influential forms of philosophical subjectivism: (1) Kantianism, (2) Hegelianism and (3) pantheism.

1. What Kant called his "Copernican revolution in philosophy" was the claim that our knowledge does not conform to a real object, but vice versa. The object conforms to the subject. Knowledge is like the projection of a movie rather than like photography. All the form, determination, specificity or knowable content comes from the mind and is projected out onto the world, rather than coming from the world and being impressed upon the mind.

Kant realized how radical this idea was; that's why he called it his "Copernican revolution in philosophy." Prior to Copernicus, the appearance of the known universe (e.g., the sun's rising and setting) was believed to result from the state of the object known (the real motion of the sun). Copernicus showed how these appearances actually resulted from the state of the earthly observer. Similarly, for Kant, our knowledge results from the way the mind of the knowing subject is constituted, not from an already constituted object.

Now, Kant would be horrified if he saw us classify his theory under the heading of "subjectivism." He thought his "Copernican revolution" was the only way to account for our scientific knowledge of the universe. He also believed all minds were constituted in the same way, so his theory was certainly not an individualism or relativism. And he believed that there was a reality that appeared *to* us, that *gave* us things to know. But he thought we could never know these "things in themselves" as they were, independent of our consciousness; for all their knowable content came from us—like a message in a bottle that washes up on the beach of a castaway's island: only it's a message he wrote himself.

Still, Kant's "Copernican revolution" is self-contradictory, just as simple skepticism is. After all, if Kant was right, how could he possibly have *known* he was right in terms of his system? He couldn't. He could never know that there *are* "things-in-themselves," onto which the knowing self projects all knowable content. That would be knowing the unknowable, thinking both sides of thought's limit.

There is a half truth in Kantianism. Some knowledge is conditioned by our forms of consciousness (e.g., colors by the eye, measurements by artificial scales and ideological positions by personal preferences). But even here there must be some objective content first that is received and known, before it can be classified or interpreted by the knowing subject.

2. Hegel's "historicism" claims that all reality is a historical process, even God, even truth. Truth changes with history, as we, its subjects, change. (This is a vast oversimplification of what is in fact a very subtle theory by an extremely complex thinker, but this is its bottom line.)

Like Kantianism, this is a half truth, but it cannot be universally true without self-contradiction. It is partly true, for the meaning of "advanced culture," for instance, in the Stone Age, could be the same as the meaning of "uncultured primitivism" in the modern age (e.g., drawing pictures on cave walls with rocks).

But as total truth, Hegel's historicism is self-contradictory for two reasons. First, you have to assume the standpoint of timeless truth in order to say that truth is determined by time *at all times*, not just at this one time. Second, you also have to say that the old theory—that truth is timeless—is timelessly false, not that it was once true and then became false. For if it was ever true that truth is timeless, then truth could never become time-bound and changing, for the timeless is by definition unchangeable. But if you say that the old "timeless truth" theory was timelessly false, you are admitting a timeless falsity, and thus also a timeless truth.

There is an important half-truth in both Kant and Hegel as applied to our knowledge of God. Our knowledge of God is limited by our minds and by our times, as the tiny range of light we can see is limited by our eye and by its movements. But the light is not *made* by the eye.

We are temporal. Even our minds are temporal. We change our minds as often as we change our clothes. Our knowledge of God is conditioned by time. Aquinas knew more about God than Jeremiah did. But *God* is not conditioned as we are. What Hegel did was to project his own temporality out onto the divine object.

3. Pantheism literally means that everything is God and God is everything; there is only one real being, and the things and persons that seem different and distinct from each other are in the last analysis really only parts or aspects or appearances of the one being, or God. As the Hindu *Upanishads* put it, "one" is the word of truth, "two" is the word of error.

According to pantheism, ordinary thinking makes three main "errors of two," or dualisms: (a) the God/world distinction, (b) the God/self distinction and (c) the self/world distinction. This last distinction is the distinction between the knowing self and the objective world known. Thus pantheism denies objective truth.

This nonobjectivity of truth also follows from the second point: that there is really no distinction between God and the self. If deep down I am God, then truth is not my object, not some preexisting thing for me to bow down to with my mind and conform to and learn. For nothing can be like that to God.

So the subjectivity of truth makes sense within pantheism. Truth is subjective to God, as the truth of "Hamlet" is subjective to Shakespeare. And if I am God, then truth is subjective to me.

But pantheism itself has one obvious problem that has no solution. Why would God forget himself and think he is me? To say the same thing from the bottom up instead of from the top down: If I'm really God, why am I so stupid, powerless and sinful? I see why a fool like me would play God, but why would a perfect God play a fool like me?

Furthermore, if all is one, as pantheism claims, and if manyness is an illusion, where did the illusion come from? If all is a dream, who is the dreamer? Why would a perfect God dream an imperfect dream? And if an imperfect, unenlightened human mind is the dreamer of this illusion of manyness, then these nondivine minds do exist, and not everything is God; thus pantheism is abandoned.

If manyness, alienation, ignorance and evil are illusions, if the only reality is one, perfect, seamless divine whole, then how can we account for the illusion? If evil is an illusion, it is really evil that I am victimized by this illusion. As Augustine says, either there is evil to fear, or the fact that we fear what is nothing is evil.

Refutation of Moral Subjectivism

Before we refute *religious* subjectivism, we should consider an extremely popular and destructive philosophy, *moral* subjectivism. Clichés like "don't be judgmental," "don't impose your values on me," "different strokes for different folks" and "alternative lifestyles" are now taken for granted in our culture. Yet every premodern culture would have regarded this subjectivism as moral insanity.

One of the reasons our culture finds moral subjectivism so congenial is that we have been conditioned to talk about moral *values* instead of moral *laws*. The very word *law* suggests something objective; we don't speak of "subjective laws." The word *values* (especially in the plural) suggests something subjective, something relative to a subject: "*my* values" or "*your* values" or "*our* values" or "*Society's* values." (Subjectivists often capitalize "Society" as we used to capitalize "God." The parallel is eerie.) The choice of words makes a real difference—Moses did not receive the Ten Values from God on Mount Sinai.

In order to participate in the modern debate we should use modern terms. So we shall defend "objective values" by refuting the most common arguments against them. (Ideally, we should use a neutral term which suggests neither subjectivism ["values"] nor objectivism ["laws"]—perhaps "right and wrong." But the language of the debate has by now been set; both sides use the term "values." So we will too, reluctantly.)

Objection 1:

Values are relative to cultures. Only provincialism and ignorance of the facts of cultural diversity blinded humanity to this truth until recently, when anthropologists discovered that there are some cultural exceptions to every supposed universal value.

Put in syllogistic form, the argument is this:

1. If cultures differ about values, then values are subjective and relative.
2. Cultures do differ about values.
3. Therefore values are subjective and relative.

Reply: Both of the premises of this syllogism are false. The first premise is false because cultures can err just as individuals can. The fact that the Aztecs thought human sacrifice was right and the Jews thought it was wrong does not mean that it really was right for the Aztecs to murder innocent children. What is culturally relative is *opinions* about what is really right and wrong, not right and wrong themselves. The word *values* fudges this distinction.

The second premise is false because even opinions about right and wrong are not wholly relative to cultures. No culture ever existed which taught a *totally* different set of values. For example, honesty, justice, courage, cooperation, wisdom, self-control and hope were never all thought to be evil, and lying, theft, murder, rape, cowardice, folly, addiction, despair and selfishness were never all thought to be good.

The origin of the belief in objective morality is not ignorance, for the belief is compatible with and coexists with knowledge of cultural diversity. Anthropology does not discover a diversity of values, only value opinions. Anthropology is not the science of values. Ethics is.

Objection 2:
It is a psychological fact that all of us learn our values from our society; that is, society conditions our values in us. Thus the origin of values is not something outside human minds, some truth objective to all human minds, but comes from within human minds themselves—from parents and teachers and society. What comes from human subjects is subjective.
Reply: 1. Once again the subjectivist confuses values with value-opinions. Society conditions opinions in us, but not truth.

2. Nor does society *condition* us, like rats; it *teaches* us, like men and women.

3. Furthermore, the fact that we learn our moral opinions from teachers does not entail the conclusion that these opinions are merely subjective or arbitrary. Some of the things we learn from teachers are subjective fancies, like tastes in food and clothes, but others are objective truths, like 2+2=4. The objector has not yet proved that values are not in the second class.

Objection 3:
Moral subjectivism produces tolerance; moral objectivism produces intolerance. If you believe your moral values are objective, you will try to impose them on everyone else.
Reply: First, even if belief in objective values did entail intolerance, that would not prove that objective values did not exist.

Second, belief in objective values does *not* entail intolerance. In fact, the real, objective value of tolerance and evil of intolerance is something the objectivist can take more seriously than the subjectivist. If all values are only subjective, so is the value of tolerance.

Third, the subjectivist is really presupposing objective values, a real right and wrong, in demanding that we be tolerant, not intolerant. Or else he is being intolerant and imposing his own subjective value of tolerance on others.

Fourth, that is exactly what the subjectivist does when he preaches "cultural diversity" and yet scorns the foundational belief of every culture in history except our own: the belief in objective values. He is being intolerant and imposing his subjectivism.

Fifth, most cultures in the past did not value tolerance. Should we tolerate this intolerance? If the subjectivist answers no, he is either appealing to the objective value of tolerance or being intolerant in imposing his personal value of tolerance on other cultures. If his answer is yes—if we should tolerate intolerance—then the subjectivist has no reason to quarrel with the supposed intolerance of objectivists.

Sixth, the very meaning of the concept of tolerance presupposes moral objectivism. For we tolerate only real evils, in order to prevent worse evils. We do not tolerate good; we promote it. A patient will tolerate nausea as a side effect of chemotherapy in order to avoid the worse evil of death by cancer. A foreign language teacher will tolerate mistakes by beginners in order to encourage attempts to master the language and to avoid the worse evil of giving up. Such judgments presuppose real evils and real goods.

Objection 4:

"Situation ethics" shows us that situations are so diverse and complex that no moral rule can be universal. We can always imagine some situation where it would be right to lie, to steal, even to kill.

Reply: Even if this argument were valid, it would not prove subjectivism, only situational relativism. It would still be *objectively* right to lie to the Nazis about hiding Jews, or to kill in self-defense, or to steal a maniac's weapon.

However, the argument does not even prove relativism, only that absolute principles must be applied to different situations. The fact of different applications presupposes the truth of the principle. Morality consists of three factors: absolute and objective principles, relative and objective situations, and subjective motives. All three must be right, not just one.

Objection 5:

Good motives alone are enough to make a person moral, and this is subjective. One who does a good deed with a bad motive or intention is not a good person, and

one who does a bad deed by accident with a good intention is a good person.
Reply: We need to be good persons, but we also need to do good deeds. Motives cannot be isolated from deeds. For instance, the motive of love is necessarily connected with the objective deeds of benevolence, not murder or rape.

Objection 6:
If we are not free to create our own values, we are not truly free.
Reply: Freedom presupposes values, it does not create them. First, it is assumed by the objector that freedom is a real (objective) value, thus presupposing objective values. Second, freedom, if it is really good must be freedom from something really bad. This also presupposes real, objective values (good vs. bad). Third, "creating your own values" is meaningless. It is impossible. No one has ever done it, and no one ever will. It is like creating a new universe, or a new number or a new color. All who supposedly "created new values" either rediscovered old, forgotten values (like Jesus' Sermon on the Mount) or created new horrors (like the French, Bolshevik or Nazi revolutions).

Objection 7:
Moral values must be subjective because they cannot be discovered by science, the senses or mathematical reasoning.
Reply: The presupposition of this argument is that whatever cannot be discovered by science, the senses or mathematical reasoning is not objectively real. This premise is self-contradictory, for it itself cannot be discovered by science, the senses or mathematical reasoning.

The deeper problem with this objection is that it stems from a failure of insight, the failure to "see" right and wrong because the objector reduces "seeing" to physical seeing. He is morally blind. Anyone who "sees" values with the inner eye of conscience understands that true values are objective. We cannot be bound in conscience by fantasies that we invent, however lovely they may be.

Objection 8:
Morality can be adequately explained simply as an evolutionary device for survival. Tribes that treated each other morally (kindly, justly, honestly, etc.) survived; immoral tribes died out. Killing, stealing, raping and lying didn't work. Morality can be explained by natural selection, "the survival of the fittest." There's nothing more, nothing mysterious to it.

Reply: The objection reduces morality to a biological instinct, learned through trial and error. Cooperation "works" so it becomes "the herd instinct." This reduction of obligation to instinct simply does not square with our moral experience. We do not experience morality as an instinct, but as a law which tells us which instinct to follow in which situations. No instinct is in itself always right, but morality is always right, therefore morality is not just an instinct. Rather, morality transcends instincts, as sheet music transcends the notes on a piano. Instincts are notes; the moral law tells us how and when to play these notes.

It is also logically impossible to reduce morality to biological instinct because that would be deriving more from less, "ought" from "is." The premise or ground or source of morality for the instinctualist is simply "this is an instinct," and the conclusion is "therefore this ought to be done." But this syllogism is invalid unless you add the second premise "all instincts ought to be followed." That premise is obviously false and impossible, since our instincts often contradict each other.

Perhaps we cannot prove the existence of objective values; perhaps they just have to be "seen," like colors. However, we can certainly refute all objections to them.

Refutation of Religious Subjectivism
Religious subjectivism really means religion is made by us, dependent on us, "true" only as a fantasy is "true." This is a polite way of saying that God is just an adult version of Santa Claus and that religious believers are just adults who never grew up.

The claim is too sweeping and vague to be fair. It cannot even be argued about until it becomes specific. It is like the claim that "science" has disproved "religion." The reply has to be: Which science? Which discovery? By whom? When? What is the proof of it? Which religion? Which doctrine? What does this doctrine really mean, really claim? And are these two truth-claims then logically contradictory or not?

As we suggested above (in chap. 2, on faith and reason, and in chap. 5, on miracles), each specific challenge can be refuted. There are *no* contradictions between science and religion. The natural laws of physics do not refute supernatural miracles. Evolution does not refute creation. Each specific contradiction claim can be answered. What is left is a vague, general ideology or prejudice that "science" contradicts "religion."

The claim that religious truth is "subjective" is in exactly the same situation. Once it becomes specific, it can be answered. For instance, the claim that Christ's resurrection was not an objective fact but a subjective fable, can be refuted by argument and evidence (see chap. 8). The claim that "God" is only "all the good in humanity" can be refuted by proving the existence of an objective God (chap. 3).

At this point the subjectivist may go on the offensive and ask: "All right, if there is objective truth in religion, where is it? Religion is a complex thing, with many aspects. Are you reducing it to something like mathematics? There are certainly subjective elements in it; how do you disentangle the so-called objective truth from the subjective?"

In answer, we notice that all religions have three aspects: creeds, codes and cults; theology, morality and liturgy; beliefs, values and rites; words, works and worship. The first speaks mainly to the intellect, the second to the will, and the third to the feelings and imagination. Thus religion addresses our whole being: as knowers of truth, as choosers of good, and as creators of beauty.

In the first area, religion is as objective as physics (though much more mysterious and harder to prove; there is no simple method in religion like the scientific method). Its verbal *formulations* of truth are changing, and so is the amount or degree of truth it knows at any time. But this is equally true of physics or any science.

In the second area, the moral goods or values that religion directs us to are just as objective as the goods of medicine. Just as medicine points us to real, objective health and healing for the body, so religion points us to real, objective health and healing for the soul: salvation, sanctity, enlightenment, spiritual health, reconciliation with God. Health varies a little among different individuals, for not everyone is an athlete or an infant. So does morality, for not everyone has a womb or is a priest: celibacy is right for priests, but wrong for spouses. But though there are some individual variations, these are additions to rather than subtractions from the universal rules. There are universal rules for holiness just as there are universal rules for health, because both are objectively real.

Not only truth and goodness but even beauty—the third area in religion—is not wholly subjective. Beauty is not wholly "in the eye of the beholder." If it were, we could never argue about it, or teach about it (e.g., music appreciation). Beauty is much more subjective than truth or goodness, but not wholly. Now religious liturgy is more than art, but it is also art. And what is true of all art is true of liturgy too.

The most important reason for liturgical worship is not beauty but truth and goodness. We worship God first of all because it is true that he exists and deserves our worship; second, because it is good to do so. And truth and goodness have already been shown to be objective.

We often forget that there can also be truth or falsity in that deep, mysterious part of our soul that is not just intellect or will but intuition or imagination. To feel awe at paper clips but not at sunsets, at Madonna but not at *the* Madonna, is to be untrue to reality, ontologically insane.

In answering the legitimate question "Just where is objective truth in religion?" we should also be careful to distinguish truth from its human forms of expression. These are subjective, relative and changing. Thus we can make two opposite errors: absolutizing the relative formulations or relativizing the truth itself. These two errors are usually born from each other, as reactions to each other.

The same distinction is crucial in ethics. If we keep clearly in mind the distinction between absolute moral principles and relative, changing applications to changing situations, we will neither relativize the absolutes nor absolutize the relativities.

The Origin of Subjectivism
We conclude with a guess about the psychological origin of subjectivism, especially in morality and religion. The apologist should not substitute psychoanalysis for refutation, but having refuted an idea, it is legitimate to ask where it came from. And in waging spiritual warfare it is helpful to know how the Enemy can tempt people to embrace the lie of subjectivism.

1. Perhaps the primary origin of subjectivism today, at least in America, is the desire to be accepted, to be "with it," fashionable, avant garde, "in the know," rather than "square," "hokey" or "out of it." We all learned this as children—to be embarrassed is the absolutely primary fear of a teenager—but we put more sophisticated, scholarly disguises on it when we become adults.

2. A second origin of subjectivism, especially in morality, is the adolescent desire to contradict and shock one's elders. Many adults in our culture are psychologically still adolescents, for we live in a youth culture, not one that respects old age, tradition or wisdom.

3. Surprisingly, a third origin of subjectivism, despite its praise of "change" and its denial of timeless truth, is the fear of radical change—that is, the fear of conversion, being "born again," consecrating one's whole life and will to God's will. Subjectivism is much more comfortable, like a womb, or a dream, or a narcissistic fantasy.

4. Finally, subjectivism usually originates in materialism, both in theory and in practice. In theory, it usually begins in empiricism, as Plato shows in his "Theaetetus"; for empirical appearances are indeed relative (the same orange tastes bitter to you, sweet to me). In practice, subjectivism usually begins in America's two favorite materialistic occupations: consumerism and eroticism, greed and lust. Almost always, the practice comes before the theory; moral sensualism precedes epistemological sensualism. Addicts cannot see objective truth clearly. One form of love—cupidity—is indeed blind. The other form—charity—is the opposite of blind. It is the road to truth, according to the man who said "I am . . . the truth" (Jn 14:6), for he also said: "Blessed are the pure in heart [love], for they will see God" (Mt 5:8).

Questions for Discussion

1. Why is objective truth doubted today more than in the past?

2. What could "that's true for you but not for me" possibly mean?

3. If denial of objective truth undercuts argument in all fields, not only religion, why doesn't it in fact extend to all fields? What other fields do its proponents extend it to? What fields is it never extended to?

4. Why would anyone disagree with the commonsense things C. S. Lewis says (p. 363) about how destructive subjectivism is?

5. Do you think most subjectivism comes from misunderstanding of terms? Why?

6. How can we say we will give the "true" definition of truth without falling victim to circularity, assuming our definition before we give it? What kind of circularity is always to be avoided? What kind is not?

7. If you have read William James's "Pragmatism," how would he reply to our and Moore's rather simple criticism (point 1, pp. 364-65)?

8. Is the definition we give for the empiricist theory of truth the same as the correct definition of empiricism as a theory of knowledge? Was Aristotle an empiricist?

9. How would an empiricist answer the argument in paragraph 2, p. 382, to avoid the consequence of subjectivism?

10. How would a rationalist try to answer the self-contradiction argument against rationalism (point 3, pp. 365-66)? What of the next argument?

11. How would one who holds to the coherence theory try to answer the argument in point 4, page 366?

12. Are all mistaken theories of truth self-contradictory?

13. If universal skepticism is immediately self-contradictory (p. 367), how can anyone hold it?

14. Can the "probablist" defend skepticism against the argument on page 367?

15. Can the subjectivist avoid the simple self-contradiction argument (p. 367)?

16. Is it true that religious subjectivism simply ignores religion's fact-claims? How

might a subjectivist interpret them? How would you argue about such an interpretation?

17. Does the reply to objection 1 (p. 368) prove that no one can be in total error, or error all the time?

18. How has the position in reply to objection 2 (p. 369) been criticized? (It is often called "foundationalism.")

19. Are the "first principles" mentioned here mere empty, formal, verbal tautologies? Why?

20. Concerning objection 3 (p. 370), on whom do you think the burden of proof rests, the believer or the unbeliever? Why?

21. What is "absolute certainty" (objection 4, p. 370)?

22. Can you imagine any other form of skepticism that is not self-contradictory, as is claimed in paragraph 3, page 371?

23. Do you think most religious skeptics really mean only to oppose dogmatism, not knowledge, and are really groping toward the notion of mystery rather than simple skepticism?

24. Which is more popular today, subjectivism or skepticism? Why? Has this always been so?

25. How would a Kantian defend Kant's "Copernican revolution" against the critique of it on pages 372-73?

26. How would a Hegelian defend Hegel's historicism against the critique of it (pp. 373-74)?

27. If our minds are temporal (p. 374), why isn't truth also temporal? (Compare Augustine on this.)

28. How would a pantheist answer the criticisms on pages 374-75?

29. Are there any other important arguments for moral subjectivism besides the eight mentioned here (pp. 375-79)?

30. How might the argument proceed if a subjectivist read and replied to each of the eight replies?

31. Do you think there is a positive proof for objective values (not just answers to objections against them, as here)? If so, what is it?

32. Is it true that we seek psychological rather than logical explanations of an idea—*causes* rather than *reasons*—only after we are convinced that the idea is false or even absurd? Give examples. How does this differ from "the genetic fallacy"?

We urge our readers to consider very carefully the eight arguments for moral subjectivism and our replies. We think this is an issue of unparalleled practical importance for everyone, and one of literal life or death for the society that holds such a view.

CHAPTER 16
The Bottom
Line

WHOEVER YOU ARE, YOU WHO ARE READING THIS BOOK, YOU ARE EITHER (1) a Christian—in which case you are reading this book not to find out whether Christianity is true or false, but to try to understand it better and to learn how to argue for it and persuade others of its truth; or (2) not a Christian—in which case you are probably reading this book out of curiosity, to find out why Christians believe the things they believe and also, we hope, out of an honest search for truth, an open-minded wondering whether this thing is really true after all.

The following remarks about the search for truth are addressed to both categories of people. Believers can interpret these remarks as practical battle plans, for they have already chosen sides. Nonbelievers can interpret them as a travel agent's layout of the stages ahead on the Christian road, what travelers who choose to go further down this road will be in for.

Four Steps in Becoming a Christian
We must distinguish four steps in becoming a Christian.

1. The first step is mental belief. This is first because you cannot take any other step toward a goal unless you believe it exists. You cannot seek or deal with a Person you do not believe exists. You cannot pray to a God you think is dead.

The next three steps are (2) repentance from sin; (3) saving faith, faith in a more than mental sense, acceptance of Christ as Savior; and (4) living out the Christian life. These three steps all presuppose the truth of the God to whom you repent, in whom you believe and with whose real presence and help you now live.

This book is designed to persuade you to take that first step, if you have not already taken it, by means of rational arguments. If you have taken that step and believe Christianity is true, this book is designed to help you to persuade others to take that first step.

But that first step is a mere beginning. Much, much more is in store for the believer. The first step is like believing in the accuracy of a road map; the next three steps are like actually using the map.

2. Step two is called repentance. This means not merely feeling guilty or sorry for your sins, but choosing—with that most fundamental and deep-down part of your soul, your will—to turn *out* of the road you are now traveling down, because you have been convinced that it is not the right road, the true road, the road designed for you by God, the road that leads to God. In the full sense, repentance means renouncing the lord of your present road—the "evil one" (Mt 13:19), the "father of lies" (Jn 8:44) and the "ruler of this world" (Jn 14:30)—so that you can give yourself instead to Christ, your rightful lord. Repentance cannot be adequately understood only psychologically, as something within yourself; it is ontological, it is a real transaction between you and your lord, a change of fundamental allegiance. It is like changing sides in a war, or like divorce and remarriage. It is traumatic.

3. The third step, which is the other side of repentance, is faith, in the biblical sense: not just mental belief (that was step one) but accepting and receiving Christ as God and Savior and Lord of your soul, your life, your destiny.

The first step is believing the road map; the second is turning out of your present road; the third is turning into another road. That other road is a Person: the one who said, "I am the way . . . no one comes to the Father except through me" (Jn 14:6).

4. The fourth step is traveling down his way, actually living the Christian life. Step three is faith, step four is works—good works, works of love. The two necessarily go together. In step three the tree of Christ's life is planted in you; in step four it bears fruit. For "faith without works is dead" (Jas 1:26).

This fourfold scheme puts into proper perspective the modest ambitions of this book. Our hope is only to persuade your honest reasoning that Christianity is true. This is necessary but not sufficient. No one will launch a boat thinking the sea is only a myth; but believing in the sea is not sufficient to become a sailor.

The Will to Believe

Even for step one, the intellect alone is not enough. The will has a necessary part to play too. For no one *will* believe unless they are *willing* to believe. This does not necessarily mean prejudice. It takes the will to open the mind as well as to close it. You do not need a positive push or predilection for Christianity, but you do need a positive predilection for objective truth wherever it may be found. No, stronger than a predilection, you need a definite, deliberate choice to love and seek and find and know the truth wherever it is.

This is much harder and rarer than we think. It entails humility and the renouncing of the habit of intellectual pride that we are all tempted to. Intellectual pride means looking at an idea as my idea, taking personal pride in it, being prejudiced in its favor just because it is part of *my* mental furniture, and being prejudiced against opposing ideas because they are *not* "mine." We all think of ourselves as right, as wise, as reliable in judgment. This is a prejudice. Just as we must renounce prejudice as the obstacle to truth in science, we must renounce it for the same reason in religion.

Finding the truth is in one way like seeing the light, and in another way it is not. It is like seeing the light in that you must deliberately open your eyes, renouncing your previous state of closed-eyes. Once you do, the light itself does the work. You don't make the light, you just receive it. But you must *will* to receive it first. What the eye is to light, the mind is to truth.

But finding the truth is very different from seeing the light. For no one can miss the light, but many can miss the truth. God did not shine down the truth about himself as unmistakably as sunlight. You have to seek God in order to find him (Jer 29:13; Mt 7:7). You don't have to seek the sunlight to find it.

Why does God do this? Why doesn't he give us all the blinding light of the noonday sun about himself? Why does he give us clues to follow instead, data to interpret, winding roads to travel?

Because God respects our freedom. He will not compel our minds as the light compels our eyes. If and only if we want it, will we find it. If and only if we *love* the truth, with our heart and soul and mind, will we find the truth about God. There is enough light for those who love and seek him, but not enough to compel nonseekers against their will. Thus God arranged it so that the heart and will and love, rather than the intellect, is what ultimately decides our destiny. The dividing line between those who know God and those who do not is not the dividing line between the clever and the simple, the brilliant and the slow. This is as it should be, for cleverness is not wholly under our control and freedom and responsibility; they are largely gifts we are born with. They are not free. But the choice to seek for the truth is a free choice. And all seekers find.

The Skeptic's Prayer

This claim—that all seekers find—is testable by experience, by experiment. If you are an honest scientist, here is a way to find out whether Christianity is true or not. Perform the relevant experiment. To test the hypothesis that someone is behind the door, knock. To test the Christian hypothesis that Christ is behind the door, knock.

How do you knock? Pray! Tell Christ you are seeking the truth—seeking *him*, if he is the truth. Ask him to fulfill his promise that all who seek him will find him. In his own time, of course. He promised that you would find, but he didn't promise a schedule. He's a lover, not a train.

But—you may reply—I don't know whether Christ is God. I don't even know whether there is a God. That's all right; you can pray the prayer of the skeptic:

God, I don't know whether you even exist. I'm a skeptic. I doubt. I think you may be only a myth. But I'm not certain (at least not when I'm completely honest with myself). So if you do exist, and if you really did promise to reward all seekers, you must be hearing me now. So I hereby declare myself a seeker, a seeker of the truth, whatever it is and wherever it is. I want to know the truth and live the truth. If you are the truth, please help me.

If Christianity is true, he will. Such a prayer constitutes a scientifically fair test of the Christian "hypothesis"—that is, if you do not put unfair restrictions on God, like demanding a miracle (your way, not his) or certainty by tomorrow (your time, not his). The demand that God act like your servant is hardly a scientifically fair test of the hypothesis that there is a God who is your King.

But all this King asks for at first is honesty, not faking a faith you do not have. Honesty is a choice of the will—the choice to seek the truth no matter what or where. This is the most momentous choice you can make. It is the choice of light over darkness, ultimately heaven over hell.

Honesty is infinitely more momentous than we often think. It is also much harder than we think. Our culture trivializes honesty into merely "sharing your feelings," telling others about the state of your nerve ends. That's not the opposite of dishonesty, that's just the opposite of *shame*, or shyness. Shallow honesty seeks "sharing," deep honesty seeks truth. Shallow honesty stands in the presence of others, deep honesty stands in the presence of God.

This book has appealed to the intellect; our last chapter, our "bottom line," is something infinitely more important: the appeal to the will to be honest and open to truth and to its instrument, reason; and thus to follow the argument wherever it may go, like a guide through the forest.

To reinforce this appeal, we conclude with what we think is the most effective essay written by the most effective Christian apologist of the twentieth century, C. S. Lewis. It is called "Man or Rabbit?" and as the title suggests, it is ultimately about the choice between two identities, two kinds of being, two fundamentally different kinds of people each of us can choose to be—eternally.

Man or Rabbit?

"Can't you lead a good life without believing in Christianity?" This is the question on which I have been asked to write, and straight away, before I begin trying to answer it, I have a comment to make. The question sounds as if it were asked by a person who said to himself, "I don't care whether Christianity is in fact true or not. I'm not interested in finding out whether the real universe is more like what the Christians say than what the Materialists say. All I'm interested in is leading a good life. I'm going to choose beliefs not because I think them true but because I find them helpful." Now frankly, I find it hard to sympathize with this state of mind. One of the things that distinguishes man from the other animals is that he wants to know things, wants to find out what reality is like, simply for the sake of knowing. When that desire is completely quenched in anyone, I think he has become something less than human. As a matter of fact, I don't believe any of you have really lost that desire. More probably, foolish preachers, by always telling you how much Christianity will help you and how good it is for society, have actually led you to forget that Christianity is not a patent medicine. Christianity claims to give an account of *facts*—to tell you what the real universe is like. Its account of the universe may be true, or it may not, and once the question is really before you, then your natural inquisitiveness must make you want to know the answer. If Christianity is untrue, then no honest man will want to believe it, however helpful it might be; if it is true, every honest man will want to believe it, even if it gives him no help at all.

As soon as we have realized this, we realize something else. If Christianity should happen to be true, then it is quite impossible that those who know this truth and those who don't should be equally well equipped for leading a good life. Knowledge of the facts must make a difference to one's actions. Suppose you found a man on the point of starvation and wanted to do the right thing. If you had no knowledge of medical science, you would probably give him a large solid meal; and as a result your man would die. That is what comes of working in the dark. In the same way a Christian and a non-Christian may both wish to do good to their fellow men. The one believes that men are going to live forever, that they were created by God and so built that they can find their true and lasting happiness only by being united to God, that they have gone badly off the rails, and that obedient faith in Christ is the only way back. The other believes that men are an accidental result of the blind working of matter, that they started as mere animals and have more or less steadily improved, that they are going to live for about seventy years, that their happiness is fully attainable by good social services and political organizations, and that everything else (e.g., vivisection, birth control, the judicial system, education) is to be judged to be "good" or "bad" simply insofar as it helps or hinders that kind of "happiness."

Now there are quite a lot of things which these two men could agree in doing for their fellow citizens. Both would approve of efficient sewers and hospitals and a healthy diet. But sooner or later the difference in their beliefs would produce differences in their practical proposals. Both, for example, might be very keen about education; but the kinds of education they wanted people to have would obviously be very different. Again, where the Materialist would simply ask about a proposed action, "Will it increase the happiness of the majority?," the Christian might have to say, "Even if it does increase the happiness of the majority, we can't do it. It is unjust." And all the time, one great difference would run through their whole policy. To the Materialist things like nations, classes, civilizations must be more important than individuals, because the individuals live only seventy-odd years each and the group may last for centuries. But to the Christian, individuals are more important, for they live eternally; and races, civilizations and the like, are in comparison the creatures of a day.

The Christian and the Materialist hold different beliefs about the universe. They can't both be right. The one who is wrong will act in a way which simply doesn't fit the real universe. Consequently, with the best will in the world, he will be helping his fellow creatures to their destruction.

With the best will in the world . . . then it won't be his fault. Surely God (if there is a God) will not punish a man for honest mistakes? But was *that* all you were thinking about? Are we ready to run the risk of working in the dark all our lives and doing infinite harm, provided only someone will assure us that our own skins will be safe, that no one will punish us or blame us? I will not believe that the reader is quite on that level. But even if he were, there is something to be said to him.

The question before each of us is not, "Can *someone* lead a good life without Christianity?" The question is, "Can *I?*" We all know there have been good men who were not Christians; men like Socrates and Confucius who had never heard of it, or men like J. S. Mill who quite honestly couldn't believe it. Supposing Christianity to be true, there men were in a state of honest ignorance or honest error. If their intentions were as good as I suppose them to have been (for of course I can't read their secret hearts), I hope and believe that the skill and mercy of God will remedy the evils which their ignorance, left to itself, would naturally produce both for them and for those whom they influenced. But the man who asks me, "Can't I lead a good life without believing in Christianity?" is clearly not in the same position. If he hadn't heard of Christianity he would not be asking this question. If, having heard of it, and having seriously considered it, he had decided that it was untrue, then once more he would not be asking the question. The man who asks this question has heard of Christianity and is by no means certain that it may not be true. He is really asking, "Need I bother about it? Mayn't I just evade the issue, just let sleeping dogs lie, and get on with being 'good'? Aren't good intentions enough to keep me safe and blameless without knocking at that dreadful door and making sure whether there is, or isn't someone inside?"

To such a man it might be enough to reply that he is really asking to be allowed to get on with being "good" before he has done his best to discover what *good* means. But that is not the whole story. We need not inquire whether God will punish him for his cowardice and laziness; they will punish themselves. The man is shirking. He is deliberately trying not to know whether Christianity is true or false, because he foresees endless trouble if it should turn out to be true. He is like the man who deliberately "forgets" to look at the notice board because, if he did, he might find his name down for some unpleasant duty. He is like the man who won't look at his bank account because he's afraid of what he might find there. He is like the man who won't go to the doctor when he first feels a mysterious pain, because he is afraid of what the doctor may tell him.

The man who remains an unbeliever for such reasons is not in a state of honest error. He is in a state of dishonest error, and that dishonesty will spread through all his thoughts and actions: a certain shiftiness, a vague worry in the background, a blunting of his whole mental edge, will result. He has lost his intellectual virginity. Honest rejection of Christ, however mistaken, will be forgiven and healed—"Whosoever shall speak a word against the Son of man, it shall be forgiven him." But to *evade* the Son of man, to look the other way, to pretend you haven't noticed, to become suddenly absorbed in something on the other side of the street, to leave the receiver off the telephone because it might be He who was ringing up, to leave unopened certain letters in a strange handwriting because they might be from Him—this is a different matter. You may not be certain yet whether you ought to be a Christian; but you do know you ought to be a man, not an ostrich, hiding its head in the sand.

But still—for intellectual honor has sunk very low in our age—I hear someone whimpering on with this question, "Will it help me? Will it make me happy? Do you really think I'd be better if I became a Christian?" Well, if you must have it, my answer is "Yes." But I don't like giving an answer at all at this stage. Here is a door, behind which, according to some people, the secret of the universe is waiting for you. Either that's true, or it isn't. And if it isn't, then what the door really conceals is simply the greatest fraud, the most colossal "sell" on record. Isn't it obviously the job of every man (that is a man and not a rabbit) to try to find out which, and then to devote his full energies either to serving this tremendous secret or to exposing and destroying this gigantic humbug? Faced with such an issue, can you really remain wholly absorbed in your own blessed "moral development"?

All right, Christianity will do you good—a great deal more good than you ever wanted or expected. And the first bit of good it will do you is to hammer into your head (you won't enjoy *that!*) the fact that what you have hitherto called "good"—all that about "leading a decent life" and "being kind"—isn't quite the magnificent and all-important affair you supposed. It will teach you that in fact you can't be "good" (not for twenty-four hours) on your own moral efforts. And then it will teach you that even if you were, you still wouldn't have achieved the purpose for which you were created. Mere *morality* is not the end of life. You were made for something quite different from that. J. S. Mill and Confucius (Socrates was much nearer the reality) simply didn't know what life is about. The people who keep on asking if they can't lead a decent life without Christ, don't know what life is about; if they did they would know that "a decent life" is mere machinery compared with the thing we men are really made for. Morality is indispensable; but the Divine Life, which gives itself to us and which calls us to be gods, intends for us something in which morality will be swallowed up. We are to be re-made. All the rabbit in us is to disappear—the worried, conscientious, ethical rabbit as well as the cowardly and sensual rabbit. We shall bleed and squeal as the handfuls of fur come out; and then, surprisingly, we shall find underneath it all a thing we have never yet imagined: a real Man, an ageless god, a son of God, strong, radiant, wise, beautiful, and drenched in joy.

"When that which is perfect is come, then that which is in part shall be done away." The idea of reaching "a good life" without Christ is based on a double error. Firstly, we cannot do it; and secondly, in setting up "a good life" as our final goal, we have missed the very point of our existence. Morality is a mountain which we cannot climb by our own efforts; and if we could we should only perish in the ice and unbreathable air of the summit, lacking those wings with which the rest of the journey has to be accomplished. For it is *from* there that the real ascent begins. The ropes and axes are "done away" and the rest is a matter of flying.

(C. S. Lewis, in *God in the Dock: Essays on Theology and Ethics*)

Bibliography

Note: No information, beyond the title, is given for items that are widely known and easily available, or for items that have been previously cited.

Chapter 1: The Nature, Power & Limitations of Apologetics

There are several classic works of apologetics that our readers might wish to consult: Justin Martyr's *First* and *Second Apology* and the *Dialogue with Trypho;* Augustine's *Confessions* (the translation by F. J. Sheed [published in a new edition by Hackett, 1993] is the best we know) and Book 19 of *The City of God;* Aquinas's *Summa Contra Gentiles* (5 vols., University of Notre Dame Press, 1975) and of course the *Summa Theologiae* (in numerous easily available editions, but the novice might find helpful the *Summa of the Summa,* edited with many explanatory notes by Peter Kreeft [Ignatius Press, 1990]); Pascal's *Pensées* (we have used the translation by A. J. Krailsheimer [Penguin Books, 1966]; readers might wish to consult *Christianity for Modern Pagans,* an edition of the *Pensées* together with commentary by Peter Kreeft [Ignatius Press, 1993]); books I and II of John Calvin's *Institutes of the Christian Religion;* and William Paley's *Evidences of Christianity.* Among modern works, C. S. Lewis's *Mere Christianity* is still perhaps the best of its kind. We urge all our readers to consult G. K. Chesterton's *Orthodoxy* and *The Everlasting Man,* Dorothy Sayers's *Christian Letters to a Post-Christian World* (Eerdmans, 1969; reissued by Macmillan in 1978 as *The Whimsical Christian*), F. J. Sheed's *Theology and Sanity* (new ed., Ignatius Press, 1993) and, among more recent works, W. L. Craig's *Apologetics: An Introduction* (Moody Press, 1984) and J. P. Moreland's *Scaling the Secular City* (Baker, 1987). We have found much helpful material in Norman L. Geisler's *Christian Apologetics*

(Baker, 1976) and in his and Ron Brooks's *When Skeptics Ask: A Handbook of Christian Evidences* (Victor Books, 1990). The following volumes by Peter Kreeft touch on general apologetic themes: *Yes or No?* (2nd ed., Ignatius Press, 1991); *Fundamentals of the Faith* (Ignatius Press, 1988); *Socrates Meets Jesus* (InterVarsity Press, 1987).

Chapter 2: Faith & Reason
Our reflections derive mostly from Aquinas's *Summa Contra Gentiles* I, 1-9 and *Summa Theologiae* I, 1, 1-10. There is a helpful secondary source in Etienne Gilson's *The Spirit of Medieval Philosophy*, chaps. 1-2 (Sheed and Ward, 1936) and *Reason and Revelation in the Middle Ages* (Scribner, 1938). Also of interest is Gilson's essay, "The Intelligence in the Service of Christ the King" (in *The Gilson Reader*, ed. Anton Pegis [Doubleday: Image Books, 1957]). John Henry Newman's *Essay in Aid of a Grammar of Assent* is a classic though difficult treatise on the act of faith; readers might be helped by Martin D'Arcy's critical exposition of Newman in *The Nature of Belief* (rev. ed. Herder, 1958). For a markedly different (existentialist) approach see Kierkegaard's *Philosophical Fragments*. See also the first chapter of W. L. Craig's *Apologetics*. A most helpful (though badly printed) account of Reformed speculation about the relation of faith and reason is Kelly James Clark's *Return to Reason* (Eerdmans, 1990). Clark has edited a superb collection of testimonies by Christian philosophers about the way faith and reason have come to coexist in their lives: *Philosophers Who Believe* (InterVarsity Press, 1993).

Chapter 3: Twenty Arguments for the Existence of God
Hans Küng's *Does God Exist?* (Doubleday, 1980) is a surprisingly learned and useful historical survey. Arguments 1-5 correspond (pretty much) to Aquinas's Five Ways from the *Summa Theologiae*. For two excellent commentaries on them, see E. L. Mascall's *He Who Is* (rev. ed., Darton, Longman and Todd, 1966) and Peter Geach's chapter on Aquinas in *Three Philosophers* by G. E. M. Anscombe and P. T. Geach (Cornell University Press, 1961). Our approach to the reading of Aquinas has been enormously influenced—well beyond the point of plagiarism!—by the writings and teaching of Herbert McCabe. We urge all our readers to study his book, *God Matters* (Geoffrey Chapman, 1987). On the first cause argument (2), see pp. 83-93 of Brian Davies's *An Introduction to the Philosophy of Religion* (2nd ed., Oxford University Press, 1993). On the argument from time and contingency (3), see Lawrence Dewan's "The Distinctiveness of St. Thomas's 'Third Way' " *(Di-*

alogue 19 [1980]) and "The Interpretation of St. Thomas's 'Third Way' " (in A. Lobato [ed.] *Littera, Sensus, Sententia* [Massimo (Milan), 1991]). An illuminating discussion, with excellent bibliographical references, of the design argument (5), can be found in Brian Davies's *Thinking About God* (Geoffrey Chapman, 1985); a convenient sampling of the classic assessments of it can be found in John Hick's collection, *The Existence of God* (Macmillan, 1964). W. L. Craig has given a full account of the kalām argument in his *The Kalām Cosmological Argument* (Barnes and Noble, 1979) and *Apologetics* (see esp. pp. 73-81); also excellent is J. P. Moreland's treatment in chap. 1 of *Scaling the Secular City*. A bit disappointing but still worth a look is *Theism, Atheism, and Big Bang Cosmology*, a debate (of sorts) between Craig and Quentin Smith (Clarendon Press, 1993). The argument from contingency (7), is discussed at great length in Germain Grisez's *Beyond the New Theism* (University of Notre Dame Press, 1975); Stuart Hackett recasts the argument in an impressive but sometimes needlessly obscure way in his remarkable book, *The Resurrection of Theism* (Moody Press, 1957); Martin D'Arcy's presentation of the argument in *Mirage and Truth* (Macmillan, 1935) and Richard Taylor's in chap. 7 of his *Metaphysics* (Prentice Hall, 1963) are both well-written and persuasive. An interesting statement of the argument from consciousness (10) can be found in Richard Swinburne's *The Existence of God* (Clarendon Press, 1979) and in chap. 3 of J. P. Moreland's *Scaling the Secular City*; see also chap. 7 of Richard Taylor's *Metaphysics*. The best statement of the moral argument (14) is still found in C. S. Lewis's opening chapters of *Mere Christianity*; but readers would profitably consult Robert M. Adams's *The Virtue of Faith* (Oxford University Press, 1987), chap. 9 of Peter Geach's *God and the Soul* (Schocken, 1969), and an article by George Mavrodes, "Religion and the Queerness of Morality" (in *Rationality, Religious Belief, and Moral Commitment*, ed. Robert Audi and William J. Wainwright [Cornell University Press, 1986]). Religious experience (18) is discussed with impressive acumen by J. P. Moreland in chap. 8 of *Scaling the Secular City*. On the central place of religion in human history and in the growth of culture, a broadening of the common consent argument (19), see Christopher Dawson's masterful *Progress and Religion* (Sheed and Ward, 1929). Our discussion of the ontological argument (13) has been heavily influenced by the writings of Charles Hartshorne; of his many books, see especially *Anselm's Discovery* (Open Court, 1965). Alvin Plantinga edited an excellent collection called simply *The Ontological Argument* (Doubleday: Anchor Books, 1965); his own defense of the argument is presented with clarity and rigor in *God, Freedom and Evil* (Harper & Row, 1974). C. S.

Lewis's statement of the argument from desire (16) is, of course, better than ours; readers might be well advised to skip our account of it and go directly to his much-reprinted sermon, "The Weight of Glory" (or to the less moving but dialectically richer account in his preface to *The Pilgrim's Regress*). Peter Kreeft's *Heaven, the Heart's Deepest Longing* (2nd ed. Ignatius Press, 1989) is an extended version of the argument (see esp. the appendix, "C. S. Lewis's Argument from Desire"). Our version of Pascal's Wager (20) was first developed by Stephen Schwarz in his "Faith, Doubt and Pascal's Wager" *(Center Journal* [Summer 1984]). Finally, there are two printed debates on the existence of God which we urge our readers to study. The first is the much-anthologized one-on-one between Bertrand Russell and Frederick Copleston (it can be found in John Hick's collection, *The Existence of God)*; the second is the exchange between Kai Nielsen and J. P. Moreland, published under the title *Does God Exist?* (new ed., Prometheus Books, 1993). Readers may also be interested in the *lived* argument of an atheist-turned-Christian in the autobiography of C. S. Lewis, *Surprised by Joy* (Harcourt Brace, 1955), and Charles Colson, *Born Again* (Chosen Books, 1976).

Chapter 4: The Nature of God

Our principal source for this chapter has been Herbert McCabe's interpretation of Aquinas; see the entire first part of his above-cited *God Matters*. Also helpful are Grisez's *Beyond the New Theism*, Davies's *Thinking About God* and Thomas Gornall's *A Philosophy of God* (Sheed and Ward, 1963). Thomas V. Morris uses "Perfect Being Theology," lots of intuition and a Pelikan 800 fountain pen to discuss the divine nature in his up-to-date textbook, *Our Idea of God* (InterVarsity Press/University of Notre Dame Press, 1991). On how the words of creatures can apply to the Creator, see Norris Clarke's "Analogy and the Meaningfulness of Language about God" *(The Thomist* [June 1976]). The all-time classic *Confessions* of St. Augustine (Sheed translation recommended, Hackett Publishing) shows how the issue of the nature of God can be profoundly personal and existential.

Chapter 5: Four Problems of Cosmology

On evolution, we highly recommend Michael Denton's *Evolution: A Theory in Crisis* (Adler and Adler, 1986). Also worth a look is Phillip Johnson's *Darwin on Trial* (InterVarsity Press/Regnery Gateway, 1991). On predestination and free will, much—far too much, we believe—has been written. Our readers may already be familiar with the classic works by Augustine *(On Grace and Free Will)* and Boethius *(The Consolation of Philosophy* [esp.

chap. 5]). A brief and balanced treatment is Mark Pontifex's *Freedom and Providence* (vol. 22 of the Twentieth Century Encyclopedia of Catholicism [Hawthorn Books, 1964]). W. L. Craig has done his best to present a position that is both intellectually satisfying and pastorally sensitive in *The Only Wise God* (Baker, 1987). The same thesis is argued at much greater length and with an impressive flourish of formal notation in his *Divine Foreknowledge and Human Freedom* (Brill, 1991). For a very different view, see William Hasker's *God, Time, and Knowledge* (Cornell University Press, 1989). On Miracles, the best treatment remains C. S. Lewis's in *Miracles*. But we were greatly influenced by Grisez's treatment in chap. 22 of his *Beyond the New Theism* and by several articles in Richard Swinburne's excellent collection, *Miracles* (Macmillan, 1989). Perhaps the most impressive article in that collection is R. L. Purtill's "Miracles: What If They Happen?" (excerpted from chap. 5 of his book, *Thinking About Religion* [Prentice Hall, 1978]). See also Francis J. Beckwith's *David Hume's Argument Against Miracles: A Critical Analysis* (University Press of America, 1989) and pp. 99-125 of W. L. Craig's *Apologetics*. On Angels, the one thing really worth reading is Aquinas's treatment in the *Summa Theologiae* (we recommend the translation with notes and appendices by Kenelm Foster in vol. 9 of the Blackfriars Edition [published by McGraw-Hill]). Mortimer Adler gives an adequate synopsis of Aquinas in *The Angels and Us* (Macmillan, 1982). C. S. Lewis paints an excitingly imaginative picture of angelic power and activity in his novels, *Out of the Silent Planet, Perelandra* and *That Hideous Strength*. The quotation from Benedict Ashley comes from chap. 13 (section II: "Persons Without Bodies") of his astonishingly learned *Theologies of the Body* (The Pope John XXIII Medical-Moral Research and Education Center, 1985).

Chapter 6: The Problem of Evil

Our principal source here has been C. S. Lewis. See his *The Problem of Pain* and *Till We Have Faces*. But see also John Hick's impressive *Evil and the God of Love* (Harper & Row, 1966), Martin D'Arcy's *Pain and the Providence of God* (Bruce, 1935), Austin Farrer's *Love Almighty and Ills Unlimited* (Collins, 1962), and chaps. 19 and 20 of Grisez's *Beyond the New Theism*. G. K. Chesterton's fantasy, *The Man Who Was Thursday*, is both suggestive and disturbing. We highly recommend the relevant sections of Alvin Plantinga's *God, Freedom and Evil*. A fascinating attempt to supplement Plantinga with a positive theodicy is Eleonore Stump's "The Problem of Evil" (*Faith and Philosophy* [October 1985]). A bit technical, but well worth studying, is Kelly James Clark's "Evil and Christian Belief" (*International Philosophical Quarterly* [June 1989]). Some readers may be helped by Peter Kreeft's *Making Sense out of Suffering* (Servant, 1986) and chap. 2 (on Job) of his *Three Philosophies of Life* (Ignatius Press, 1989).

Chapter 7: The Divinity of Christ

Our argument was inspired primarily by C. S. Lewis's *Mere Christianity* (Book 2; and see his introduction to *The Problem of Pain*). Also powerful is G. K. Chesterton's *The Everlasting Man*. An imaginative variation on Lewis's themes can be found in Peter Kreeft's *Between Heaven and Hell* (InterVarsity Press, 1982) and *Socrates Meets Jesus* (InterVarsity Press, 1987). For a somewhat old-fashioned but still exciting debate that touches on much more than the divinity of Christ, see *Is Christianity True?* by Arnold Lunn and C. E. M. Joad (Eyre and Spottiswoode, Ltd., 1933). Joad later became a Christian. Readers may also want to explore the personal, existential dimension of this issue in *Jesus According To* (St. Paul Books, 1992).

Chapter 8: The Resurrection

There are two classic works on the resurrection: Frank Morison's *Who Moved the Stone?* (Faber & Faber, 1930) and W. L. Craig's *The Son Rises* (Moody, 1981; reissued with some [dubious] additions as *Knowing the Truth About the Resurrection* [Servant, 1988]). Both deserve careful study. Readers are also urged to consult the debate between Gary Habermas and Antony Flew, *Did Jesus Rise from the Dead?* (Harper & Row, 1987), as well as Habermas's earlier *The Resurrection of Jesus: An Apologetic* (Baker, 1980). John Wenham's *Easter Enigma* (Academie Books, 1984) is a detailed and fascinating attempt to show the mutual consistency of the resurrection narratives. For a dramatic reconstruction of what happened on the first Easter, see the twelfth play ("The King Comes to His Own") of Dorothy Sayers's *The Man Born to Be King* (Ignatius Press ed., 1990).

Chapter 9: The Bible: Myth or History?

There is currently a great deal of upheaval in biblical studies. A riveting sense of it can be found in *Biblical Interpretation in Crisis* (ed. Richard John Neuhaus [Eerdmans, 1989]) and in *Hermes and Athena: Biblical Exegesis and Philosophical Theology* (ed. Eleonore Stump and Thomas P. Flint [University of Notre Dame Press, 1993]). J. A. T. Robinson's *Redating the New Testament* (SCM Press, 1976) and *Can We Trust the New Testament?* (Eerdmans, 1977) are very much worth reading and pondering. Also helpful are F. F. Bruce's *The New Testament Documents: Are They Reliable?*, Josh McDowell's *Evidence That Demands a Verdict* (Here's Life Publishers, Inc., 1972), Craig Blomberg's

The Historical Reliability of the Gospels (InterVarsity Press, 1987), C. F. D. Moule's *The Birth of the New Testament* (3rd ed. Harper & Row, 1981), R. T. France's *The Evidence for Jesus* (InterVarsity Press, 1986), chap. 5 of E. L. Mascall's *The Secularization of Christianity* (Holt, Rinehart and Winston, 1965) and chap. 2 of his *Theology and the Gospel of Christ.*

Chapter 10: Life After Death

We have been greatly influenced by the works of H. D. Lewis. See his *The Elusive Mind* (Humanities, 1969), *The Self and Immortality* (Seabury, 1973), *Persons and Life After Death* (Macmillan, 1978) and *The Elusive Self* (Westminster, 1981). See also Richard Swinburne's *The Evolution of the Soul* (Clarendon Press, 1986), the final chapters of J. C. Eccles and Daniel Robinson's *The Wonder of Being Human* (Free Press, 1984), Gary Habermas and J. P. Moreland's *Immortality* (Moody, 1991) and chap. 3 of Moreland's *Scaling the Secular City.* Of possible interest are Mortimer Adler's *Intellect: Mind over Matter* (Macmillan, 1990), William Barrett's *The Death of the Soul* (Doubleday, 1986) and Peter Kreeft's *Love Is Stronger Than Death* (Harper & Row, 1979). See also Mark C. Albrecht's *Reincarnation: A Christian Critique of a New Age Doctrine* (2nd. rev. ed., InterVarsity Press, 1987) and Sheldon Vanauken's *A Severe Mercy* (Harper, 1977), a real-life love story, conversion story and life-after-death story.

Chapters 11 and 12: Heaven and Hell

The obvious sources are C. S. Lewis's *The Problem of Pain* (chaps. 8-10), *The Great Divorce* and "The Weight of Glory." But no reader should miss Harry Blamires's *Knowing the Truth About Heaven and Hell* (Servant, 1988). We have found Martin D'Arcy's little book *Death and Life* (Longmans, Green, and Co., 1942) instructive. Also instructive, though in a different way, is Charles Williams's frightening novel *Descent into Hell.* Peter Kreeft (surprise!) has written a few books on this topic as well. See his *Heaven, the Heart's Deepest Longing* (2nd ed., Ignatius Press, 1989) and *Everything You Ever Wanted to Know About Heaven* (2nd ed., Ignatius Press, 1989).

Chapters 13 and 14: Salvation and Other Religions

Though Huston Smith's *The World's Religions* is a good introduction to other religions, we have not found anything on Christianity and other religions that has satisfied us. But we have been deeply influenced and greatly helped by the writings of R. C. Zaehner. See his *Concordant Discord* (Clarendon Press, 1970) and *Christianity and Other Religions* (vol. 146 of the Twentieth-Century Encyclopedia of Catholicism [Hawthorn Books, 1964]).

Chapter 15: Objective Truth

We recommend Mortimer Adler's *Ten Philosophical Mistakes* (Macmillan, 1985), C. S. Lewis's essay "The Poison of Subjectivism" (in *Christian Reflections* [Eerdmans, 1967]), his *The Abolition of Man* (Macmillan, 1947) and chap. 12 of Peter Kreeft's *The Best Things in Life* (InterVarsity Press, 1984).

Subject Index

Scripture Index